Small Talk

LANGUAGE IN SOCIAL LIFE SERIES

Series Editor: Professor Christopher N Candlin

Chair Professor of Applied Linguistics

Department of English

Centre for English Language Education & Communication Research

City University of Hong Kong, Hong Kong

For a complete list of books in this series see pages *v* and *vi*

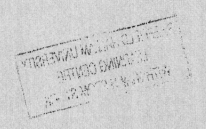

Small Talk

Edited by Justine Coupland

Longman

An imprint of **Pearson Education**

Harlow, England · London · New York · Reading, Massachusetts · San Francisco · Toronto · Don Mills, Ontario · Sydney
Tokyo · Singapore · Hong Kong · Seoul · Taipei · Cape Town · Madrid · Mexico City · Amsterdam · Munich · Paris · Milan

Pearson Education Limited
Edinburgh Gate
Harlow
Essex CM20 2JE
England

and Associated Companies throughout the world

Visit us on the World Wide Web at:
www.pearsoneduc.com

First published 2000

ISBN 0–582–41427–X CSD
ISBN 0–582–41426–1 PPR

British Library Cataloguing-in-Publication Data

A catalogue record for this book is available from the British Library

Library of Congress Cataloging-in-Publication Data

A catalog record for this book is available from the Library of Congress

Set by 35 in 10/12pt Janson
Produced by Pearson Education Asia Pte Ltd.
Printed and bound by CPI Antony Rowe, Eastbourne

LANGUAGE IN SOCIAL LIFE SERIES

Series Editor: Professor Christopher N Candlin
Chair Professor of Applied Linguistics
Department of English
Centre for English Language Education & Communication Research
City University of Hong Kong, Hong Kong

Contents

Preface

Each of the chapters in this book argues a perspective on small talk which is supported by analyses of interactional data in specific social settings. A range of methodological approaches is brought to bear on talk in private and public contexts, face-to-face and on the telephone, mainly naturally occurring but including talk in film and literature and in automated telephone systems. The chapters share in building a new representation of small talk as functionally multifaceted, central to social interaction as a whole, but even having direct relevance to transactional and institutional goals.

The contributing authors have all taken on the task of assessing the theoretical and practical significance of a notion of 'small talk' for the work they are doing. The perspectives they adopt are all broadly sociolinguistic, but span Discourse Analysis and Pragmatics, Communication and Conversation Analysis. I am grateful to authors for their willingness to reorient their research towards a topic of interest to me personally, and for creating a much broader and richer perspective on it than I could have done alone.

List of Contributors

Shoshana Blum-Kulka The Hebrew University of Jerusalem, Israel

Christine Cheepen British Telecom, England

Kathy Chilton University of York, England

Jennifer Coates University of Surrey Roehampton, London, England

Nikolas Coupland Cardiff University, Wales

Paul Drew University of York, England

Marie Flindall University of Canterbury, New Zealand

Janet Holmes Victoria University of Wellington, New Zealand

Adam Jaworski Cardiff University, Wales

Koenraad Kuiper University of Canterbury, New Zealand

Michael McCarthy University of Nottingham, England

Julie M. Naughton Alexandria, Virginia, USA

Sandra L. Ragan University of Oklahoma, USA

Karen Tracy University of Colorado, Boulder, USA

Virpi Ylänne-McEwen Cardiff University, Wales

Publisher's **Acknowledgements**

We are indebted to Warner Bros Publications Inc for permission to reproduce extracts from the film *WHO'S AFRAID OF VIRGINIA WOLF*.

General Editor's **Preface**

It is a measure of the smallness of the consideration given generally to *small talk* that its importance as evidenced in this new contribution to the *Language in Social Life Series* has had to wait some time for recognition. Perhaps people have confused *small talk* with *unimportant talk*. Until this book, we have not had a comprehensive and considered account of its ubiquity, its significance to the theory and practice of several related disciplines including interactive sociolinguistics, discourse analysis, communication theory, the ethnography of speaking and cross-cultural pragmatics, its potential for illuminating differences of social orientation towards discourse, nor have we had any systematic and studied evaluation of its place in the explanation of participants' transactional and relational goals.

Justine Coupland's admirably edited collection of newly-commissioned original papers from a wide spectrum of distinguished contributors from a range of fields, social and cultural contexts of situation, and theoretical orientations, makes up for this gap. The papers draw on a range of descriptive and socially explanatory approaches to discourse analysis, and in so doing, offer readers much practical accounting of research methodologies in discourse analysis and interactive sociolinguistics, valuable in themselves to aspiring researchers in the field.

This is not to say, of course, that small talk has lain entirely unacknowledged. At least since Malinowski, who appears here justifiably enough somewhat in father-figure guise, (though of course persons and individuals have been engaging in small talk since presumably Adam and Eve), the field of this topic has been addressed by scholars, though nowhere in this comprehensive fashion. The organisation of the book speaks to this range, scoping the subject as it does from theoretical, procedural, social and instrumental perspectives. Dr Coupland provides the reader with a well-judged, comprehensive and targeted analysis of the small talk phenomenon in social interaction in her opening Introduction, and each section of the book has a similar valuable orientation for the reader.

Rather than recounting or re-emphasising her own well-made and well-argued arguments for the significance of small talk, let me as a way of acknowledging the importance of the book address in this General Editor's Preface some issues of theoretical and practical significance by way of some personal examples, now entirely and freshly informed by her and her contributors' analyses in this remarkable collection.

I do this by reference to four small, even tiny, examples which seem (though this is always debatable, and constitutes an identification problem) to be *small* enough to qualify. The first is from a study into the interaction between lawyers and clients in conferencing activities in lawyers' (i.e. solicitors') chambers in New South Wales, sponsored by the Law Foundation of New South Wales, the second is from a study into the discourse of psychotherapists/psychiatrists and borderline personality disorder patients in New South Wales, sponsored by the Australian National Health and Medical Research Council, the third is from a study into the interaction between doctors and patients in HIV/AIDS clinics, once again in New South Wales, and also funded by the Australian National Health and Medical Research Council, and the fourth is from a study into dentist–patient communication in hospitals and private practice conducted some time ago now in the north-west of England, sponsored by the General Dental Council of England and Wales.

> Extract 1   Lawyer: ...that means the mum's not going to crack or something
>
>   Mother: that's right
>   Lawyer: ...*and mums do don't they*

(from a solicitor to a female client with a small baby who had attended his chambers seeking legal redress against a runaway husband)[i]

> Extract 2   *Patient: ....I don't know, maybe it's sort of delusion, escape that I*
>   *– y'know I just felt just this – it was just living and breathing was*
>   *just a little bit easier, y'know. (2) er*
>   *Doctor: ..mayb- living and breathing was easier*

(from a psychiatrist to a borderline personality disorder patient in a clinical consultation session)[ii]

> Extract 3   *Doctor: I'll give you – this one here, Indinavir, is really easy to take.*
>   *You take it before you eat*
>   *Patient: You reckon that's easy!*
>   *Doctor: Right*
>   *Patient: Look at that, avoid food one hour before and two hours after*
>   *taking it? Basically, if you were trying to do that, you'd never eat.*
>   *I'd take it in the morning and then .. two hours later I'd be able to*
>   *have my breakfast?*

> Doctor: *That's right*
> Patient: *It'd never work. Couldn't do it*
> Doctor: *Couldn't do it. All right. OK*

(from a clinical consultation involving a doctor and a patient living with HIV and AIDS)[iii]

Extract 4   Dentist: ......*hang on, can't stop, got someone unfreezing on the second floor right, right?*

(from a dentist in private practice, suddenly, in the middle of a casual conversation during a recording session)[iv]

The issues I want very briefly to highlight through these small extracts are ones which are canvassed in the book and which appear to me to be central to its themes. I have singled them out because they both complement the arguments so cogently formulated by Justine Coupland and because they suggest to me ways in which this book may have particular applied linguistic and discourse analytical value.

The first issue addresses the locating of small talk in the pragmatic space between and among the transactional and the relational functions of talk. Many papers in this collection highlight this issue and do so very clearly, raising questions of the connections between what Tracy and Naughton in their paper neatly call small talk as *tool* and *trait*. As the papers generally indicate, determining which of these functions an instance of small talk is performing at any one time, or both, is a key interpretive and explanatory issue. Although there will be instances where the distinction is marked, as in a study I once conducted with a colleague at the University of Lancaster into engineering lecture discourse, and where the distinction was associated not so much with any single linguistic or discursive feature but with a multimodal complex of signifying features of selected lexical and grammatical structures, prosodic patterning and kinetic action, the distinction is nonetheless very frequently hard to draw. In part, this is due to the interactants' natural (and sometimes trained) capacity to manage two planes of discourse at the same time, the ideational and the interpersonal, keeping in touch with their main topical themes and content while also keeping channels open to one's co-participants, and in part because the ambiguity is a characteristic feature associated with the multi-disciplinary goals of much professional activity, and evidenced by a consequent interdiscursive and intertextual realisation.

Take Example 1: here a local and country New South Wales solicitor is talking to a woman who has just had a baby and is living in very poor circumstances in a rented caravan on a park. Her husband has disappeared with another woman. She is seeking legal redress in terms of financial support for herself and her baby. Up to the point where the lawyer says what he says in the extract, he has been laying out the legal circumstances of her case and her possible legal action, much as lawyers typically lay out a legal matter, translating the relational narrative of the client into legal terms. We should note at once that the term *relational* is here of genre-specific interest. It is so, because typically in the study of lawyer–client communication such relational talk has been generally held to be the province of the client. The client relates, the lawyer transacts. As we shall see, such an assumed association of the relational to the client can bias the analysis. The lawyer also relates. The issue is less the form of the relational talk than its significance in the context of the interaction. So, here, the lawyer comes to this exemplified remark, said with a shift of prosody and timbre to a more intimate, small talk conversational, relational style, as a *quasi* aside. Why is this small and relational talk transactionally significant? In subsequent discussion with the lawyer, it was clear that it constituted a specific, chosen action on his part. The intention was to alert the mother carefully, indirectly and casually almost, to a situation he felt that she might be led into, where in her despair she might batter her child. The small talk aside was, thus, at once relational but also a consciously-made selection from the extended interdiscursive repertoire of the family solicitor, whose chief role as a lawyer, in his own admission, frequently blurred with his secondary role as counsellor. It was thus also transactional.

What does one draw from this? Not only that the pragmatic space of small talk always potentially encompasses the relational/transactional, but that too surface an analysis might suggest that such a small talk utterance was an example of *relational* small talk within the legal *transactional* matrix, when, I argue, the intervention was also *transactional* within an extended discursive complex of the lawyer/(counsellor). At the heart of this example is the discussion between what is *core* and what is *marginal* which runs through the papers in this volume, and, more pointedly, the debate whether 'relational stuff' can be in fact 'real stuff'. To this lawyer at least, it clearly was. On this example, then, the important question is not whether relational talk deviates from normal transactional practice but that it is centrally contingent to professional practice. This is a point made, in particular, by the papers in the final section of the present volume.

The second issue I would like to derive from a reading of these papers has to do with the issue of the connection that may be drawn between small talk and professional expertise. Exploring expert talk and the links to be made between discursive choice and the display of expertise seems to me a prime area for current applied linguistic and discourse analytical research, if only because so many professional and institutional actions are mediated or constituted through and by talk (and writing), and identify talk (and writing) as a signal characteristic of competence. Such research would be identifying what the place of discursive competence was as an acknowledged feature in the appraisal and evaluation of expertise, and how such discursive competence was to be described. For example, small talk is linked in one paper in the collection to the ability to 'work a room' (as part of an apparently recognised Clintonian mastery of discursive competence in the political context). The question is then, what does 'working a room' actually imply small-talk-wise, and how do other contexts of situation differentially define this professionally and institutionally significant expertise?

Example 2 provides a case in point. Data from consultations with borderline personality disorder patients/clients reveal that these patients/clients often experience severe difficulties in identifying and expressing their emotions. In consequence, their discourse is characteristically marked by a monotonous prosody and a continual recounting of a restricted set of mundane everyday activities, expressed typically without particular personal engagement of emotion and affect. In this context, psychiatrists and some branches of psychotherapist who are involved with such patients/clients, see their role as essentially providing a non-judgmental and non-interventionist encouragement to further patient/client talk, in short, a kind of minimalist relational smalltalk, eschewing in general more overt forward-directed, extended and transactionally strategic talk. In discussion with such professionals, however, it became clear to my research project colleagues and myself that they actually construed their conversational action as co-occurring on two planes, a strategic plane and a tactical plane. Strategically, any such consultation interaction was one in a series and sequence of such time-bound (usually around 50 minute) interactions and was itself subject to a locally strategic management of what might be achievable within the individual 50 minute session. Tactically, however, the psychiatrist or psychotherapist was ever watchful and conscious of the need to maintain the flow of the interaction and to judge where a non-standard tactical intervention might serve a strategic purpose, locally and within the span of the series of sessions. In fact, strategic and tactical action were terms that such professionals employed in describing what they did. How then are we to understand this extract? On the surface it is a socially cohesive conversational remark, characteristic of relational small talk. In one sense this is exactly what it is, an utterance doing important interpersonal relational work. Seen as a momentary and tactical realisation of a professional strategic plan in relation to the exploration and gradual amelioration of this psychiatric disorder, however, it takes on more transactional significance. Though based on the voices of ordinary conversation, such interventions are subordinate to a professional plan of talk. What the intervention does is to seek to exploit an opening in the borderline personality disordered patient/client's talk where, for once, the patient/client enters into an unusual, if temporary, recount of a personally significant change in her feelings about herself, which the doctor seeks to open further by his remark, allowing the patient/client, however briefly, the space to move into a happier speculative world away from the narrating of mundane everyday experience. At this point, then, we may argue that the relational becomes, and is, transactional, and is acknowledged as such by the psychiatrist as part

of his or her expert competence. Thus here, the variable relational and transactional pragmatic space of small talk constitutes an arena in which such
small talk is not only seen as an instance of professional action but also as a
marker of a recognisable and valued professional identity.

The third issue suggested by my reading of these important papers is
taken up in my Example 3. It has to do with the co-construction of meanings
through joint relational talk. Current ideologies surrounding the practices
of doctor–patient interaction display a shift towards what has been termed,
metaphorically, a *concordance* or a *therapeutic alliance* between doctor and
patient. Such an alliance is advocated as a means through which the joint
expertise and experience of both parties can be conjoined in the common
enterprise of securing optimal healthcare outcomes for the patient. The
means by which this alliance is to be forged and tested is through the joint
discursive work of the co-participants. In the terms of this alliance, therefore, we may expect some sharing of the discursive power among both parties, in particular in terms of rights to engage in transactional or relational
talk, or, as we have seen in relational-as-transactional talk. In the example
illustrated (Example 3) we see this co-construction at work with both parties
engaging in transactional and relational talk, and where the relational functions both relationally and transactionally.

What inferences can we draw for the themes of this book from this
exchange? Firstly, I believe, we should not be misled into assuming that the
distribution of relational and transactional talk among the parties in an exchange is some inevitable given, the choice of which mode of talk necessarily
favouring inevitably the powerful in an interaction. In HIV and AIDS medicine and healthcare the distribution of power, in terms of knowledge and
experience at least, is not the natural prerogative of the doctor. Some
patients are highly informed and intensely experienced. The ability to engage
in professional transactional talk is the property of them both. Moreover, the
necessary long-term engagement of a doctor and patient in the treatment of
this disease fosters an interpersonal relationship in which the relational (as
interpersonal talk) is naturally engendered by the extent and nature of the
established contact between the parties. Such talk is again the potentially
activatable property of them both. Secondly, we may note that both doctor
and patient engage in talk whose transactional or relational significance (or
both) is an ongoing interactional accomplishment of both parties. What we
have here, then, is not so much layered talk in terms of planes, evidenced
sometimes by transactional and sometimes by relational talk, but a situation
where any given utterance, whether apparently relationally or transactional
in character, can potentially serve both interpersonal and ideational goals,
both of which are significant for the treatment of the disease. The so-called
concordance or *therapeutic alliance* between the parties, crucial for the management of HIV and AIDS given the importance of mutual understanding and
empathy to the appropriate conformity to drug regimes, simply necessitates

talk in which the micro management and the micro interpretation of all talk, relational and transactional, is necessarily joint and where distinctions between smallness and bigness of talk may have little explanatory value.

Throughout the book, reference is made in Justine Coupland's sectional Introductions and many of the papers themselves, to the Faircloughian and ultimately Habermasian assertion that distinctions between the public and private worlds of speakers and hearers are currently being confused (even deliberately confused) by a creeping *conversationalisation* of discourse. I draw on the text of my final Example 4 for an elaboration of this significant aspect of the arguments contained here. It would appear from this assertion that small is not only beautiful, it has become aggressive. Certainly, several of the papers in this collection point to the need to take what Fairclough in a number of papers and books has identified as an explanatory or critical approach to the analysis of discourse. On his reading, instances of small talk are to be regarded as potential evidence of a gradual collapsing of public and private boundaries, and, beyond this, as evidence of a masked but hegemonic colonising and a recruitment-like absorption of less powerful participants to the ideological-discursive formations of those in power. That there is some truth in this argument is evidenced in some of the papers in the collection.

Two related issues arise from this. The first is that we need to be exceptionally careful in assuming that some surface interactive cooperativeness, in a Gricean sense, evidenced by the mutual and complementary exchange of relational small talk, necessarily asserts some deeper-going cooperativeness in terms of shared goals among the participants and a commitment by them to some shared outcomes. The one does not necessarily guarantee the other. Entrenched and often institutionalised disequilibriums of power easily may outlive the smooth surface co-construction of an interaction. This is especially true in my experience of doctor–patient and nurse–patient talk as we suggest in relation to Example 3 above. Relational talk can thus be merely a surface indication of some apparent but deeply unfulfilled harmony. Secondly, and more poignantly in my professional memory as far as this particular Example 4 text is concerned, relational talk when reproduced in some descriptive account of professional and institutional discourse, can be seen by some as invested with much greater ideological significance than the analyst may assume. Thus this reported offhand remark of a local dentist abandoning a casual conversation and running upstairs to an unfreezing patient in a surgery which was notable even in the local profession for having three floors of patients – all possibly at one time at different stages of treatment, and itself arguably the product of the privatisation of dentistry – occasioned some considerable disquiet, I recall at the time, among the dental authorities for its apparent besmirching of the good name of dentistry. One cannot be too careful about the potential bigness of small talk, as this book reminds us. Here in this example, relational talk was seen not as an instance of some well-judged expertise as in Example 2 above, or as we took it to be, the casual offhand friendly remark by a dentist to researchers whose attention then quickly shifted to the need to pay out an inadequate recording wire, but, when recorded, served for some official readers as an unfortunate datum for the regrettable commercialisation of private dentist practice, itself much more subject to the time-bound economies of patient throughput than doctoring was at that time (and perhaps still is) even before the age of Thatcher. Relational talk may thus become politically suspect, as it has unfortunately come to be seen as too costly to the healthcare system in many healthcare sites in the growing world of timed and quantifiable case management, where the transactional has come to rule.

I have taken some time in this Preface, following the excitingly illustrated pattern of the papers collected in the book, to highlight the personal relevance of the analyses of small talk presented here, stimulated very clearly by Justine Coupland's scholarly and impressive command of the literature and its data, and her own extensive and well-published research. It would be trite, however, only to close with an acknowledgement of the imaginative and convincing arguments raised in the papers, however genuine and appreciative this is. Following this book, small talk is now on the interactive sociolinguistic agenda; the task now is to document further its functional purposes in a range of sites, to chart the systemic networks of significant choice among these purposes, and understand from the papers in this book how in all sociolinguistics, small is *always* significant.

Christopher N. Candlin
General Editor
Centre for English Language Education & Communication Research
City University of Hong Kong

---

[i] From: Y. Maley, C. N. Candlin, J. Crichton and P. Koster (1995) Orientations in lawyer–client interviews. *Forensic Linguistics*. 2,1 (42–55)

[ii] From: M. Garbutt (1996) *Figure talk: reported speech and thought in the discourse of psychotherapy*. Unpublished PhD thesis. Department of Linguistics. Macquarie University, Sydney

[iii] From: C. N. Candlin, A. Moore and G. Plum (1998) *From compliance to concordance: shifting discourses in HIV medicine*. Paper presented at the International Pragmatics Conference. Rheims. France (July)

[iv] From: C. N. Candlin, H. Coleman and J. Burton: (1981) *Dentist–Patient Communication*. Report to the General Dental Council of England & Wales. Department of Linguistics and Modern English Language. University of Lancaster, Lancaster, UK

Introduction: sociolinguistic perspectives on small talk
Justine Coupland

Although the boundaries of types of talk are always uncertain, the term 'small talk' has a recognised currency in several traditions of sociolinguistics, semantics and communication studies, and certainly in popular perceptions. 'Small talk' has widely been taken, from both academic and popular perspectives, to be a conventionalised and peripheral mode of talk. It seems to subsume 'gossip', 'chat' and 'time-out talk', for example, although it is not helpful to try to impose firm and final definitions on these generic labels.[1] What the labels point to is a range of supposedly minor, informal, unimportant and non-serious modes of talk, linked to the general communicative function sometimes characterised as 'talking to avoid other problems' (see Robinson 1972). In this book we explore the interactional dynamics of small talk and associated modes of discourse in many different social contexts. But we also reassess the social and cultural implications of small talk, and the values and assumptions that naturalise this concept. How is it, we have to ask, that some episodes and styles of social interaction can be deemed 'small', and in what senses? What social functions are realised by speech events and practices identified by the attribution 'small talk'? How should we orient to it, theoretically and analytically? And behind all of this, *is* it an 'it'?

In this Introduction I shall firstly outline and review the main research traditions where a conception of small talk has surfaced. Then I shall begin the work of identifying some of the contexts, discursive characteristics and social implications of small talk, as I have approached them in my own research. The main burden of filling out such details, and of linking them to a range of theoretical issues, falls on the chapters assembled in the body of the book.

Small talk as phatic communion

Malinowski introduced the concept of 'phatic communion' in 1923 (reprinted in 1972), and this is both the earliest and the prototypical formulation of small talk as a communicative mode – the establishment of human bonds or communion, 'merely', as Malinowski wrote, by talking. For Malinowski, hallmarks of phatic communion were its ritualised and apparently purposeless character. He described it as 'language used in free, aimless, social intercourse' (1972: 149). In his famous dictum, phatic communion is 'a type of speech in which ties of union are created by a mere exchange of words', when people 'aimlessly gossip' (p. 151); 'the function of speech in mere sociabilities'; 'purposeless expressions of preference or aversions, accounts of irrelevant happenings, comments on what is perfectly obvious' (p. 150). On the assumption that the need for the mere presence of others is 'one of the bedrock aspects of man's [sic] nature in society', speech can be seen as 'the intimate correlate of this tendency' (p. 150). Therefore, communion among humans will often be marked in speech – 'phatically'.

Malinowski was interested in small talk as discourse operating in a limited domain, dislocated from practical action and from what he thought of as 'purposive activities' (which included hunting, tilling soil and enacting war in 'primitive' societies). Nevertheless he did recognise phatic talk to be a form of action, serving 'to establish bonds of personal union between people brought together by the mere need of companionship' (p. 151). Even though it may 'not serve any purpose of communicating ideas', phatic communion, for Malinowski, is functional in defusing the threat of taciturnity (p. 150). We infer that phatic talk is space-filling talk, a minimalist fulfilment of a basic communicative requirement.

There are no illustrative examples of any detail in the original treatment, although Malinowski notes there is a preference for affirmation and consent in phatic talk, perhaps mixed with an incidental disagreement which creates the 'bonds of antipathy' (p. 150). These oblique remarks begin to suggest some strategic uses of small talk. He implies that achieving social bonding through phatic talk may be reflexive on the part of small talkers. In the same vein, he hints at listeners operating strategically behind the veneer of small talk. He gives us the image of speakers offering personal accounts of their views and life histories, to which, he says, 'hearers listen under some restraint and with slightly veiled impatience, waiting for their own turn to speak'. He continues:

> But though the hearing given to such utterances is as a rule not as intense as the speaker's own share, it is quite essential for his pleasure . . .

(pp. 150/1)

For Malinowski, phatic communion is therefore 'talking small' in the further sense that it is potentially communicatively suspect or at least dissimulative (see also Sacks 1975). Malinowski certainly felt there was a fundamental indirectness in phatic exchanges:

> Are words in phatic communion used primarily to convey meaning, the meaning which is symbolically theirs? Certainly not! . . . A mere phrase of politeness . . . fulfils a function to which the meaning of its words is almost completely irrelevant. Inquiries about health, comments on the weather, affirmations of some supremely obvious state of things – all such are exchanged, not in order to inform, not in this case to connect people to action, certainly not in order to express any thought.

(p. 151)

Unfortunately, these brief comments about the social pragmatics of small talk remain undeveloped in the original treatment.

The legacy of Malinowski's treatment is therefore a systematically ambivalent view of small talk, talk which is aimless, prefatory, obvious, uninteresting, sometimes suspect and even irrelevant, but part of the process of fulfilling our intrinsically human needs for social cohesiveness and mutual recognition. In many later uses of the term 'phatic communion' it is the negative valuation that dominates, with recipients evaluating it as 'phoney' (Wolfson 1981) and analysts seeing it as 'dull and pedestrian' (Leech 1974) or semantically 'empty' (Turner 1973). But this ambiguity is only one of many obscurities and dilemmas about how we should read small talk which remain to be addressed. Can a sociolinguistic focus support a conception of everyday language as banal? Who is to judge the banality or significance of talk? In fact, whose designation of 'smallness' is captured in the label 'small talk'? Should the argument be that even talk which is banal for participants, or at least wholly unexceptional for them at the moment of its production and reception, is nevertheless socio–culturally significant as a performed routine? If the evaluation of small talk is made from participants' own orientations, will its interpersonal significance be revealed to us? Are there sociolinguistic environments when 'everyday social discourse' takes on a particular significance, perhaps as a symbolic retreat from more serious, challenging or even oppressive modes of talk? And therefore how should we model the relationship of small talk to other 'non-small' modes of talk? Is the cultural framing of small talk changing, and might there be new, less obviously socially cohesive, purposes to which 'everyday talk' can be put? Are we prepared to subscribe to the view that talk can be ranked on a scale of 'authentic' to 'suspect', and does doing so require us to endorse Habermas's (1984) idealism of non-strategic 'communication'? These are some of the more contemporary questions which this book will address.

Sociolinguistics and the celebration of the everyday

What is core and what is marginal in communication is a matter of perspective. The assumption that small talk is a marginal mode of discourse certainly runs counter to several dominant trends in the academic study of language and human communication. If we think of terms like 'casual conversation', 'desultory conversation' and 'everyday talk', these are the concepts which define the data at the heart of sociolinguistics as a whole. From many different positions it has been argued that what is sociolinguistically important is what is commonplace. We can think of Labov's insistence (Labov 1972) on the regularity and social significance of vernaculars, and of Schegloff's commitment (Schegloff 1986) to revealing the mechanics of everyday conversational exchanges as the cornerstone of how social order is realised. Labov's and Schegloff's positions are similar in that they agree that there is a systematicity and orderliness about everyday language which, they would argue, needs to be the main focus for their (very different) technical approaches to analysis. Everyday language is the 'best data'.

An extension of this position is the argument that everyday conversation is the norm from which other forms of discourse deviate. As Heritage points out (1997), it was Goffman's belief too that the 'institutional order' of everyday interaction itself underlies the operation of all other institutions in society. To this extent again, 'simple, desultory conversation' has a significance that is anything but marginal. Whether or not it is inherently the best data for theory building, it defines an important norm. It defines the basic parameters and possibilities of social exchange, and talk in more 'specialist' social contexts – such as in business, commerce, education, medicine or the law – needs to be analysed as deviating from underlying, everyday practice. This deviation approach to the analysis of institutional talk is a methodological necessity. We can scarcely avoid analysing talk in specific work settings, for example, in terms of how the institution restricts or extends the range of 'normal' interactional possibilities. For example, hierarchical, asymmetrical relationships, as doctor–patient relationships have often been held to be, are interactionally achieved by restricting patients' turn management options (who can speak when) or by restricting the sorts of acts they can realise (e.g. they have limited questioning rights). Teacher talk affords teachers 'comment' or 'follow-up' turns after students' classroom responses, allowing teachers to legislate on what is correct or appropriate. The distinctiveness of institutional talk will often be apparent only through an explicit or implicit contrast with everyday conversational norms (Drew and Heritage 1992).

At the same time, it is too limiting to equate small talk with everyday conversation. For one thing, as I noted earlier, small talk has specific functions within 'specialist' or 'institutional' settings. Small talk is sociolinguistically more interesting and more diverse than being a generic baseline for the analysis of 'big talk' in specific situations. There is a great deal we need to discover about the local dynamics of small talk in its specific domains – how small talk is achieved interactionally, turn by turn, and what it therefore achieves for participants *in situ*. This emphasis on the insiders' perspective, which is so vociferously promoted within Conversation Analysis, is vital in terms of providing micro-level detailing to macro-level theorising about genre and interaction practices. Even so, Conversation Analysis has generally resisted engaging with the social particularities of speakers. For example, Schneider (1988) offers a perspective on small talk which has as its aim the development of 'sociopragmatic competence' in the language learning context. Thus, his focus is mainly on description of forms, structures and topics rather than the explanation of social functions which small talk may achieve for interlocutors. Eggins and Slade (1997) have offered an insightful formal and strategic analysis of the social achievements of 'casual conversations' between friends, workmates and family members. But what is conversationally achieved by and for participants through small talk is likely to be different depending on the specific contextual constitution of the speech event. While it is important to recognise what Schegloff (1992) calls the 'contexting' power of talk, the value and social significance of small talk is nonetheless highly 'contexted'. Many of the later chapters show a classically sociolinguistic concern for time, place and participation, and for how these factors impinge on the social significance of small talk.

In a series of papers (1974, 1975, 1981), Laver analysed the discourse structure and function of (what he explicitly refers to as) phatic communion among familiars in casual conversational settings. Parts of Laver's analysis are a direct echo of Malinowski. Consistent with Malinowski, he comments on phatic sequences, especially at the margins of conversations, as means of establishing and maintaining social relationships and means of achieving transitions – into, within and out of more 'content-oriented' talk. He writes about the exploratory and propitiatory functions of small talk (cf. Robinson's 'avoiding other problems', mentioned above). Laver also argues that the linguistic form of a phatic initiative both constrains the thematic development of the interaction (that is, it is meaningful in the way it sequences a social encounter). But he also argues that it confers crucial indexical meanings, that is, it is socially diagnostic, perhaps of speakers' social identities and stances. Laver sees sociolinguistic significance in phatic talk, at least in how it provides for interactants to size each other up and establish the footing on which talk will proceed. Phatic talk may happen sequentially at the margins of conversations, but it does work relevant for the whole interaction.

What is most compelling in Laver's work is his demonstration of the verbal and non-verbal ordering of conversational openings and closings, in ways that cross-refer interestingly to conversation analysts' accounts of these sequences. Laver's perspective is indebted to Firth's work (1972) on greeting and parting as ritual and patterned routines (see below). But he also introduces a speculative predictive mechanism, specifying how speakers are able to stake claims about solidarity/intimacy and status relationships through particular encoding choices within phatic talk. Again these are classically sociolinguistic readings of language and the marking of social relationships. This insight would seem to have found its full flourishing in Brown and Levinson's (1978, 1987) politeness model, and in their suggestion that cultural grand rites find their origins in conventional, local demonstrations of person-respecting and relational management (Goffman 1959).

The ritualised character of conversation openings and closings is only apparent through detailed micro-analysis, but the variability of mini-rituals of small talk is apparent only when we closely examine many different sociolinguistic environments. We know, for example, that telephone conversations will be structured differently from face-to-face conversations because of channel constraints and effects (Cheepen, this volume; Drew and Chilton, this volume; Hopper 1992; Schegloff 1986). There is also cultural variation in telephone talk sequencing rules (Carroll 1987) which cannot be so mechanically explained. But what of the many other social encounters where small talk is embedded, sometimes minimalistically, into non-verbal interactional practices, such as in brief buying/selling exchanges at stalls and kiosks (Merritt 1975), more extended service encounters (N. Coupland and Ylänne-McEwen; and McCarthy; both in this volume), and supermarket checkout counters (Kuiper and Flindall, this volume)?

Encounters we normally define as transactional or instrumentally motivated, and of course the commercial and professional worlds of talk at work, are interactionally constituted partly on the basis of social talk. More particularly, institutional discourse typically involves a dialectic between institutional (e.g. medical, legal, pedagogic or commercial) frames and sociorelational frames for talk. The reinstatement of small talk norms in a medical interaction, say after a sequence of talk involving diagnosis and prescribing, takes its social value from the frame shift that occasions it. In that setting, small talk is likely to be seen as a marked or deviant mode, rather than unmarked or normative. Several discourse analytic studies have been concerned with the interplay of social and transactional goals as reflected in the structuring of talk at work (Coupland, Robinson and Coupland 1994; Fisher 1991; Ragan, this volume; see also the final section of this Introduction). A further complexity is that, in professional and commercial domains, small talk needs to be interpreted not only in terms of its relational function (establishing rapport between professionals and clients), but in terms of how that rapport furthers or contests the instrumental and transactional goals of the institution (Coates and Holmes, both in this volume). Small talk, as several chapters of this volume clearly show, cannot be segregated from the 'mainstream' concerns of talk at work. It is an intrinsic part of the talk at work complex.

Small talk and feminist sociolinguistics

A recurrent trend in feminist sociolinguistics has been to (re)invest talk which is primarily geared towards 'communion' and the fulfilment of social goals, rather than in pursuit of 'task' or instrumental or transactional goals, with positive communicative value (e.g. Coates 1986, this volume; Jones 1990; Tannen 1989). In feminist sociolinguistics, small talk is important because it is 'small'. This line of research expresses ideological resistance to Malinowski's views about the suspect and inauthentic nature of phatic communion. At the same time, it lends ideological support to his view that phaticity defines the social essence of humankind, although specifically in a gendered context. Since it has often been women rather than men who have been stereotypically associated with generating small talk and 'gossip', the deprecation of small talk and the deprecation of women have been mutually reinforcing social processes.

Feminist ideology has inverted social evaluations of women's communicative norms, and part of this has been to argue, in one of Malinowski's directions, that women's small talk in private domains has distinct social utility (at least for women) and inherent importance. Women, it is suggested, are indeed more socially engaged, cooperative and constructive than men, and this is all to the good. Women's talk is a model of ecologically sensitive communication, able to resist the worst excesses of men's competitiveness and obsessive concern with facticity and material achievement. The world of 'big talk' is a self-created man's world, and the 'big talk'/ 'small talk' distinction is either mythological or more evidence of men's obsession with size (or both). In this way of thinking, 'gossip' is rescued from being a sociolinguistic stereotype of women's unproductive, demeaning, scheming and inauthentic communication. It becomes a source of female identity and power, and certainly enjoyment (Guendouzi 1998; Coates, this volume).

Although much of feminist sociolinguistics takes an 'intergroup' line on gender relations in this way, entering the battle to redistribute the social evaluations of men's and women's communicative roles and functions, its significance may well be broader than this. What primarily emerges from feminist critiques is the fact that western societies have whole-heartedly accepted that communication is in fact value-gradable, on a scale from most-to-least authentic, or most-to-least valid. If the term 'small talk' has not come into prominence, it is because it is the overshadowed antithesis of 'real' or 'full' or 'serious' or 'useful' or 'powerful' talk. Whether or not 'real talk' has been held to be a man's exclusive domain is, from this perspective, less significant than the fact that an evaluative public conception of communication itself is strongly in place. Real talk is talk that 'gets stuff done', where 'stuff' does not include 'relational stuff'. Within this ideology, sociality is marginalised as a 'small' concern, and language for transacting business and other commercial or institutional instrumentalities is foregrounded.

This consumerist model evokes Bourdieu (1991), but with a less meta-phorical reading of the capital value of language. Through a focus on small talk, sociolinguistics is able to position itself against those cultural forces which assert that communication deserving of attention – in life and in research – must be 'big': talk comprising or incorporating factual informa-tion exchange, instrumental goals, serious key, and unwavering commitment to openness, truth and disclosiveness (again see Coates, this volume). In this way the feminist initiative needs to be taken much further, into reconcep-tualising the functions and diversity of relationally oriented, informal talk in many different communicative environments, public as well as private, male as well as female, in varying cultural contexts.

Scollon reminds us of how central the relational function of talk is to us:

> Linguists . . . sociologists . . . anthropologists . . . linguistic pragmatists . . . sociolinguists . . . and critical discourse analysts have all pointed out that any social encounter, including any of those in which talk is engaged, has as its logically first and interactionally ongoing highest priority to position the participants in the social encounter in relationship to each other. What-ever else we do in speaking to each other, we make claims about ourselves as a person, we make claims about the person of our listeners, we claim how those persons are related to each other at the outset of the encounter, we project an ongoing monitoring of those multiple relationships, and as we close the encounter we make claims about what sort of relationships we expect will hold upon resuming our contacts in future social encounters.

> (Scollon 1998: 33)

We do not have to endorse Scollon's claim about which functional dimen-sion of talk has the 'highest priority'. But it does seem necessary to insist that social encounters are pervasively organised around multiple interactional goals that go well beyond, for instance, the transmission and reception of factual information (see Tracy 1990; Tracy and N. Coupland 1991). Other-wise, we fall back into Malinowskian assumptions about the 'mereness' of small talk and the putative sub-genres it includes – phatic communion, chat, gossip, banter and so on. Talk where people pay (sometimes sustained) topical attention to the superficial, the safe, the immediate situation and the local environment can move from the margins to the centre of our 'academic gaze' (Tracy and Naughton, this volume) when we begin to read it for its relational and social identity functions.

Cheepen and Monaghan (1990: 19) have a nice instance of speakers representing what we might call the 'value in emptiness' of small talk encounters:[2]

Extract 1

A: Have a good weekend?
B: Yes, quite nice. Spent Saturday evening with Sue.
A: What did she have to say?
B: Nothing really.

As Cheepen and Monaghan point out, speaker B does not seem to be implying that the evening's conversation with Sue was actually empty or even dull,
but that, topically at least, nothing about it would be of interest to A at the
time of the transcribed exchange. They say that such conversations have 'a
purely private value, in that [they are] satisfying and worthwhile only to the
participants' (ibid.: 20). Some of their other illustrative data show protracted
conversations involving mutual exploration of detailed accounts, commentaries and narratives. They include, for example, a very lengthy sequence of
conversation about the Christmas trees the two participants have seen and
bought that year (1990: 140–4). To a non-participant, and perhaps even to a
sociolinguist commentator, the talk might appear repetitive, redundant, even
inane or banal. Yet at the time of conversing, and at some level, the way the
participants work together to sustain the topic seems to indicate a mutual
agreement that the topic and their sharing of it *matters*. Eggins and Slade
(1997: 16) also comment on participants in casual conversation reporting that
'nothing happens', which they call the 'central paradox of casual conversation'.

'Nothing happening' conversationally within small talk encounters can
subsume an enormous amount of creative, collaborative meaning-making.
It is conceivable that the evening conversation with Sue included episodes
similar to the following, which involves three young men, Chris (31), James
(24) and Gary (22). They have arranged to meet for a drink and are sitting
around a table in a bar. Chris and James know each other better than either
of them knows Gary. (The exchange was observed and transcribed by Crispin
Thurlow, who kindly gives me permission to include it here.)

Extract 2

```
 1 C: oh I got some really nice you must see these I got for my Christmas these people I
 2    stayed with the other day some really amazing shot glasses (describing the shape
 3    with his hands) really thick short shot glasses=
 4 J: = (ironically) oh yeah?=
 5 C: =and I said (.) hey I was just talking about these the other day (turning to
 6    Gary) that's cos=
 7 J: =we got=
 8 C: =James bought some nice
 9 J: we got a bulk buy of uh twenty shot glasses
10 C: twenty shot glasses
11 J: we can line them up they were fifty pence each
12 G: where's that from?
```

13 J: from (silly voice) yurgh Habitat
14 C: in Bristol
15 J: (imitating a Bristolian accent) in Brissol
            [
16 C: (imitating a French accent) dans Bristol=
17 J: =dans=
18 G: =I erm (.) borrowed one once from this hotel in (.) <u>Rhodes</u>
                                                        [
19 C: (smiling) <u>borrowed</u>
20 G: (laughing slightly) yeah I borrowed <u>two</u> actually they're really nice=
21 J: (ironically) =oh yeah?=
22 G: =slightly= (describes their shape with his hands)
23 C: (2.0) these are amazing these came in a little tin (.) a little silver tin=
24 J: (ironically) very posh=
25 C: with like red stuffing inside and shot glasses four shot glasses they're <u>really</u> <u>nice</u> you'd=
26 J: =you'll have to get some friends now=
27 C: =you'd really like them (.) (noise in amusement at J's comment) yerrh!
                                                        [
28 G: ((3 sylls))
29   ((he's got four on his own)) (tapping the table as if downing four shots in
30   succession)
31 C: exactly who needs friends when you've got four shot glasses?
32 G: (in mock drunkenness) uuuurgh!
33   (joint laughter)
34 C: (mock drunkenness again) I don't need fucking friends urgh!
35   (J and G laugh)
36 J: what are you going to do? put your Babycham in them?
37 G: (very quietly) I might do (.) I got given (.) about two three years ago this
38   incredible bottle of super duper tequila from Mexico . . .

The extract shows small talk in its guise as recreational activity among friends/intimates. Thurlow comments in his contextual notes (made as a participant observer) that much of the sequence was 'embedded in personal-historical relationships'. This is evidenced in the shared knowledge (e.g. about speakers' likes and dislikes) but also in the styling of the talk, in how speakers are able to orient to each other. The tenor is one of mildly competitive verbal play. The triadic exchange of banter, the rapid turn taking and the shifting confederations show a mutual, eager enjoyment of talk in its communing function. Verbal duelling such as this has been seen as a particularly male talk activity (Johnson and Finlay 1997; Schwebel 1997), but the dominant relational effect in this instance is collaboration and enjoyment of a co-constructed discourse event. It perhaps fills out Malinowski's oblique suggestion of 'bonds of antipathy' (see above). The topics carried through the talk, realised as verbal play, are 'unimportant' ones, unlikely to seriously threaten any of the participants if one-upmanship results in a relational imbalance.

The extract is largely organised as narrative, and narrative in general offers rich relational opportunities in small talk settings (see Cheepen 1988;

Eggins and Slade 1997). Firstly there is collaborative storytelling in James's and Chris's story about their acquisition of shot glasses, lines 1–17. This is thematically developed by Gary's story (lines 18–22). Sociality is displayed via the process of telling linked stories. Throughout the extract, speakers do various playful voicings (cf. Bakhtin 1986), for example in James's self-mockery for pretentiousness (line 13). Accent shifting (lines 15 and 16) and code shifting (line 16), teasing in the form of mock insults (lines 19, 21, 24 and 26) and feigned drunkenness (lines 32 and 34) all cue the speakers' enjoyment of their joint spoken performance. The sequence also constructs and confirms intimacy. For example, commenting on fine detail (lines 23 and 25) presumes willingness on the listener's part to engage with detail. The 'smallness' of the talk is a key to the intimacy it achieves. Speakers also project other times spent together, retrospectively or prospectively (line 1, *you must see these*, and line 11, *we can line them up*). Friendship is constructed in these utterances by speakers orienting to the actual 'we-ness' of shared activities, or to individual actions which will let them share perspectives, or to the likelihood of shared responses. References to Chris's lacking and needing friends (lines 26 and 31) work as ironic expressions precisely because they are interspersed between so much friendship-building talk.

Small talk, economic discourse and social change

Considering the institutional functioning of small talk raises the issue of its strategic use – the relational in the service of the institutional, as mentioned above. Fairclough (1995) has built on this observation to suggest there may be a general social trend towards the conversationalisation of public dis-courses. He considers how and why public encounters, including media talk, tend to be colonised by informality and pseudo-intimacy (see also Candlin, forthcoming). Giddens (1991) and others have also theorised the new and heightened significance of intimate relationships in late modern societies, which lack the stability previously associated with predictable lifespan positions and roles.

The blurring of traditional lifeworlds – e.g. 'the world of work' vs. 'the world of leisure' becoming less distinct in the information society, but also in the redefinition of some forms of 'leisure' as 'work' – adds salience. In these ways too, small talk merits sociolinguistic attention. Small talk may be expected to feature in the new communicative domains, particularly those of the ever-growing service industries, which have come to recognise the need for 'relational sensitivity' in the way they market and conduct their activities (cf. Cameron 1995; Sarangi and Slembrouck 1996). This gives us another strong argument for developing richly contextualised accounts of small talk, as part of a critical orientation to language in social life.

An exchange I took part in, in a dentist's surgery, illustrates the potentially shifting priorities for small talk in the workplace. It is worth mentioning that I have been visiting this dentist for twenty years, first as an NHS patient and more recently (and, as is common enough, after some coercion) as a privately insured patient. I was sitting in the designated waiting corner of the treatment room; D is the dentist.

Extract 3

J: are you busy at the moment?
D: no not too bad (.) you didn't have to wait longer than five minutes did you?

To me, my question was an archetypally phatic initiative, between long-standing acquaintances, designed to fill silence at a liminal moment, incorporating a safe topic relevant to a shared local environment. I expected a formulaic reply, along the lines of the one produced before D's pause. But D's continuing question indicated that he drew an inference of possible complaint from my question, about the delay in the waiting area. As a now paying patient, my question about being busy seemed to open up an agenda of publicised waiting times, privileges and responsibilities. My intended safe and neutral small talk, recontextualised into the commercial world of private dental care, is no longer safe and neutral but liable to be interpreted as part of the transaction. This process is the reverse of Fairclough's (1995) conversationalisation of public discourse or pseudo-intimacy. It is the commercialisation of small talk.

This set of political and moral issues deserves more attention. It could be illuminated by reconsidering sociological debates about the basis of social action in general. Transactional (e.g. selling) encounters seem to be constructed on a basic principle of 'means–ends rationality' (Cohen 1997). In entering a transactional encounter (say to buy a sweater or book a holiday), both server and customer through their talk assume speaking and acting positions in order to achieve desired and planned outcomes. Talk is structured around these goals, roles and anticipated outcomes. By contrast, the same individuals, outside of the buying/selling frame, might converse with each other with far less, or far less evident, means–ends rationality. They may simply be 'being sociable'. If this mode of discourse follows a rational principle it could be termed 'value-rational' (Cohen 1997). The structuring of the speakers' (small talk) encounter will display the lack of commitment to reasoned outcomes. But, following Fairclough's argument about conversationalisation, we can also conceive of small talk and 'goallessness' being appropriated into the means–ends rational frame, and pressed into service, e.g. to oil the commercial wheels or to engineer trust and commitment (see N. Coupland and Ylänne-McEwen; also Cheepen; both in this volume). It should be possible to establish, on the basis of interactional evidence, whether 'small talk' is being enacted in one rather than another of these two broadly distinct social formats.

It is also useful to study metacommentaries on small talk, and how even *they* can be put to commercial use. A recent British Telecom booklet, titled *Talk Works: How to get more out of life from better conversations*, uses some of the intrepretive lines we have considered in this Introduction. On a page entitled 'Conversations that make a difference' the last paragraph invites readers to 'Suppose Gail wants to have a chat about nothing in particular'. The text goes on to provide a way of reasoning about the value of small talk:

> It may be just Gail's way of saying 'I like you. I value your company.' To dismiss this kind of conversation – small talk, as we call it – as unimportant is to deny Gail the opportunity to demonstrate her friendship.

> (British Telecom 1997: 15–16)

The booklet finishes with '25 top tips', number 23 of which reads: 'Respect small talk. It's an important way to establish and demonstrate our closeness to people . . .' British Telecom marketing staff appear to have read Scollon more than Malinowski. But their 'tips' seem geared towards boosting telephone talk time more than telephone users' social relationships.

Small talk and social ritual

From the few instances I have considered above, it is obvious that defining small talk too rigidly as a bounded mode of talk will constrain the analysis of its social functions. Certainly, Malinowski and Laver located phatic communion outside of the communicative mainstream, and some other studies have maintained this tradition. Schneider (1988) and Eggins and Slade (1997), as I noted earlier, locate 'phatic discourse' (in the case of the first) and 'casual conversation' (in the case of the second) as modes of discourse distinct from working talk and give a detailed lexico-grammatical accounts of it. What such approaches miss is the subtleties of discursive renegotiation – where, within a given speech event, speakers' orientations, framings and footings shift, reflecting their changing local priorities as talk proceeds.

At the same time, local creativity is a counterpoint to communicative predictability. It is only because so many facets of small talk are routinised (Coulmas 1981) that its styles and formats can be evoked creatively in other contexts of interaction. In his book *Smooth Talkers* (1996), Kuiper makes the distinction between routine(s) and ritual(s). Routines are more general, and any repeated activity is a routine. Rituals are routines which have assumed specific socio–cultural significance – like television debates, funerals and playing the dozens (Labov's ritual insults). This definition suggests that many structural, referential and stylistic features of small talk are routine (conventional conversational openings and closings, talking about the weather or updating on recent personal happenings, signalled prosodic engagement) (see Schneider 1988), but they are not necessarily invested with cultural significance as rituals. Some small talk events, alternatively, may reach this level of recognition and be culturally identified, for example in 'gossiping' (where ratified participants are carefully monitored and highly significant socio–cultural activities such as moral policing are mutually achieved).

In fact, one unifying strand of argument in the chapters of this volume is that small talking – whether we use the terms ritual or routine to identify its sub-practices – typically has a very broad if under-analysed cultural significance. The range of conversational work that Brown and Levinson (1987) subsume under the rubric of positive and negative politeness is certainly routinised, even formulaic, and a defining characteristic of everyday social talk. But Brown and Levinson also see politeness as a series of mini-rituals systematically linked to, and evocative of, socio-cultural grand rites. That is, in local conversational routines, people actively recreate the bonding and respecting behaviours that are the social fabric of their communities. This in turn suggests that even stigmatised small talk events – those with labels like 'nattering', 'chewing the fat' and 'gossiping' – can be examined as means of cultural reproduction (see Blum-Kulka, this volume). Their value is apparent when we find striking cross-cultural variation in the significance afforded to interactional routines (see Nwoye 1992; Matsumoto 1988 and Jaworski, this volume). One example is the social standing attached to the observed performance of *taearof*, realised as the issuing of repeated and insistent social invitations in Persian (Koutlaki 1997).

Any approbation that small talk has attracted can easily be associated with the long-standing belief that rituals are, at least at an abstract level, socially productive. As we have seen, conversation analysts' arguments that everyday conversation constructs the social order mesh well with Malinowski's early claims about the value of 'mere talk' in establishing social communion. As Cohen says in her commentary on Garfinkel (1997: 128), Garfinkel's case was that 'normal practices produce intelligible forms of social organization, an order in events that actors take for granted in their everyday lives'. Garfinkel, says Cohen, held an 'embargo on consciousness' (p. 127), suggesting that social actors know how to produce social action but don't know what they know. The analysis of conversation, and its routine structures, therefore captures the quality of the social structure.

But order, organisation and predictability are a two-edged sword in social life, and 'the social order' is not always experienced as a neutral set of invisible, socially productive norms. Correspondingly, small talk can be seen to have more specific socio-structural potential, for better or worse. Interactional routines can provide reassurance and enjoyment through their predictability, as in retelling family stories, singing familiar songs or cycling through familiar conversational routines. They can evoke a normality and permanence of social relationships. At a lower level, conversation closing routines explicitly refer to on-going relationships, next meetings and retrospect on pleasurable social contact (*it's been nice to talk to you . . . , see you soon . . . , I'll call you*). But routines can also be dull and even stultifying. They can stifle involvement and creativity, for example in the dreaded predictability of 'safe' topics of talk in western first-acquaintance interactions (the local environment or the weather) or, in situations I don't need to specify, updating formulas (*how did you get here today?*; *are you taking a holiday this year?*, *my goodness how you've grown*).

There are risks in endorsing the cult of the everyday to the extent of ruling out evaluative reactions to small talk. This at least might be where academic and lay evaluations part company. We need to acknowledge that formulaicity, while serving norms of politeness behaviour, can be tedious and communicatively incompetent. Artful speakers may regularly seek to avoid or deflect it, in order to break through to a mode of small talk which is more creatively designed and personally focused (Kuiper and Flindall, this volume). This is nicely illustrated by a fragment of talk I overheard in a small neighbourhood post office (Extract 4). A customer is paying for a couple of postage stamps with a £5 note. The Clerk's metacomment in turn two and the Customer's response both show awareness of the limits of conventional small talking, as if both have read Malinowski.

Extract 4

Customer: I'm sorry I haven't got anything smaller
Clerk: (starting to smile) you're not sorry at all
Customer: (chuckling) no but it seems like the right thing to say doesn't it?

Contextual loadings of small talk: the case of old age

It is easy enough to demonstrate that the loading of small talk, or (in N. Coupland and Ylänne-McEwen's term, this volume) the extent and nature of its 'mattering', is contextually variable. At the time of writing, a local radio station is running an advertisement, at the start of which we hear a young man asking a young woman some questions about her recent holiday. Did she enjoy it? Who had she been with? The young woman replies that she is too tired to talk, and this far, listeners are likely to judge the talk to be pretty mundane. The tape of their conversation is then run again, this time with the background noises of the aftermath of a traffic accident or urban disturbance. We are made aware that the young man is a Special Constable looking after an injured woman, and the 'small talk' is intended to keep her awake and conscious. Our assessment of how much and how the talk about the holiday matters is shifted by the altered frame in which we understand the situation in which it occurs.

If small talk as a way of speaking has typically been adjudged insignificant or banal (and we have seen that some linguists have taken this view), this has been based on an assumption that contents and styles of talk can be graded in absolute terms (see above). The assumption is challenged by Tannen (1989: 148), who cites 'an instance of private language reported to me by a woman whose family refers to grandmother as "I had a little ham, I had a little cheese"'. Tannen's informants had described the 'boring way that grand- mother reports insignificant details such as what she had for lunch. They wish she gave fewer details, or did not report her lunch at all, since they regard the topic not worth telling about.' Tannen's argument is that the telling and sharing of details is at the centre of the pursuit and confirmation of rapport and intimacy in relationships, much as I have argued earlier in this chapter. Another of Tannen's instances (ibid.) is a woman in her 70s who cried tears of gratitude when a male friend asked her on the phone what she had worn out to dinner that evening. The aunt reported that no one had shown that sort of interest in her for a very long time, and interpreted her friend's elicitation of details as an expression of interest and commitment.

But there is a special salience in instances like these which probably generalises not so much to old age itself as to circumstances of loneliness and social isolation. It happens that, at least in the UK, these circumstances do tend (but by no means universally) to be associated with advanced old age. With colleagues, a good deal of my own research has been concerned with the sociolinguistic correlates of ageing (Coupland, Coupland and Giles 1991; Nussbaum and Coupland 1995), and small talk takes on a distinctive flavour in the context of old age.

Sacks's idea of the 'private calendar' helps us establish the issue theoret- ically. What private calendars do (Sacks 1987: 222) 'is to provide for the locating of, not only events within relationships, but events of the world in general by reference to the relationship'. Private calendars provide a way for people to conceptualise together 'what matters to us', and to talk about their lives in the world through reference to experiences they have shared in their mutual histories. People who share private calendars which are busy, active and eventful, will have a lot to share in their talk, and a lot to 'catch up on' when they meet after a separation. Sacks in fact muses on elderly people who have few or no regular social contacts and therefore little to fill out their private calendar, and few contacts to share talk with in any case. Much of small talk is topically founded in response to change (see N. Coupland and Ylänne-McEwen, Drew and Chilton, Jaworski, Kuiper and Flindall, McCarthy, all in this volume). Recent past events (e.g. visits, news), changes to present circumstances (e.g. health), and future plans and intentions are all grist to the topical small talk mill. We noted earlier how small talk among acquaintances conventionally builds on conversation openings such as *what've you been up to?*, *what's been happening?*, or *doing anything nice at the weekend?*

Two contrasting data extracts from our earlier research on ageing (N. Coupland, J. Coupland, Giles and Henwood 1988: 18) show the potential effect of different private calendars on small talk. In each case, I (identified as J in the transcripts) am involved in conversation with an elderly female relative, sitting drinking tea during a regular visit. Extract 5 illustrates my exchanges with the relative (fictionalised as Emily) with whom I share a relatively full private calendar. Emily is a well, active 83 year old. She is recounting the aftermath of a recent family visit at which we had both been present.

Extract 5

```
1 E: um (.) what else (.) and er er I rang M____ last
2     night I was in a panic=
3 J: =why?
4 E: when I came home from (.) er from er (.) Gloucester (.)
5     from K___'s birthday I took some snaps while I was there
            [   ]
6 J:        mm
7 E: (.) and I couldn't find my camera and I looked and looked
                              [ ]
8 J:                          ah
```

Emily's *what else* in line 1 marks this segment as one in a sequence of tellings between us. Her account is marked as newsworthy, or sufficiently 'mattering' to tell, by the implication of a need to disclose, the framing within a narrative sequence (lines 4–7) and the dramatising force of *in a panic* (line 2) as narrative work-up. The event being described (the temporary loss of a camera) is perhaps mundane enough, but comes about in the context of family birthday celebration (line 5). The wider context is Emily's having travelled to the party and having change to report.

In contrast, lack of change in Doris's life impacts on the nature of small talk she and I can achieve, see Extract 6. Doris is a relatively unwell, immobile 85 year old. Doris has initiated talk on 'the price of things today', specifically referring to biscuits (not for the first time in conversation with me).

Extract 6

```
1 D: but in all ways prices are crazy (.) now (.) er for example
2     at breakfast (.) I never could eat breakfast (.) a couple
3     of biscuits are all I like for my breakfast=
4 J: =mm
5 D: I like a plain biscuit I like an Osborne biscuit (.) well Edna
```

```
 6      got them for me (.) um (.) oh until two or three months ago
 7      (.) she said to me well she said (.) I had a real shock today
 8      (.) she said she'd always got the biscuits at such and such
 9      a place but she went into another supermarket that she
10      doesn't often go into (.) and the same packet of biscuits (.)
11      Osborne biscuits which she had been paying twenty-five
12      pence for (.) in this shop were fifteen (1.0) now a packet
13      of biscuits and ten pence variation on them
14 J:   gosh (.) that's a lot isn't it?
                     [
15 D:                      I think there should be some
16      price control
17 J:   mm (.) mm (.) there isn't though (.) is there?
```

Doris's detailing about breakfast (lines 2–3) is very reminiscent of Tannen's 'bread and cheese' example. The detailing of the story of Edna (the home care assistant)'s discovery, with the reported speech (lines 7–8) details of the new location for shopping (lines 9–10) the type of product (line 11) and the price difference (lines 13–14) assumes a newsworthiness evaluation which I did not share. An exhaustive, unsolicited, subsequent account of Doris' daily routine, plus an anecdote rehearsed (I happened to know) on several previous occasions (about a relative helping with some house repairs) were also part of the conversation. A combination of limited topic repertoire, infrequent social contacts and a largely non-changing milieu may lead some small talkers to misjudge the extent to which what matters to them will also be seen as mattering to their interlocutor. There may be serious inter-individual and intergroup consequences, such as avoiding contact and confirming ageist stereotypes. Yet it is very likely that small talk like mine with Doris does matter, both because such encounters may constitute relatively important events in Doris's calendar and perhaps because it allows her to fend off more troubling and problematic topics.

Earlier in the chapter I mentioned the complex inter-relation between social and professional frames in medical discourse. Data from Geriatric Outpatients clinics (from my work with colleagues) again show how ageing issues can re-weight the significance of small talk in that setting. Extract 7 was originally reported in Coupland, Robinson and N. Coupland 1994 (but see also Coupland, Coupland and Robinson 1992; Coupland and Coupland 1997, 1998, 1999). This is the first meeting between the male doctor (D) and this elderly female patient (P). The sequence takes place immediately after the initial greetings and dispositional talk at the opening of the consultation.

Extract 7

```
1 D: you've been seeing=
2 P: =doctor=
```

```
 3  D:  =doctor Brown haven't you (.) the Australian doctor
                            [      ]
 4  P:                      ((yes))
 5  P:  yes ((well)) she's gone hasn't she?
                                     [
 6  D:                               she's gone back to
 7      Australia so you'd have a long way to go to see her
                            [     ]
 8  P:                      yes
 9  P:  yeah (chuckles)
10  D:  where did you get the (.) the ((armband))?
11  P:  which one? (.) which one?
                                  [
12  D:                            the gold one?
13  P:  the gold one? (.) why?
                        [     ]
14  D:                  yeah
15  P:  Saudi
16  D:  Saudi?
17  P:  ((Sau er)) that's their er (.) emblem
18  D:  that's right yeah
                    [
19  P:              ((got a)) son there
20  D:  your son?
21  P:  he got a big jobs you know
22  D:  has he?
23  P:  he's goes around doing big jobs his own business
               [      ]
24  D:         that's erm right
25  P:  he was out there for four months
26  D:  and he brought you home that?
27                        [     ]
28  P:                    and see the only thing about
29      it they couldn't have a (.) drink out there (.) and there's
30      no drink out there see
                         [
31  D:                   yeah no Brain's Dark (a local brew of beer)
32  P:  (laughs) er
               [
33  D:         how are you anyway? tell me
```

Generally in these data, consultations open in a predominantly social frame, where relational concerns are given precedence over (at least overtly) instrumental medical concerns. Most of the openings we examined exhibited conventional norms of politeness and (what Laver called) exploration and propitiation. Occasional instances of teasing, complimenting and personal noticings (such as the one in Extract 7, line 10) are more likely to be heard as expressions of genuine interpersonal involvement than as conventional formulas. They are certainly more extensive and more diverse in our data than in most doctor–patient corpora (see Ragan, this volume).

At line 6 the doctor begins to indulge in some gentle teasing of the patient about Doctor Brown ('the Australian doctor')'s move. At line 10, at a point where the patient might have expected the social frame to have lapsed and the medical business now to be attended to, the doctor enquires about an item of jewellery the patient is wearing. The patient's *why?* at line 13 may indicate her surprise at the personal focus of the question in this context. How could the armband and where it came from matter to the doctor? But the doctor actively sustains the patient's account in response. They develop the topic together and establish it as an area in which they have some shared experience. The doctor's *that's right* at line 18 has the form and placement of a 'professional' follow-up third-move, but this talk remains non-professionally framed. Later, at line 20, where the doctor again has an opportunity to move the talk onto medical matters, he continues to support the patient in the telling of personal details, now about her son (lines 22, 26 and 31). They come to share a joke about the importance of the local beer.

Another extract (the final one we shall consider) shows how negotiating frames in the geriatrics context can be difficult to manage. The patient in Extract 8 is a female, aged 80, overweight and with diabetes. She is accompanied by her daughter (identified as Da) to the clinic. The three have met on several previous occasions. At the start of the extract, greetings and dispositional talk have been dispensed with and the doctor has obtained permission to record; this is the topic in place at the outset of the extract.

Extract 8

```
 1 D:  any (.) no secrets you want to tell me=
 2 Da: = (laughs)
            [
 3 P:     no I haven't ((doctor))
                [
 4 D:         oh I'm disappointed (.) I'm disappointed
 5 Da: (laughs loudly)
                                      [
 6 P:                                 are you?
 7     (all three laugh together)
 8 D:  (recovering) ahh! how was Bournemouth? (rustles case-notes)
 9 P:  oh lovely
10 D:  mm
11 Da: yeah came home ((fitter))
            [
12 P:       really nice
13 D:  enjoyed yourself
```

14 P: yes nice and quiet
        [
15 D: I can see that I can see that you have enjoyed yourself
                         [
16 Da: (laughs)
17 P: <u>can</u> you?
18 D: (teasing voice) yes the blood sugar is a little on the <u>high</u> side (2.0)
19 Da: well (hurriedly) the er on the last visit
             [
20 D: (laughs at length and heartily)
21 Da: (laughs briefly) you said er (laughs)
22   (all three laugh together)
23 Da: on the (laughs) on the last visit (more seriously) the doctor we saw (.) he
24   prescribed them (tablets she is putting on the table) for mam but she was
25   bilious

From line 1, the doctor develops a strategy of eliciting somewhat inappropriate confidential details of the patient's life, to initiate a mildly flirtatious, teasing sequence. This, together with its response, lasts to line 6. At line 8 the doctor invokes their shared private calendar in his enquiry about a recent holiday the patient and her daughter have taken. His appraisal at lines 15 and 18 looks to be very much in the same mode of verbal banter as before, but when he extends this into commenting on the patient's blood test results (line 18), there is a dissonance and a frame ambiguity. What agenda the doctor is speaking to, and therefore what matters in the talk, at line 18 and in the discourse space which follows it, is delicately poised. The hearable uptake is first a two-second pause, and then the daughter's account of her mother's medication problems, starting on line 19.

My role as a participant-observer allowed me to notice the doctor's 'twinkling' demeanour during line 15, which is apparently picked up and responded to (at first hesitantly) by the daughter (in line 21), and then by her mother. The mutual laughter at line 22 confirms that they are now all orienting to the doctor's blood sugar comment as *not* mattering in the biomedical domain, but as part of talk in the social domain, in relation to how they enjoyed the holiday. The patient and daughter must expect the doctor to assume his professional role as a 'health caretaker' (which presumably involves 'policing' blood sugar levels) at some point. But whether that point has arrived, in the development of the discourse, at line 15 is the source of the daughter's uncertainty. There is an audible stylistic shift out of 'smile voice' during line 23. In the following turns (beyond the transcribed portion), talk is framed and oriented to by all three as 'serious medical business'.

There are important reasons in the theory and ideology of geriatrics why socio-relational talk of the sort we see in Extracts 7 and 8 *needs* to be part of geriatric medical consultation discourse. Many of the health problems confronting older people have to do with life circumstances and morale, as much as specific bio-medical conditions. Talk about social circumstances and family connections may trigger discussion of environmental matters which could be relevant to the clinic's and the doctors' professional responsibilities. The fact that various socio-relational themes (family contacts and alcohol in Extract 7, and holidays and diet in Extract 8) have surfaced in the social frame for talk may mean that they will be easier to reinstate later as topics for 'medical' consideration (see also Candlin 1995). Again, the solidarity and social support it achieves, in itself, can reasonably be thought of as part of the 'treatment'. The age context does not redefine consultation talk in the social frame to be something other than social talk. Rather, age issues introduce another layer of potential relevance upon it.

Overall, in age-related discourse contexts, we find one set of social considerations which force us to develop relatively complex readings of small talk practice. In various ways, small talk involving elderly speakers (more specifically, those with possibly limited social networks or with health problems linked to their social circumstances) can be an important human and even medical resource. These are reasons to challenge the presumed 'smallness' of small talk, and this is a theme I have emphasised throughout this Introduction.

In the following chapters, other contributors make equally powerful arguments for richly contextualised readings. The methodological approach of the volume can broadly be characterised as discourse analytic; but chapter authors' use of a variety of theoretical frameworks demonstrate the broad church into which discourse analysis, over the last twenty years, has evolved. The theoretical backdrop which informs many of the analyses can be broadly defined as interactional sociolinguistics, which is to say that the analysts here make use of a range of ideas including social anthropology, discursive psychology, pragmatics and critical linguistics (see especially Holmes, Coupland and Ylänne-McEwen, Jaworski, Coates). But there are analyses which are influenced in addition by USA-style Communication theory, with its influences from psychology in general and social psychology in particular, as evidenced in Tracy and Naughton and Ragan. Some of the chapters in the book also make use of the ethnomethodologically driven conversation analytic approach, which is most apparent in Drew and Chilton, but also shows its influence in Cheepen and in Coupland and Ylänne-McEwen. McCarthy's work here has grown from the theory of spoken genre; extending the traditional transactional focus into the relational arena. Kuiper and Flindall's chapter can most clearly be identified with the ethnography of speaking, in that they demonstrate the constraints of culture on linguistic performance. Blum-Kulka and Jaworski's chapters also exemplify cross-cultural pragmatics. Taken together, the chapters range over a wide array of social and cultural settings, but move their analyses forward through examining the relationship between function and form within those contexts, as is classically the case with discourse analysis.

Notes

1. I am grateful to Jackie Guendouzi, with whom I shared many discussions about timeout talk, to Pam Perkins for providing me with material and to Nik Coupland and Gordon Tucker for comments on earlier drafts of this work.
2. Transcription conventions used in Extracts 2–8 are:

(.)	un-timed short pause
(1.0)	pause timed in seconds
(quietly)	informal commentary on style or context of following utterance(s)
?	indicates question function (not grammatical interrogative)
[	overlapping speech
[ ]	entirely overlapped speech
Underlining	shows unusually heavy emphasis
=	shows 'latching' (utterances following each other without perceptible pause)

References

Bakhtin, M. M. (1986) *Speech Genres and Other Late Essays.* Trans. V. W. McGee. Austin, Texas: University of Texas Press.

Bourdieu, P. (1991) *Language and Symbolic Power.* Cambridge: Polity Press.

British Telecom (1997) *Talk Works: How to get more out of life through better conversations.*

Brown, P. and Levinson, S. (1978) Universals in Language Usage: Politeness phenomena. In E. N. Goody (ed.) *Questions and Politeness.* Cambridge: Cambridge University Press, pp. 56–289.

Brown, P. and Levinson, S. (1987) *Politeness: Some Universals in Language Usage.* Cambridge: Cambridge University Press.

Cameron, D. (1995) *Verbal Hygiene.* London: Routledge.

Candlin, S. (1995) Towards excellence in nursing: An analysis of the discourse of nurses and patients in the context of health care assessment. Unpublished PhD thesis, University of Lancaster.

Candlin, S. (forthcoming) New dynamics in the nurse–patient relationship?

Carroll, R. (1987) *Cultural Misunderstandings: The French-American experiences.* Chicago: University of Chicago Press.

Cheepen, C. (1988) *The Predictability of Informal Conversation.* London: Pinter.

Cheepen, C. and Monaghan, J. (1990) *Spoken English: A Practical Guide.* London: Pinter.

Coates, J. (1986) *Women, Men and Language.* London: Longman.

Cohen, I. J. (1997) Theories of action and praxis. In B. Turner (ed.) *The Blackwell Companion to Social Theory.* Oxford: Blackwell Publishers, pp. 111–42.

Coulmas, F. (1981) *Conversational Routine: Explorations in Standardized Communication Situations and Prepatterned Speech.* The Hague: Mouton.

Coupland, J., Coupland, N. and Robinson, J. (1992) 'How are you?': Negotiating phatic communion. *Language in Society* 21: 201–30.

Coupland, J., Robinson, J. and Coupland, N. (1994) Frame negotiation in doctor-elderly patient consultations. *Discourse and Society* 5, 1: 89–124.

Coupland, N. and Coupland, J. (1997) Discourses of the unsayable: Death-implicative talk in geriatric medical consultations. In A. Jaworski (ed.) *Silence: Interdisciplinary Perspectives*, pp. 117–52.

Coupland, N. and Coupland, J. (1998) Reshaping lives: Constitutive identity work in geriatric medical consultations. *Text.* 18, 2: 159–89.

Coupland, N. and Coupland, J. (1999) Ageing, ageism and anti-ageism: Moral stance in geriatric medical discourse. In H. Hamilton (ed.) *Language and Old Age*. New York: Garland Publishing, pp. 177–208.

Coupland, N., Coupland, J. and Giles, H. (1991) *Language, Society and the Elderly: Discourse, Identity and Ageing*. Oxford: Blackwell.

Coupland, N., Coupland, J., Giles, H. and Henwood, K. (1988) Accommodating the elderly: Invoking and extending a theory. *Language in Society* 17: 1–41.

Drew, P. and Heritage, J. (1992) *Talk at Work: Interaction in Institutional Settings* (Studies in Interactional Sociolinguistics 8). Cambridge: Cambridge University Press.

Eggins, S. and Slade, D. (1997) *Analysing Casual Conversation*. London: Cassell.

Fairclough, N. (1995) *Critical Discourse Analysis*. London: Longman.

Firth, J. R. (1972) Verbal and bodily rituals of greeting and parting. In J. S. La Fontaine (ed.) *The Interpretation of Ritual*. London: Tavistock, pp. 1–38.

Fisher, S. (1991) A discourse of the social: medical talk/power talk/oppositional talk? *Discourse and Society* 2 (2): 157–82.

Garfinkel, H. (1963) *Studies in Ethnomethodology*. Englewood Cliff, NJ: Prentice Hall.

Giddens, A. (1991) *Modernity and self-identity: Self and Society in the Late Modern Age*. Cambridge: Polity Press.

Goffman, E. (1959) *The Presentation of Self in Everyday Life*. New York: Anchor Books.

Guendouzi, J. (1998) Negotiating socialised gender identity in women's time-out talk. Unpublished PhD thesis, University of Wales, Cardiff.

Habermas, J. (1984) *Theory of Communicative Action*, vol.1: *Reason and the Rationalisation of Society* (translated by T. McCarthy). London: Heinemann.

Heritage, J. (1997) Conversation analysis and institutional talk: Analysing data. (Paper presented at the Cardiff Round Table on Sociolinguistics and Social Theory.)

Hopper, R. (1992) *Telephone Conversation*. Bloomington: Indiana University Press.

Johnson, S. and Finlay, F. (1997) Do men gossip? An analysis of football talk on television. In S. Johnson and U. H. Meinhof (eds) *Language and Masculinity*. Oxford: Blackwell, pp. 130–43.

Jones. D. (1990) Gossip: Notes on women's oral culture. In D. Cameron (ed.) *The Feminist Critique of Language: A Reader*. London: Routledge.

Koutlaki, S. (1997) Politeness and facework in Persian. Unpublished PhD thesis, University of Wales, Cardiff.

Kuiper, K. (1996) *Smooth Talkers: The Linguistic Performance of Auctioneers and Sportscasters*. Mahwah, NJ: Lawrence Erlbaum Associates.

Labov, W. (1972) *Sociolinguistic Patterns*. Philadelphia: University of Pennsylvania Press.

Laver, J. (1974) Communicative functions of phatic communion. *Work in Progress* 7: 1–17.

Laver, J. (1975) Communicative functions of phatic communion. In A. Kendon, R. M. Harris, and M. R. Key (eds) *The Organisation of Behavior in Face-to-Face Interaction*. The Hague: Mouton, pp. 215–38.

Laver, J. (1981) Linguistic routines and politeness in greeting and parting. In F. Coulmas (ed.) *Conversational Routine*. The Hague: Mouton, pp. 289–304.

Leech, G. (1974) *Semantics*. Harmondsworth: Penguin.

Malinowski, B. (1923) The problem of meaning in primitive languages. In C. K. Ogden and I. A. Richards (eds) *The Meaning of Meaning*. London: Routledge and Kegan Paul, pp. 146–52.

Matsumoto, Y. (1988) Reexamination of the universality of face: Politeness phenomena in Japanese. *Journal of Pragmatics* 12: 403–26.

Merritt, M. (1975) On questions following questions in service encounters. *Language in Society* 5: 315–57.

Nussbaum, J. and Coupland, J. (eds) (1995) *Handbook of Communication and Aging Research*. Mahwah, NJ: Lawrence Erlbaum Associates.

Nwoye, O. (1992) Linguistic politeness and sociocultural variations of the notion of face. *Journal of Pragmatics* 18: 309–28.

Robinson, W. P. (1972) *Language and Social Behaviour*. Harmondsworth: Penguin.

Sacks, H. (1975) Everyone has to lie. In M. Sanches and B. G. Blount (eds) *Sociocultural dimensions of language use*. New York: Academic Press, pp. 57–80.

Sacks, H. (1987) You want to find out if anybody really does care. In G. Button and J. R. Lee (eds) *Talk and Social Organisation*. Clevedon: Multilingual Matters.

Sarangi, S. and Slembrouck, S. (1996) *Language, Bureaucracy and Social Control*. London: Longman.

Schegloff, E. (1986) The routine as achievement. *Human Studies* 9: 111–51.

Schegloff, E. (1992) On talk and its institutional occasions. In P. Drew and J. Heritage (eds) *Talk at Work: Interaction in Institutional Settings*. Cambridge: Cambridge University Press, pp. 101–34.

Schiffrin, D. (1994) *Approaches to Discourse*. Oxford: Basil Blackwell.

Schneider, K. (1988) *Small Talk: Analysing Phatic Discourse* Marburg: Hitzeroth.

Schwebel, D. C. (1997) Strategies of verbal duelling: How college students win a verbal battle. *Journal of Language and Social Psychology*, 16, 3: 326–43.

Scollon, R. (1998) *Mediated Discourse as Social interaction: A Study of News Discourse*. London: Addison Wesley Longman.

Tannen, D. (1989) *Talking Voices: Repetition, Dialogue and Imagery in Conversational Discourse*. Cambridge: Cambridge University Press.

Tracy, K. (1990) The many faces of facework. In H. Giles and W. P. Robinson (eds) *Handbook of Language and Social Psychology*. Chichester: John Wiley, pp. 209–26.

Tracy, K. and Coupland, N. (1991) *Multiple Goals in Discourse*. Clevedon: Multilingual Matters.

Turner, G. (1973) *Stylistics*. Harmondsworth: Penguin.

Wolfson, N. (1981) Invitations, compliments and the competence of the native speaker. *International Journal of Psycholinguistics* 8: 7–22.

Locating small talk theoretically

Introduction to **Part I**

Justine Coupland

All chapters in the volume introduce new data and, through their analyses and interpretations of it, help to reformulate theory. Matters of sociolinguistic contextualisation, discourse organisation, social implications and applications are common to all contributions. To that extent, the four-part structure of the book overstates distinctions between chapters – into 'theoretical', 'procedural', 'social' and 'applied' aspects, respectively. At the same time, there are differences of emphasis within the chapters.

The four I have placed in this first section include particularly helpful discussions of small talk as a generic phenomenon. They continue, clarify and elaborate the discussion I opened up in the Introduction. They attempt categorisations and bring forward criteria for particular definitions of small talk phenomena, whether these are for academic usage or in popular perceptions. They examine small talk alongside and in contrast to other discourse phenomena and practices.

Holmes discusses the distribution, structural positioning and functioning of small talk in the workplace. She conceptualises types of talk as existing along a continuum, with 'core business talk' and 'phatic communion' interspersed by 'work-related' and 'social' talk. Her argument is that the status of an exchange as small talk, and the complex functions that such talk serves in the workplace, can only be established in a rich contextual analysis. We need, for example, to consider the purposes of particular social exchanges in particular contexts, and the symmetrical or asymmetrical statuses of the participants. Functionally, Holmes finds small talk to be a versatile resource in the institutional setting (here, a government office). A large number of data extracts display small talk being used among colleagues as a transitional device, at liminal moments, and in longer stretches of talk to enact friendship or collegiality. But, notably, it is also used to constitute power in the workplace via the management of small talk, with superiors delaying, withholding or constraining such talk with their subordinates.

Tracy and Naughton also examine institutional interaction, but they ask how lay and academic conceptual 'lenses' for looking at talk guide how talk is perceived. Their academic lens provides us with a review of how communication theory in the United States has distinguished types or genres of talk. Their data are from meetings – an academic research colloquium and a hospice case review. The 'lay lens' is illustrated by examining popular usage of the term small talk, as used in newspaper articles about business, politics and the media. The lay lens yields a focus on instrumentality, with small talk largely seen as a skill or accomplishment needed to make connections and to succeed generally. Tracy and Naughton's close analysis of extended stretches of talk within two institutions, as viewed turn-by-turn through four academic lenses, reveals small talk to be the medium via which individual and especially group-level identities and aspects of relationships within the group are supported or contested. Tracy and Naughton argue, as does McCarthy in the following chapter, for placing the interpersonal and relational functions of all talk at 'centre stage', when viewing through the academic lens.

McCarthy's chosen social contexts are ones where interactants are locked into dyadic co-presence – a driving lesson and a session at the hairdresser's. His theoretical focus is the relationship between spoken genres and how the values of 'transactional or task oriented talk' and 'relational' or 'participant-oriented' talk are weighted in different environments. McCarthy argues that theorists need to give greater priority to the relational values expressed in small talk as a way of generating more satisfactory models of spoken genres. Rather like Holmes's categorisation, he distinguishes four broad 'types of talk', ranging from phatic exchanges through relational (including small) talk to transactional-plus-relational talk and finally transactional talk. But he emphasises that functional values vary along different, concurrent dimensions in the whole range of talk he studies, with individual realisations seen as polyphonic. Thus, in each of his four types of talk he finds and displays for us a degree of relational focus.

McCarthy's 'sealed' social contexts are ones where small talk might be the preferred alternative to silence – talk (as Robinson construed it, and as discussed in the general Introduction) 'to avoid other problems'. Even talk which participants might define, as McCarthy says, to be 'banal or tiresome' might be less troublesome than silence. McCarthy does in fact show us how the topics introduced by the clients and their service providers are of some transactional relevance to the participants. He also echoes Tracy and Naughton's point that these speakers are at least giving voice to their social identities and their relationships. But in McCarthy's analysis, it is the talk/silence contrast that primarily drives small talk.

Jaworski's theoretical argument, based around authors' representations of talk from dramatic texts, gives us a very different account of talk and silence. His case is that small talk and silence can function as communicative equivalents, as well as sometimes standing in opposition to each other. As we saw in the Introduction, traditional treatments of phatic communion, from Malinowski on, have imbued small talk with negativity, precisely because it is 'merely' the avoidance of silence. But Jaworski's analysis shows how dramatists have constructed fictional characters who find solidarity and intimacy, more than threat or alarm, in silence. Along with other contributors to the book, Jaworski argues for a multi-layered approach to small talk, taking into account the full dynamics of speech events, including participant characteristics and goals. His chapter also considers cross-cultural variation in the use and interpretation of both small talk and silence. While both small talk and silence are directly involved in the negotiation of social distance, and differently across social and cultural groups, Jaworski gives us a more elaborate theoretical account of their inter-relationships.

1

Doing collegiality and keeping control at work: small talk in government departments[1]
Janet Holmes

Introduction

Extract 1[2]

Context: Diana enters Sally's office at the beginning of the day to collect mail
1 D: good morning Sally lovely day
2 S: yes don't know what we're doing here we should be out in the sun
3 D: mm pity about the work really
4 S: how are your kids?
5 D: much better thank goodness any mail?

This short exchange raises a number of the issues which will be explored in this paper. It looks like a classic example of 'small talk' but we cannot be sure of its exact status, nor of the precise functions it is serving, without knowing a great deal more about the context in which it occurs. Diana's opening utterance constitutes a ritual greeting and a conventional reference to the weather – prototypical small talk fitting most analysts' definitions (see Schneider 1988). Sally's response, *don't know what we're doing here we should be out in the sun*, is not quite so conventional (though increasingly becoming so), and might well qualify as small talk between equals. The fact that Diana is Sally's boss is information which allows for an alternative reading. The response can be read as a (humorous) complaint: Sally is 'here', at least to some extent, because Diana, her manager, requires her to be, as Diana's reply acknowledges. From an equal, the response *pity about the work really* would be unambiguously interpreted as ironic and humorous; from a superior, there is a potentially 'repressive' reading (see Holmes 1998).

The enquiry about Diana's children is also open to alternative interpretations. Conventional enquiries about the addressee's health (e.g. *how are you?*) constitute canonical small talk (Coupland *et al.* 1992); an enquiry about the health of family members conveys a slightly higher level of interest. A ritual reply – one which confirmed the status of the enquiry as small talk – would typically have taken the form *fine* or *great*. Diana's reply provides more information: we infer that her children have been sick and that this has been inconvenient and/or a source of worry. A further possible inference from the fact that she immediately asks *any mail* is that she does not wish to discuss the matter (though, without a great deal of additional information, it is fruitless to speculate on possible reasons for this). As the superior she has the right to signal the end of the small talk phase of the interaction. The status of an exchange as small talk, and the variety of complex functions that such talk serves in everyday interaction in the workplace, are far from straightforward issues, as this chapter will demonstrate.

Most discussions of small talk begin from Malinowski's definition of 'phatic communion' (1949: 216). But the concept has proved so valuable that it has developed to cover a wider range of discourse, and considerable attention has been paid to its complex functions (see Justine Coupland's Introduction to this volume). Coupland *et al.* note that Malinowski's discussion has given rise to a disparaging view of small talk as 'dissimulative', involving a 'fundamental indirectness' (1992: 209), a view which they challenge, noting the strategic advantages of discourse which avoids precise commitment to a particular position.

The negative perception of small talk as marginal or purposeless reflects to some extent the way it is often defined, explicitly or implicitly, as talk which is *not* concerned with information, which is not 'purposive' or task-oriented. Schneider (1988: 1), for example, quotes Schlieben-Lange's (1979: 98) distinction between 'instrumental' talk, focussed on information and intentions, and phatic or small talk which has a more sociable primary function.[3] Yet, as the discussion of Extract 1 suggested, things are often more complicated. While the exchange clearly serves the social function of establishing initial contact between two co-workers on a particular day, it also serves a range of other functions, both affective and referential. It is not generally possible to parcel out meaning into neat packages of referential on the one hand and social or affective on the other. Talk is inherently multifunctional. Examining politeness strategies in women's and men's speech, the same point emerged; the structure of the model of interaction I adopted was designed to emphasise the fact that every interaction 'simultaneously expresses both propositional content and affective meaning' (Holmes 1990: 254; see also Tracy 1991, Tracy and Coupland 1991, Holmes 1995).

A social constructionist framework highlights the dynamic implications of this observation in on-going interaction. In every social encounter we are unavoidably involved in maintaining and modifying the interpersonal relationship between ourselves and our addressee(s). Adopting this perspective, 'small talk' cannot be dismissed as a peripheral, marginal or minor discourse mode. Small talk is one means by which we negotiate interpersonal relationships, a crucial function of talk with significant implications for on-going and future interactions.

Although phatic communion has been the focus of considerable theoretical discussion, there has been relatively little research examining its relation to small talk and its occurrence in 'natural situations'. Noting this point, Coupland *et al.* (1992) suggest that the issue of 'how phatic and transactional priorities are merged in, for example, service encounters and institutional settings is one worth pursuing' (Coupland *et al.* 1992: 227). This paper draws on a range of examples from one particular institutional setting, namely, government departments. Following a brief description of the database and the methodology, the analysis examines the relationship between 'core business talk' i.e. highly focused, on-task talk in relation to the defined objectives of an interaction (see below) – and more social talk in the workplace. The distribution and structural positioning of small talk are then discussed, and the final section of the paper focuses on the various functions of 'small talk' in the business organisations examined.

Database and methodology

The database from which the extracts discussed in this paper have been drawn consists of 330 interactions involving 251 people (152 women and 99 men) in four government departments. 114 of the participants are New Zealand Pakeha, 111 are Maori, and 26 are from other ethnic groups, such as Samoan, Chinese or Thai.[4] In total we recorded 121 hours of material. In each workplace a group of key personnel, representing a range of roles and levels within the organisation, recorded their everyday interactions with a variety of interlocutors across a range of work settings. A number of larger meetings in each workplace were also video-taped.[5]

The methodology developed for the project was designed to give participants maximum control over the data collection process. A group of volunteers from each workplace tape-recorded a range of their everyday work interactions over a period of about two weeks. Some kept a recorder and microphone on their desks, others carried the equipment round with them. All those involved provided information on their ethnic background, home language, age, etc., contextual information and permission for the data to be used for linguistic analysis. Throughout the process participants were free to edit and delete material as they wished. Even after they had completed recording and handed over the tapes, they could ask us to edit out material which they felt in retrospect they did not wish us to analyse. By handing over control of the recording process in this way, we developed an excellent research relationship with our workplace participants, based on mutual trust. Over a period of time, people increasingly ignored the recording equipment, and there are often comments at the end of interactions indicating people had forgotten about the tape recorder.[6] Also over time the amount of material they deleted, or which they asked us to edit out, decreased dramatically. As a result, in return for guarantees of anonymity and confidentiality, our volunteers trusted us with a wide range of fascinating material.

One of the consequences of this methodology for the analysis of small talk is that observations about the distribution of small talk must be treated with some caution. Although we emphasised that we were interested in ALL types of talk in the workplace, including social talk and personal talk, it is clear that participants often assumed that we were most centrally interested in the talk they classified as 'work', i.e. transactional talk of various kinds (cf. also Willing 1992). Hence, especially in the early stages of the project, they sometimes did not turn on their recorders until what they considered the 'real' beginning of a meeting, and they stopped the tape when they considered they had reached the end of the meeting. Despite such patterns, we did collect a good deal of small talk in the workplace, but the inevitable limitations of the data represented in our sample should be borne in mind, especially in relation to comments on the distribution of small talk. On the other hand, we are not aware of any other extant corpus which has been collected with a greater possibility of including naturally occurring spontaneous small talk in the workplace.

The requirements of the methodology also generated regular 'off-task' or non-work related discussion. Especially on the first occasion someone was recorded, there was often talk about the project itself, as well as talk related to filling in a background information sheet. One interesting consequence of this was that over time the topic of the recording process *developed into a legitimate topic of small talk*. In other words, the recording process became so 'normal' for some participants that it was relegated to the periphery of their attention and reference to it became routinised and formulaic. Consequently, ritual references to the project came to function in the same way as ritualised greetings (cf. what Coupland *et al.* (1992: 217) call ' "how are you?" (HAY) utterances').

Extract 2

Context: Ruth (manager) is talking to her personal assistant, Carol

1 R: [to tape recorder] conversation with Carol [laughs] come over here
2   I'm just gonna drive everyone insane with this tape recorder
3   /okay\
4 C: /oh well\ we'll let you off
5   right there's the phone number for you to call
6 R: okay ta
7 C: now look at these faxes these are- these are people whom we haven't
8   heard from [tut] so instead of bothering Mary to get her to sign

Ruth switches the tape recorder on as she approaches Carol's desk. She identifies the conversation for the purposes of the project as a *conversation with
Carol*, and then comments on the fact that she is doing a lot of recording.
This kind of comment occurs regularly in Ruth's recordings and other data
collectors similarly comment in a formulaic way on the recording process
on tape again, recording as usual and so on. Such comments become part of a
perfunctory ritual, reflecting the fact that the recording process has been
thoroughly integrated into people's work routines.

Analysing small talk at work

The analysis which follows is in three sections. The first section discusses
and illustrates some of the problems of identifying and defining 'small talk'
in the workplaces which were the focus of study. The second section discusses
features of the distribution, structural positioning and extent of small talk in
a variety of different contexts within these workplaces. The third section
explores the complex functions of small talk in the workplace, demonstrating
how apparently peripheral and innocuous phatic exchanges can serve pivotal
roles in furthering the interpersonal (and sometimes transactional/instrumental)
goals of those involved.

Identifying small talk in the workplace

One might expect that it would be relatively straightforward to identify
small talk in the workplace, that it would clearly stand out from surrounding
transactional 'work talk' or 'business talk'; but this is not the case. Many
aspects of the social and discourse context are crucial in defining small
talk. As Coupland *et al.* point out, the phatic function of talk emerges from
'its local sequential placement in particular contextualized episodes' and is
contingent upon 'the momentary salience of particular interactional goals'
(1992: 215).

In approaching the definition of small talk at work, it is useful to conceptualise types of talk in terms of a continuum with 'core business talk' at one
end and phatic communion at the other. (See Figure 1.1.) This conceptualisa-
tion assists in making explicit the criteria used to assign different sections of
an interaction to a particular point on the continuum. 'Core business talk' is
relevant, focussed, often context-bound, on-task talk, with a high information content. 'Relevance' is an important criterion. 'Relevant' here means
relevant to the organisation's core business: the underlying assumption is
that the 'proper' focus of workplace discourse is the business at hand. Busi-

CORE BUSINESS TALK ———————————————— PHATIC COMMUNION

Relevant 'on-topic' talk	Atopical talk
Maximally informative	Minimally informative
Context-bound	Context-free
Transactional	Social

Figure 1.1   Criteria for distinguishing business talk from phatic communion

ness talk directly serves the organisation's interests. 'Informativeness' is another useful criterion: core business talk is well-focussed, referential talk with high information content. A third criterion is the extent to which talk is context-bound: a full understanding of core business talk typically involves a great deal of background knowledge.[7] There is also, typically, a specific agenda for core business talk, though this may not be written or even explicit.

So, talk which qualifies for classification at the core business end of the continuum is crucially informative, highly focused and 'on-topic' in terms of the agreed meeting agenda for that particular meeting in that particular workplace, and it directly serves the organisation's goals. In Extract 3, for example, it is clear that Greg and Dan are heavily involved in the discourse of their workplace. They are centrally on-topic, communicating useful information to each other which only members of their workplace team could understand: this is core business talk furthering the objectives of their organisation.

Extract 3

Context: Pre-arranged meeting in manager's office
1 D: what they have in mind there the other issue with regard to this is
2   um they've also been sent a draft copy of the statement that New
3   Zealand's going to give deliver to the um Human Rights
4   Commission in Geneva
5 G: right
6 D: in a few weeks + now they don't require our input just yet
7   but they said that there may be a requirement for us to do a quick
8   summary of ++ or update where we're at with decade activities
9 G: yeah

At the other end of the continuum is phatic communion. At the extreme, this is talk which is independent of any specific workplace context, which is 'atopical' and irrelevant in terms of workplace business, and which has relatively little referential content or information load.[8] Extract 4 provides an example.

Extract 4

Context: Jock and Pam pass in the corridor.
1 J: morning Pam
2 P: hi Jock nice day
3 J: yeah great

There is nothing about this exchange to locate it in terms of workplace or participants; and it is minimally informative. Nevertheless, such social or collegial talk may be very important in terms of its affective components, and so serve the organisation's goals indirectly by maintaining good relationships between employees. The extent to which such talk is tolerated, encouraged or obligatory is one distinguishing feature of different organisational cultures. Although the extremes are relatively easy to identify, the point of suggesting that a continuum is involved is to highlight the fact that many workplace interactions do not fit neatly into the core categories of business talk and phatic communion. And, in particular, what I want to call 'small talk' extends a considerable distance along the continuum from phatic communion towards core business talk. Figure 1.2 illustrates this point.

The criteria used to allocate talk to a particular category are clearly gradable. Relevance is a matter of degree rather than a feature which is simply present or absent. Typically, the discourse of a meeting (at least in this database) does not develop in a neat linear progression; rather talk moves on and off topic (as defined in relation to the agreed core business) throughout the meeting. 'Topic drift' (Wilson 1989; Sollitt-Morris 1996) through explanations of terms, clarifications of intention, short side sequences and longer digressions from the main purpose of the meeting is common. Talk may gradually shift or drift along the continuum from on-topic business talk to talk which is not strictly relevant to the agenda for the interaction, but which is nevertheless work-related. Similarly, the information content of an interaction is not a matter of all-or-none. Measurement is crucially context-sensitive; so, for example, the current background knowledge of participants about relevant topics and issues is just one variable which will determine how informative an interaction is. And the extent to which a verbal exchange is tied to a particular context is also clearly variable. So an exchange may involve 'work talk', but not be strictly on-topic for the particular interaction in which it occurs. During a meeting to discuss the membership of an appointment panel, for example, the participants digressed to discuss the personality of a manager, a topic which was not strictly relevant to their task,

Core ——————————— Work ——————————— Social ———————— Phatic
business talk   related talk   talk   communion

←——————— SMALL TALK ———————→

Figure 1.2   Locating small talk on the continuum

but which was clearly a work-related topic. In Extract 5, the talk is strictly off Rose's intended topic, but again the topic is work-related talk.

Extract 5

Context: Rose, a senior manager, enters the office of an administrative assistant, Lisa, in search of information about someone's address

1 L: maybe you know the answer
2 R: what's that?
3 L: why was *ms* introduced instead of *missus* or *miss* +++
4 R: that's an interesting question ++ thought it had something to do with
5   um it's more sort of neutral you know in terms of the other one depicts
6   a particular status

As Rose enters the room, she is met by a request from Lisa to resolve a query (line 1). She responds *what's that* and there follows a discussion of an issue which is strictly 'off-topic' or irrelevant in relation to Rose's reason for being there. Although the request derails Ruth temporarily from her transactional goal, the topic is relevant to the department's business in the wider organisational context. The discussion thus provides an interesting example of talk on the continuum between business talk and social talk. Though it is strictly off-topic in terms of Ruth's intended business, it is nevertheless work-related business talk.

At the other end of the continuum, phatic communion drifts gradually towards social talk as the content of the exchange becomes more context-specific, and relates more precisely to the individuals involved. In such talk, the specific topic is backgrounded and contact *per se* is foregrounded, but the topic may not be totally divorced from the work context. So, meeting in the lift, Matt and Bob are clearly exchanging small talk but, with its reference to work, it is slightly less context-free than Extract 4.

Extract 6

Context: Two male colleagues of equal status, Matt and Bob, in the lift

1 M: hi how's things
2 B: hi good good + haven't seen you for ages how are you
3 M: fine busy though as always + must meet my performance
4   objectives eh [laugh]
5 B: [laugh] yeah me too
Lift arrives at Bob's floor
6   ah well see you later
7 M: yea bye

The exchange thus illustrates the permeability of the boundaries between social and personal talk. The integration of the corporate script into the phatic exchange provides a specific example of the 'conversationalisation' of work discourse (see Fairclough 1995, and further discussion below). More-over, the colleagues' laughter suggests some self-consciousness as well, per-haps, as some shared scepticism, of these relatively new features of their workplace culture.

Similar examples occur when a number of people gather together for a meeting. Sitting around in silence would be socially embarrassing: if people work together, it is expected that they should have topics to talk about. Phatic talk serves Malinowski's canonical function of avoiding silence, filling the gap while people wait for the meeting to begin.[9]

Extract 7

Context: People are gathering for a meeting and chatting as they wait for others. Monica is the chair. Helen is to do a presentation.

1 L: I met your um friend Marie Cross last night
2 M: oh good + how is she
3 L: she's fine really lovely
4 M: what was that at
5 L: that was at that thing um (the) international institute thing. . . .
6 M: [inhales] okay + this is everybody isn't it except Gavin when he comes. . . .
7 H: just tell me Monica when you think you're ready for my bit
8 M: yeah really I just wanted to sort of + um sort of just use this opportunity
9   to get a bit of a review on where we're at with. . . .

Extract 8 illustrates a further point along the continuum towards social talk. This talk occurs at the beginning of the day as the two young women re-establish contact.

Extract 8

Context: Two office workers at the beginning of the day

1 C: I went to Nelson over the holidays you know
2 N: oh this holiday?
3 C: mm
4 N: oh okay
5 C: first time for + well to have a look around it

After about four minutes discussing the holiday area, they move to a core business topic.

Yet another step along the continuum is exemplified in Extract 9. Meg's university course is off-topic talk with a personal component.

Extract 9

Context: Iona and Meg are discussing aspects of a project they are working on

1 M: that'll be enough for them to be going on with for a start though eh
2 I: mm (with) the stuff that I'll be getting them as well Max seems quite

3   [clears throat] really good at getting things together
4 M: there's a couple of articles that I've got photocopied off and I think
5   I took them home 'cause I wanted them for my varsity so I'll
6   have to dig those
7 I: mm
8 M: for my varsity notes
9 I: are you stud- you're studying at the moment
10 M: yeah [clears throat] [tut] I'm in my second year of my um masters of
11   social science research
12 I: mm
13 M: and I was using one of the papers was Walker's paper on Maori usage
14   yeah
15 I: it's hard
16 M: so it was sort of directly relevant for [laughs] my masters so I took it
17 I: yeah
18 M: this one + Maori usage methods in (. . . .) but we've got the journal
19   at work anyway so I can photocopy another one and all these
20   um publicat- oh reports in the back
21 I: mm
22 M: I have to make sure that + I have to speak to the people that are
23   the project managers

The discussion is brief and the shift back to core business talk is relatively smoothly accomplished, because the reports discussed at the end of the exchange are relevant both to Meg's university study and to her work, since she has to make the reports available to the project managers. Further examples occur regularly in discussions of business travel plans in one organisation. During a meeting between Esther and Paddy, two policy analysts, for example, the official topic of talk is the necessary preparations for a business trip to Korea. However, the initial stage of the meeting involves some discussion of travel by others in the same section; like the discussion of *ms* in Extract 5, this is workplace talk, but not strictly on-topic core business for this meeting. At a later point the discourse moves to Esther's social plans for a weekend in Japan on the way to the business meeting in Korea.

Extract 10

Context: Esther and Paddy are planning the details of an overseas business trip on which Esther will accompany a senior member of the Ministry
1 E: um and also then he gets there on a Tuesday afternoon or something
2   I think and we'd have the Monday then we thought we could
3   perhaps look at some [*word deleted for reasons of confidentiality*]
4   protection stuff in Japan /before\ he turns up
5 P: /mm\ okay
6 E: it also gave us a weekend in between in which we could just sort of
7   go [exhales] [acts out collapsing] [laughs]=/
8 P: yeah
9 E: so for a day and a half or so and then pick up when AJ came back

10 P: mm and Japan is an interesting place
11 E: and I got a really good I mean it'd be ideal for me in terms of I've
12   really good friend who left and is living there at the moment I
13   haven't seen her for months
14 P: which er which er area
15 E: um she's in + in Nagata or some it's you know where Tokyo is
16 P: mhm
17 E: it's sort of straight up. . . .
18   so I mean if I got a chance to go and see her that would be ideal
19 P: yeah yeah
20 E: and I'll perhaps do that over a weekend

The discussion has drifted further along the continuum from work-related talk towards social talk. However, the comments are related closely to the 'official' topic of the discourse, and, again, the transition back to the core business topic is smoothly achieved via a discussion of the ways in which the work programme is so intense before and after the planned weekend in Japan.

The exchange also illustrates the fact that the functions of talk are not fixed but rather they emerge out of the developing discourse. Exchanges develop in a variety of not always predictable ways, as Extract 11 illustrates.

Extract 11

Context: Manager, Hana, with her PA, Beth, who has just returned after a holiday
 1 H: well it's nice to have you back welcome back
 2 B: yes had a very good holiday [tut]
 3 H: and feel well rested? so where did you go
 4 B: no [laughs]
 5 H: oh well
 6 B: it's just just been busy with my mum and then she had me take her
 7   there and take her there and [laughs]
 8 H: oh
 9 B: so no it was good I didn't have to worry about meals I didn't have to
10   worry about bills or kids or um work or anything just me
11 H: (just) a holiday for you
12 B: yeah + [tut] it was UNREAL [laughs]
13 H: now listen are you going to be wanting to take time off during the
14   school holidays

This is typical of the way people who work together re-establish contact after a time gap and it illustrates very nicely how small talk can lead into work-related talk: *now listen are you going to want to take time off during the school holidays* (line 13).

These extracts illustrate the inextricability of business talk from small talk: the continuum identified in our data is clearly an essential characteristic of talk in the organisations we examined. The data demonstrates the artificiality of any firm boundary between business talk and social talk, illustrating

Fairclough's (1995) claims about the 'conversationalisation of public discourse' and the ways in which the different 'lifeworlds' of work and leisure overlap. In exploring the distribution and functions of small talk in the workplace, this aspect of the data will be evident.

Distributional features of small talk at work

Small talk is typically, but not exclusively, found at the boundaries of inter-action, as well as at the boundaries of the working day. Greeting and parting exchanges which typically occur in the opening and closing phases of inter-actions are obvious manifestation of small talk. In the workplace, the first encounter of the day between work colleagues could be considered an obligat-ory site for small talk. Its absence at this point would be marked, justified perhaps by an emergency requiring urgent attention to a specific task. Initial encounters are typified by references to the weather (*lovely day*), recent shared activities (*great concert last night*) and ritual enquiries after well being (*how's things?*). Such exchanges between work colleagues occur in passing, as well as at the beginning of planned activities, and they appear to resemble small talk in other contexts in most crucial respects.

At the beginning of meetings in our data, for example, as people gathered together, small talk was common. In addition to its social functions (dis-cussed in the next section), small talk filled in time while participants waited for the meeting to begin. This was evident from the fact that, as soon as a sufficient number of people were present, the small talk was generally inter-rupted by the person chairing the meeting. See Extract 7 above. One of the main functions of Monica's small talk with Leslie is to fill in time until sufficient people have gathered to justify starting the meeting. This is evid-ent from Monica's framing discourse marker *okay* (line 6) which signals a shift from pre-meeting talk to the opening of the meeting (Stenstrom 1994).

At the end of interactions, small talk was also common. It might be a brief *see you later* or *give us a bell* ('phone me'), or a more protracted disengage-ment, serving a range of functions, especially attention to positive face needs (see below for discussion of some extended examples). Small talk provides a transition assisting people to 'come back to earth' as one contributor put it, after a session of hard work, or sometimes to re-establish cordial relations following an intense and perhaps heated debate. Even after a mundane, regular session of delegating tasks, small talk served to re-orientate people to their personal rather than their role relationship.

Extract 12

Context: Helen has been delegating jobs to Rebecca, her PA
1 R: I finally got + the the names transferred from the cvs onto the +
2   ont- onto the labels to send out the thank you letters yesterday

3 H: oh good (let's) get that one done . . .
4 R: okay
5 H: okay
6 R: and how's Sam
7 H: he's just fine

The preclosing sequence (lines 4–5) *okay okay* signals that the work is completed. Rebecca starts to leave and as she gathers up her papers asks about Helen's partner (line 6), a typical example of small talk at the end of a meeting. In this position small talk has the potential for development into more extended social talk, but equally it can be brief and formulaic, simply marking the end of the encounter.

Another point at which small talk can occur is when the personnel involved in an interaction changes – when someone leaves or someone new arrives to join an interaction. In some respects, these 'change' points parallel openings and closings but, because they are often 'interruptions' to the business of the continuing participants, any small talk is generally minimal and may be confined to routine phrases such as *how's things*, *how are you* which in this context elicit routine minimal replies such as *fine*, *good*, or in some cases no overt response.

Although small talk occurred most typically at the peripheries of workplace interactions, it also surfaced within work encounters (cf. Coupland *et al.* 1992: 213). Within meetings, people regularly digressed from the topic, and sometimes social discourse displaced task-orientated or work discourse. The discussion in Extract 10 above, concerning Esther's plans for her weekend in Japan, provides one example. Other examples involved talk which introduced strictly irrelevant information ('gossip') about people whose names came up in the course of a business-orientated discussion.

A related distributional point concerns the nature of the transitions from small talk to task-focussed discourse. People often move very skilfully and subtly from discourse which is clearly 'core business' to talk which is social in its motivation, and back again. While the transition in Extract 7 is clear-cut, with M clearly deciding it is time to start the meeting (line 6: *okay + this is everybody isn't it except Gavin when he comes*), the transition is often less abrupt, with business talk at the end of an encounter shifting after a mutually negotiated completion to social interpersonal discourse as in Extract 12, or small talk at the beginning of an encounter gradually shifting to work talk, as in Extract 13.

Extract 13

Context: Two young women meeting to discuss a joint project
1 I: so how are things (amongst) your um +
2   your holiday how was your holiday
3 M: oh it was really funny the holiday was like really really awesome

 4 I: right
 5 M: and then my first day back I was just like kicking back + in my desk just
 6   just still really relaxed and I
 7 I: trying to get back into it [laughs]
 8 M: yeah and a girl from (my-) a woman from my section came up and
 9   said oh [inhales] do you want to do this horrible speech that I have
10   to give in front of students for work day they had career work day
11   thing and the students have to come in to the building and I said
12 I: yeah
13 M: yeah yeah sure I'll do it and she goes [surprised tone] really I thought
14   I'd have to get down on my knees and BEG and I was going oh no
15   no it's cool and I'm sure it was because I was just you know still
16   in holiday mode 'cause I don't normally like speaking in front
17   of anyone [laughs] but
18 I: yeah
19 M: yeah I agreed (to) and it was fine
20 I: so you might have um taken er a while
21 M: so [laughs]
22 I: longer t- to come to the decision (would you) [laughs]
23 M: yeah oh yeah I would have gone no no go away
24   but yeah it was really good
25 I: it was a good trip oh (okay)
26 M: yeah but now back into it again
27 I: yeah things are pretty full on here
28 M: yeah I can imagine
29 I: mm sort of working I just did my first submission + for the minister

This extract illustrates very nicely both in form and, as it happens, in content, the gradual shift from formulaic small talk in which Ilsa enquires about Mary's holiday to discussion of a submission for the Minister, a topic which is firmly in the work domain. It is accomplished in this case via a discussion of the effects of a holiday on Mary's attitude to a work request. The ending of the interaction, in particular, illustrates very clearly the conversational skill with which the two negotiate the transition back to work talk. Mary's evaluative comment (line 24) *but yeah it was really good* marks the end of her answer to Ilsa's question (line 2) *how was your holiday*. Ilsa's reformulation (line 25) *it was a good trip*, indicates agreement to the topic closure. Mary acknowledges the closure *yeah*, (line 26) and then (literally) moves the topic to work *but now back into it again*. The topics of their talk thus mirror the chronological progression holiday and then back to work. Ilsa then picks up the topic and starts to bring Mary up to date with where things are at.

In such cases, small talk serves as a bridge to the main business of the encounter. There are many examples where the transition from small talk to the business of the meeting is similarly skilfully accomplished. As Coupland *et al.* note, small talk is flexible and malleable; phatic exchanges have 'unique bridging potential – relationally and interactionally' (1992: 226) and are thus very useful tokens of interactional discourse. They enable speakers to move painlessly from social to transactional talk.

However, perhaps the one feature which distinguishes workplace discourse most clearly from social discourse in many other contexts is the fact that task-related interactions may open without small talk of any kind. While we must beware of making assumptions in this respect because of the limitations of our data, nevertheless there is evidence that interactions often began as follows:

Extract 14

Context: Kate, a relatively senior person in the organisation addresses Anne, the computer adviser, as Anne walks through the office
1 K: can I just talk to you
2 A: yeah
3 K: I got your message saying that you'd set up the Turner ID for me
4 A: yep
5 K: but I can't log on to it yet 'cause I don't have a + code number or anything

The preamble, checking availability, satisfies minimal politeness requirements. The discussion then continues with Anne explaining how to resolve the problem. Clearly small talk is not obligatory in some types of work transactions. Most obviously in our data, initial 'greeting' small talk seems to be treated as dispensable in transactions which are signalled as brief requests for assistance or information, or where an agenda has been set in advance, and/or where participants are working according to agreed explicit time constraints. Initial small talk may also be dispensed with when participants have had some contact earlier on the day of a meeting. It is possible that this is a feature which distinguishes small talk in the workplace from its occurrence in other contexts; determining the exact form of these constraints is an obvious area for further research.

Interestingly, however, when initial small talk is dispensed with in this way, attention to face needs may surface later. So, Kate apologises later in the interaction for having accosted Anne so directly at the opening of the encounter: *sorry I'm a bit mean doing this and when you're just walking in*. Kate then goes on to introduce another request for advice – the apology, in other words, is used to 'legitimise' an extension of the interaction beyond the brief request for assistance first requested. At a later point, however, Anne introduces personal talk and Kate is captured; she cannot politely avoid listening to an account of Anne's personal problems (see discussion of Extract 21 below).

Finally the length of small talk exchanges reflects a wide variety of factors. The place and time are obvious influences. Where it occurs in the corridors in passing, it will be typically brief, performing its canonical function of creating and maintaining social relations within a broader context in which the primary avowed goals of the organisation predominate. So colleagues passing in a corridor tend to keep small talk exchanges brief, as illustrated in Extract 4 above, and in Extract 15.

Extract 15

Context: Tom and Graeme pass in the corridor as Tom comes into the building
1 T: nice day out there
2 G: yeah great

Where it occurs in social venues such as morning tea or lunch breaks, small talk may be relatively expansive, providing a natural bridge to personal and social relationship discourse, as well as to the 'shop talk' which dominates many tea and coffee breaks.[10] Office-based small talk tends to reflect the influence of other factors such as how well the participants know each other, the relative status of participants and how busy they are, as well as the norms of the organisational culture. Some of these factors are discussed further below.

Functions of small talk at work

Small talk as a discourse strategy

Discussion of the distribution of small talk has inevitably drawn attention to one of its most obvious functions: small talk often marks the boundaries of interactions. It is one of a number of discourse strategies available for managing social interaction. The way phatic communion functions in the opening and closing phases of interactions has been discussed very thoroughly by Laver (1975). Drawing on 'informal observation of everyday social encounters' by himself and his students (1975: 216), Laver suggests a range of social functions of phatic communion, one end of the small talk continuum in Figure 2 above (see also Coupland's Introduction). Within the opening phase he identifies three main functions: firstly, a 'propitiatory function in defusing the potential hostility of silence in situations where speech is conventionally anticipated' (1975: 220); secondly, an 'exploratory function', in that phatic communion 'allows the participants to feel their way towards the working consensus of their interaction' (1975: 221); and, thirdly, an initiatory function, 'it allows the participants to cooperate in getting the interaction comfortably under way' (1975: 221). In the closing phases of an interaction, phatic communion facilitates a cooperative parting, assuaging 'any feelings of rejection' and 'consolidating the relationship' (1975: 231). All of these social and interpersonal functions of phatic communion or small talk are very relevant in workplace interaction, as I will illustrate below.

Another aspect of the boundary-marking function of small talk is its role as a transitional device or 'time-filler' between different activities, as illustrated in Extract 7 above. One of the most interesting features to emerge from the analysis of the distribution of small talk was its elasticity, flexibility and adaptability. It can expand or contract according to need. It can be picked up and dropped with minimal discoursal effort. It can be used to fill 'dead' time in the workplace, or to fill a gap between planned activities.[11] In our data, small talk occurred in the workplace between people waiting for a meeting to start, between a policy analyst and a manager's PA while the analyst was waiting to see the manager, and between people waiting for a xeroxing or scanning job to be completed. Small talk occurred between people waiting for a visitor to arrive, and between colleagues waiting for a third person to finish a phone call. In all these cases, small talk filled a time gap with acceptable, and indeed valuable, relationship-maintaining social interaction, while also avoiding problematic disengagement issues when the 'main activity' could be commenced or resumed. Because it is undemanding in terms of topic and intellectual content, and infinitely flexible in terms of length, small talk is ideally suited for these varied functions.

Social functions of small talk at work

While small talk clearly serves to mark boundaries and transitions in workplace interaction, it simultaneously serves important social functions, constructing, expressing, maintaining and reinforcing interpersonal relationships between those who work together. In the workplace, this not only involves the solidarity-orientated functions discussed by Laver (1975, 1981), it also involves attention to the way people 'do power' at work (see Holmes 1997, Holmes, Stubbe and Vine 1999). The analysis below illustrates ways in which apparently peripheral and innocuous phatic exchanges can serve pivotal roles in furthering the interpersonal, and sometimes instrumental, goals of those involved.

Doing collegiality in the workplace

Paying attention to the face needs of others is a crucial component of 'doing friendship' (see Holmes 1995, Coates 1996). In the workplace, the equivalent activity can perhaps be described as 'doing collegiality'. Our data suggests that the amount of attention paid to facework in the workplace is influenced by a wide range of factors, including the weight placed on interpersonal relationships in particular workplace cultures, different theories about effective management, the ethnic background and the gender of participants, and so on. These difference are not explored in this paper, though they will be the focus of future analysis. Where facework is valued, however, small talk plays a part.

'Doing collegiality' involves, in particular, paying attention to the positive face needs of participants, and small talk is an obvious example of discourse which is oriented to the addressee's positive face needs. Indeed, small talk might be considered a core example of positively polite talk. Like complimenting behaviour, it is designed to signal that the addressee's wants, 'or the actions/acquisitions/values resulting from them' (Brown and Levinson 1987: 101) are appreciated and shared by the speaker. Small talk typically serves to establish, maintain or renew social relationships (Laver 1975, 1981). In the workplace the exchange of greetings, complaints about how busy life is, promises to get in touch for lunch, coffee and so on, are examples of small talk tokens that serve this positive politeness function.

Extract 16

Context: Joan and Elizabeth pass in the corridor
1 E: hi Joan
2 J: hi how are you
3 E: oh busy busy busy
4 J: mm terrible isn't it

Extract 17

Context: Jon and May pass on the stairs
1 J: hello hello /haven't seen you for a while\
2 M: /hi \
3   well I've been a bit busy
4 J: must have lunch sometime
5 M: yea good idea give me a ring

In these extracts, small talk enables these workmates to 'do collegiality'. They indicate mutual good intentions as they construct, maintain, repair or extend their collegial relationships. Jon's use of 'sometime' in his invitation is an indication of the largely symbolic status of the interchange, and this is ratified by May's equally non-specific suggestion that he ring her; no precise time or date is mentioned (cf. Wolfson *et al.* 1983 on invitations). Reference to how busy one is serves in the workplace as an ideal small talk token. It indicates an orientation to the 'proper' goals of the workplace, while also providing an acceptable account of why social relationships receive less attention than might be expected of good colleagues: in other words 'busyness' is an acceptable excuse for perfunctory attention to interpersonal relationships at work.

As mentioned above, positively polite small talk can also serve a valuable bridging function, a means of transition to the main business of a workplace interaction. Small talk warms people up socially, oils the interpersonal wheels and gets talk started on a positive note.[12] Extracts 8 and 13 above illustrate workers warming up for the day's work interactions. Talk about holidays and leisure activities provide a gentle introduction to work talk. In these extracts, small talk serves what Laver calls an initiatory function of 'getting the interaction comfortably underway' (1975: 221; see also Tannen 1994: 65).

Within an interaction, too, small talk can serve the positively polite function of oiling the interpersonal wheels. Extract 10 above provides a relevant illustration. The discussion of Esther's plans for using her free time in Japan serves a variety of mainly positively polite purposes. Esther is offering Paddy personal information in the midst of the work discussion, and in so doing she strengthens their interpersonal relationship. Another example occurs in the middle of an interaction between a manager and her PA who has been away for a period. The manager is recounting some of the problems she had explaining the filing system to the temporary replacement and she then says with a sigh of relief *oh it's nice to have you back*. This appreciative comment inserted in the middle of task-oriented talk has the function of providing social oil, reasserting the importance of the sound and effective working relationship which has been developed between the two women. In such contexts, the small talk is clearly distinct from phatic communion; it is more than the production of a linguistic routine, a mere form of words. Rather it is a creatively adapted form of social talk.

The end of a workplace interaction is another important position for small talk which is attending to positive face needs. Laver suggests phatic communion mitigates a possible sense of rejection and 'consolidates' the relationship (1975: 232). It serves the function of easing the transition from transactional, work-focussed, on-task talk about a particular topic to more relational talk. Extract 13 above exemplifies this point and Extract 18 provides another example. Although it looks superficially as if it is a greeting at the opening of an interaction, this occurrence of *welcome back* comes at the *end* of a concentrated interaction focussing on what Hana needs her PA to do, an interaction in which she says several times that it is nice to have Beth back.

Extract 18

[content precedes and overlaps with Extract 11 above]
Context: Hana, a manager, is briefing her PA, Beth, on jobs to be done
1 B: (and) the election briefing
2 H: yeah oh ++ I think we've cancelled that ++ you might need to check
3 B: yeah
4 H: I'm fairly sure that's been cancelled ++ the panel on Friday afternoon's
5   been cancelled so everyone will just have to + cope on their own
6 B: (pardon)
7 H: well it's nice to have you back welcome back
8 B: yes had a very good holiday [tut]
9 H: and feel well rested? so where did you go?

Hana finishes the 'work' talk and then shifts to interpersonal social talk via a formulaic small talk greeting (line 7) *it's nice to have you back welcome back*. In the absence of the evidence that such authentic data provides, one would never predict that a greeting such as *welcome back* would occur at the *end* of such an interaction. Its positioning suggests it is a signal of relaxation at the end of the task. Hana switches from a style associated with managing the task to paying more attention to the personal relationship between her and her interlocutor. The small talk serves as a bridge to more extended social discourse. Hana's questions (line 9) *and feel well rested? so where did you go?* provide the addressee with an opportunity to elaborate and extend the social talk well beyond formulaic phatic communion.

Small talk is, then, an obvious means of 'doing collegiality' in the workplace. It enables colleagues to pay appropriate attention to the positive face needs of their colleagues. The data suggests that, although social talk can emerge from particular topics (such as travel or personalities) within a transaction, canonical small talk or phatic communion is typically confined to the margins of interactions. In this position it can serve as a formulaic nod towards collegiality where appropriate, or alternatively it can provide a bridge to more extended social or interpersonal discourse between those with more deeply rooted collegial relationships.

Doing power in the workplace

Discourse in the workplace involves the construction not only of collegiality but also of power relationships. Every interaction involves people enacting, reproducing and sometimes resisting institutional power relationships in their use of discourse (e.g. Crawford 1995, Davies 1991). Pateman (1980) examines power relationships from the perspective of 'oppressive' and 'repressive' discourse, while Fairclough uses the term 'coercive power' (Fairclough 1989, 1995). 'Oppression' is the open expression of power, while 'repressive discourse' is a covert means of exercising 'top-down' or coercive power, in which superiors minimise overt status differences and emphasise solidarity in order to gain their interlocutor's willing compliance and goodwill (see also Sollitt-Morris 1996).

Fairclough notes that it is the people in positions of power who decide what is correct or appropriate in an interaction. He comments that they also have 'the capacity to determine to what extent . . . [their] power will be overtly expressed' (1989: 72), and that in recent years the overt marking of power has been declining. Along with this decline has gone a reduction in formality (Fairclough 1992), and a process of 'conversationalising' public discourses (Fairclough 1995). Similarly Ng and Bradac (1993: 7) discuss strategies for 'depoliticising' the message in order to exercise covert influence over the attitudes and behaviour of others. Power, it is suggested, is increasingly expressed covertly and indirectly; it is hidden.

Holmes, Stubbe and Vine (1999) describe a variety of ways, both overt and covert, in which people 'do power' in the workplace. One obvious means of directly expressing power or status is the use by senior staff of overt discourse strategies for controlling an interaction. So, for example, in our data the senior participants generally set the agenda, gave direct orders, expressed explicit approval of the actions of others and summarised decisions. But they also employed a variety of less direct, less overt and more subtle means of 'doing power', one example of which was the way they generally 'managed' the small talk. In many New Zealand workplaces, in response to an egalitarian work ethic, rather than being relinquished, power seems to have gone underground (Sollitt-Morris 1996). The management of small talk could be regarded as one example of subterranean power construction.

Apart from the first contact of the day, small talk is usually optional. But it is generally the superior in an unequal interaction who has the deciding voice in licensing it (cf. Hornyak cited in Tannen 1994: 223–4). Except at breaks, there is often little or no small talk between people who are involved in an on-going work relationship: e.g. a senior policy analyst walked into the office of his administrative assistant saying *can you ring these people for me Joe*. Similarly a manager delivered a pile of papers to her PA saying *can you send these out, they need to go by this afternoon*. In such contexts these superiors did not use or expect small talk, and it did not occur. No overt flaunting of power is involved; the superior's definition of the situation simply prevails.

On the other hand, as suggested in the previous section, those in positions of power may use small talk to ease the transition to work-related topics, or to develop or maintain good social relations between themselves and their subordinates. Hence small talk can be used to reduce the social distance between superiors and their subordinates. Small talk topics do not reflect expertise or specialist knowledge. Topics such as the weather, holidays, child care problems and problems with transport are mundane and accessible to all, and so lend themselves to an emphasis on equality. But the positive politeness functions of small talk may be manipulated as well as used for sincere and genuinely positive affective functions.

The management of small talk may thus provide insights into the ways in which superiors manage interaction with their subordinates. In unequal encounters, the senior person typically sets the agenda. Similarly the senior participant generally determines how much small talk there will be at the beginning and end of an interaction. The extent to which the discourse of work may be de-institutionalised, the extent to which the world of leisure will be permitted to encroach on the world of work is largely in the hands of the superior, In the following extract Carol, Ruth's PA, uses the topic of the tape recording, which has become routinised in this workplace,[13] as a small talk token. Ruth, however, does not allow the topic to develop but instead moves quickly to business.

Extract 19

Context: Ruth walks in to give her PA some typing which needs correcting
1 R: hello
2 C: hello missus- Ms Tape [laughs]
3 R: huh?
4 C: I said hello Ms Tape
5 R: who's Ms Tate?
6 C: TAPE
7 R: TAPE oh yeah yeah I'll drive everyone up the wall
Pointing to the typing Carol has done for her
8   is that a space or not + it is a space
9 C: [quietly] no it's not a space it's not a space

The superior has the right to minimise, or cut off small talk and get on to business, and Ruth here resists attempts to use small talk as a bridge to an extended session of social talk. Because of the routine character of small talk it is possible to use it equally as a transition to work talk as well as to social or personal discourse. By responding formulaically and minimally, Ruth keeps the small talk to a ritual function.

It is also possible for those in more powerful positions to deliberately use small talk to 'manage' or influence the behaviour of others. So, for example, because small talk is associated with the peripheries of interaction, a senior person can use small talk as a strategy for bringing an interaction to an end. In Extract 18, Hana, a manager, signals to her PA that the business of the interaction is completed by switching to small talk. This leads to more extended interpersonal social talk but Hana keeps it relatively brief by introducing (via the discourse marker *now listen*) a related issue involving work arrangements.

Extract 20

[section of Extract 11 repeated here for convenience]
B: so no it was good I didn't have to worry about meals I didn't have to worry about bills or
    kids or um work or anything just me
H: (just) a holiday for you
B: yeah + [tut] it was UNREAL [laughs]
H: now listen are you going to be wanting to take time off during the school holidays

By contrast, in a similar interaction with Jocelyn, an equal, the social talk is more extensive and the transition to a closing is carefully negotiated between the two women. Jocelyn's account of her 'time out' is not cut by Hana, and she responds to Hana's potential pre-closing *that's neat* by indicating she is ready to go.

Extract 21

Context: Hana and Jocelyn, two managers, are finishing a planning meeting
They have been chatting about Jocelyn's non-work activities.
1 H: excellent
2 J: it was good + very good
3 H: oh excellent oh
4 J: yeah
5 H: great Jocelyn that's neat
6 J: must go
7 H: mm okay
8 J: all right?
9 H: okay thanks

By suggesting that those in positions of power tend to manage and often to limit small talk, this discussion has assumed that subordinates have a greater vested interest in developing small talk with their superiors than vice versa. This interpretation is supported by American research using a questionnaire to study small talk in two business organisations (Levine 1987). The results suggested that, while employees appreciate the opportunity to engage in small talk with their bosses, the employers preferred to restrict small talk to non-personal topics. There was evidence in our data that subordinates tended to respond very positively to small talk initiated by superiors, and often endeavoured to extend it in the direction of more personal talk, while superiors tended to respond more circumspectly maintaining a degree of social distance.

The workplace data also provided evidence that subordinates in an interaction do not always accept their superior's construction of a situation. Talk is a potential site of resistance and challenge (Bergvall and Remlinger 1996); talk can be characterised as a 'resistant political activity' (Kingfisher 1996: 536). So there was sometimes a suggestion of resistance to a superior's repression of social talk, especially if the subordinate had reason to feel exploited or manipulated, a victim of 'repressive discourse'. The interaction between Kate and Anne, introduced in Extract 14 above illustrates this point. Kate, the superior, initiates the interaction pretty much head-on without any small talk to ease into her request for assistance (which is also an indirect complaint). Anne is faced with a problem when she has scarcely settled back to work after some time away. As mentioned above, Kate later apologises, but uses the apology as a licence to introduce a second problem. Once she has responded to both problems, Anne asserts her right to some consideration, and she uses small talk as a channel to social talk which enables her to air her personal problems.

Extract 22

Context: Anne, computer adviser, and Kate, a more senior policy advisor
1 A: yeah it was a real bummer me not coming in yesterday

2   /but I was absolutely wrecked\
3 K: /[oh don't worry I worked it out\ for myself and I didn't need to use it

Kate responds to the first part of the comment and overlaps the more personal discourse. Effectively, she focuses on the transactional aspect of the utterance. Anne persists:

Extract 22 (continued)

1 A: I got up and I I just was so exhausted and I thought
2   gee I just wanted to cry
3 K: oh you poor thing

At this point Anne has moved from small talk to very personal self-disclosure. Kate is faced with the option of being overtly and explicitly rude or of listening to Anne – the price, perhaps, of trying to obtain advice more speedily than if she had booked Anne's time. She responds sympathetically to Anne's self-revelation. Anne then continues with her story of stress. She has effectively resisted Kate's attempts at repressive discourse and asserted her own interests. The interaction ends only when Kate's PA interrupts.

Extract 23

1 N: would you like to speak to Mr D?
2 K: oh yes I would
3 A: okay
4 K: thanks

The interaction then winds up with references back to Kate's problem and Anne offers to come round and check it later. Other similar examples involve small talk used by a subordinate as a precursor to a request for a day's leave, before requesting support for a promotion and before asking for permission to leave work early one day. The subordinate uses the small talk to reduce social distance and emphasise their good relationship with their superior, before requesting a 'good' that only the superior can bestow. Superiors vary in the extent to which they respond to such talk. Finally, they have the right to cut it short, and proceed to business, as illustrated in Extract 24.

Extract 24

Context: Tom enters Greg's office to request a day's leave
1 T: can I just have a quick word
2 G: yeah sure have a seat
3 T: [sitting down] great weather eh
4 G: mm
5 T: yeah been a good week did you get away skiing at the weekend

6 G: yeah we did + now how can I help you
7 T: I was just wondering if I could take Friday off and make it
8   a long weekend

Tom's small talk (line 5) focuses on common areas of interest, reducing social distance and de-emphasising status differences, but Greg effectively resists the invitation to extend the small talk with his brief responses.

Though I have focused in this section on the relationship between differential status and the management of small talk, there are obviously many other relevant factors which account for the precise ways in which interactions progress, and the degree of explicitness with which people 'do power' in interaction. So, for instance, the urgency of the task at hand may override all social niceties, or the closeness of the relationship between two people may override any status difference. Conversely, people may dispense with small talk when they are not concerned to nurture or develop the social relationship. Contextual factors must always be considered.

The analysis has suggested that the management of small talk is a clear but generally indirect and polite manifestation of workplace power relations. Superiors typically determine whether and to what extent there will be any small talk in an interaction, and they may explicitly use small talk as a means of managing a variety of aspects of an interaction. Subordinates use small talk to do power too, but the extent to which they are successful is finally determined by their superiors.

Conclusion

The distinction between business talk and small talk is sometimes difficult to draw; there is a continuum from one to the other, with many different kinds of 'off-topic' discourse functioning in interesting ways in between. Moreover, the term small talk covers a range of different types of social talk, from narrowly defined formulaic greeting and parting exchanges to more expansive personally oriented talk. Crucially, small talk must be identified in context, defined by the way the participants orientate to the discourse and the often subtle and ambiguous functions they achieve through its use. The first section of this paper examined the extent to which definitions are inextricably context-bound, involving considerations of the purposes of particular social exchanges in particular contexts between specific participants, and suggesting the extent to which distinctions between transactional and social talk, between business talk and phatic communion, are matters of degree rather than firmly bounded categories.

The second section of the paper explored some of these distributional characteristics of small talk, as well as their related social implications. Small talk tends to occur at the boundaries of social encounters, though it may also occur at transition points within an interaction, or serve as a brief social intermission in a 'full-on' work session.

The third section of the paper considered the functions of small talk. Small talk in the workplace functions like knitting. It can be easily taken up and easily dropped. It is a useful, undemanding means of filling a gap between work activities. Small talk oils the social wheels. At the beginning of an interaction, it assists the transitions from interpersonal or social talk to work or task-oriented talk. At the end of an interaction, it provides a means of finishing on a positive note, referring, however briefly, to the personal component of the relationship following a period when work roles and responsibilities have dominated the interaction. Small talk is flexible, adaptable, compressible and expandable. It can be as formulaic or as personal as people wish to make it. These characteristics make small talk eminently attractive as a construction tool in managing workplace relationships. It expresses and reinforce solidarity; it is a way of 'doing collegiality'. But it may also serve as an overt or covert expression of power relationships: people use and respond to small talk as one strategy for 'doing power' in the workplace. Management of small talk is one way in which superiors constitute their organisational control, though subordinates may challenge, resist or subvert the discourse.

The discussion in this paper has exemplified some of the ways in which small talk in the workplace serves interpersonal goals. But, as sociolinguists have repeatedly demonstrated, most discourse is multifunctional. Analysing small talk in health interviews, Coupland *et al.* say:

> even our most instrumental, transactional encounters are pervasively organized around *multiple* interactional goals that go well beyond the transmission and reception of factual information.

> (1992: 211)

Conversely, small talk, a fundamentally social kind of talk, can serve transactional as well as interpersonal goals. This is one of many aspects of small talk in our workplaces which await further analysis. There is an extensive literature arguing the positive and negative aspects of organisational gossip (e.g. Brown 1988, Mishra 1990, Brady 1992, Noon and Delbridge 1993). The ways in which small talk (in the form of the 'grapevine' and/or gossip) tends to serve or undermine the goals of our focus workplaces is an obvious area for further analysis.

There are also indications that different ethnic groups and different genders regard the function of small talk differently. The very label 'small talk' suggests that this kind of talk is not valued very highly in male-dominated, western cultures. It is typically regarded as peripheral and marginal, and supremely dispensable. Yet in other cultures, the social formalities are not so dispensable, and their omission can cause grave offence (e.g. Metge and Kinloch 1978, Case 1988, Cushner and Brislin 1996). In New Zealand, researchers have repeatedly emphasised the importance that Maori people place on proper attention to rituals of social contact (Salmond 1974, Metge 1986, 1995). It seems likely that ethnicity will prove an area of potential contrast in the analysis of workplace discourse. For similar reasons, gender will be an interesting factor to consider in further research on the functions of small talk. Paying attention to the positive face needs of others is one means of constructing an identity which is perceived as predominantly 'feminine' in western cultures. Moreover, there is a popular conception that '[m]any women mix business with talk about their personal lives and expect other women to do so too' (Tannen 1994: 64; cf. also Willing 1992; Clyre 1996). Workplaces where both women and men play influential managerial roles are obvious sites for examining such claims.

In conclusion, then, this analysis of small talk in the workplace provides valuable ethnographic data which confirms discoursal and functional pattens previously lacking a firm empirical base. It also suggests that the analysis of workplace discourse in context will provide a rich source of further insights concerning the ways in which people use language to achieve multiplex objectives.

Appendix

Transcription conventions

All names are pseudonyms.

YES	Capitals indicate emphatic stress
[laughs]	Paralinguistic features in square brackets
[drawls]	
+	Pause of up to one second
++	Two second pause
..../......\...	Simultaneous speech
..../.......\...	
(hello)	Transcriber's best guess at an unclear utterance
?	Rising or question intonation
publicat-	Incomplete or cut-off utterance
-----	Some words omitted

Notes

1. I would like to express appreciation to Justine Coupland for her invaluable and perceptive suggestions for improving this paper, and to Maria Stubbe and Bernadette Vine who commented helpfully on earlier drafts. I also thank those who allowed their workplace interactions to be recorded and analysed. The research was made possible by a grant from the New Zealand Foundation for Research Science and Technology.

2. Throughout the paper, names have been changed to protect people's identity. Extracts have sometimes been slightly edited for ease of reading – e.g. precise position of overlaps is generally not marked. See Appendix on p. 58.

3. Participants in our project also shared this view of small talk as peripheral. Although we emphasised our interest in *all* the talk in which they engaged in the workplace, they generally assumed that this only included talk on work topics. So they taped morning tea chat, because they acknowledged that they often talked work during breaks, but they tended to turn the tape recorder on after the small talk which opened a transactional encounter, and off before the small talk which ended it. This point is discussed further in the methodology section below.

4. Pakeha is a Maori word used in New Zealand to refer to people of European (usually British) descent.

5. The term 'meeting' is used in this chapter to include any workplace interaction involving two or more people which has a work-related objective.

6. Mott and Petrie (1995: 329) who adopted a similar methodology make the same point.

7. Note that core business talk does not necessarily entail a traditional 'work' setting such as office or board room. The type of talk and especially its relationship to organisational goals are the crucial factors (cf. Duranti and Goodwin 1992).

8. Justine Coupland (pc) helpfully suggested that phatic communion is 'atopical' rather than 'off-topic'.

9. Laver (1975: 220) elaborates on this *propitiatory* function where small talk defuses 'the potential hostility of silence in situations where speech is conventionally anticipated'. 'Hostility' is too strong a word for this context, but the point is otherwise relevant. Silence could suggest people did not get on well together, undermining the assumption of collegiality apparent in all our participating workplaces.

10. Note that, as some organisations recognise, social talk and the networking that it facilitates is just as important to the achievement of the organisation's goals as business talk – though its importance is not always acknowledged.

11. Linde (1988) describes how helicopter crews pick up and drop social chat as the demands of work ebb and flow.

12. This is a very important function of talk in Polynesian and Asian cultures.

13. The extent to which talk about recording has become routinised and acquired the status of small talk is evident from the fact that Ruth's response echoes almost exactly her response in Extract 2, i.e. it has become formulaic and ritualised.

References

Bergvall, Victoria L. and Remlinger, Kathryn A. (1996) Reproduction, resistance and gender in educational discourse: the role of Critical Discourse Analysis. *Discourse and Society* 7 (4): 453–79.

Brady, Teresa (1992) Effective small talk makes for big success. *Supervisory Management* 37: 1–3.

Brown, Edward (1988) Maladies which will weaken any organization. *Management Quarterly* 29 (3): 7–11.

Brown, Penelope and Levinson, Stephen C. (1987) *Politeness: Some Universals in Language Usage*. Cambridge: Cambridge University Press.

Case, Susan Schick (1988) Cultural differences not deficiencies: an analysis of managerial women's language. In Suzanna Rose and Laurie Harwood (eds), *Women's Careers: Pathways and Pitfalls*. New York: Praeger, 41–63.

Clyre, M. (1996) *Intercultural Communication at Work: Cultural values in discourse*. Cambridge: Cambridge University Press.

Coates, Jennifer (1996) *Women Talk*. Oxford: Blackwell.

Coupland, Justine, Coupland, Nik and Robinson, Jeffrey D. (1992) 'How are you?': Negotiating phatic communion. *Language in Society* 21 (2): 207–30.

Crawford, Mary (1995) *Talking Difference*. London: Sage.

Cushner, Kenneth and Brislin, Richard W. (1996) *Intercultural Interactions. A Practical Guide*. London: Sage.

Davies, B. (1991) The concept of agency: a feminist poststructuralist analysis. *Social Analysis* 30: 42–53.

Duranti, A. and Goodwin, C. (eds) (1992) *Rethinking Context: Language as an Interactive Phenomenon*. Cambridge: Cambridge University Press.

Fairclough, Norman L. (1989) *Language and Power*. London: Longman.

Fairclough, Norman L. (ed.) (1992) *Critical Language Awareness*. London: Longman.

Fairclough, Norman L. (1995) *Critical Discourse Analysis: Papers in the Critical Study of Language*. London: Longman.

Holmes, Janet (1990) Politeness strategies in New Zealand women's speech. In Allan Bell and Janet Holmes (eds) *New Zealand Ways of Speaking English*. Clevedon: Multilingual Matters, 252–76.

Holmes, Janet (1995) *Women, Men and Politeness*. London: Longman.

Holmes, Janet (1997) Analysing power at work: an analytical framework. Paper presented at Sixth International Conference on Language and Social Psychology, University of Ottawa, Ottawa, Ontario, 16–20 May 1997. ERIC document.

Holmes, Janet (1998) No joking matter: the functions of language in the workplace. *Proceedings of the Australian Linguistics Society Conference 3–5 July 1998*. Brisbane: University of Queensland.

Holmes, Janet, Stubbe, Maria and Vine, Bernadette (1999) Constructing professional identity: 'doing power' in policy units. In Srikant Sarangi and Celia Roberts (eds), *Discourse in the Workplace: Communication in Institutional and Professional Settings*. Berlin: Mouton De Gruyter.

Kingfisher, Catherine Pélissier (1996) Women on welfare: conversational sites of acquiescence and dissent. *Discourse and Society* 7 (4): 531–57.

Laver, John (1975) Communicative functions of phatic communion. In A. Kendon, R. M. Harris and M. R. Key (eds) *The Organization of Behaviour in Face-to-Face Interaction*. The Hague: Mouton, 215–38.

Laver, John (1981) Linguistic routines and politeness in greeting and parting. In Florian Coulmas (ed.) *Conversational Routine*. The Hague: Mouton, 289–304.

Levine, Deborah Clark (1987) Small talk: A big communicative function in the organization? Paper presented at the Annual Meeting of the Eastern Communication Association. Syracuse. EDRS. ED283228.

Linde, Charlotte (1988) Linguistic consequences of complex social structures. *Proceedings of the Fourteenth Annual Meeting of the Berkeley Linguistic Society*. Berkeley, CA: Berkeley Linguistics Society, 142–52.

Malinowski, Brontislaw (1949) The problem of meaning in primitive languages. Supplement 1 in C. K. Ogden and I. Richards *The Meaning of Meaning*. 10th ed. London: Routledge and Kegan Paul, 269–336.

Metge, Joan (1986) *In and Out of Touch: Whakamaa in Cross-Cultural Context*. Wellington: Victoria University Press.

Metge, Joan (1995) *New Growth from Old: The Whaanau in the Modern World*. Wellington: Victoria University Press.

Metge, Joan and Kinloch, Patricia (1978) *Talking Past Each Other: Problems of Cross-cultural Communication*. Wellington: Victoria University Press/Price Milburn.

Mishra, Jitendra M. (1990) Managing the grapevine. *Public Personnel Management* 19 (2): 213–28.

Mott, Helen and Petrie, Helen (1995) Workplace interactions: women's linguistic behavior. *Journal of Language and Social Psychology* 14 (3): 324–36.

Ng, Sik Hung, and Bradac, James J. (1993) *Power in Language: Verbal Communication and Social Influence*. Newbury Park, CA: Sage.

Noon, Mike and Delbridge, Rick (1993) News from behind my hand: gossip in organizations. *Organization Studies* 14 (1): 23–36.

Pateman, Trevor (1980) *Language, Truth and Politics: Towards a Radical Theory for Communication*. Sussex: Jean Stroud.

Salmond, Anne (1974) Rituals of encounter among the Maori: sociolinguistic study of a scene. In Richard Bauman and Joel Sherzer (eds), *Explorations in the Ethnography of Speaking*. Cambridge: Cambridge University Press, 192–212.

Schlieben-Lange, B. (1979) *Linguistische Pragmatik*. 2nd revised ed. Stuttgart: Kohlhammer.

Schneider, Klaus P. (1988) *Small Talk: Analysing Phatic Discourse*. Marburg: Hitzeroth.

Sollitt-Morris, Lynnette (1996) Language, gender and power relationships: the enactment of repressive discourse in staff meeting as of two subject departments in a New Zealand secondary school. Unpublished PhD thesis, Victoria University of Wellington, New Zealand.

Stenstrom, Anna-Brita (1994) *An Introduction to Spoken Interaction*. London: Longman.

Tannen, Deborah (1994) *Talking from 9 to 5*. London: Virago Press.

Tracy, Karen (ed.) (1991) *Understanding Face-to-Face Interaction*. Hillsdale, NJ: Lawrence Erlbaum.

Tracy, Karen and Coupland, Nikolas (eds) (1991) *Multiple Goals in Discourse*. Clevedon: Multilingual Matters.

Tulin, Mary Fewel (1997) Talking organization: possibilities for conversation analysis in organizational behavior research. *Journal of Management Inquiry* 6 (2): 101–19.

Willing, K. (1992) *Talking it Through*. Sydney: NCELTR.

Wilson, John (1989) *On the Boundaries of Conversation*. Oxford: Pergamon.

Wolfson, Nessa, D'Amico-Reisner, Lynne and Huber, Lisa (1983) How to arrange for social commitments in American English: the invitation. In Nessa Wolfson and Elliot Judd (eds), *Sociolinguistics and Language Acquisition*. Rowley, Mass.: Newbury House, 116–28.

2

Institutional identity-work: a better lens
Karen Tracy and Julie M. Naughton

Although there is considerable disagreement (e.g. Bhaskar 1986, 1989; Shotter 1993) about the degree to which language and other discursive forms shape people's social worlds (people's noticing, thinking, definition of an exchange and the situation, relationships, meanings attributed to another and so on), virtually no one would argue that there is no influence. In this chapter we consider the significance of this linkage for terms about communication: How do the meta-talk terms (the words used to distinguish kinds and purposes of talk) used in scholarly communities and everyday talk affect what is seen to be occurring in interaction? The site upon which we focus is gatherings in institutional settings. Specifically, we consider how popular and academic meta-talk concepts direct intellectual gaze. How, we ask, do the conceptual lenses for viewing talk guide what is noticed or ignored in institutional occasions where people come together for work purposes?

The chapter begins by exploring the dominant lay lens – small talk. Focusing on a sample of articles from the popular press, we describe lay conceptions of small talk, as well as small talk's understood significance. Then, we turn attention to the most frequently used academic lenses, starting with phatic communion (Malinowski 1923), the closest relative of small talk, and proceeding to examine more distant cousins – 'task-socio-emotional' (Bales 1950a, 1950b), 'content-relational' (Watzlawick, Beavin and Jackson 1967), and 'message/meta-message' (Tannen 1984). Finally we discuss 'identity-work' (Tracy 1997; Tracy and Naughton 1994), an intellectual grandchild of these earlier terms, and the one we use in our own research. To ground our critique of academic lenses, we consider interaction in two institutional gatherings: (1) a research colloquium in a university department, and (2) a weekly meeting of Hospice staff in which the status and care of patients is discussed. In the chapter's conclusion, we summarize key differences among lay and academic lenses, and argue why identity-work is an especially useful lens for viewing talk in institutional settings.

The lay lens: small talk versus talk

In everyday parlance some interactions go unlabelled and other kinds get referred to as *small talk*. But what exactly do lay language users mean by small
talk and how is it different from talk in its unmarked form? To develop a
profile of small talk's meanings and significance, we examined popular articles in which references to small talk appeared. Because we were interested
in interaction in institutional settings rather than in dating relationships,
family gatherings and other informal occasions, we used the Dow Jones
Index, a database that catalogues newspaper and magazine articles appearing
in US political and business-related sources. Included in the Index are articles from newspapers and magazines such as the *Washington Post*, *Newsweek*
and the *Wall Street Journal*. The articles came from a two-year time-span
running from May 1996 to May 1998. In choosing articles, we selected the
first 100 articles in which small talk was attributed to an actual person or
group, or articles which provided a prescriptive discussion, such as 'how to
do' small talk. Furthermore, we limited articles to those focused on institutional settings (mostly government or business), eliminating from consideration any that focused on personal relationships.

News articles in the popular press framed small talk in two ways: as a tool
and as a trait. In framing small talk as a tool, it was treated as something to
be used to accomplish interactional goals. In this frame the questions about
small talk were 'who did it?', 'when?' and 'how was it used?'. Small talk was
also written about as if it were a trait. Similar to traits like extroversion or
aggressiveness, small talk habits were treated as an enduring personality
characteristic. Individuals either were prone to small talking or avoided it.

Small talk as a tool

Instrumentality was the overriding focus of the lay lens. News articles high-
lighted small talk's usefulness in helping individuals accomplish social goals
such as managing impressions, putting people at ease, building connection,
winning approval and predisposing a listener to one's perspective. One article
wrote about small talk as evidence of 'renewed harmony'[1] for a hostile board
of directors. When applied as a tool, the articles suggested small talk was a
catalyst for the big talk. Small talk had a prime-the-pump function for the real
talk, also called 'information exchange',[2] 'formal remarks'[3] or 'real business'.[4]

Of interest was the fact that most articles used the term without a clear
indication of what the tool entailed. That is, what small talk is was regarded
as so transparently obvious that nothing more needed to be said. In those
articles that gave examples, talk about the weather was the most common
topic. One article referenced weather talk as the most 'conventional small

talk'.[5] Other mentioned topics of small talk included pets, clothing, sports and shopping. In sum, when small talk is treated as a tool, the social function of talk comes to the foreground and the specific content recedes into the background.

Although articles had little to say about what small talk was, they had much to say about its functions and value. The dominant opinion was that small talk was a necessary and good skill in work settings. Of the 44 examples that displayed a clear valence 73 per cent (33) included positive treatments of the concept and 27 per cent (11) were negative. By and large, small talk was treated as a necessary element of institutional success at any level. When individuals failed to engage in small talk, it was considered a problem. The failure to make small talk was framed as making conversational interlocutors uncomfortable, as in the case of the manager who was described as refusing to engage in the 'smallest small talk'.[6]

Some articles offered specific advice about how to use small talk. In an article on how foreign business people can succeed in a small American town, the foreigner was cautioned that, 'At cocktail parties it is best to stick to "small talk" rather than getting involved in long discussions about serious matters.'[7] Another article urged those who would skip a company holiday party to attend as a way to 'score points with your boss'.[8] For these parties, employees are informed that the first rule of manners is, 'Make small talk. Don't get into an analysis of the company budget or gossip about co-workers. Keep it light.'

At the same time, not to engage in small talk was portrayed negatively. There was a story about Marguerite Ables, a 68 year old woman, who was having trouble rejoining the work force after years as a homemaker. By her report, she lost a job because she 'didn't join in with the others with their small talk' and accordingly didn't 'get along well with coworkers'.[9] An 18 year old who 'made no small talk, no attempt to fit in' was labelled a social outcast.[10]

In articles offering behavior recommendations, employees are urged to take special care in making small talk with the boss. An example of this is one article that gives advice about taking advantage of chance meetings with superiors in an elevator. The employee is urged to make meaningful small talk that may impress them and to avoid 'conventional small talk'[11] like the weather. Small talk, then, is treated as a good way to 'get ahead' in business. The lower level employee is encouraged to use small talk, and use it skillfully to shape a positive impression of the self for the more powerful people. Stated bluntly, small talk is not a discretionary activity for lower-ranked employees. Of the nine stories about lower-ranked employees, the seven who engaged in small talk were evaluated positively and the two who did not (examples noted above) were evaluated negatively.

If one had already 'gotten ahead', however – i.e. occupied a high organizational rank – the functions of small talk, and whether it was mandatory, were seen a bit differently. Most noteworthy was the greater complexity in the evaluative picture of small talk among high-ranking officials. Similar to their lower-ranked counterparts, small talk was seen as a desirable and necessary skill. It was generally expected that high-ranking people had the social skills to 'work a room'[12] and appear sophisticated in a social setting. This, in fact, was the unmarked form, what was routinely expected, albeit not always done. High-ranking people such as members of a fund-raising dinner, commission members, diplomats, government officials, power brokers, negotiators and so on were supposed to engage in gracious talk with lower-ranking others.

Interestingly though, references to high-ranking people who did not engage in small talk (57 per cent) were more frequent than those who did (43 per cent). We interpret this as evidence that being an effective small-talker was the unmarked state for high-ranking officials. Reporters saw it as requiring comment when a powerful person did not engage in skillful small talking. Negative portrayals treated small talk as 'a waste of time',[13] 'mundane',[14] and as 'very small talk'[15] that was 'only',[16] 'mere'[17] small talk. From these articles it becomes apparent that everyday communicators scale small talk. At one end are instances that are significant, important 'a big deal';[18] at the other are exchanges that are trivial, extraneous and 'a waste of time'.[19]

Timing also played an interesting role in how articles used the concept of small talk. The lay lens of small talk exhibited a noted bias toward beginnings. Articles predominantly referred to the small talk which preceded the primary interaction. Few mentioned small talk following the main talk event. This is surprising because small talk could be expected to come both before and after the unmarked talk of professional interactions. Of 20 articles where chronology was evident only 12 per cent (3 articles) referred to small talk following the unmarked talk. A bias toward beginnings makes sense when small talk is treated as a tool. In other words, when small talk is seen as laying the groundwork for the accomplishment of other goals, then once the big talk is completed, small talk becomes extraneous. There is no reason to mention postlude small talk.

Viewing small talk as a tool makes endings less visible. The lay lens draws attention away from the fact that endings are a key part of maintaining relationships that, in most cases, extend beyond immediate instrumentality. The lay lens makes less visible that all talk is embedded in ongoing relationships. This can be contrasted with the content-relational lens (Watzlawick, Beavin and Jackson 1967) and the message-metamessage lens (Tannen 1984) which highlight the effect of messages on ongoing relationships.

Small talk as a trait

Beyond featuring small talk as a tool, it was also featured as a trait. Popular press articles used small talk as a descriptor, implying 's/he's the kind of person who does/doesn't do small talk'. The tendency to use or avoid small talk was framed as an enduring, personal characteristic. While academic lenses, soon to be discussed, tend to abstract small talk out of particular situations, a feature of the lay lens is the tendency to attach small talk to individuals.

Evidence for our interpretation is found in articles that were biographical descriptions. Business news services routinely run biographies of important participants in the international business scene, as well as obituaries which describe a person's character posthumously. In these descriptions, a person's orientation toward small talk was presented as an enduring trait. Of interest was the fact that disdain for small talk was a frequent descriptor of high-ranking males, whereas being skilled at small talk was not mentioned. Statements such as these were made about the reticent: 'a monkish distaste for small talk',[20] 'not warm and fuzzy',[21] 'ill at ease',[22] 'trademark growl',[23] 'That's the problem with [him], no small talk',[24] 'avoids small talk, even with his oldest buddies'.[25]

While being skilled at small talk is expected and valued for high-ranking persons, it is not categorically desirable. Small talk has a down side. This is illustrated by analyzing the media references to two high-profile politicians with diametrically opposed talk styles: Bill Clinton, President of the United States and Steve Forbes, a presidential candidate. Bill Clinton is widely known to be an avid and skilled practitioner of informal conversation with all kinds of people in many types of situations. Steve Forbes, despite his public visibility as a businessman and politician, is regarded as a highly private person who is reticent to talk on topics other than politics. The two are on opposite ends of the small talk spectrum: Clinton is a skilled user; Forbes is a known avoider. What are the implications for each man's identity? Let us consider Clinton first.

Known to be socially skilled, one could say that Bill Clinton is the consummate small talker. Indeed press coverage reinforces this image. News articles refer to small talk occasions he managed with a neutral or admiring tone. One writer described Clinton's 'legendary ability to work a room'.[26] The ability to make small talk is treated by one writer as a typical trait for Clinton. In commenting on a tape of Clinton, a news articles notes the nonverbal behaviors that accompany his small talk, 'The footage is vintage Clinton. Some guests get handshakes, while others get a grasp on the shoulder. All get a moment or two of presidential eye contact.'[27] Another article recounts how 'Clinton adroitly chats away with someone else about golf'.[28] In these instances Clinton is shown to be engaged in small talk behaviors and they are portrayed as effective. While not blatantly admiring, the reports are not critical of these behaviors and convey a favorable evaluation through their choice of words like 'adroitly' and calling his a 'legendary ability'. The ability to engage in effective small talk appears to have become a trait of Clinton, one that also runs the risk of being seen as overly smooth and insincere.

The opposite side of the small talk coin is represented by businessman cum politician Steve Forbes whose 'leaden' or 'wooden' style has become his hallmark. Just as Clinton's conversational style demands attention, so too does that of Forbes. Steve Forbes is a man who defies the expectation that one should engage in small talk. One article describes how high-visibility members of the press (e.g. Larry King, Ted Koppel, Walter Shapiro) were mystified by his unwillingness to engage in small talk. Attempts to probe his personal thoughts or aspiration elicited a pat answer about the flat tax, economic growth, etc. These visible media hosts expressed frustration with his unwillingness to engage in small talk. Bob Schieffer, the commentator on a televised interview show, *Face the Nation*, recalled, 'He simply will not engage in a conversation. He did not volunteer any information, not even the smallest small talk.'[29] Avoidance of small talk was not just a behavior Forbes did with the media but was also typical of his conduct with business associates. A close business associate of Forbes commented, 'he's one of these people who likes to come to your office instead of having you come to his, because then he can get out when he wants'.[30]

An aversion to small talk, then, is a central part of Forbes's public persona. While journalists expressed frustration, as noted above, Forbes's aversion of small talk was also a source of respect. One commentator noted, Steve Forbes appeared to be winning the war with the press by playing by his own rules, and interviewer Ted Koppel explained, 'if you try to jar him off his message you simply look evil in the public's eye. You can't push Mr Forbes too hard or you simply look like a bully, while he looks like a tolerant, benign future president of the United States.'[31] Reflected in these media portrayals is a certain respect for Forbes's persistent refusal to deviate from his own plan and engage in informal talk. From analysis of these two examples, we conclude that the identity of a high-ranking individual can be promoted either with or without displays of small talk. Both Clinton and Forbes were admired for their behaviors; both were also criticized, one as 'slick' the other as 'wooden'. In sum, small talk use is discretionary for those at the top of the power hierarchy. Powerful people have the right to choose whether or not to engage in small talk; lower ranking, less powerful people, in contrast, are expected to bow to the demands of small talk. Embedded in the descriptions of powerful people who do small talk, and powerful people who do not, is an ambivalence about small talk that surfaces in a variety of venues. Put baldly, small talk is important and a waste of time, vital but mundane; performing important functions and at the same time belittling and pandering.

To sum up the popular press's view of small talk: (1) People know what it is so there's no point laboring the obvious; (2) Small talk varies in kind from 'small' small talk to 'big' or meaningful small talk; (3) Small talk is most often done at social occasions, around coffee pots and elevators (see Holmes, this volume), and at the start of other talk activities; (4) Being an effective small talker is valuable for everyone, although especially low-ranking employees, and (5) There is a down side to being an effective small talker. Exceptionally good small talkers run the risk of being seen as slick, insincere or superficial.

Academic lenses for viewing institutional exchanges

To facilitate examination of different academic lenses, let us begin by examining one instance of the kind of talk in which we are interested. Presented below is an excerpt from a university colloquium. The colloquium occurred in a communication department at 'State U', a research university in the United States. State U's colloquium was a weekly meeting that brought post-graduate students and faculty members together to discuss the research of one of the people in the departmental group. The colloquium involved 15 to 20 participants, eight or nine of whom were faculty members, and the rest of whom were students. Presentations could involve highly polished projects (recently published papers) but typically were 'work in progress'. Students working on their doctoral degree were required to present a paper at colloquium before completing their formal course work. This paper was referred to as 'the colloquium paper'. Colloquium papers went through an official feedback and rewrite process before coming to the group for presentation. In a usual semester, two or three graduate students would present their 'colloquium papers'.

At State U's colloquium, students and faculty would begin assembling 5–10 minutes before the scheduled start time. During the group's assembling time multiple friendly conversations (small talk?) occurred. The start of a meeting was marked by the colloquium chair (an assigned responsibility for one faculty member) calling the group to order. The call to order was accomplished by the Chair raising his voice and telling the group it was time to get started. It was at this point that audio-taping of colloquia started. (For details see Tracy 1997, Tracy and Baratz 1994; Tracy and Carjuzaa 1993; Tracy and Naughton 1994.) Consider the first several minutes of one meeting's opening after the Chair's initial call to order.[32]

Excerpt 1

Opening Minutes of State U's Colloquium[33]

```
1 FM Chair:  ((tape starts)) These four graduate students
2            who have been to uh, I think Ted's been to
3            every- no Ted's missed one, who have been to
4            every colloquium
5 GS1 (Ted): that's pretty observant.
6 Group:     ((light chuckles))
7 FM Chair:  Oh I'm making notes
8 FM2:       What about
```

```
 9 FM Chair:  It goes into your permanent record.
10 Group:     ((louder and more extended chuckles and murmurs))
11 FM2:       (                                    )
12 FM Chair:  Her ( . ) her tape recorder's here.
13 Group:     ((simultaneous talk and laughter))
14 FM Chair:  So this goes into your permane- this goes
15            into your permanent record Ted. I bet you
16            didn't know I was taking attendance every
17            day.
18 Group:     ((light laughter))
19 FM3:       Does this go- Is it the heading ( . ) called
20            ( . ) foolish enough to go indiscriminately to
21            colloquia?
22 Group      ((light laughter))
23 FM Chair:  I think it's uh, I think it's uh, wuh we need
24            fran-, you know this might not be the forum
25            for it but uh somehow we need to get ( . )
26            better about it ( . ) graduate student
27            attendance
28 ?:         Yea:h
29 FM Chair:  Uh and we may have take some kind of uh more
30            formal (pause)
31 FM4:       We hold the organizer responsible for that.
32 FM3        >>wait a minute<<                    '
33 Group:     ((murmuring))
34 FM Chair:  Well I don't, I was going to say, I don't
35            don't, I don't believe that it's the quality
36            of the progra:ms.
37 FM4:       Your merit increase is dependent upon the
38            number of graduate students [attending]
39 FM3:       Now wait a minute ( . ) you've got a background
40            in linguistics, right? Did you hear the
41            sentence ( . ) We need to determine, something
42            about ( . ) bet⌈ter graduate student⌉
43            attendance right?
44 ?                         ⌊better graduate student⌋
45 Group:     ((light chuckles))
46 FM Chair:  You don't want the worst grad students
47            attending
48 Group:     ((loud laughter))
49 FM Chair:  Only the better ones.
50 Group:     ((Chuckles))
51 FM3:       Right.
52 GS2:    .  You're not satisfied with what's here?
53 Group:     ((laughter))
54 FM Chair:  Is this, is this why we only have five people
55            here? Is that-
56 GS2:       Why are you ignoring me Rich? [colloquium
57            chair's name]
58 FM Chair:  Let's start. Um this is uh this is the first
```

59   of uh in fact this is the first of, was gonna
60   be three, now it's gonna be uh two, the first
61   of uh a couple of colloquium papers that
62   we're gonna hear this semester. I guarantee
63   you next semester we'll hear several. I, I
64   can safely make that prediction.
65 FM2:   Others (.) weren't colloquium papers?
66 Group: ((loud laughter))
67 FM Chair: Official, official uh official colloquium
68   papers, part of the uh right, the requirement
69   (pause) graduate student requirement.
70 FM3:   You know you've only got two feet and you've
71   stuck three in your mouth
72 Group: ((laughter))
73 FM Chair: Uh this is Layton. Are you ready Layton?
74   Layton is . .

If we use the lay distinction between talk and small talk to understand this interactional segment, we would be hard pressed to decide what was going on. Given that joking and laughter are visible and the talk's purpose seem non-serious, we could view it as small talk. Yet to label this exchange small talk seems a forced fit. Not only is the content of the talk (problems about attendance, information about upcoming events) not commonly regarded as small talk topics, but the talk occurred in an event/time slot (within the confines of an institutional meeting) not associated with this genre. Although we might shoehorn this instance into the small talk category, it is not a good fit.

Lay uses of the term, small talk, lead attention away from the specifics of interaction, implicitly treating talk so labeled as not in need of analysis. Simply put, using the lay label of small talk legitimates minimal reflection about what is occurring. Unlike the communicative acts of negotiating a contract, giving performance feedback or leading a meeting, interaction labeled as small talk needs little elaboration. Other than reminding people to do it, little more need be said. Fostering insight into communicative exchanges is neither a goal nor necessarily a reasonable expectation to make of everyday meta-talk terms. For academic ones, though, it is reasonable expectation. Consider, now, how different academic meta-talk terms enable and limit interactional noticing.

Phatic communion versus communication

Phatic communion is the closest relative to the lay concept of small talk. To quote Malinowski (1923: 318), the originator of the term, phatic communion 'serves to establish bonds of personal union between people brought together by the mere need of companionship and does not serve any purpose of communicating ideas'. Similar to small talk, phatic communion's implicit contrast is with an unmarked counterpart, whether it be labeled 'talk' or 'communication'. Communication in its unmarked form, what Coupland and her colleagues (1992) label ' "true" communication', is about conveying information for serious purposes. Phatic communion does not convey information but, as Malinoski initially argued, and others have shown in more detail (e.g. Laver 1975, 1981; Rintel and Pittam 1997), has significant social functions, helping to smooth interaction and connect people.

In an academic world where the purpose of language was assumed to be representation, Malinowski's position was truly radical, a precursor of the speech as action view that appeared several decades later in Austin's work (1962). Yet while a harbinger of ideas to come, phatic communion reinforced a notion that talk was either giving information ('communication'), or doing something social ('phatic communion'). In addition, in defining phatic communion first and foremost in terms of what it is missing (serious information), it implicitly devalued the alternative function it was said to serve (J. Coupland, N. Coupland and Robinson 1992).

Malinowski offered more detailed thoughts about what counts as phatic communion than we saw in the popular press's use of small talk. Phatic communion includes greetings, 'purposeless expression of preference or aversion, accounts of irrelevant happenings, comments on what is perfectly obvious'. Furthermore it involves 'always the same emphasis of affirmation and consent, mixed perhaps with incidental disagreement' (1923: 314).

When we look at talk from this colloquium exchange, the phatic communion/communication lens gives us a cloudy scene. While companionship and solidifying interpersonal bonds do seem to be a function of this colloquium exchange, the talk also is conveying ideas. Even in these opening minutes, the talk was not 'mere' connecting. Embedded in the joking (e.g. lines 14–17, 37–38) is a reference to a consequential problem the group must think about and solve (getting graduate students to attend regularly). Too, this joking appears to encourage problem reflection, something phatic communion is not routinely expected to do. In short, this exchange has features of both phatic and non-phatic communication. Although parts of Malinowski's essay treats these two forms of talk as co-existing or on a continuum, his dominant position – seen in the above description – was to treat the talk types as mutually exclusive. Thus, for this meeting excerpt, using phatic communion and communication to view what is happening does not direct gaze in especially insightful ways.

Task versus social-emotional behaviors

A second way of analyzing talk developed by social psychologist Robert Bales in the 1950s (Bales 1950a; 1950b; see Hare 1976 for a review) gives relational functions a more equal footing with information ones. Developed to facilitate the analysis of small group interaction in American society, Bales's starting site has more direct relevance to institutional meetings, our

Table 2.1   Bales's categories for interaction process analysis

Task functions	
PROBLEM-SOLVING ATTEMPTS	QUESTIONING
Gives suggestions: direction, implying autonomy for another	Asks for suggestions: direction, possible ways of acting
Gives opinion: evaluation, analysis, expresses feeling, wish	Asks for opinion: evaluation, analysis, expression of feeling
Gives information: orientation, repeats, clarifies, confirms	Asks for information: orientation, repetition, confirmation
Social-emotional functions	
POSITIVE REACTIONS	NEGATIVE REACTIONS
Shows solidarity: jokes, raises other's status, gives help, reward	Shows antagonism: deflates other's status, defends or asserts self
Shows tension release: laughs, shows satisfaction	Shows tension: asks for help. Withdraws 'out of the field'
Shows agreement: passive acceptance, understands, concurs, complies	Shows disagreement: passive rejection, formality, withholds help

focal interest, than Malinowski's (1923) concepts which grew out of his study of pre-industrial, agrarian, fishing communities.

Bales argued that talk – what he thought of as 'verbal behavior' – was of two main types. It was a kind of task behavior or it was socio-emotional behavior. Within each type were six kinds which were further grouped into two subsets. Task behaviors could involve either problem-solving attempts or questioning, and social-emotional actions could involve either positive or negative reactions. Table 2.1[34] displays the twelve categories.

Bales's system was influential in research through the 1970s, but for a variety of reasons has fallen into disuse. It remains, however, a staple idea presented in college level communication textbooks about small group interaction (e.g. Ross 1989; Schultz 1989). Bales's concepts were elaborated within a quantitative coding system that has a number of drawbacks for scholars interested in understanding talk's significance in everyday interchanges (Potter and Wetherell 1987). For our analytic purpose, consider how the key terms guide noticing and thinking about talk.

In contrast to the concepts, phatic communion (communication) and small talk (talk), the task/socio-emotional dichotomy with its sub-categories offers more detailed guidance about what to look for. Although there can be problems in applying Bales's system we would easily be able to see instances of all four types of task (problem solving and questioning) and socio-emotional actions (positive and negative) in this colloquium exchange. That is, Bales's system encourages seeing multiple actions across a strip of talk. In addition, it not only draws attention to the fact that talk can be about socio-emotional functions, but it explicitly recognizes that talk does interpersonally negative relational work. In elaborating equal numbers of categories for each function (6 task, 6 socio-emotional) and giving each main category a name that is not derivative of the other, Bales's concepts enable a rich kind of noticing.

At the same time, the task/socio-emotional dichotomy guides thought into two problematic channels. In a conceptual system that assigns an utterance to one and only one function, attention is directed away from thinking about the multiple functions of talk (Tracy and Coupland 1990). If multi-functionality is a typical rather than an exceptional property of talk, this is a serious misdirection. For instance, is FM3's utterance (lines 19–21) 'Does this go- Is it the heading (.) called (.) foolish enough to go indiscriminately to colloquia?' asking others for their opinion as to the worth of colloquium? Expressing his own opinion of colloquium's worth? Showing solidarity through a joke? Or showing antagonism by being critical of an activity that another person is responsible for planning? All of these seem plausible parts of what FM3 meant. In addition, the functions Bales identified leave out several important kinds of actions people give attention to in meetings, the particulars of which we elaborate in the discussion of identity-work.

Content/relational and message/metamessage

A third set of meta-talk terms, content/relational and message/metamessage extend Bateson's earlier idea of report and command (Ruesch and Bateson 1951). Content/relational, meta-talk terms especially visible in communication, were developed by Watzlawick, Beavin and Jackson (1967). According to the authors, the content level of a message is the information conveyed by an utterance, with a caveat that the information need not be accurate or true. The relational level of a message refers to what a message implies about the relationship between the communicators. 'Relationship statements are about one or several of the following assertions: "this is how I see myself . . . this is how I see you . . . this is how I see you seeing me" and so forth' (p. 52).

A similar set of terms, also drawing on Bateson but more prevalent in linguistics, is the distinction between the message and meta-message (Tannen 1984). The message is the information, the conventional semantic meaning whereas the metamessage refers to the message about the message, how what is said is to be taken. Metamessages such as 'Understand what I just said as ironic' are cued by 'a combination of intonation, voice quality, facial expression, gesture, plus the expectation that such usage is appropriate to the situation' (Tannen 1984: 23).

In both sets of terms, the first term of the pair (i.e. 'content' and 'message') line up neatly with each other, but the second terms ('relational' and 'metamessage') do so less well. Whereas psychologists Watzlawick, Beavin and Jackson elaborate the different identities and relationships talk may implicate, they leave undeveloped the discourse particulars that would accomplish different relational states. In contrast, sociolinguist Tannen elaborates the features of the code that do the work of cueing attitudes but offers little thought as to how these features of code also implicate an identity. Presumably, for instance, irony relies upon and thereby cues shared background, therein implicating collegial relations or friendship, rather than a stranger relationship.

If we use these sets of terms as lenses on the colloquium exchange, we can see considerably more than was possible with the other meta-talk terms. In particular, both sets of terms draw attention to exchanges always doing both informational and relational (or attitude cueing) work. Stated another way, the terms lead us to ask of any colloquium exchange: What information is being conveyed and what views of self and relationships are being established through these ways of talking?

Using these concepts as the analytic lens, might lead us to notice that the FM Chair's comments about Ted's attendance (lines 1–3, 7, 9), the joke about graduate student attendance being recorded where no mention is made of faculty attendance (lines 14–17), his announcements about upcoming colloquia (lines 58–64) his command to start (line 58) and his introducing of Layton (line 73) are conversational moves that enact his status as a faculty member (i.e. not a graduate student) and as a situationally high-ranking one at that (i.e. the faculty member in charge of the occasion).

Furthermore we are likely to notice that FM4's comments (line 31) about holding the colloquium organizer responsible for graduate students' attendance, as well as suggesting that attendance be a criterion on which the colloquium chair's salary decisions be made (lines 37–8), are jokes, teasing statements not intended to be taken literally, a way to mark that the two have a friendly collegial relationship At the same time, the comment about salary, coming as it does from the department chair, a person centrally involved in this kind of institutional decision, can be seen as a reminder, albeit subtle, that the speaker is not just another faculty member, but has a status others do not possess.

These meta-talk terms direct attention to a large array of interesting social actions, but they do steer observation toward people as individuals and away from group-level identities and functions.

Talk as identity-work

The last meta-talk concept, the one we have adopted in our own work to analyze different kinds of institutional discourse, builds upon these intellectual predecessors, although especially the content/relational and message/meta-message distinctions. Identity-work refers to the way talk implicates self, partners' identities and, where relevant, the institutional group identity or that of non-present others. As we state elsewhere (Tracy and Naughton 1994: 286), identity-implicative analysis brings two questions to the foreground:

'What facet(s) of identity is made salient by talking in just this particular way?' [Then the conversational practices that do this identity work are uncovered by asking:] 'What aspects of discourse, in particular and specifically, lead to these identity inferences?'

Although indebted to earlier concepts, identity-work departs from them in three ways. First, as just mentioned, the notion of identity applies to groups in addition to individuals. Thus, in organizational settings, besides asking how talk does identity-work for individuals, it also makes sense to consider how it is enacting and reflecting an identity for the group. That is, it leads us to ask what institutional identities are constructed by and reflected in group members talking in a particular ways.

Second, our conception of identity-work presupposes that the identities that individuals and groups desire (or desire to avoid) are multiple and frequently in competition with each other. Hence, communicators routinely face dilemmas and much talk is geared to navigating among competing desirable or undesirable identities. For example, many groups, such as was true in this colloquium group, are concerned to have relationships of equality and recognize each members' expertise. Stated another way, they wish to use their experts wisely while avoiding strong hierarchical relations. Billig and his colleagues provide an illuminating analysis of how this works in a health care team, highlighting the considerable interactional effort given to showing the staff from the children's playrooms and the nurses (but not the physicians) that they were 'equal'. As Billig *et al.* (1988) note, 'It is precisely those whose expertise is deemed unequal who must be reassured that personally they are just as valuable as anyone else' (p. 75).

Finally, rather than having a contrast term that foregrounds the informational function of communication (content or message), arguably privileging this term since it is always mentioned first, task and information activities get folded into identity functions. Assertions or questions about a proposed course of action, for instance, become viewable as moves a person uses to establish self as a 'competent accountant', 'skeptical peer', 'deferential junior manager' and so on. For instance, greetings at a meeting's start become more than just small talk or phatic communion; they become visible as interactional moves to clarify participants' relative status or relationship well-being. Among the Swahili, for example, the extensiveness of one's greeting is a key way people inform each other of whether a person is in good standing with the speaker (Yahya-Othman (1994). A greeting, then, can do the work of showing disapproval or hostility, not just creating a common bond.

As with greetings, so too with other conversational moves. Teases, complaints, inquiries are parts of many institutional identities, and enact the individual and group identities in complex ways. In organizational settings, however, identities are not just enacted in talk but are also brought to it (Aronsson 1998). At State U's colloquium before one word was uttered, participants existed and were seen as graduate students, faculty members, the colloquium chair, the department chair. Yet although these identities existed at the outset, their situated meanings did not. Rather, through their talk State U participants constructed and contested what it meant to be each of these categories of people. An upshot of folding content/information into identity-work functions is that it highlights talk as being about the perform-ance of social acts – establishing who people are, how they see others, what kinds of relationships they have and what kind of group they are.

In an analysis of the colloquium group from which this excerpt was taken, Tracy (1997) describes a constellation of identities sought by the State U group. Members of this department colloquium wanted to establish that their group was a set of people who took ideas seriously, cared about each other and were actively working to be an 'intellectual' community that was both supportive and critical. For identities that reference relatively intang-ible interactional group qualities, such as 'see this group as a reasonably functioning intellectual community', the identity-work processes are espe-cially subtle. Multiple comments were made to FM Chair (e.g. lines 31, 37–8, 52, 56, 70–1) that could have been taken as instances of personal criticism. In letting these comments pass without counter-arguing, the FM Chair treated them as teases and thereby helped construct the group as a friendly, banter-ing community. Moreover, because both graduate students and faculty mem-bers participated in the exchange about better and worse grad students (lines 39–57), the group constructed itself as a place in which there was a casual-ness and lack of formality about status differences. These conversational actions, then, are forms of institutional (i.e. group-level) identity-work. When these moves are combined with other conversational actions the group did (i.e. making claims, commenting, questioning, challenging and counter-arguing) we are led to see a group enacting its desired identity as a working intellectual community.

To highlight and summarize the advantages of looking at talk with an identity-work lens, let us examine interaction in another institutional setting.

Identity-work at Hospice team meetings

Hospice, now a well-established institution, began as a social movement whose purpose was to make the process of dying more humane for patients and families. In contrast to mainstream medicine which tends to equate health care with physical treatment, the institution of Hospice is committed to holistic care – addressing patients' physical, spiritual and psycho-social needs. Hospices vary in terms of whether they are distinct facilities (i.e. a home for the dying) or deliver care to patients and their caretakers in a patient's home. At City Hospice, the site we studied (see Naughton 1996 for details), nurses and other hospice staff cared for patients in their homes. Weekly meetings, held to keep all staff abreast of what was happening with patients and staff meetings, were one of the few times Hospice personnel were in the same place. The agenda for these meetings was to discuss patients' physical condition, medications and the adequacy of their caregiver situation. However, beside providing information and evaluations relevant to these topics, staff members often expressed personal reaction to a patient or family.

Third party comments – personal remarks about a non-present third party (usually a patient but sometimes a family member) – in fact, occurred in 17 per cent of patient discussions.[35] Instances of third party comments included statements such as: 'She's a dear soul', 'a lovely couple', and 'I just love her'. Of the third party comments observed in six hours of team meetings (40 comments), the vast majority were positive (87 per cent). What are these positive third-party comments doing? Are they no more than a brief moment of small talk or gossip in a sea of information? The comments do not have a clear information function relevant to a patient's care so why do staff say these kinds of remarks? To what kind of group-level identity, might these comments be attending?

These positive comments, we suggest, are one important way hospice professionals display their commitment to an institutional philosophy that commits them to care for the mind and soul of patients in addition to their bodies. In other words, it was through making comments such as 'he's a charmer', 'such a dear', and 'so sweet', that hospice staff members enacted themselves as caring professionals, people who saw a patient as a 'whole person', as more than malfunctioning physical organism.

These expressions worked in two directions. Not only did they enact a speaker as concerned, they also served as eliciting devices to get other staff members to affirm that a third party comment-maker was, indeed, caring. Consider Constance, a nurse who was particularly effusive in her expressions of devotion to a patient whose mouth was disfigured from cancer. At one meeting, Constance said of this patient, 'Uh, she's a wonderful, just a real sweetheart, never complains, things are wonderful, just a real dear soul.' Constance's string of accolades followed a summary of the patient's medications and preceded a question about the woman's pain level. As such they might seem an off-topic aside. When viewed in terms of the identity-work the comment may be performing, though, a function becomes obvious. Constance's talking in this manner was one way to display for peers that in the work she did alone with these patients she was a compassionate nurse. At another meeting one of Constance's expressions of affections was followed by another nurse commenting that the patient was 'lucky' to have Constance as her primary nurse. That is, Constance's expression of affection for patients seems to have been treated as evidence by others that Constance was a 'good' Hospice nurse. In a setting such as City Hospice where most of the care was given in patients' homes outside the view of fellow staff, the way a staff person talked about patients becomes an important sign of her (or his) job skill and commitment to the Hospice philosophy.

Another example of how third party comments function as eliciting devices can be seen in an exchange that occurred between the centre's medical director and a nurse. The medical director, Cal Jones, ended discussion of one patient (Mildred) and started discussion of another (Emma) by saying:

Excerpt 2

Dr Jones: These are three of my favorite people, Emma Toot, Mildred Carew and uh
Nurse: She, she loves you. ((team members giggle)) I mean as expressive as, as expressive as this little old lady gets, which isn't very expressive, she, she said that Cal Jones, he has the best Irish humor.
((Loud laughs from the team))

Of note is that Cal's comment about 'favorite people' opened a conversational space for the nurse to comment about the patient's liking for the doctor. In this way, the third party comment not only enacted that the doctor was caring but gave another staff member a place to affirm that Cal was beloved by a patient, statements very difficult for staff to make about themselves. To the extent that statements of liking indicate, trust, respect and cooperation, then staff comments about patients' liking of other staff become one of the ways the institution marks and sustains itself as an alternative-care institution.

Individually these third party comments support team members' identities as concerned professionals. Cumulatively the comments do group-level identity work, sustaining City Hospice's sense of itself as a caring hospice. In Excerpt 3 the chaplain, Susan, tells how several family members expressed gratitude for City Hospice's care.

Excerpt 3

Ch: He can't say enough about hospice and what we did for him and he said that in Connecticut people are very good on the surface but underneath, you know, they're somewhat removed or distant from you. He said, BOY, he said, not [name of Western US state in which City Hospice resides]
Team: ((loud laughter))
Ch: He said they're just, you know, he said, it's almost, it's almost more than you know what to do with. And Jed [another family member] said yeah, they care about you and they're right in your face.
Team: ((loud laughter))
(two sentences deleted)
N1:   We care about you and we're right in your face.
Team: ((loud laughter))
N1:   That could be our slogan.

In this excerpt the family members had corroborated the group's identity as caring. Through the laughing responses and the quick adoption of the family member's pithy prose, the staff displayed delight in this characterization of their group. In this manner, the Hospice group identity was enacted and supported through third party comments. In making these comments, team members showed that they cared about their patients. The comments gave all members of the group evidence that team members were attached to their patients; their talk lived out that there was nothing 'removed and distant' about the way this team gave care to their terminally ill patients.

To label third party comments 'small talk', 'phatic communion', or to view them only in terms of individual-level functions would be to overlook the crucial role these comments play in accomplishing the work this group is about – being an alternative care institution. The comments were not merely passing the time of day congenially (i.e. phatic communion), nor were they straightforward 'socio-emotional comments', rather they did important institutional identity-work. The credo of City Hospice was to give unconditional accepting care to the dying patients they served. Positive third party comments were a conversational practice to accomplish this task. Each expression of positive sentiment and appreciation gave life to this hospice credo, and gave the group evidence that it was living its commitment.

Conclusion

Lenses make visible what otherwise might go unnoticed, as well as draw attention away from features of a scene that might deserve more careful scrutiny. Sometimes, such as can happen with a good pair of contact lenses, a wearer forgets that his or her vision is being shaped by lenses. Although for the physical process of seeing, some individuals do not need glasses, this is never true for interactional meanings. There is no such thing as 20–20 vision for interaction; lenses of one kind or another are required to see.

In this chapter we considered the effects of lay and academic meta-talk lenses on what becomes visible in institutional interactions. The lay lens, small talk versus talk, is broadly used and broadly useful to distinguish among occasions for talk and among potential topics. For non-experts (i.e. non linguistic or discourse analytic scholars) it is the lens of choice because of its ease of wear and its multi-functionality. For discourse specialists, however, the talk/small talk lens is not adequate. Seeing the specifics of interaction requires meta-talk lenses developed to facilitate reflection and analysis. Each of the academic lenses we examined in this chapter – phatic communion and communication, task and socio-emotional, content and relational, message, and meta-message, and institutional identity-work – encourages reflection, bringing details of social scenes into focus that remain fuzzy when viewed with the lay lens. Although all these lenses produce sharper pictures for studies of institutional interaction, we have argued for the especial suitability of identity-work. In contrast to the other meta-talk terms, identity-work draws attention to functions of talk that go beyond individual intentions. Institutions, too, have identities and talk is a central means through which these group-level identities are supported or contested. Viewing talk as identity-work not only insures that interpersonal and relational functions are recognized but places these functions center stage. Talk is fundamentally, not just occasionally or incidentally, the place in which people establish and challenge who they are as individuals and as groups.

Notes

1. Pae, P. (1998, 8 January). Myers praised for unity plea: Board urged to stop bickering. *Washington Post*, p. V01.
2. Ginsberg, S. (1997, 12 October). For more workers, it's a schmooze they can use. *Washington Post*, p. H2.
3. Chen, E. (1996, 18 May). Dole focuses on his war injuries in medical center tour. *Los Angeles Times*, p. 11.
4. Firestone, D. (1998, 20 February). Soft money socializing with the president. *New York Times*, p. 2.
5. Prager, J. (1997, 30 July). Consultant offers a few pointers on making small talk with a boss. *Wall Street Journal*, p. B1.
6. Kurtz, H. (1996, 5 February). Presidential Timber. Steve Forbes is as wooden as they come. *Washington Post*, p. C01.
7. Gepfert, K. (1996, 27 November). Come and see us sometime. *Wall Street Journal*, p. S2.
8. Carter, D. (1997, 16 December). Score points with the boss, go to the party but behave. *Rochester Democrat and Chronicle*, p. 5.
9. Moss, M. (1997, 24 September). Leaving home: Marguerite Ables, 68, finds her life's work. *Wall Street Journal*, p. A1.
10. Vick, K. and Mooar, B. (1996, 30 May). Defendant's peer describe troublemaker. *Washington Post*, p. A01.
11. Prager, J. (1997, 30 July). Consultant offers a few pointers on making small talk with a boss. *Wall Street Journal*, p. B1.
12. Land, D. (1997, 16 October). Quiet but thrusting approach. *Financial Times*, p. 8.
13. Hanson, C. (1996, 14 April). The boss ignores you? How to foster feedback. *Chicago Tribune*, p. 7.
14. Escobar, G. and Ordonez, J. (1997, 18 August). Beam plunges from bridge over Rock Creek. *Washington Post*, p. A01.
15. Edwards, O. (1996, 7 October). The basicilica chip. *Forbes*, p. S140.
16. Koziol, N. (1998, 10 May). Plant manager Floyd Swink is an icon in the Midwest's conservation movement. *Chicago Tribune*, p. 1.
17. Skelton, G. (1996, 25 March). A campaign war story sheds some light. *Los Angeles Times*, p. 3.

18. Roberts, R. (1996, 1 October). The gold standard: When 10,000 financiers gather it's obvious money doesn't walk. *Washington Post*, p. D01.
19. Hanson, C. (1996, 14 April). The boss ignores you? How to foster feedback. *Chicago Tribune*, p. 7.
20. Powell, M. and Williams, V. (1997, 29 March). D. C. Council chairman David A Clarke dies. *Washington Post*, p. A1.
21. Powell, M. and Williams, V. (1997, 29 March). D. C. Council chairman David A Clarke dies. *Washington Post*, p. A1.
22. Barnes, B. (1997, 1 January). George W. Mitchell dies at 92: Federal reserve board official. *Washington Post*, p. C4.
23. Shulins, N. (1996, 18 July). For the children: A warrior on the page. *Associated Press*. Retrieved May 20, 1998 from Dow Jones Interactive on-line database.
24. Gapper, J. (1998, 10 February). Always ready for a bit of rough and tumble. *Financial Times*, p. 2.
25. McWilliams, G. (1998, 2 March). Dick Cheney ain't studyin' war no more. *Business Week*, p. 84.
26. Nichols, B. (1997, 6 October). Tape shows coffee talk. *USA Today*, p. 9A.
27. Nichols, B. (1997, 6 October). Tape shows coffee talk. *USA Today*, p. 9A.
28. Duffy, M. and Tumulty, K. (1997, 27 October). It's groundhog day: The Clinton tapes roll on and on and on, but every now and then a tantalizing detail emerges. *Time Magazine*, p. 43.
29. Kurtz, H. (1996, 5 February). Presidential Timber? Steve Forbes is as wooden as they come and it's driving the media crazy. *Washington Post*, p. C1.
30. Kramer, F. (1996, 16 February). Quiet and unassuming, Forbes leads from behind the scenes. *Associated Press*. Retrieved May 20, 1998 from Dow Jones Interactive on-line database.
31. Presidential Timber? Steve Forbes is as wooden as they come and it's driving the media crazy. *Washington Post*, p. C1.
32. Note FM stands for faculty member and GS stands for graduate students. Participants are numbered in terms of their entrance into the discussion. The audio-taping began a few seconds into the Chair's opening remarks.
33. Talk is transcribed using a simplified version of the symbols used in conversation analysis (Atkinson and Heritage 1984). Micro-pauses (approximately .2 of a second are indicated by (.) and longer pauses are indicated by (pause). Punctuation indicates intonation where a question mark (?) indicates rising intonation, a period = falling intonation, and a comma (,) indicates a continuing or listing intonation. Hyphens (tak-) indicate an abrupt cut-off. Speech that is faster than the surrounding talk is enclosed with greater than and less than symbols (>>faster talk<<). Off-set square brackets (⌐) indicate the start and finish of overlapping speech. Colons indicate prolonged sounds. Single parentheses mark unclear stretches of speech and double parentheses (( )) are used for non-speech sounds. Square brackets mark information needed to interpret what a person is saying.
34. This table is based on one presented by Hare (1976).

35. Of 240 staff comments, this practice occurred in 40 of them. Names have been changed to preserve participant confidentiality.

References

Aronsson, K. (1998) Identity in interaction and social choreography. *Research on Language and Social Interaction*, 31: 75–89.

Atkinson, J. M. and Heritage, J. (eds) (1984) *Structure of Social Action: Studies in Conversation Analysis*. Cambridge: Cambridge University Press.

Austin, J. L. (1962) *How to Do Things with Words*. Oxford: Oxford University Press.

Bales, R. F. (1950a) A set of categories for the analysis of small group interaction. *American Sociological Review*, 15: 257–63.

Bales, R. F. (1950b) *Interaction Process Analysis: A Method for the Study of Small Group Interaction*. Cambridge, MA: Addison-Wesley.

Bhaskar, R. (1986) *Scientific Realism and Human Emancipation*. London: Verso.

Bhaskar, R. (1989) *Reclaiming Reality: A Critical Introduction to Contemporary Philosophy*. London: Verso.

Billig, M., Condor, S., Edwards, D., Gane, M., Middleton, D. and Radley, A. (1988) *Ideological Dilemmas*. London: Sage.

Coupland, J., Coupland, N. and Robinson, J. (1992) How are you: Negotiating phatic communication. *Language in Society*, 21: 207–30.

Hare, A. P. (1976) *Handbook of Small Group Research* (2nd edition) New York: The Free Press.

Laver, J. (1975) Communicative functions of phatic communication. In A. Kendon, R. M. Harris and M. R. Key (eds) *The Organisation of Behaviour in Face-To-Face Interaction*. The Hague: Mouton.

Laver, J. (1981) Linguistic routines and politeness in greeting and parting. In F. Coulmas (ed.) *Conversational Routine: Explorations in Standardised Communication Situations and Prepatterned Speech*. The Hague: Mouton.

Malinowski, B. (1923) The problem of meaning in primitive languages. In C. K. Ogden and I. A. Richards (eds), *The Meaning of Meaning*. New York: Harcourt, Brace and World.

Naughton, J. M. (1996) Discursively managing evaluation and acceptance in a hospice team meeting: A dilemma. Ann Arbor, MI: UMI Dissertation Services.

Potter, J. and Wetherell, M. (1987) *Discourse and Social Psychology*. London: Sage.

Rintel, E. S. and Pittam, J. (1997) Strangers in a strange land: Interaction management on Internet relay chat. *Human Communication Research*, 23: 507–34.

Ross, R. S. (1989) *Small Groups in Organizational Settings*. Englewood Cliffs, NJ: Prentice Hall.

Ruesch, J. and Bateson, G. (1951) *Communication: The Social Matrix of Psychiatry*. New York: Norton.

Schultz, B. G. (1989) *Communicating in the Small Group*. New York: Harper and Row.

Shotter, J. (1993) *Conversational Realities: Constructing Life through Language*. Thousand Oaks, CA: Sage.

Tannen, D. (1984) *Conversational style: Analyzing Talk among Friends*. Norwood, NJ: Ablex.

Tracy, K. (1997) *Colloquium: Dilemmas of Academic Discourse*. Norwood, NJ: Ablex.

Tracy, K. and Baratz, S. (1994) The case for case studies of facework. In S. Ting-Toomey (ed.), *The challenge of facework*. Albany: SUNY Press.

Tracy, K. and Carjuzaa, J. (1993) Identity enactment in intellectual discussion. *Journal of Language and Social Psychology*, 12: 171–94.

Tracy, K. and Coupland, N. (1990) Multiple goals in discourse: An overview of issues. *Journal of Language and Social Psychology*, 9: 1–13.

Tracy, K. and Naughton, J. M. (1994) The identity work of questioning in intellectual discussion. *Communication Monographs*, 61: 281–302.

Watzlawick, P., Beavin, J. H. and Jackson, D. D. (1967) *Pragmatics of Human Communication*. New York: Norton.

Yahya-Othman, S. (1994) Covering one's social back: Politeness among the Swahili. *Text*, 14: 141–61.

3

Mutually captive audiences: small talk and the genre of close-contact service encounters
Michael McCarthy

1 Introduction

In the study of spoken genres, service encounters (both public, of the consumer-oriented type) and more private (e.g. professional counselling, therapy and more institutional types) have a long pedigree. This chapter looks at two contexts of consumer service, the hairdresser's and the driving lesson, and tries to understand the significance of elements of small talk (defined here as non-obligatory talk in terms of task requirements) that occur in such data. The framework for examining the small talk presupposes a model (or at least a general theory) of spoken genres, and broad analytical frameworks for the description of transactional (i.e. 'business- or task-oriented' talk) and relational (i.e. participant relationship-oriented) talk. Within this broad definition of 'relational', segments of talk that fall into conventional categories of phatic communication will also be considered, in the spirit of recent studies of phatic communication such as Coupland, Coupland and Robinson (1992) where, building on Laver's important work (e.g. Laver 1975), phatic exchanges are dealt with in a genuinely exploratory way, and not dismissed as in some way communicatively 'deficient'. This chapter takes the view that the data cannot be fully accounted for by a crude separation of these broad-brush labels for types of talk. Adopting a definition of genre that incorporates participant relations and goal-orientation, and using real corpus data, I argue that genre models based predominantly on transactional achievements cannot account for the kinds of variation immanent in corpus data and cannot account for participants' commitment to relational talk even when such talk may appear unmotivated.

2   Spoken genres

No theory of spoken genre can ignore the foundational work of Mitchell (1957), whose study of the buying and selling discourses at markets in Cyrenaica, based on data gathered in 1949, still stands as a seminal account of the staging and sequencing of extended spoken events. Mitchell, although not explicitly concerned with genre, lays out the most basic features of context that cannot be ignored in the examination of data (or, in his case, at a time when portable tape-recorders were rare, close observation in the field). Mitchell included the spatio-temporal features of context (the 'where and when' of speech events), the activities being performed (e.g. lecturing, eating, buying and selling), the 'attitude' (p. 33) of participants (including the kinds of speech acts performed, such as boasting, blaming, cursing, etc.), their professions, social class, etc, as relevant features in his analysis. With the benefits of a healthy literature in sociolinguistics and discourse- and conversation-analysis, it is perhaps hard for us entering a new century to appreciate how radical Mitchell's proposals were, but they still remain as one of the clearest statements of the relevance of contextual features to the understanding of lexico-grammatical and other choices at the formal levels. Mitchell traced the variation in language that occurred in market and shop transactions and market auctions, showing, among other things, how the utterances of buyer and seller regularly correlated across the different types of selling events, yet with significant features of variation, that is to say, although many aspects of the language were constant across the different settings, other features were not. Market transactions, but not shop ones, might include an enquiry as to whether the goods on view were for sale or not; greetings, normal in shops, might not necessarily occur in markets; in markets, either seller or buyer might name a price for the goods, while in shops the seller invariably initiated the price-naming. Despite these elements of variation, Mitchell was able to observe recurring sequential stages in the events, typically including elements such as *salutation – enquiry as to the object of sale – investigation of the object of sale – bargaining – conclusion*. Within each stage, there was considerable variation (for example, different spatial relations between the participants resulted in different proxemics: in this respect, open air markets were different to enclosed shops). The enduring value of Mitchell's proposals is that they enable us to explain why utterance-types in different classes of service encounter might vary when other things appear to be equal (i.e. in Mitchell's case that all the traders were market traders, all the goods were basic commodities and foodstuffs, there was a broad cultural unity, etc.). We shall return to this theme below. Mitchell's work offered the possibility of the construction of a theory of spoken genre that went beyond the evidence of the residual text (i.e. the transcript) of a spoken event, and which explicitly admitted the goals and relationships of the interaction into the reckoning, over and above the sequential elements that construct the text, however predictable and reliable in their sequence those elements might be.

Bakhtin (especially Bakhtin 1986) is clearly also an important figure for the development of theories of spoken genre. Bakhtin's conception of genre focuses on the *utterance*, a unit of talk which may vary in length from one brief speaker-turn to a whole extended monologue; the defining feature of the utterance is that it ends at a point where an interlocutor may make a response.[1] The Bakhtinian utterance reflects the conditions and goals of different human activities, via their 'compositional structure' (1986: 60). Utterances are locally configured and individual, but 'each sphere in which language is used develops its own relatively stable types of these utterances' (ibid.), and these are what constitute genres. A prime example of this Bakhtinian principle might be the types of stability observed over time and space in academic and scientific writing, even though individual writers construct individual utterances to suit their unique circumstances and arguments (see Swales 1990). But genres, crucially, also partake of interpersonal aspects: 'each speech genre in each area of speech communication has its own typical conception of the addressee, and this defines it as a genre' (ibid. 95). One further significance of Bakhtin's work to the present chapter is that it removes the distinction between language as the possession of the individual psyche and language as a social construct, a resource shared among participants.

Hymes (1972) also conceives of genre as a higher-order feature of speech events, emphasising their dynamic characteristics, and separating them from speech events *per se*: genres *may* coincide with speech events, but they can also occur within speech events, and the same genre can exhibit variation in different speech events. Duranti (1983) shares this dynamic view of genre: the same genre may be played out in different ways, depending on the identity and purposes of speakers, where the genre occurs in the whole speech event, etc. Walter (1988: 2–3), seeking to characterise the genre of courtroom jury summations, also homes in on the setting in which the talk occurs as a crucial variable. Dynamism and variability are recurring themes in major work on genres, and in the studies that are of greatest relevance to the present chapter, i.e. those investigating service encounters, they preoccupy researchers faced with variation within superficially homogeneous data sets. Indeed, service encounters have proved to be amongst the most fertile of soils for those delving into spoken genres, and not surprisingly, since they seem to be based on a very primeval commonality (the transaction of information, goods and services) that lends itself to over-arching modelling of shared, obligatory features (such as those exemplified from Mitchell 1957), above, and yet are so different from case to case in their actual realisations. It is to studies of service encounters that we now turn in greater detail in our efforts to trace the emergence of a general theory of speech genres that will serve the data in the present study.

3   Service encounters

Since Mitchell, many others have investigated service encounters of the public, buying-and-selling type (this chapter excludes as beyond its scope the services of professionals such as therapists, counsellors, medical practitioners, lawyers, etc.). Key studies include Merritt (1976), who looked at variability in question-answer and question-question sequences in server-customer talk in a small university campus general store. Merritt's study showed how questions may follow questions in the strategic pursuit of a successful serving outcome, though her study did not focus on the relational aspects of talk which concern the present study. Hasan also worked with service encounter data in the 1970s, a good discussion of which was later made widely available in Hasan (1985). Hasan looked at transactions at a greengrocer's and argued for the primacy of obligatory elements (such as *sale request, sale compliance, sale, purchase* and *purchase closure*) in the defining of the generic structure potential (GSP) of any language event, while admitting the participants' (contextually limited) rights to add optional elements. While Hasan focused on the transactional elements of her data, her chosen extracts display utterances not 'obligatory' in any sense to the service encounter, and which could only have a relational purpose (e.g. customers giving reasons for their choice). N. Coupland (1983) looked at travel agency encounters and focused on non-obligatory elements such as explicit boundary marking and strategies for making purpose plain. Coupland had a sociological aim, the correlation of language variables with socio-economic ones, but his study also showed some interesting examples of what he calls 'encounter evaluations' (p. 472) (where participants comment on and evaluate the ease or difficulty with which the encounter has proceeded), which are clearly relationally oriented and which are relevant to the types of elements to be discussed in our data below.

Ventola (1987) spreads her net further to include, in addition to travel agency discourse, talk in a post office and a gift shop. Like Hasan, she too is concerned with differentiating obligatory (e.g. sale request) and non-obligatory elements (e.g. greetings) (pp. 51ff), and recognises the fluidity and dynamism of even the most banal everyday service conversations. Working with the tripartite Hallidayan model of Field, Tenor and Mode, Ventola's main interest is the Field (i.e. the more content- and transactionally-oriented features of the discourse), rather than the Tenor (what we are interested in here: the relational/interpersonal features), and how agnate features occur across the different spatial settings, offering the analyst the possibility of formulating a generic structure potential for any given genre. Ventola (1983), using Finnish and Australian English data, looks at some cross-cultural differences in schematic expectations in service encounters in a travel agents and a post office.

Lamoureux (1989) wades even deeper into the turbid waters of retailing and refers to data that includes recordings from bookshops, a fabric shop, a record shop, a card shop, markets, a department store, a fish shop, a bakery and a drugstore, with interesting observations on how participants work conversationally to align 'customer needs with server potential' (p. 106), another theme relevant to the data of the present chapter. Perhaps even more directly relevant to our present concerns is Lindenfeld's (1990) study of talk in French urban marketplaces, which devotes two sections to small talk and to the trading of jokes and playful insults between sellers and customers. Such talk is defined as 'remarks varying in length which are not essential for the accomplishment of the business at hand, and occasional narratives which are even further removed from instrumental talk' (p. 105). Interestingly, small talk is differentially distributed as between seller and buyer, especially as regards topic, with buyers favouring discussions of food storing and eating, anticipated pleasure in consumption, personal informa- tion, vacation patterns, etc. and vendors eschewing personal talk except where they echo or match information proffered by a customer. On the other hand, Lindenfeld found that both buyers and sellers engaged in the banter- ing of jokes and playful insults.

A whole raft of informative studies has emerged from the Italian-based PIXI project, using recordings made in British and Italian bookshops. These include in their aims the teasing-out of cross-cultural differences in inter- active styles in English and Italian, which are posited to be based on cultural schemata and expectations and which leave their trace in the text in the form of different sequencing of the elements of requesting and negotiating ser- vice, and differences in the explanations and justifications of particular beha- viours engaged in by participants (see Aston 1988, 1991; Brodine 1991; Zorzi Calò 1991; Anderson 1994; Gavioli 1995). The PIXI project also spawned George's (1990) study of complaint-making based on data recorded at a tourist resort, once again with a cross-cultural Italian-English perspect- ive. Cross-cultural concerns also underlie Bailey's (1997) study of the racial tensions that can arise from different perceptions of what constitutes soci- able behaviour in the service encounter, based on data recorded in liquor stores with Korean vendors and Korean and African American customers.

Among those that have given a special focus to relational talk as opposed to just transactional talk in service encounters, apart from Lindenfeld (see above), are several studies not directly concerned with the 'shop' contexts I have reported so far. Lieverscheidt, Werlen and Zimmermann (1989), whose data, as does some of that in this chapter, comes from the hairdresser's salon, examine the types of talk found in two different social settings: a 'traditional' hair salon patronised by the local community, and a 'trendy' salon patronised by young, left-wing intellectual types. The researchers found that more ritualised conversation dominated in the traditional salon and, while conversa- tional topics were similar in both salons, there was greater topic elaboration in the 'trendy' setting. At the same time, overall, there seemed to be less pressure and obligation to engage in small talk in the trendy salon, and there was in total less small talk than in the traditional setting. Lieverscheidt *et al.*'s research reinforces both the social dimension and the spatio–temporal factors, with carefully drawn diagrams of the two salons indicating the disposition of chairs and the general layout. Barbers are included, along with beauticians and pharmacists in a study of conversations in service encounters by Beinstein (1975), in which her focus is on the topics of conversation engaged in when 'persons who do not ordinarily see each other come together to carry out a task for mutual benefit' (p. 86). Beinstein's study was based mostly on interviews, supplemented by observation and some recorded conversational data. Holidays, social problems, health problems, economic matters, food, entertainment and fashion were highest ranked as most frequent conversational topics, followed by politics and world affairs, and personal problems. The barber's ranked slightly differently, with sports and fashion occupying a higher position. Beinstein speculated that orientation towards these topics might be important where a stable clientele had not yet been established, 'to ensure continued patronage' (p. 91); in other words, a link can be perceived between business-like motives and non-task oriented talk in the chosen settings.

In a different setting, Schneider's (1989) study of small talk during hotel registration sessions between receptionists and guests shows a pattern of information exchanges that construct an identity for guests; such talk does not just fill up time. Similarly, Komter's (1991) study of the discourse of job interviews examines the small talk that usually takes place at the beginning of an interview, and concludes that it is an important and legitimate phase in the interview process, rather than just an optional extra. Iacobucci (1990), who looks at customer calls to a phone company concerning billing queries, is also concerned to elevate the importance of 'apparently relational-oriented talk' (p. 97) to a level where it is integrated with 'task concerns' (ibid.) to align with accepted institutional frameworks. Iacobucci's subjects often seemed to give unnecessary explanations and background information about their purpose in ringing the company, but these are clearly shown to be not merely interpersonally motivated but strategic elements in the achievement of the caller's goal. Most recently, an indepth study of travel agency discourse by Ylänne-McEwen (1997) returns to the theme of how relational talk is far from tangential to the task of selling and buying travel and holidays.

A common theme in the service encounter literature is the tension between the basic, primordial elements of service transaction and other, more optional elements (whether phatic, such as greetings and closing routines, or relational in the broader sense exemplified in the studies referred to in this section). This natural tension springs from a desire to establish differentiated genres with as deterministic and predictable a set of norms as possible, but it is by no means a given that deterministic models can best capture spoken interaction, where the construction of relationships, and the formulation of goals, are emergent rather than predetermined (Tracy and N. Coupland 1990). In the data which follow, I hope to show that a more satisfactory model of spoken genre is one that accepts the emergent role of relational discourse as of equal relevance to the achievement of goals as the transactional 'staging' of predictable elements, and that much data simply cannot be accounted for unless we take such a line.

4   Data

The data for this study come from the CANCODE spoken corpus. CANCODE stands for 'Cambridge and Nottingham Corpus of Discourse in English'; the corpus was established at the Department of English Studies, University of Nottingham, UK and is funded by Cambridge University Press, with whom the sole copyright resides. The project is jointly directed by Ronald Carter[2] and the present author. The corpus consists of five million words of transcribed conversations. The corpus tape-recordings were made in a variety of settings including private homes, shops, offices and other public places, and educational institutions (though in non-formal settings) across the islands of Britain and Ireland, with a wide demographic spread. For further details of the corpus and its construction, see McCarthy (1998).

The chosen extracts for the present study come from two types of service encounter: a hairdresser's salon and a driving lesson. To date, and to my knowledge, only one published study completely devoted to hairdresser talk exists (Lieverscheidt, Werlen and Zimmermann 1989; see above), and none devoted to driving lessons. The hairdressing data comes from a cutting session at a women's salon in the north of England in 1995.[3] Customer and cutter are both female; the customer is in her forties, the cutter in her thirties. The session also includes conversation with a younger female assistant who washes the client's hair before the main cutting phase. The driving lesson was recorded in Dublin, Ireland in 1997, and includes a female learner in her twenties and her older, male instructor.[4] What the data sets have in common is that they are a particular type of service encounter where server and served are in close proximity in a physically limited space for a defined length of time; in short, the participants are each other's captive audience. What is more, in both cases, service provider and client know each other from previous encounters; it is not their first time together, and in both recordings the atmosphere is friendly and informal. Both encounters last approximately 45 minutes. In the spirit of Mitchell (1957), I shall not ignore the effects these contextual features are likely to have on (a) the amount of talk, and (b) the distribution of transactional versus relational elements.

There are crucial differences between the two types of encounter, however, which also affect the amount and nature of the talk. The hairdresser's is a one-sided 'language-in-action' affair: the hairdresser is very physically active, the customer passive and restricted to sitting still in the chair and only moving the head when asked to do so. In the driving lesson, the learner is the active one in the sense that it is she who does the driving, but the instructor is also verbally and mentally active, informing and instructing his client, keeping one eye on her movements and keeping a steady eye on the road in case of problems. The driving lesson is much more of a 'language-in-action' event for both participants. One of the things directly affected by the intimate tie between language and action which both these types of encounter display is silence; in the CANCODE corpus, conversations where the language is primarily in the service of physical activities regularly display long silences which would be otherwise unacceptable in casual conversation (see the language-in-action extracts in Carter and McCarthy 1997 for several examples of this).[5] The silence factor will be seen to be important in the distribution of relational talk in both our data situations.

5 Types of talk in the data

5.1 The hairdresser's: generic types

Unsurprisingly, the hairdresser data contains a good deal of conversation of all three principle kinds that concern us (phatic, transactional and relational), unsurprisingly because the reputation of barbers and hairdressers as talkers has been recognised for centuries. In his entertaining article on representations of hairdressers over time, Herzog (1996), writing as a cultural historian, offers evaluations of hairdressers by, among others, diarists and literary writers of the eighteenth and nineteenth centuries, which include references to 'the chattering dexterity of a friseur',[6] a hairdresser 'with a voluble tongue',[7] 'agreeable discussions'[8] with the barber, and the barber's 'continued babble'.[9] Most of us have, at one time or another, been the captive audience in the hair-cutting chair, and many people, when asked informally, claim to 'know the script' well, such that hairdresser talk has become stereotyped in everyday perceptions. The overall staging (or generic structure) of the hairdressing session consists of the following phases, marked both verbally and non-verbally (by physical activity) by the participants:

1. Arrival and checking in for appointment (just inside the salon, with cutter doubling as receptionist)
2. Invitation to 'come through' (i.e. move to the washing chair)

3. Initial discussion of how the client's hair is to be cut (washing chair, with client's regular cutter)
4. Hair washing (washing chair, with different server)
5. Move to cutting chair, with an invitation to coffee
6. Hair cutting (cutting chair, with cutter)
7. Payment/closure (at cash desk, cutter acting as cashier)

These are the stages in this particular extract where, in a small provincial salon, servers may take on more than one role. In busier salons, it is likely that the role of receptionist/cashier may be filled by someone not involved in the washing and cutting, and it is also the case that washing may happen at a different chair from the cutting chair. Equally, stages 3 and 4 above are often reversed, but the general pattern is probably widely applicable to (at least female) hairdressing service encounters in many parts of the world.

The transactional talk clearly orientates towards these phases, for example:[10]

Extract 1

(Moving from reception area to cutting chair)
1 <Server> Would you like to come through.
2 <Client> Ya.

Extract 2

(Beginning of washing session)
1 <Server> Would you like to pop your head back.
2 <Client> Thanks.
3 <Server> Is that alright for you?
4 <Client> Yes that's fine thanks.

Extract 3

(Closure)
1 <Server> That's £16.50 then please.
2 <Client> Thank you.
3 <Server> Did you have a jacket with you?
4 <Client>   └No I didn't.

Also necessary in the transactional talk are local requests and/or instructions concerning the hair washing, cutting and styling, for example:

Extract 4

1 <Server> Do you have conditioner on your hair?
2 <Client> You could put a little bit on yeah.

Extract 5

1 <Server> Are we taking it over to the side or back or?
2 <Client> I don't mind.
3 (5 secs)
4 <Client> Maybe start off straight back because it tends+
5 <Server> $^{\llcorner}$To go flop.
6 <Client> $^{\llcorner}$to flop erm it's
7   certainly thickened up now.

However, other than these necessary transactional exchanges, long periods of activity take place where no strictly transactional talk is necessary. There are a number of long silences during the recording, e.g. 45 seconds while the client is waiting for the washing assistant to approach the chair at the basin, intermittent silences of between 10 and 20 seconds while the head is partially submerged or drenched while being washed or rinsed, 40 seconds while the hair-dryer is running, etc., in other words, occasions when talk would be difficult or impossible. Despite this, some 5,000 words of non-transactional talk occur during the 45-minute session. The task-oriented transactional talk accounts for approximately 400 words. The percentages are thus approximately 7.5 per cent transactional and 92.5 per cent non-transactional.

Before we turn to the nature of the non-transactional talk, it is worth noting that even the overtly transactional talk can break its bounds and reveal relational concerns. The cutter and client know each other from previous encounters, and the cutter acknowledges this relationship in a metastatement (lines 3–6) right at the start of the discussion with her client as to how she wants her hair done (note the use of communal *we*, which is often heard in friendly service encounters). The conversation begins with a phatic exchange:

Extract 6

1 <Server> Are you all right?
2 <Client> I'm fine thanks and you?
3 <Server> I'm fine thank you yes [<Client> [Laughs]] **are we cutting it as**
4   **normal or anything different or**?
5 <Client> Erm any suggestions or [laughs]?
6 <Server> **I always ask you that [laughs].** Without touching the back+
7 <Client> $^{\llcorner}$Ya.
8 <Server> I mean you could go very wispy into the neck and sort of have a wedge.
9 <Client> Yeah.
10 <Server> Keep that back wedge keep that very into the neck like sort of wedge.

This is clearly a case of what Lamoureux (1989) referred to as aligning customer needs with server potential. Here the server reflects on the routine nature of the encounter, the moment when she offers her client the opportunity to decide something different from the normal. Such reflexive moments may be seen as important evidence of the participants' conscious engagement in the construction of the emerging genre; in this case the cutter acknowledges the relationship she has built with her client on this particular negotiable aspect of the regular hairdressing process. Equally, there are non-obligatory comments accompanying transactional events, as in line 2 of Extract 7:

Extract 7

(Referring to the protective gown worn by the client)
1 <Server> There's some armholes in the gown.
2 <Client> Oh is there [laughs] oh there [laughs] **a bit like batman otherwise**
3   [laughs].

Extract 8

(Referring to the shampoo)
1 <Client> That's a nice smell.

Extract 8 is an example of 'noticings about the shared local environment' (see Drew and Chilton, this volume).

There is, too, what N. Coupland (1983: 472) called an 'encounter evaluation' (see section 3 above) at the end of the session, which serves to satisfy all parties that the encounter has been pleasant, successful, free of problems, etc.

Extract 9

(End of the cutting session)
1 <Client> Oh that's lovely.
2 <Server> Better isn't it?
3 <Client>   ⌐Mm that's smashing.

In this exchange, as well as it being a conventional marker of termination of the cutting phase, participants can show varying degrees of enthusiasm for the new haircut which will consolidate or otherwise a good, ongoing service relationship between them. The session then closes, after payment, with a phatic exchange, an almost identical example of which we shall find in the driving lesson data, where the client refers to how many other customers the server has to deal with before finishing work, which seems to have become a ritualisation of concern for the server in such situations. Here the server breaks the phatic bounds and expands the ritual with a friendly dig (line 3) at her colleagues:

Extract 10

1 <Client> You nearly finished now?
2 <Server> I've just got one more and then time to go home at half past five
3   [<Client> [Laughs]] **just letting these lot know 'cos they're here**
4   **until seven** [laughs].

Thus transactional and phatic elements are additionally marked by orientation towards the ongoing client–server relationship, and this would seem to be particularly important in 'captive audience' types of encounters between server and served, more so perhaps than those of short duration (e.g. shops), where boundary marking of the phases of the encounter may well be more business-like. I have also noted that both the data sets involve participants who are not transacting service for the first time; King and Sereno (1984) see the distinction between long-term and 'zero-history' relationships (p. 271) as an important factor in how relational meaning is co-constructed by participants in talk, and this would certainly seem to be relevant here. These contextual features might explain why researchers using data from short-encounter situations such as post offices and general stores have found more to comment on in the transactional structure than in the relational, and why their modelling of genre is heavily transaction-biased (e.g. Hasan 1985; Ventola 1983, 1987). In part this bias is an artefact of the analytical model used; systemic functional analysis operating as it does with moves which are move conveniently related to transactional stages. It also accounts for the much richer relational data found in studies such as Ylänne-McEwen (1997), where the extended travel-agency encounters depended for their success in no small part on the achievement and maintenance of a satisfactory relationship between server and customer.

5.2   The hairdresser's: relational topics

Those parts of the hairdressing session not filled by phatic, transactional (or transactional-plus-relational) talk or by silence (see also Jaworski, this volume) are given over to casual conversation. The topics covered are listed in Table 3.1 below, together with a note on which of the two participants initiates them:

Each participant initiates topics, but the subjects revolve mostly around the life and situation of the washer and cutter; the client asks the washer and cutter a lot about herself but returns relatively little about her own life and situation, except in the topics of what part of town she lives in, and some minor contributions about her own experiences of the topics of childbirth and hair loss (this last topic being less 'casually' occasioned and more related to the task at hand). This may be more than personal reticence: the cutter is often physically in a better position to engage in talk, while the customer

Table 3.1

Topic	Initiated by
The weather	C
Washing assistant's training and career	C
Holidays	C
What part of town client and washing assistant live	S
Driving and mobility, driving lessons, cost	C
Cutter's illness and absence from work	C
Cutter's pregnancy	C
Work reorganisation with the forthcoming birth	S
The cutter's other child, Charlotte	C
Anecdotes about Charlotte	S
Family birthdays	S
The cutter's husband	S
Cutter's daily routine	S
A customer who suffered hair loss	S
Women versus men wearing wigs	S

S = server   C = client

may be discomforted for extended periods (e.g. with her head bowed and/or wet). It is the cutter, for instance, who engages in extended anecdotes about her child. The importance of such personal anecdotes has recently been demonstrated by Schiffrin (1996), for whom such stories about oneself relate 'a matrix of actions and beliefs that together display a social identity'. Social identity is clearly felt by participants to be relevant in the co-construction of genres, including service encounters, but there is no rule that says each participant must contribute equally to this kind of personal disclosure, and different spatio-temporal and socio-cultural features of context will generate different distributions of such talk, as Lindenfeld (1990) noticed in her study of market trading (see section 3 above).

The conversational topics do not in fact stray much beyond matters relevant to the washer's and cutter's work situation (the washer's training and living situation vis-à-vis the job; the cutter's illness and the problem of reorganising work due to her pregnancy; the cutter's other child and its care; her husband's role in making things work, her daily routine; a customer who suffered hair loss; wigs). Thus although there seems to be a good deal of 'casual conversation', the field is circumscribed by those topics relevant to the business at hand, and to topics that construct and reconstruct the satisfactory ongoing client–server relationship. For example, in discussing the forthcoming new birth, the cutter is at pains to explain when she will be on maternity leave, so as not to inconvenience the client:

Extract 11

1 <Client> So how long will you be off for?
2 <Server> Em be about 12 weeks again+
3 <Client>   ⌐Oh yeah.
4 <Server> so have another haircut before I go.
5 <Client> [Laughs] if I come in say the beginning of June.
6 <Server> Yes you'll be fine then.
7 <Client> [Laughs] yes.
8 <Server> Then you can wait until I come back.

In the present data, at least, there is little to justify labelling the cutting chair conversation as prattle or babble, as the quotes from Herzog (1996) might have suggested; important information is exchanged through the medium of sociable chat which vouches for the current situation of the participants and gives them useful perspectives on their server–client relationship. Although the small talk may adhere to a well-worn 'script', it is far from pointless. The scale of functional values apparent in the whole range of talk, from that directed at the efficient execution of the business at hand, via information exchange on organisational matters for the present and future, via personal data, all the way to the more general and diffuse sense of conviviality and sociability that the small talk engenders is polyphonic, and it is difficult to separate the different functions along the scale. However, analysis enables us to model the data at a more theoretical level, which provides templates for predictive power and replicability across different data sets. Although the types of talk apparent here are on a continuum (see also Holmes, this volume), it is possible to characterise their typical realisations, so long as one does not forget that their actual realisations are polyphonic. Our hairdressing data, therefore, raises important issues for defining genres. The most basic issue is: what do we achieve by only identifying transactional elements in genres such as service encounters? We can certainly do this, as I have attempted to show, for the hairdresser's salon, but then so little of our data (in terms of minutes, or numbers of words) would be accounted for (less than 10 per cent of the spoken words, as we saw above), a situation which surely cannot be satisfactory to the genre analyst, especially if one's notion of genre includes a strong element of goal-orientation. Do people stray lazily from their task-related goals, or only address them at staging-points in the discourse? This would seem unlikely, and the best solution for all the missing data in a more integrated view of genre would seem to be to put the relational exigencies at centre-stage alongside the transactional in the emergence and achievement of goals.

5.3   The driving lesson: generic types

Phatic exchanges at greeting and parting are brief in the driving lesson, and the talk throughout the 45-minute session is overwhelmingly transaction-oriented.

This is not surprising, since the driving instruction is delivered primarily through the verbal channel, and participants must remain on task whenever the car is moving, not least from the safety angle; it is a classroom on wheels. Silences are frequent and lengthy, punctuated only by instructions to turn corners, change gear, park, etc. and by evaluations of the learner's driving by the instructor or occasionally by the learner herself. Examples typical of the transactional talk include direct instructions:

Extract 12

1 <Instructor> Er turn right here again.
2 <Learner>   Uhuh.
3 (5 secs)
4 <Instructor> Okay keep turning.

Extract 13

1 <Instructor> Er left turn here. Use your brake as when you're changing down you
2   see slow down [<Learner> Yeah] put in a lower gear. Keep turning left
3   that's okay.

More indirect advice is also given related to general driving rules and to the exigencies of the official driving test:

Extract 14

1 <Instructor> Even with the green light in your favour you've got to check your right
2   side.
3 <Learner>   ⌐Yeah sure of course. You
4   could easily make a mistake.
5 <Instructor>   ⌐If you don't on the test they'll mark it down
6   okay.
7 <Learner>   Yeah. Okay.

Self-evaluations by the learner occasionally accompany the driving tasks. These are not obligatory, and would seem to be a way of giving salience to the personal elements that might possibly affect both the transactional and the relational aspects of the encounter (e.g. tiredness accounting for poor driving performance, as well as potentially for unfriendliness or irritability):

Extract 15

(At the conclusion of a three-point-turn)
1 <Instructor> All right.
2 <Learner>   [Laughs] **The exertion yeah it is hard work.**
3 <Instructor>   ⌐Yeah.

Extract 16

(After a reversing manoeuvre)
1 <Learner>   **Yeah the reversing+**
2 <Instructor>   └Sorry?
3 <Learner>   **is not without its tension.**
4 <Instructor> Oh yeah

As in the hairdresser's salon, further opportunities are taken to break out of the transactional by non-obligatory commenting on relevant features of the situation; these provide for occasional 'interactional moments' during the transactional flow:

Extract 17

1 <Learner>   Hard to see now.
2 <Instructor> **Pretty strong sun isn't it?**
3 <Learner>   Mm.
4 <Instructor> Sure is.

Extract 18

1 <Instructor> You're improving a lot now actually.
2 <Learner>   Good [laughs] **now is the time I've got to do something really**
3   **stupid like have the engine cut out.**
4 <Instructor> Well it's minor actually. That can happen to any driver on the road.

During the lesson, occasional encounter evaluations take place. In Extract 19, we see that the evaluation (lines 1–6) is accompanied by an account (an explanation of behaviour; lines 7–10), which is personal and which occupies a fuzzy territory between the transactional and the relational:

Extract 19

1 <Instructor> But no you're progressing all the time [<Learner> Yeah] so it basically
2   co-ordinates you know.
3 <Learner>   Yeah well I feel that even today+
4 <Instructor>   └Yeah you feel it yourself actually yeah.
5 <Learner>   is better than say last week+
6 <Instructor>   └That's right.
7 <Learner>   **em cos I'd had a break of about two weeks** [<Instructor> Right] **and**
8   **I think it's definitely beneficial+**
9 <Instructor>   └Right it's better.
10 <Learner> **to do a lesson every week at least.**
11 <Instructor>   └That's right it is.

At the conclusion of the lesson, an obligatory evaluation encounter occurs, obligatory, that is, for the instructor, but to which the learner might be expected to contribute in some way:

Extract 20

```
 1  <Instructor>  All right?
 2  <Learner>     [Sighs] yeah [laughs].
 3  <Instructor>              └Well done, Maria, you did well on that lesson you can
 4                switch off now.
 5  <Learner>     Yeah great thank you very much.
 6  (Extract 21 intervenes here)
 7  <Instructor>  So how d'you find it okay?
 8  <Learner>     Yeah it was great actually+
 9  <Instructor>              └That's good.
10  <Learner>     I really enjoyed it I thought I was more in control.
11  <Instructor>                         └You've come on a lot on
12                that lesson actually.
13  <Learner>     D'you think so?
14  <Instructor>  Yeah. Since the last one even you know.
15  <Learner>     I think the last one was a bad one though. [<Instructor> Yeah] I mean I
16                felt I wasn't patient you know.
17  <Instructor>                     └Yeah but you see you had a gap before
18                that.
19  <Learner>     That's why.
20  <Instructor>  That's what was wrong [<Learner> Yeah] really.
21  <Learner>     Yeah I think so.
22  <Instructor>  Yes.
```

Also, as at the end of the hairdressing session, the ritual concern for the server's workload is expressed and, as in the hairdresser's, the opportunity is taken to expand the phatic exchange beyond its minimal content with a humorous remark, this time by the client:

Extract 21

```
1  <Learner>     There you go. Have you got another one to go?
2  <Instructor>  I have indeed. One more to go.
3  <Learner>     I can let go now can't I?
4  <Instructor>              └Sorry?
5  <Learner>     I can let go now can't I? [laughs]
6  <Instructor>  Relax exactly yeah.
```

But, given that talk itself is at a premium owing to the long silences when both parties are concentrating on the road and the driving tasks, the transactional, task-driven instructions along with lengthy silences overwhelmingly dominate the 45 minutes. It is only when the car is for one reason or another

held up in its normal progress along the highway that predominantly relational talk occurs.

5.4   The driving lesson: relational topics

The weather provides opportunities for non-task-orientated talk, as the driving
lesson takes place on a beautiful spring day. The first such occasion is initiated by the instructor during a phase where the car is cruising safely on an
open stretch of road, and taken up by the learner with reference to spring
flowers:

Extract 22

```
 1 <Instructor> It's a nice day now actually isn't?
 2 <Learner>                          └Oh it's beautiful yeah.
 3 (2 secs)
 4 <Learner>    Makes you full of the joys of spring doesn't it?
 5 <Instructor> It does yeah.
 6 <Learner>    I em walk through Merrion Square usually in the mornings
 7              [<Instructor> Right] so you can tell the progress every morning
 8              [<Instructor> Yeah] cos er you've got the crocuses out last week
 9              [<Instructor> Oh of course yes] and you've got the trees budding
10              [<Instructor> Yeah] the cherry blossom.
11 <Instructor> Oh yeah it's a nice time of the year.
12 <Learner>    Oh yeah it's great.
13 <Instructor> Back down to third again.
```

Typically, such episodes are curtailed by the necessity for the instructor to
issue commands and advice, as in line 13. Inevitably, during a driving lesson
in a busy urban environment, the car will occasionally get held up at lights,
road works and other obstructions. It is at these otherwise inactive points
that the participants break out of the primarily transactional mode into
relational talk. Again, as in the hairdresser's, the talk is no free-for-all, but
addresses topics of direct or indirect relevance to the participants and their
social identities as 'driving animals'. Two such enforced stops occur, the first
of which (Extract 23) is at a rather slow set of traffic lights, where the
weather (cf. the hair-washing phase at the hairdresser's) is commented on by
the instructor, who relates it to driving conditions:

Extract 23

```
1 <Instructor> Yeah it's nice now isn't it.
2 <Learner>    Mm it's lovely really bright and clear.
3 <Instructor>                          └Nice sky.
4 <Learner>                                     └Yeah.
5 <Instructor> Good day for driving.
```

6 <Learner>   Yeah well apart from the glare [laughs].
7 <Instructor> The glare is a bit of a problem yeah.

At the other enforced stop, the car is held up for a considerable time at roadworks. It is here that the only extended relational episode occurs, and both parties exchange personal information, though still circumscribed by the general topic framework of roads. The episode is reproduced in its entirety here:

Extract 24

 1 <Instructor> They're always digging up roads.
 2 <Learner>   ⌐Yeah aren't they yeah.
 3 <Instructor> Ah it's a very botched job here.
 4 <Learner>   Mm I presume they're not going to leave it like that.
 5 <Instructor> Hopefully not.
 6 <Learner>   Mm.
 7 <Instructor> I wonder why they'd have to leave it like that initially though.
 8 <Learner>   Yeah I know, just a big lump of+
 9 <Instructor>   ⌐I could level it off a little bit better
10   myself than that.
11 <Learner>   tar [laughs] yeah I know yeah.
12 <Instructor>   ⌐Yeah.
13 (5 secs)
14 <Learner>   Out where my parents live they've been er knocking down the or taking
15   away the cherry blossom trees. [<Instructor> Oh right really] I was
16   wondering have you noticed this around at all no?
17 <Instructor>   ⌐No where's that again?
18 <Learner>   Well it's in Blanchardstown [<Instructor> Oh really] but I noticed it
19   around Donnybrook as well.
20 <Instructor> Why are they doing that? Cherry blossoms?
21 <Learner>   And they're lovely big mature trees.
22 <Instructor> [Inaudible]
23 <Learner>   Yeah and I was wondering that. Me mum was saying that er.
24 <Instructor>   ⌐Is that a
25   disease or something?
26 <Learner>   No the roots are spreading out underneath the pavement and cracking
27   the pavement [<Instructor> Aha] and the walls so. Erm.
28 <Instructor> They're dodgy yeah.
29 <Learner>   That's a bit dangerous yeah so anyway they decided to take up the trees
30   but they're planting again other different trees [<Instructor> Yeah] that
31   don't have such a big root system.
32 <Instructor> So cherry blossom spreads a lot.
33 <Learner>   Apparently yeah I mean you're talking maybe two metres [<Instructor>
34   Yeah] anyway from where they are [<Instructor> Yeah] to the wall.
35 (4 secs)
36 <Learner>   It's a pity.
37 <Instructor> We've a few big trees at the back of our garden actually.
38 <Learner>   Have you yeah.

39 <Instructor> Sycamore and a [inaudible] trees.
40 <Learner>   Oh very nice.
41 <Instructor> Well they're the kind that spread as well unfortunately.
42 <Learner>   Yeah.
43 <Instructor> Sycamore a very fast fast growing tree. Can't control it.
44 <Learner>   Mm can't do much with the roots I don't know if they have a big root
45   system do they?
46 <Instructor> Eh?
47 <Learner>   Do they have a big root system?
48 <Instructor>   ⌊Well sycamore's a fair size.
49 (They are clear to move off)
50 <Instructor> Far side, that's right okay we'll turn left at the lights.

Two long silences (5 seconds and 4 seconds) are broken by the learner, once with a piece of personal information (line 14) and on the second occasion with a retrospective comment on the lapsed topic (line 36), which prompts a piece of personal information from the instructor. Both are working hard to talk during this otherwise threatening delay to normal operations. The conversation lasts only as long as the hold-up, and is immediately truncated when the roadworks traffic lights change and the task demands of the driving take over again. The conversation starts with the instructor referring to the problem of roadworks, but both parties personalise the topic, the instructor with a joke about being able to do the work better than the road workers, and the learner with her story about her parents' street and the loss of trees, which the instructor matches with an account of his own tree problems. This is in line with Lindenfeld's (1990) finding that market traders only gave personal information as an act of matching personal information provided by customers.

What purpose does such a conversation serve? The imperative is to fill an inactive silence, but the participants eschew other possibilities (e.g. such as talking about driving techniques, or the car itself) and opt for a wider conversational topic which enables them to advance their personal knowledge of each other. As in the hairdresser's, they seem to be expressing a need to maintain a good, sociable, ongoing relationship, one which must last the test of several more 'captive' encounters within the confines of the small metal box that is the car, from which neither party can escape for 45 minutes, just like the hairdresser's chair. Whether consciously or not, participants seem to know that successful construction of this kind of service genre and achievement of its goals is as much to do with relational aspects as with getting the tasks done, and opportunities to consolidate the relational level are grasped by whichever party or parties is in a position to do so, as determined by the precise spatio–temporal nexus of circumstances which either facilitates (e.g. customer's head in a comfortable position at the hairdresser's, driver relaxed at roadworks) or militates against (noisy hair-dryer in operation, learner heavily focused on a difficult driving manoeuvre) non-transactional talk.

Such spatio–temporal factors, in relation to tasks and goals, bring us back to Mitchell's (1957) accounts of the variability in talk that he observed in different spatial settings and in different buying-and-selling task types.

6   Conclusion

The data we have looked at display some remarkable similarities, as well as crucial differences, in the pattern of talk. In both cases, we may distinguish four broad types of talk:

1. Phatic exchanges (greetings, partings)
2. Transactional talk (requests, enquiries, instructions)
3. Transactional-plus-relational talk (non-obligatory task evaluations and other comments)
4. Relational talk (small talk, anecdotes, wider topics of mutual interest)

It is only in the second type, transactional talk, that task demands are predominantly focused on, and even here, as we observed in section 5.1, participants do not hesitate to reinforce the relational context. In all the other types, participants work to build and consolidate their personal relationship. In the phatic exchanges that may be expected regularly to occur in such service encounters, and which can, in many situations, serve as a sort of minimal courtesy-level acknowledgement of the human encounter, we have seen how, in both cases presented here, opportunities for lightheartedness are taken. We have also seen how in our third type, transactional-plus-relational, it has been impossible to separate task-orientated language from non-obligatory personal comments and accounts. In the fourth type, that which is purely relational (in the sense that no task-oriented language occurs), we have seen that the spatio–temporal constraints of our two 'captive audience' sessions delimit the opportunities for relational talk, and how these are grasped when they present themselves.

The hairdresser's salon offers the maximum time and space for relational talk, and that, put simply, is why it occurs. The perception of such talk by clients is, as we have seen, a cultural issue; but Herzog's diarists and literary authors of past centuries (see section 5.1 above) are not alone in complaining about being the trapped victims of the hairdresser's or barber's chair, as we all know from our personal conversational experience. Equally, one can only wonder how the average client would feel if his/her hairdresser said nothing apart from the purely transactional instructions and requests for 30 or 45 minutes, and how satisfactory such an encounter would be. We are all, in our daily lives, thrown into situations where we are obliged to talk to people we might otherwise not choose to cultivate; the dilemma upon whose horns we perch uneasily in those situations is that talk may be an effort, may be banal and tiresome for one or all parties, but that the alternative, silence, is even more threatening and unacceptable. The driving lesson is different, with the spatio–temporal dimensions being filled with the business at hand for both parties; continuous small talk would probably be considered by most to be a positive danger in a situation where concentration on the task is everything. Yet even here, as we have seen, in those windows of opportunity offered by slow traffic lights and roadworks, both parties immediately orientate towards non-task talk.

I have stressed from the beginning that such data as that presented here offers not only fascinating and entertaining social insight, but should bring us up short if we are inclined to build a model of genre that ignores its relational aspects or relegates them to a second-order position. There are indeed stages/phases in each transcript that define the progression through time and space, obligatory elements that characterise both events (e.g. particular manoeuvres that are expected in the driving lesson – one would hardly expect to be required to do a handbrake about-turn as beloved of joyriders, for instance), and these are indeed important measures for the definition of generic structure potential. Linguists naturally focus on boundary phenomena in describing structure, but, arguably, it is the data in between the boundaries that most needs explaining.

The present data have raised two basic questions that need answers: why do such similar types of non-transactional talk occur in these two settings, and why is it so different in quantity? Only an account of genre that takes spatio–temporal correlates into account, as Mitchell proposed so long ago, and which sees goal-orientation as a multi-levelled, emergent phenomenon going beyond transactional activities, as indeed it is in the goal-orientation literature such as Tracy and N. Coupland (1990), will be able to account for large amounts of data which might otherwise be dismissed as 'small talk', but which are clearly not so small at all (see also Tracy and Naughton, this volume). Ochs's (1996) account of 'socializing humanity' makes a highly relevant observation here:

> . . . in all societies, members have tacit understandings of norms, preferences, and expectations concerning how situational dimensions such as time, space, affective stance, epistemic stance, social identity, social acts, and social activities cluster together.

(p. 417)

What Ochs is describing here as a universal human phenomenon is clearly what our data have shown: the spatio–temporal constraints of salon and motor-car, the attitudes of participants, their self-positioning with regard to assertion/tentativeness (their 'epistemic stance': cf. data examples 16–18 above), their construction and reinforcement of social identities, their experience of the tasks at hand, all cluster harmoniously, rather than unfold sequentially.

What is needed in spoken genre studies is an expansion of the kinds of data analysed, as well as a willingness to take into account a broader range of situational features. For instance, this chapter takes no account of gender in the two interactions: notions such as the construction of a 'collaborative floor' between women interlocutors, as discussed by Coates (1997) might illuminate differences in relational talk in similar service encounters with different gender mixes. Age and social class (see the review of N. Coupland (1983) in section 3 above) may also be relevant (age certainly seems to have informed the conversation between the client and younger washing assistant at the hairdresser's, which centres round the younger woman's career hopes), along with inter-cultural factors (see the references to the PIXI project studies in section 3, and also Jaworski, this volume) and inter-ethnic ones (Bailey 1997; see also Sarangi 1996). Despite its own spatio–temporal limits ('8–9,000 words and let's have it by Christmas!' said the volume's editor), this chapter sets out to offer a small contribution to a better theory of spoken genres; its contribution, I hope, will be considered as positive in the larger, developing picture of spoken language studies.

Notes

1. See Hasan (1992) for a critique of the ambivalence of some of Bakhtin's categories. Hasan justly criticises Bakhtin's theories as difficult to operationalise.
2. Thanks are due to Ron Carter for some insightful and useful comments on an earlier draft of this chapter. This volume's editor, Justine Coupland, also provided constructive criticism and suggestions for improvement of the first draft, and I thank her too.
3. I am very grateful to Jodie Looker, formerly of the Department of English Studies, University of Nottingham, for permission to use the data. Jodie kindly donated her recordings to the CANCODE corpus.
4. The data were collected as part of the CANCODE project by Fiona Fay, who is responsible for the Southern-Irish English segment of the corpus. The CANCODE team are grateful for her work.
5. A typical example from Carter and McCarthy (1997) is one where four people are assembling a child's portable cot. Silences of more than five seconds and up to 12 seconds occur six times during the 600-word/274-second extract. In total, there are 99 seconds of silences which exceed one second, that is to say, 36 per cent of the total time.
6. Diary of Benjamin Haydon, 1820, quoted by Herzog (1996: 32).
7. Richard Graves, 1774, quoted by Herzog (1996: 32–3).

8. Charles Lamb, 1818, ibid.
9. Walter Scott, *The Fortunes of Nigel*, ibid.
10. The transcription conventions I shall use in this paper are a simplified version of the rather complex markings entered in the CANCODE corpus data for the purposes of computational analysis of things such as speaker information, turn-end, overlaps, etc. (see McCarthy 1998: chapter 1.6 for examples and a discussion). The conventions used here are:

< >   Speaker identity
.   End of turn or perceptible pause of up to one second during a turn
?   Rising intonation with questioning function
+   Speaker's turn continues after overlap or interruption
L   Overlap or interruption
[ ]   Back-channel
( )   contextual information (e.g. silences over 1 second)

References

Anderson, L. (1994) Accounting practices in service encounters in English and Italian. In H. Purschel, E. Bartsch, P. Franklin, U. Schmitz and S. Vandermeeren (eds) *Intercultural Communication*. Frankfurt: Peter Lang, 99–120.

Aston, G. (ed.) (1988) *Negotiating Service: Studies in the Discourse of Bookshop Encounters*. Bologna: Editrice CLUEB.

Aston, G. (1991) Cultural norms of conversational procedure in pedagogic perspective. In S. Stati, E. Weigand and F. Hundsnurscher (eds) *Dialoganalyse III: Referate der 3. Arbeitstagung Bologna, 1990, I and II*. Tübingen: Niemeyer, II: 341–51.

Bailey, B. (1997) Communication of respect in interethnic service encounters. *Language in Society* 26: 327–56.

Bakhtin, M. (1986) *Speech Genres and Other Late Essays*. C. Emerson and M. Holquist (eds). Austin: University of Texas Press.

Beinstein, J. (1975) Conversations in public places. *Journal of Communication* 25: 85–95.

Brodine, R. (1991) Requesting and responding in Italian and English service encounters. In S. Stati, E. Weigand and F. Hundsnurscher (eds) *Dialoganalyse III: Referate der 3. Arbeitstagung Bologna, 1990, I and II*. Tübingen: Niemeyer, I: 293–305.

Carter, R. and McCarthy, M. J. (1997) *Exploring Spoken English*. Cambridge: Cambridge University Press.

Coates, J. (1997) The construction of a collaborative floor in women's friendly talk. In T. Givón (ed.) *Conversation, Cognitive, Communicative and Social Perspectives*. Amsterdam: John Benjamins, 55–89.

Coupland, J., Coupland, N. and Robinson, J. (1992) 'How are you?': negotiating phatic communion. *Language in Society* 21 (2): 207–30.

Coupland, N. (1983) Patterns of encounter management: further arguments for discourse variables. *Language in Society* 12: 459–76.

Duranti, A. (1983) Samoan speechmaking across social events: one genre in and out of a 'fono'. *Language in Society* 12: 1–22.

Gavioli, L. (1995) Turn-initial versus turn-final laughter: two techniques for initiating remedy in English/Italian bookshops service encounters. *Discourse Processes* 19 (3): 369–84.

George, S. (1990) *Getting things done in Naples*. Bologna: Editrice CLUEB.

Hasan, R. (1985) The structure of a text. In M. A. K. Halliday and R. Hasan *Language, Context and Text: Aspects of Language in a Social-semiotic perspective*. Oxford: Oxford University Press, 52–69.

Hasan, R. (1992) Speech genre, semiotic mediation and the development of higher mental functions. *Language Sciences* 14 (4): 489–528.

Herzog, D. (1996) The trouble with hairdressers. *Representations* 53: 21–43.

Hymes, D. (1972) Models of the interaction of language and social life. In J. Gumperz and D. Hymes (eds) *Directions in Sociolinguistics: The Ethnography of Communication*. New York: Rinehart and Winston, 35–71.

Iacobucci, C. (1990) Accounts, formulations and goal attainment strategies in service encounters. In K. Tracy and N. Coupland (eds) *Multiple Goals in Discourse*. Clevedon: Multilingual Matters, 85–99.

King, S. and Sereno, K. (1984) Conversational appropriateness as a conversational imperative. *The Quarterly Journal of Speech* 70 (3): 264–73.

Komter, M. (1991) *Conflict and Cooperation in Job Interviews: A Study of Talk, Tasks and Ideas*. Amsterdam: John Benjamins.

Lamoureux, E. (1989) Rhetoric and conversation in service encounters. *Research on Language and Social Interaction* 22: 93–114.

Laver, J. (1975) Communicative functions of phatic communion. In A. Kendon, R. Harris and M. Key (eds) *The Organization of Behaviour in Face-to-face Interaction*. The Hague: Mouton, 215–38.

Lieverscheidt, E., Werlen, I., and Zimmermann, H. (1989) Salongsprache: Kommunikationen beim Coiffeur. In E. Weigand and F. Hundsnurscher (eds) *Dialoganalyse II: Referate der 2. Arbeitstagung Bochum, 1988, I and II*. Tübingen: Niemeyer, I: 361–80.

Lindenfeld, J. (1990) *Speech and Sociability at French Urban Market Places*. Amsterdam: John Benjamins.

McCarthy, M. J. (1998) *Spoken Language and Applied Linguistics*. Cambridge: Cambridge University Press.

Merritt, M. (1976) On questions following questions in service encounters. *Language in Society* 5: 315–57.

Mitchell, T. F. (1957) The language of buying and selling in Cyrenaica: a situational statement. *Hespéris* XLIV: 31–71.

Ochs, E. (1996) Linguistic resources for socializing humanity. In J. Gumperz and S. Levinson (eds) *Rethinking Linguistic Relativity*. Cambridge: Cambridge University Press, 407–37.

Sarangi, S. (1996) Conflation of institutional and cultural stereotyping in Asian migrants' discourse. *Discourse and Society* 7 (3): 359–87.

Schiffrin, D. (1996) Narrative as self-portrait: sociolinguistic constructions of identity. *Language in Society* 25: 167–203.

Schneider, K. (1989) The art of talking about nothing. In E. Weigand and F. Hundsnurscher (eds) *Dialoganalyse II: Referate der 2. Arbeitstagung Bochum, 1988, I and II*. Tübingen: Niemeyer, I: 437–49.

Swales, J. (1990) *Genre Analysis*. Cambridge: Cambridge University Press.

Tracy, K. and Coupland, N. (1990) (eds) *Multiple Goals in Discourse*. Clevedon: Multilingual Matters.

Ventola, E. (1983) Contrasting schematic structures in service encounters. *Applied Linguistics* 4: 242–58.

Ventola, E. (1987) *The Structure of Social Interaction: A Systemic Approach to the Semiotics of Service Encounters*. London: Frances Pinter.

Walter, B. (1988) *The Jury Summation as Speech Genre*. Amsterdam: John Benjamins.

Ylänne-McEwen, V. (1997) Relational processes within a transactional setting: An investigation of travel agency discourse. Unpublished PhD dissertation. University of Wales, Cardiff.

Zorzi Calò, D. (1991) Le procedure per l'accessibilità e per l'acceptibilità: un confronto fra l'italiano e l'inglese. In E. Weigand and F. Hundsnurscher (eds) *Dialoganalyse II: Referate der 2. Arbeitstagung Bochum, 1988, I and II*. Tübingen: Niemeyer, II: 401–10.

4

Silence and small talk
Adam Jaworski

Było już takie milczenie.
Ale nie ma pewnośc że to pomiędzy nami.

EWA LIPSKA

Introduction

Malinowski's definition of phatic communion, the 'prototypical formulation of smalltalk' (J. Coupland, this volume) leaves us in no doubt as to his view on silence vis-à-vis the sociable nature of talk:[1]

> to a natural man, another man's *silence is* not a reassuring factor, but, on the contrary, something *alarming and dangerous*. The stranger who cannot speak the language is to all savage tribesmen a natural enemy. To the primitive mind, whether among savages or our own uneducated classes, *taciturnity means not only unfriendliness but directly bad character*. This no doubt varies greatly with the national character but remains true as a general rule. The breaking of silence, the communion of words is the first act to establish links of fellowship, which is consummated only by breaking of bread and the communion of food. The modern English expression, 'Nice day to-day' or the Melanesian phrase, 'Whence comest thou?' are needed to get over the *strange and unpleasant tension which men feel when facing each other in silence*.
>
> (Malinowski 1923: 314; my emphasis)

This is bad press for silence. It is clear that, for Malinowski, avoidance of silence is one of the central goals of social actors engaging in phatic talk. This juxtaposition of silence and phatic talk (see also McCarthy, this volume) firmly establishes the opposition between the two concepts, which is not only formal but also evaluative in favour of phatic talk. As it seems, this rationalisation of phatic talk has gone unchallenged for decades. For example, Laver (1974: 220, 1981: 301) defines phatic communion as largely confined to the opening and closing phases of conversation and its aim is to 'defuse the potential hostility of silence in situations where speech is conventionally anticipated'.

In sum, although the concept of small talk itself has been treated with a degree of ambivalence if not downright negativity, in both lay and linguistic accounts (J. Coupland, this volume), at least it has been associated with one's willingness to *communicate* with another person. Silence, on the other hand, is best avoided at all costs to prevent 'awkward' or 'uncomfortable' periods and communication breakdown (see Jaworski 1993 for references).

A comment on terminology

There are many approaches to defining small talk. This is certainly true of most other concepts in sociolinguistics and other academic disciplines, although, of course, some concepts are more established and more widely accepted than others. It seems, however, that our definitional dilemmas are most easily overcome if we apply specific terminology of the near synonyms such as *small talk, phatic communion, chit-chat, gossip, casual conversation* and the like to specific communicative situations. The everyday understanding of these terms allows for a considerable overlap among them, yet we have no difficulty in choosing one or the other to label a particular stretch of (sociable) talk.

Coupland *et al.* (1992) and J. Coupland (this volume) offer comprehensive historical overviews of these terms and I will not attempt to replicate them. However, as these sources suggest, the above-mentioned terms are often used interchangeably or to define one another, and we can apply criteria based on such attributes as sociality, informality, ritualization, liminality, etc. to account for the linguistic phenomena referred to as *phatic communion, small talk, chat, gossip, informal prattle* and so on, although, of course, intuitively and thanks to the body of existing literature we 'know' that *small talk*, for example, is a label typically associated with transitional aspects of conversation such as openings and closings, which include greetings, self-introductions, recollections of previous meetings, expressions of concern for members of addressee's family, etc. On the other hand, *gossip* is a genre label best used to describe sequences of talk about certain types of interpersonal relationships or events in situations such as a coffee break in an office. These sequences may be less ritualised than greetings, for example, but certainly they are not unstructured and no less conventionalised (see Eggins and Slade 1997).

Yet, there is room for overlap even between *small talk* and *gossip* as described above. We could argue that gossip during a coffee break in an office is a form of small talk, while enquiries about one's family members' health in an opening of a conversation is also talk 'about' relationships. But to dwell on *precise* delimitation of boundaries between such terms is futile. Instead, I postulate that we use terms *clearly*, by which I mean disambiguating their intended meaning in case of any controversy.

This is not to advocate any degree of Humpty-Dumptiness in the use of sociolinguistic terminology. I preclude this by accepting Brown and Levinson's (1987) assumption that communicators (also in academic discourse) act rationally and, consequently, use terminology in agreement with existing conventions. Where there is doubt due to multiple, competing conventions existing side by side, clarifying one's use of a given term is needed and desirable.

In their review of phaticity, Coupland *et al.* (1992: 213) argue that none of the approaches outlined by them present 'much cross-cultural insight, though the functions of phatic communion are clearly highly variable across cultures', and propose to identify phaticity in functional interactional terms:

> . . . by this account, phatic communion would cease to be associated *uniquely* with fringes of encounters (Laver) or extended chatting (Malinowski, Cheepen) and we should expect to find instances where a relationally designed and perhaps phatic mode of talk surfaces whenever relational goals become salient – even *within* sequences of transactional, instrumental, or task-oriented talk.

> (ibid.)

This approach allows one to identify stretches of phatic talk by orienting to interactants' local concerns, patterns of self-presentation and alignments whenever relational goals are foregrounded (see next section for a brief discussion of goals).

I agree with this functional approach to operationalising phaticity because it is broad enough to encompass all the forms of phatic talk discussed above, and it avoids essentialising the discussion by trying to establish one-to-one relationships between linguistic forms and their meanings. Of course, relational goals can be achieved via other routes (other than engaging in small talk), and they may be verbal, non-verbal and even non-linguistic means, e.g. accommodating to someone's accent, choice of a solidary term of address, disclosure of confidential information, offer of a 'genuine' invitation, smiling, offers of gifts and so on. On the other hand, small talk in the form of gossip, for example, may be an important means of maintaining rapport between interactants (Coates 1988), as well as have factual value by spreading information which is vital for a community and/or establishing norms of acceptable moral conduct of its members.

These are important aspects of small talk to bear in mind because, as will be demonstrated later in the discussion, it is impossible to separate completely 'doing sociability' from some kind of information exchange (e.g. giving someone your name in a self-introduction) (cf. Coupland *et al.* 1992; Žegarac and Clark 1999).

Thus, the broad definition of *phatic communion* (with all its possible variants identified as *small talk, chit-chat, gossip* and the like) which is adopted in this chapter follows Coupland *et al.*'s (1992) functional orientation emphasising (positive)[2] relational goals and a relatively low level of participants' attendance to the seriousness or factuality of talk. This functional and, admittedly, liberal approach to the definition of small talk, which centres on sociability and interpersonal distance, allows me then to identify small talk not through a pre-determined set of linguistic forms but by referring to the dynamics of the speech event, including participant characteristics, their goals and so on. For example, Extract 2 features a teasing exchange between intimates, which I consider to form part of the interactants' small talk. A similar teasing exchange between non-intimates or status unequals would be unlikely to fulfil the phatic function.

My understanding and use of the term 'silence' in this chapter is based on similar principles. Silence has been used to refer to many different communicative items. With regard to form, silence has been referred to as *pause* (including inter and intra-turn *gaps* and *lapses*), *non-talk, absence of talk* (as opposed to *absence of noise*), *nonphonation* or just *silence*. But we can also talk about silence as absence of something that we expect to hear on a given occasion, when we assume it is 'there' but remains unsaid (e.g. *ellipsis, evasion*, etc.). There are many useful ways of using the term 'silence' and 'silencing' metaphorically, for example, in reference to oppressed minorities, censorship or, by extension to a visual medium, in describing certain types of painting as *silent, quiet* or *muted* (see, for example, Jaworski 1993; Bilmes 1994; Kurzon 1998; papers in Tannen and Saville-Troike 1985; Jaworski 1997a).

Functions of silence and small talk in a cross-cultural perspective

The traditionally negative valuation of small talk, and even more negative valuation of silence, stems, in my view, from the common, folklinguistic belief that language is primarily used for information exchange, or what Halliday (1978) refers to as the *ideational* metafunction, i.e. use of language for referential purposes, such as describing people, objects, states and events, presenting ideas, expressing opinions and so on (cf. Coupland *et al.* 1992: 211). But, following Halliday's taxonomy further, language (and other semiotic systems) performs at least two other metafunctions: the *interpersonal* and the *textual*. The interpersonal metafunction has got to do with the way language both reflects and defines relationships among interactants: the speaker (sender) of the utterance, the addressee (receiver) and the possible audience. The textual metafunction gives language the capacity to refer to itself (as metalanguage) and to signal whether a given text is intended (framed) as a lecture, poem, play, joke, chit-chat or some other type of speech event.

Tracy and Coupland (1990) overview the literature on goals and introduce a distinction between 'task' or 'instrumental' goals and 'identity' or 'relational' goals. Generally speaking, the former deal with the content of what is said and the referential meaning of utterances (corresponding to Halliday's ideational metafunction), whereas the latter deal with self-presentation and face concerns of all interactants, corresponding to the interpersonal metafunction. An important point these authors make, however, is that specific utterances in discourse may fulfil more than one goal at once, and this multifunctionality of discourse applies also to small talk. For example, as has been mentioned, gossip serves primarily to create rapport between interactants (relational goal) but it may also convey new information (instrumental goal).

Although silence may be limited in performing the ideational and textual metafunctions, or fulfilling instrumental, task-oriented goals (Sobkowiak 1997)[3], it is an important strategy with respect to the interpersonal metafunction or relational goals. That makes silence rather similar to small talk, including all of its cultural, situational and idiosyncratic variation.

Small talk and silence are probably sociolinguistic universals, but there appear to be important cross-cultural differences in how they are used or tolerated. For example, in his classic paper, Basso (1972) has linked the use of silence among the Western Apaches to the notion of ambiguity, uncertainty and anxiety in interpersonal relations. Such situations are associated with high risk of face-threat which, in traditional formulations by Malinowski and Laver, prescribe small talk.

Lehtonen and Sajavaara (1985) have observed that, during meal-times, Finnish families engage in relatively less small talk than, for example, Anglo-American families. Likewise, Blum-Kulka (1997) has observed differences in the cultural and gender patterning of the distribution of (small) talk and silence across American Jewish, American Israeli and Israeli family meal-time talk. She argues that American Jewish fathers, for example, engage in more talk than males in the other two groups, but that in contrast to their American counterparts, the Israeli fathers use more phatic-orientated talk (e.g. gossip, talk about children and cooking) (cf. Blum-Kulka 1997: 91–3 and this volume).

These examples suggest that in some communities, when there is no immediate demand for instrumental talk, silence need not be perceived as awkward or uncomfortable to the degree it is perceived by members of other communities. Observations like this have been linked to the variable use of silence as a politeness strategy in different communities.

Holmes (1995: 5) defines linguistic politeness as 'an expression of good-will or camaraderie, as well as the more familiar non-intrusive behaviour which is labelled "polite" in everyday usage'. Stated in those terms, polite-ness is realised via a system of strategies designed to facilitate the fulfilment of the interpersonal metafunction (Halliday) or identity/relational goals (Tracy and Coupland).

Undoubtedly, there are cultural and other inter-group differences in the use of politeness strategies such as refraining from speaking. Sifianou (1997) argues, for example, that, other things being equal, silence in social relations is valuated more negatively in Greece than in Britain because in Greece it is perceived as a 'distancing' device in a society in which priority is given to the well-being and closeness within one's in-group. On the other hand, personal freedom, privacy and solitary activities are appreciated more in England. Thus, in Greece, expression of personal emotions, exuberance and talkative-ness are primarily associated with creating involvement, pleasant, open and sincere personality and worthy companionship. A taciturn person, on the other hand, may be regarded as indifferent, unfriendly, snobbish and even sly and dangerous. In contrast, in England silence becomes a desirable mani-festation of lack of imposition.

One empirical study which gives support to a similar relativistic view of small talk and silence in a cross-cultural context is the work of Giles et al. (1991), who examined beliefs about talk and silence cross-culturally and cross-generationally. Starting from the premise that 'beliefs include the evalu-ation of language behaviours and function at least in part to guide these', the authors have reported, in a questionnaire-based study, that Hong Kong stu-dents are more positively disposed towards small talk than their Beijing counterparts, and that the latter expressed a greater tolerance for silence than the former. On the other hand, both groups of Chinese respondents (from Hong Kong and Beijing) appeared to perceive silence as more import-ant, more enjoyable and being used to a greater degree for social control than Caucasian Americans.

Ethnographic studies of various communities contain numerous other, more or less anecdotal accounts of interpersonal silence occurring in non-transactional settings. For example, Enninger (1987) has reported that among the Amish of Pennsylvania interactive silences are much longer than among the majority of Anglo-Americans. In one conversation among three adult Amish speakers Enninger (1987: 280) has recorded 'no fewer than eleven between-turn gaps and lapses longer than twenty seconds, the longest being fifty-six seconds'. There were no signs of communication breakdown in this or other similar situations observed in the Amish culture, which attests to the commonly held view among the Amish, but not among most other (white) American subcultures that successful interactive events, such as social visits, do not necessarily involve the use of talk. According to Enninger, these extended gaps and lapses have probably influenced the perception of the Amish by American mainstream society (whatever that may be) as taciturn and uncooperative.

Likewise, Philips (1976) observes that among Warm Spring Indians an immediate answer to a question is not always appropriate or expected. The answer can be provided later, and often is. The same is true about responding to invitations. The structure of the act of inviting in this community seems to be 'less elaborate' and involves less small talk than among Anglo-Americans.

> Anglos on the reservation sometimes complain that they are never invited to Indian homes. Some Indians tell them they are welcome anytime, and mean it, but this is not treated as sufficient by the Anglos. Some Indians will tell Anglos that if they are visiting an Indian home, they should not wait to be invited to eat when a meal is served. They should assume there is a place for them and may join the others as they move to the table, if they choose to.

> (Philips 1976: 91)

The contrast between Anglo-American and Warm Springs invitations seems to lie primarily in where each community places this speech act on a scale of factuality – phaticity, and the relative amount of talk (or specific formulae) which are available and/or necessary to perform an invitation. Anglo-Americans appear to have different *norms of interpretation* (Hymes 1972) for drawing inferences about utterances of the *We must get together sometime*-type, allowing them to treat these as phatic (similar to saying *See you later* to a person the speaker is unlikely to see ever again in his/her life), whereas the norms shared within other communities may place such utterances nearer the factual end of the continuum (cf. Wolfson 1981). Likewise, Warm Springs Indians, and others, may not share the Anglo-American phatic formulae *leading* to factual invitations.

To remove any suspicion of depicting non-Anglo ways of speaking as 'deficient' or lacking in certain formulae, we may cite the opposite case of a language which uses formulae with a phatic force with no English verbal equivalents. For example, Polish speakers rather commonly exchange two formulae, one before and one after a meal, which do not have familiar equivalents in English. The former is *Smacznego!* equivalent to the French *bon appetit*, while the latter is *Dziękuję!* 'thank you'. As is common with many linguistic formulae, L2 speakers tend to borrow them freely from their L1 (Jaworski 1990), and there have been many instances when I have heard Polish speakers of English as L2 saying to startled English L1 speakers with whom they were dining together *Good appetite!* and *Thank you!* before and after a meal, respectively. It remains an open question whether these Polish-English speakers simply 'didn't know' that English speakers tend not to use such formulae, or did they simply adapt their L1 norms of polite behaviour in an attempt to avoid what they would have otherwise perceived as embarrassing, silent slots in their L2 dining interaction.

Cultural differences in the use of small talk and silence are, as has been illustrated, most easily observed in intercultural encounters. It is when someone perceives that something is 'missing' in the discourse of the other that silence becomes particularly salient. It is important to realise that, as otherwise we would seem to be suggesting that Warm Springs Indians use silence to invite, and English speakers use silence to end a meal. They don't. All that these examples suggest is that different communities use different degrees of prescribed small talk in the same types of sociable events, and that non-talk resulting from such norms is not necessarily awkward, unsociable or face-threatening.

Other studies of silence indicate that it is commonly used in other, more localised contexts to fulfil the interpersonal metafunction. For example, for conflict management (Tannen 1990), conflict avoidance (Hocker and Wilmot 1995), as a means of negotiating power relations (Gilmore 1985; Jaworski 1998a), as a face-saving strategy in impaired communication (Jaworski and Stephens 1998), and expression of reverence, awe and respect for God in ritual communication (Szuchewycz 1997). However, a more detailed discussion of these studies goes beyond the scope of this chapter.

Suffice it to say that silence and small talk do not seem so far apart in terms of their functional roles as Malinowski's definition of phatic communion suggests. In fact, they may both fulfil similar functions or, put differently, occur in communicative situations serving similar interactional communicative goals. In the rest of this chapter I will be particularly concerned with the notion of social distance as a factor in determining the use and distribution of silence and small talk.

Social distance, silence and small talk

As cross-cultural evidence points out, silence and small talk are relative communicative strategies and their interpretation is variable. This view stands in agreement with Tannen (1993: 178; see also Gal 1989), who discusses silence as only one of a number linguistic strategies, which may 'be taken to "mean" power or powerlessness, domination or subjugation'.

One of the contextual factors which affects the meaning of silence is interpersonal distance. For example, we are often forced into close proximity with others as patients in waiting rooms, passengers in train compartments, customers in self-service restaurants and so on. In such contexts, acting out the social role 'stranger' requires, for the most part, refraining from speaking (Saville-Troike 1985).

However, silence rather than small talk may also turn out to be the norm in pursuing relational goals between close intimates, even in the seemingly highly verbose Anglo-American culture. Consider the following quote from Quentin Tarrantino's film *Pulp Fiction* which expresses this kind of sentiment:

Extract 1

[33 seconds of uncomfortable silence]
Mia: don't you hate that? (2)
Vincent: what?
Mia: uncomfortable silences (2) why do you feel it's necessary to yak about bullshit (.) in order to feel comfortable? (2)
Vincent: I don't know (.) that's a good question (2)
Mia: that's when you've met somebody special (2) when you can just shut the fuck up for a minute (.) comfortably share silence

This example demonstrates the author's metapragmatic awareness of a contrast between uncomfortable silences which need to be replaced with *yakking about bullshit* (small talk) and comfortable silences which occur between close intimates.

I am not saying here that intimates never *chat* or do any other type of relational talk which is not intended to be 'serious' and 'factual'. Of course, they do, although it is almost a truism to assert that small talk between intimates is very different from that of casual acquaintances. In sum, certain manifestations of silence and small talk may be treated as functional equivalents, although they may not always be interchangeable, i.e. they appear in complementary distribution, occupying distinct (but also overlapping) points on the scale of interpersonal distance.

Silence and small talk in two dramatic works

The data examined here is derived from two literary sources: Edward Albee's play *Who's Afraid of Virginia Woolf?* and Edward Thomas's television play *Fallen Sons*. The forms of silence which are identified in the examples below include metapragmatic comments (e.g. references to silence and sulking), pauses in conversation, muteness and refusal to communicate. In functional terms, the unifying aspect of these 'silences' is that they are interactionally relevant to the dynamics of social relations between interactants, especially with regard to creating or maintaining interpersonal distance.[4] In the final section of this chapter, I draw my conclusions in reference to a broader pragmatic framework of interpersonal distance (Wolfson 1988).

Who's Afraid of Virginia Woolf?

Who's Afraid of Virginia Woolf? was first published in 1962 (film, directed by Mike Nichols, 1966). The play is set in George and Martha's living room. George is a middle-aged history professor in a small New England college. Apart from being George's wife Martha is also the daughter of the President of the College. After a party at Martha's father's, at two o'clock in the morning, Martha announces to disbelieving George that she had invited Nick and Honey (a newly-arrived, younger college couple), and that they are not going to bed just yet.

Martha and George's relationship is not easy. They argue a lot and their dialogue ranges from concurrent screaming and shouting to sulking and silence. In this section I examine two extracts,[5] which demonstrate the role of silence and small talk in managing interpersonal relations between the characters in the play.

The first example illustrates a typical (if not *the* prototypical) situation which calls for small talk: the arrival of guests at a party. Nick and Honey come to George and Martha's house but because they only met each other earlier that same night they are still in the 'getting to know each other' stage. In fact, George and Martha do not even remember their guests' names. The extract starts at a moment when Martha is screaming at George at the top of her voice and Nick and Honey come in:

Extract 2

```
 1  Martha:  [with her back to the door, turning as George opens
 2            the door and screaming at him] GODDAMN YOU [Nick and
 3            Honey appear in the door, clearly startled and
 4            embarrassed]
 5            (1)
 6  George:  [laughs with satisfaction of having Martha's
 7            explosion overheard]
 8            (3)
 9  Martha:  HI there
10  Honey:   HELLO
11  Martha:  c'mon=
12  Nick:    how are you?=
13  Honey:   here we are we've finally made it
14               [
15  George:     you must be our little guests [Honey looks at
16            him, nods, everyone begins to smile]=
17  Martha:  [laughs loudly] just ignore old sour-pussy uh c'mon
18            in kids (.) uh just hand your coats to old sour-
19            pussy [laughs]=
20  Nick:    well, now, perhaps we shouldn't have come=
21  Honey:   oh yes yes it is late
```

22 Martha: [laughing constantly] late? are you kidding? uh just
23   throw your stuff down anyplace and c'mon in
24 George: [ironically as if to himself] anywhere furniture
25   floor doesn't make any difference around this place
26 Martha: [laughs]
27   (1)
28 Nick: [to Honey] I told you we shouldn't have come
29 Martha: [admonishing] I SAID C'MON IN NOW C'MON [sits down]
30 Honey: [as she and Nick advance, giggling] oh dear
31 George: [parodying Honey] oh dear ha ha ha ha ha
32 Martha: [to George] look muckmucky you cut that out
33 George: [to Martha, innocently] Martha [to Nick and Honey,
34   matter-of-factly] Martha's devil with language she
35   really is
36 All: [intermittent, forced and embarrassed laughter]
37 Martha: uh kids sit down
38   [Nick and Honey sit down] (1.5)
39 Honey: [looks around] ah::: isn't this lovely
40   (2)
41 Nick: [prompted by Honey] oh yes indeed very handsome
42 Martha: [smiles] oh well thank you
43   (13) [George settles in an arm-chair; Nick looks at
44   him as if waiting for George to say something; smile
45   on Martha's face wanes as she looks at George who
46   appears completely disengaged; Honey looks down;
47   Nick looks around; except George, everyone seems
48   very embarrassed]
49 Nick: [points at an abstract painting] uh (.) who uh (1.5)
50   who did the painting?
51 Martha: that? oh that's by=
52 George: some Greek with a moustache Martha attacked one
53   [
54 Honey: [trying to save the situation]   ho
55   hohohoho
56 George: night in a in a [parodying Honey] hohohoho
57   (1)
58 Nick: [gets up, comes closer to the painting] it's (.) got
59   a a=
60 George: quiet intensity?
61 Nick: (.) well no a a a=
62 George: a certain noisy relaxed quality maybe?
63 Nick: (.) no what I meant was=
64 George: how about a quietly noisy relaxed intensity?
65 Honey: dear uh you're being joshed
66 Nick: I'm aware of that
67 Honey: oh
68 George: oh I'm sorry what it is actually is a pictorial
69   representation of the order of Martha's mind
70 All: [laugh loudly; Martha's laughter is loudest]
71 Martha: fix the kids a drink, George, what would you like to

72		drink kids? [George gets up and walks over to the
73		bar]
74	Nick:	Honey? (2.5) what would you like?
75	Honey:	oh::: I don't know dear (.) a little brandy maybe
76		never mix never worry
77	George:	brandy? just brandy simple simple (.) what about you
78		uh::: uh::: uhm:
79	Nick:	[turns his head and looks at George] (2) bourbon on
80		the rocks if you don't mind
81	George:	mind? I don't mind do you think I mind? Martha?
82		rubbing alcohol for you?
83	Martha:	sure never mix never worry [(7.5) during which
84		general laughter subsiding quickly] HEY hey [Martha
85		starts singing] who's afraid of Virginia Woolf
86		Virginia Woo=
87	Honey:	oh yea, [sings] Virginia Woolf wasn't that funny?
88		that was so funny [Martha and Honey laugh, Nick
89		smiles]
90	Nick:	yes it was
91	Martha:	[laughs] I thought I'd bust a gut [still laughing,
92		then seriously] George didn't think it was funny at
93		all

This extended extract is punctuated by a number of awkward silences. They do not all result from the participants' simply not doing polite small talk. The silences in lines 5, 8, 27, 57 are reactions to, rather than causes of embarrassment. The first two silences in lines 5 and 8 (in fact, one longer one filled partly by George's laughter) arise as direct reactions to Martha's screaming at George. I have called silences like this 'formulaic silences' (Jaworski 1993) as they seem to be routine responses to face threatening acts when verbal formulae are not readily available.

Martha breaks the silence in line 9 with a loud greeting, which restores the friendly footing between the hosts and the visitors. The fact that Martha initiates the greeting exchange makes it marked as, under normal circumstances, it is the person(s) arriving at someone's house that initiate(s) a greeting sequence. In this case, however, Nick and Honey's first 'greeting slot' is taken up by their (formulaic) silence triggered by an embarrassing incident a moment earlier.

The typical small talk exchange of formulaic pleasantries between the two couples is disrupted throughout this episode by George's sarcasm and ridicule of the guests. In line 14, he observes *you must be our little guests*. Honey reacts to this with a quick glance at him, nodding and silence. Nick remains silent, too. The couple's silence is strategic in view of George's sarcastic remark (imagine a response such as *We are not your little guests!*). Only Martha attempts to cover up George's *faux pas* by loud laughter and an excuse: *just ignore old sour-pussy* (line 17).

Another instance when George teases Nick is in response to his question about the painting (lines 49–50). First, Martha tries to respond to the question, which is a typical instance of phatic talk used to end a long, awkward silence (lines 43–8). However, George butts in and offers a blatantly untrue answer *some Greek with a moustache Martha attacked one night in a in a* (lines 52, 56), and later starts a parody of what Nick might have said about the painting in a typical small talk sequence had George allowed him to speak (lines 60–4). When, in line 68, George admits that he has 'joshed' Nick and apologises to him, George avoids another embarrassing silence by changing the focus of his continued sarcasm immediately and centres on Martha as a butt of his joke: *oh I'm sorry what it is actually is a pictorial representation of the order of Martha's mind* (lines 68–9). This remark is followed by general laughter (line 70), although Martha's hardest effort to laugh very loudly indicates that she is filling in another potential silence resulting from the embarrassment of being ridiculed in front of their guests.

A number of other instances of silence in Extract 2 are not direct reactions to embarrassment but themselves produce typical social awkwardness associated with lack of small talk when it is expected (these are the 'alarming and dangerous' silences invoked by Malinowski in his definition of phatic communion). Examples of such silences can be found in lines 38, 40, 43, 49, 58. The embarrassment which they produce is indicated by the participants' non-verbal behaviour (looking down, looking around the house to find something to comment on, e.g. lines 38, 46–7), and searching for new topics to restart the conversation (e.g. lines 49–50).

I have nothing else to say about these silences other than they fit the typical and widely accepted, however rather one-sided view of silence as a negative and destructive aspect of communication. Instead, I want to move to another example which illustrates how silence combines with small talk in a more positive, although not always harmonious manner.

Extract 3 is a transcript of a scene, which occurs before that in Extract 2, in George and Martha's bedroom soon after George finds out from Martha that they are going to entertain shortly. George's initial reaction is anger and dismay but then he gives up a fight and acquiesces to Martha's decision:

Extract 3

```
1 George: [resigned] ok where are they? we've got guests where
2          are they?
3 Martha: they'll be here soon
4 George: what did they do? go home and get some sleep first
5          or something? [lies down on bed]
6 Martha: they'll be here
7 George: I wish you'd tell me about something sometimes you
8          should stop ( . ) springing things on me all the time
```

 9 Martha: I don't spring things on you all the time
10   [
11 George: yes you do you really do
12   you're always (.) springing things on me (.) always
13   (1)
14 Martha: poor Georgie-Porgie put-upon pie (3) oh::: (.) what
15   are you doing? are you sulking? (.) let me see are
16   you sulking? is that what you're doing? [gets on the
17   bed, wakes up sleepy-looking and acting George]
18   hunh?
19 George: never mind
20 Martha: AWWW:::
21 George: just don't bother yourself [turns his back on Martha
22   and buries his face in the pillow]
23 Martha: AWWW:::: AWWW::: [sits on George's back] OH::: hey
24   (.) HEY:: [starts singing tapping George's back
25   rhythmically, tickles him; George moans and groans]
26   who's afraid of Virginia Woolf Virginia Woolf who's
27   afraid of Virginia Woolf Virginia Woolf [laughs; no
28   reaction from George] (1) [seriously] what's the
29   matter? didn't you think that was funny? (.) I
30   thought it was a scream
31 George: [muffled by the pillow] it was all right
32 Martha: you laughed your head off when you heard it at the
33   party
34 George: [muffled] I smiled I didn't laugh my head off
35 Martha: you laughed your goddamn head off
36 George: [still muffled but irritated] it was all right
37 Martha: it was a scream
38 George: [starts turning back, Martha gets off his back;
39   patiently] it was very funny yes
40 Martha: (.) oh you make me puke
41 George: [looks at her] what?
42 Martha: you make me puke
43 George: (.) that wasn't a very nice thing to say Martha
44 Martha: that wasn't WHAT?
45 George: a very nice thing to say
46 Martha: oh I like your anger I think that's what I like
47   about you most your:: anger [disgusted] ugh (1)
48   you're such a a simp (.) you you haven't even got
49   the the the (.) oh the what?
50 George: er er (1) guts?
51 Martha: (2) [almost cheerful] phrasemaker
52   (2) [George laughs, then Martha; she gets back on
53   the bed, lies next to George, hugs him, reaches for
54   her drink] (5)
55 Martha: you never put any ice in my drink why is that hunh?
56 George: I always put ice in your drinks Martha you eat it
57   that's all it's this habit you've got of chewing on
58   your ice cubes like a cocker spaniel (2) you'll

59   crack your big teeth
60 Martha: they're my big teeth
61 George: yeah some of them some of them
62 Martha: I've got more teeth than you have
63 George: two more
64 Martha: [sipping] hm::: (.) and you're going bald
65 George: so are you
66   [they both start laughing, Martha puts away her
67   drink, moves closer to George and puts her hand on
68   his arm] (6)
69 George: hello honey
70 Martha: [laughs quietly; puts her arm around George's neck]
71   ok go on give mommy a big sloppy kiss
72 George: no::: [turns his head away]
73 Martha: I WANT A BIG SLOPPY KISS
74 George: I don't wanna kiss you right now Martha [rises,
75   leaves Martha on the bed]

The above excerpt is particularly revealing about the variable nature of small talk. What it indicates is that, between intimates, small talk, in its common understanding of 'talk about the weather and other safe topics' is rare. On the contrary, highly face-threatening acts without any mitigating devices are common. For example, George complains to Martha that she is *springing things on [him] all the time* (line 8). Martha ridicules George *poor Georgie-Porgie put-upon pie* (line 14), and so on.

In Extract 3 Martha and George do not engage in small talk which helps them to establish or (re)define their relationship. They do not 'need' that as their relationship is solid (or, at least, stable). Rather, their small talk takes the form of verbal *banter* or *sparring* through which they negotiate temporary shifts in distance from disengagement to intimacy. In this sense, silence is an important, positive (i.e. active) strategy in generating locally relevant relational meanings.

The first example of silence in Extract 3 comes from George, who manifests detachment from Martha and her plan for a continued party that morning. George lies down on the bed and ignores Martha's insults (line 14). After 3 seconds of silence Martha notices that George has retreated from his involvement in the argument and tries to bring him back to it by making provoking, metapragmatic comments about his sulking (lines 15–16). Then, Martha tries to revive George's attention by howling (line 23), sitting on him, tickling and tapping his back (lines 25–6), and finally, singing loudly a song that was a 'scream' at the party earlier that night (lines 26–8). Despite all these efforts, George reacts with more silence and irritated moans and groans.

This exchange seems to foreground as much relational goals between Martha and George as any phatic exchange between casual acquaintances. It is not particularly serious and not orientated towards factuality. Even George's complaint about never knowing Martha's plans until the very last moment appears, at least at this time of night and with George's resigned tone, nothing more than a ritual complaint and not an attempt to change Martha's behaviour in the future.

After Martha fails to draw George back into the conversation, she engages in an argument about how funny the party song was (*what's the matter? didn't you think that was funny?*, lines 28–9). At first, this seems to be a 'serious' argument but George continues to give muffled (silenced) responses and finally admits patiently *it was very funny yes* (line 39) only to please Martha and stop the row. Martha realises that George's concession is for the sake of finishing the argument. George does not rise to the occasion of the verbal duel and Martha expresses her disgust with him (*you make me puke*, line 42). The insult is her last hope of irritating George and drawing him back into the argument. She fails again. George calmly comments *that wasn't a very nice thing to say Martha* (line 43) and by refusing to pick up Martha's challenge, he distances himself from her and angers her even more. Martha's fury peaks (lines 46ff.) but while searching for yet another insult she is lost for words and needs George's help.

The situation in which George helps Martha to find an insult to deride him is so ridiculous that the fight between them stops. In line 51 there is a brief silence followed by Martha's light-hearted comment *phrasemaker*. The following 20 seconds are filled by non-verbal interaction which restores a friendly footing between the couple: laughter, increased proximity between George and Martha, hugging (lines 52–4). The five-second silence which ends this sequence is not awkward, distancing or threatening. In fact, all the non-verbal and paralinguistic clues lead to the interpretation of this silence as comfortable and creating rapport between both interactants. And these are, of course, classic features of small talk.

The exchange following this silence continues in a good-natured, humorous tenor. Martha makes a mock accusation that George never puts ice in her drinks (line 55). This leads to a teasing exchange about which of them shows greater signs of ageing: losing teeth and hair (lines 61–5) and, eventually, to humour resulting in more laughter, even closer proximity and another, six-second long, comfortable silence (line 68). Then, George produces an instance of phatic talk: *hello honey* (line 69).

This last sequence is noteworthy because George's *hello honey*, although displaying all the properties of phaticity, is not produced to break the preceding silence. This silence is comfortable and sends to both persons signals of close affinity and harmony, so the greeting and the term of endearment are extensions of this silence rather than its antithesis. In this context, the silence also acquires a clear phatic function and with *hello honey* can be said to constitute a rather literal example of 'sweet nothings' (Cheepen, this volume). This interpretation of lines 68–9 seems accurate also in the light of Martha's accommodative next turn in which she asks for a *big sloppy kiss* (line 71).

In Extract 3, Martha and George engage in different forms of relational interaction which includes silence of disengagement, verbal abuse, benevolent banter, friendly teasing, flirtation and silence of harmony and intimacy. The main function of the whole sequence is phatic: Martha and George engage in all this talk to kill the time waiting for their guests to arrive. Otherwise, they (certainly George) would have gone to bed.

Fallen Sons

The play *Fallen Sons* lasts about 30 minutes and its script (in Welsh and English) consists of only about five hundred words.[6] The main characters of the play are the twin brothers Danny and Iorry, their mother and father, and (in the later years) Danny's family. The action of the play shifts constantly across three years and Danny and Iorry's three birthdays: 1993, Danny and Iorry's 70th birthday; 1963, their 40th birthday; 1935, their 12th birthday (and a few following days). The location is rural South Wales and Cardiff.

The central event around which the plot of the play revolves is Iorry's accidental killing of his father. The accident (Welsh: *damwain*) takes place on the day of the twins' 12th birthday. While everyone else is outside the house doing different chores, Iorry plays with his father's shotgun inside the house. The father stops chopping the wood and comes into the house to find matches to light up his pipe and as he walks into the house Iorry turns round pointing the gun in the direction of his father and pulls the trigger. Danny and his mother run into the house and find the father lying dead on the floor and Iorry standing next to him. The mother shakes Iorry angrily and slaps him in the face.

In this section I elaborate on the patterns of silence used in the play with regard to interpersonal distance (I leave out the question of *power*, but see Jaworski 1998b).

The fatal accident in which Iorry shoots his father renders the boy speechless. We cannot be sure whether it is the fact that he shot his father or that his mother slapped and, ultimately, rejected him that leaves Iorry speechless or 'in a profound state of shock', as the family doctor proclaims later. At the scene of the accident Iorry tries to say something to his mother but cannot utter a word. Consequently, he becomes the silenced member of the family literally (muted) and metaphorically, as his mother sends him away to live on his uncle's farm.

Both these forms of Iorry's silencing relegate him into some kind of social and familial oblivion. First, as a mute, he is deprived of the basic human faculty of speech, rendering him a 'non-person'. Second, his mother's decision to send him away from home turns him into an outcast within his own family. Silence here signals total rejection, severing of all links and creating detachment; it turns Iorry into a stranger in his own family. At 12, Danny is separated from his brother and maintains this separation for many years. He refuses to speak to Iorry, does not reciprocate birthday greetings, and does not even allow his son to meet his uncle.

In contrast, before the accident, Danny and Iorry are shown to be very close. However, their closeness is also portrayed without almost any dialogue taking place between them. Brief utterances and non-verbal signals form the basis of their communication in play, clowning around and helping their parents around the farm. The only longer piece of dialogue which they engage in is a brief argument at breakfast over whether Iorry knows how to skin rabbits. The argument comes abruptly to an end when their mother declares *No arguing on your birthday*. The father (who remains silent throughout the play) does not even take any notice of their argument. To me, the ease with which the boys come in and out of the argument and slip back into silence emphasises their closeness, too (not unlike the rapid switches between Martha and George's arguments and silence).

The second example of a bonding use of silence between Danny and Iorry takes place on the day of their 70th birthday. Danny, feeling left out and let down by his son and his family, decides to pay Iorry a long overdue visit. In the closing scenes of the play, Danny finds his brother on a small sailing boat. The two old men get on the boat, drink whisky from one bottle and Iorry finally manages to say the word which he has been trying to say all his life: *damwain* 'accident'. There is no more talk between the brothers, only the silence of reconciliation to which they finally come after fifty-eight years of separation.

The intimacy of the brothers' re-started relationship rests largely on their engagement in silence. It is as if the pendulum of their relationship swung back to the extreme closeness end and, apart from Danny's accommodative repetition of Iorry's *damwain*, smiling and a shared bottle of whisky, it is only silence that they need in order to share the close proximity of each other's company. They do not engage in a reassessment of all the years since the accident, and do not do any 'catching up', only a silent celebration of their birthday and brotherly bond.

Interestingly, silence in *Fallen Sons* does not contrast with any extended talk or small talk. In fact, different types of silence contrast with one another. In this way, the play is a good illustration of the complementarity of silence and small talk: situations in which silence unambiguously delineates interpersonal closeness and detachment create no need for small talk.

Conclusion

In this chapter I have argued that silence and small talk may sometimes be treated as partly overlapping, functional equivalents. Their forms and meaning depend largely on the situational context, especially, interpersonal distance between social actors. Thus, this chapter offers some basis for a revision of our understanding of phaticity and small talk in relation to silence, which until now have been constituted as formal opposites with silence being conceptualised as socially awkward and undesirable. In fact, I have argued that in certain types of interpersonal relations, most notably *intimacy* and *detachment*, silence is common and/or desirable and/or a possible vehicle of phaticity.

Invoking seemingly opposite types of interpersonal relations which are best 'served' by the same type of linguistic communication (silence) is no contradiction. In her model of social interaction based on the dimension of interpersonal distance, Wolfson (1988) suggests that rules of spoken communication are similar between intimates, status unequals and strangers, as opposed to nonintimates, status unequal friends, co-workers and acquaintances.[7] She argues that

> when we examine the ways in which different speech acts are realized in actual everyday speech, and when we compare these behaviors in terms of the social relationships of the interlocutors, we find again and again that the two extremes of social distance – minimum and maximum – seem to call forth very similar behavior, while relationships which are more toward the center show marked differences.
>
> (Wolfson 1988: 32)

According to Wolfson, this pattern of verbal behaviour (referred to as the bulge theory) is based on the perceived stability and fixedness of intimate and distant social relations, on one hand, and the perceived volatility of casual relations, on the other. Interactants in the former type of relationship find little need for elaborate, verbal negotiation of their respective statuses, while those in the other group operate in relationships which invite more negotiation of social status through verbal exchange.

In support of her theory, Wolfson cites numerous examples of ethnographic studies of the realisation of different speech acts in American English. For example, with regard to the speech act of invitation she notes that the data fall into two clear-cut categories:

> The first consisted of unambiguous, complete invitations giving time, place, activity and a request for response. These unambiguous invitations occurred most frequently between intimates and between status unequals – the two sets of interlocutors whose relationships with the speaker were at the extremes of social distance. The second category of invitations consisted of ambiguous or incomplete references to the possibility of future social commitments. Once a large body of data had been collected, it was possible to recognize these so-called invitations as 'leads'. Utterances such as 'We really must get together sometime' or 'Let's have lunch together soon' are

typical examples. But in order for a social commitment to result from a 'lead', it was nearly always the case that both parties to the interaction took part in negotiating the arrangement. And what was particularly interesting about these 'leads' was that they occurred between status-equal nonintimates – that is, between speakers whose relationships are most open to redefinition.

(Wolfson 1988: 33)

The use and distribution of silence in the two plays analysed here can be explained by analogy to the bulge model. All the instances of intimate relations between George and Martha, and Danny and Iorry are marked or constructed with different forms of non-threatening silence. Likewise, withdrawal, detachment and hostility are equally frequently signalled through silence. Interestingly, silence in contexts of increased distance may be less confrontational and threatening than talk. 'Polite' small talk about the weather between a husband and wife or brother and sister is more likely to signal discord than foreground positive, relational goals (see Note 2 on p. 130).

Consistent with the bulge model, small talk is characteristic of the relationships towards the centre: nonintimates, status unequal friends, co-workers, acquaintances, or strangers brought into co-presence in close proximity (McCarthy, this volume). An example of a situation which calls for small talk appears in Extract 2, in which the two couples are precisely in a nonintimate, status unequal relationship. In Extract 3 and in the play *Fallen Sons*, however, we see that the extreme ends of the distance continuum are not equally likely to result in small talk between the participants, and if small talk does occur it is likely to be different than towards the centre.

Finally, one comment on the use of literary data is in order. It is obvious that literary material offers a stylised approximation of the so-called naturally occurring talk. However, I agree with Lakoff and Tannen (1984: 345) that the examination of fictional, literary dialogue is useful for theorising communication in general because it 'enables us to inspect pragmatic competence – speakers' abstract knowledge of what is expected of them in discourse'. There is no reason to assume that (good) authors' metapragmatic awareness and representation of communication is in any way inferior to that of linguists. Besides, assuming that literary texts are often based on their authors' extensive research or experience, we can gain access to the representations of situations which might otherwise have been unavailable to us.

Notes

1. I thank Justine Coupland for useful comments and discussion of earlier drafts of this chapter.

2. I believe that 'positive' relational communication of small talk tends to mean narrowing the gap in interpersonal distance. However, in some situations, conventional scripts for small talk may signal *increased* distance, e.g. between angry partners.

3. This is not to say that silence cannot perform the ideational and textual metafunctions. For example, Bilmes (1994) offers a compelling argument for the study of silence as the absence of specific talk. This is the realisation of the ideational function as *concealment*. Silence (e.g. pausing) may also be used to perform the textual metafunction, e.g. as a keying device in introducing verbal performance (Bauman 1977; Jaworski 1997b, 1997c).

4. Discussion of how silence and small talk may be used for social control and power goes beyond the scope of this chapter.

5. Extracts 2 and 3 are transcripts of the dialogues from the film version of *Who's Afraid of Virginia Woolf?* (Warner Home Video S001056). The transcription conventions are as follows:

   lower case throughout except for proper names
   CAPS   extra loudness/emphasis
   [overlapping speech
   [laughs]   paralinguistic and non-verbal information
   ?   rising intonation
   =   contiguous speech
   ah::   lengthening
   (.)   pause shorter than 1 second
   (2)   pause of approximately 2 seconds

6. This section is based on the video recording of the play produced by Wales Playhouse for BBC Wales in 1993. I am grateful to Edward Thomas for allowing me to use this material and to Mary Rose Peate for her assistance in this matter and for sharing her ideas and the transcript of the play with me.

7. Wolfson's original work and theory were based on the data collected among white, middle-class, urban Americans, but the model can be extended to other speech communities (see, e.g., Holmes 1995 on gendered New Zealand English).

References

Albee, E. (1965 [1962]) *Who's Afraid of Virginia Woolf?* London: Penguin.

Basso, K. H. (1972) 'To give up on words': Silence in Western Apache culture. In P. P. Giglioli (ed.) *Language and Social Context*. Harmondsworth: Penguin, 67–86.

Bauman, R. (1977) The nature of performance. In R. Bauman (ed.) *Verbal Art as Performance*. Rowley, MA: Newbury House, 3–58.

Bilmes, J. (1994) Constituting silence: Life in the world of total meaning. *Semiotica* 98: 73–87.

Blum-Kulka, S. (1997) *Dinner Talk: Cultural Patterns of Sociability and Socialization in Family Discourse*. Mahwah, NJ: Lawrence Erlbaum Associates.

Brown, P. and Levinson, S. C. (1987) *Politeness: Some Universals in Language Usage.* Cambridge: Cambridge University Press.

Cheepen, C. (1988) *The Predictability of Everyday Conversation.* London: Pinter.

Coates, J. (1988) Gossip revisited. In J. Coates and D. Cameron (eds) *Women in their Speech Communities: New Perspectives on Language and Sex.* London: Longman, 94–122.

Coupland, J., Coupland, N. and Robinson, J. D. (1992) 'How are you?': Negotiating phatic communion. *Language in Society* 21: 207–30.

Eggins, S. and Slade, D. (1997) *Analysing Casual Conversation.* London: Cassell.

Enninger, W. (1987) What interactants do with non-talk across cultures. In K. Knapp, W. Enninger and A. Knapp-Potthoff (eds) *Analyzing Intercultural Communication.* Berlin: Mouton de Gruyter, 269–302.

Gal, S. (1989) Between speech and silence: The problematics of research on language and gender. *Papers in Pragmatics* 3: 1–39.

Giles, H., Coupland, N. and Wiemann, J. M. (1991) 'Talk is cheap' but 'My word is my bond': Beliefs about talk. In K. Bolton and H. Kwok (eds) *Sociolinguistics Today: Eastern and Western Perspectives.* London: Routledge, 218–43.

Gilmore, P. (1985) Silence and sulking: Emotional displays in the classroom. In D. Tannen and M. Saville-Troike (eds) *Perspectives on Silence.* Norwood, NJ: Ablex. 139–62.

Halliday, M. A. K. (1978) *Language as social semiotic: The social interpretation of language and meaning.* London: Edward Arnold.

Hocker, J. L. and Wilmot, W. W. (1995) *Interpersonal Conflict.* 2nd ed. Madison, WI: Wm. C. Brown and Benchmark Publishers.

Holmes, J. (1995) *Women, Men and Politeness.* London: Longman.

Hymes, D. (1972) Models of the interaction of language and social life. In J. J. Gumperz and D. Hymes (eds) *Directions in Sociolinguistics.* New York: Holt, Reinhart and Winston, 35–71.

Jaworski, A. (1990) The acquisition and perception of formulaic language and second language teaching. *Multilingua* 9/4: 397–411.

Jaworski, A. (1993) *The Power of Silence: Social and Pragmatic Perspectives.* Newbury Park, CA: Sage.

Jaworski, A. (ed.) (1997a) *Silence: Interdisciplinary Perspectives.* Berlin: Mouton de Gruyter.

Jaworski, A. (1997b) Aesthetic, communicative and political silences in Laurie Anderson's performance art. In A. Jaworski (ed.) *Silence: Interdisciplinary Perspectives.* Berlin: Mouton de Gruyter, 15–35.

Jaworski, A. (1997c) 'White and white': metacommunicative and metaphorical silences. in A. Jaworski (ed.) *Silence: Interdisciplinary Perspectives.* Berlin: Mouton de Gruyter, 381–401.

Jaworski, A. (1998a) Talk and silence in *The Interrogation. Language and Literature* 7/2: 99–122.

Jaworski, A. (1998b) The silence of power and solidarity in *Fallen Sons. Studia Anglica Posnaniensia* 33: 141–52.

Jaworski, A. and Stephens, D. (1998) Self-reports on silence as a face-saving strategy by people with hearing impairment. *International Journal of Applied Linguistics* 8/1: 61–80.

Kurzon, D. (1998) *Discourse of Silence.* Amsterdam/Philadelphia: John Benjamins.

Lakoff, R. Tolmach and Tannen, D. (1984) Communicative strategies and meta-strategies in a pragmatic theory: the case of *Scenes from a Marriage*. *Semiotica* 17(3–4): 323–46.

Laver, J. (1974) Communicative functions of phatic communion. In A. Kendon, R. M. Harris and M. Ritche Key (eds) *Organization of Behavior in Face-to-face Interaction*. The Hague: Mouton, 215–38.

Laver, J. D. M. H. (1981) Linguistic routines and politeness in greeting and parting. In F. Coulmas (ed.) *Conversational Routine: Explorations in Standardized Communication Situations and Prepatterned Speech*. The Hague: Mouton, 289–304.

Lehtonen, J. and Sajavaara, K. (1985) The silent Finn. In D. Tannen and M. Saville-Troike (eds) *Perspectives on Silence*. Norwood, NJ: Ablex, 193–201.

Malinowski, B. (1923) The problem of meaning in primitive languages. Supplement to C. K. Ogden and I. A. Richards *The Meaning of Meaning*. London: Routledge and Kegan Paul, 146–52.

Philips, S. U. (1976) Some sources of cultural variability in the regulation of talk. *Language in Society* 5: 81–95.

Saville-Troike, M. (1985) The place of silence in an integrated theory of communication. In D. Tannen and M. Saville-Troike (eds) *Perspectives on Silence*. Norwood, NJ: Ablex, 3–18.

Sifianou, M. (1997) Silence and politeness. In A. Jaworski (ed.) *Silence: Interdisciplinary Perspectives*. Berlin: Mouton de Gruyter, 63–84.

Sobkowiak, W. (1997) Silence in markedness theory. In A. Jaworski (ed.) *Silence: Interdisciplinary Perspectives*. Berlin: Mouton de Gruyter, 39–61.

Szuchewycz, B. (1997) Silence in ritual communication. In A. Jaworski (ed.) *Silence: Interdisciplinary Perspectives*. Berlin: Mouton de Gruyter, 239–60.

Tannen, D. (1990) Silence as conflict management in fiction and drama: Pinter's *Betrayal* and a short story, 'Great Wits'. In A. Grimshaw (ed.) *Conflict Talk*. Cambridge: Cambridge University Press, 260–79.

Tannen, D. (1993) The relativity of linguistic strategies: Rethinking power and solidarity in gender and dominance. In D. Tannen (ed.) *Gender and Conversational Interaction*. New York: Oxford University Press, 165–88.

Tannen, D. and Saville-Troike, M. (eds) *Perspectives on Silence*, Norwood, NJ: Ablex.

Tracy, K. and Coupland, N. (1990) Multiple goals in discourse: an overview of issues. In K. Tracy and N. Coupland (eds) *Multiple Goals in Discourse*. Clevedon: Multilingual Matters: 1–13.

Wolfson, N. (1981) Invitations, compliments and the competence of the native speaker. *International Journal of Psycholinguistics* 8: 7–22.

Wolfson, N. (1988) The bulge: A theory of speech behavior and social distance. In J. Fine (ed.) *Second Language Discourse: A Textbook of Current Research*. Norwood, NJ: Ablex, 21–38.

Wolfson, N., D'Amico Reisner, L. and Huber, L. (1983) The analysis of invitations in American English. In N. Wolfson and E. Judd (eds) *Sociolinguistics and Language Acquisition*. Rowley, MA: Newbury House, 116–28.

Žegarac, V. and Clark, B. (1999) Phatic interpretations and phatic communication. *Journal of Linguistics* 35, 2: 321–46.

Procedural aspects: participants' orientations to and organisation of small talk

Introduction to **Part II**

Justine Coupland

Chapters in the second section of the book examine in detail how participants organise small talk encounters and manage shifts between small talk
and talk of a more obviously 'full' or newsworthy nature, or talk which
carries forward business transactions. Sequencing and structure are therefore
important considerations in all these analyses. In each of these chapters,
researchers analyse how formulaic, boundarying talk and more individually
designed relational sequences are managed conversationally.

Drew and Chilton analyse a series of telephone calls among family members, whose overall purpose is the maintaining of social relationships – to
exchange news or to share 'the small events and concerns which make up
their daily lives'. Drew and Chilton are interested in how conversationalists
organise their talk in the early phases of these calls, to negotiate and ultimately determine the type of call any one instance is to be. So, the initial
small talk of the calls displays participants' orientation to the routine, or
occasionally the exceptional, nature of the call. The topics addressed by
most calls studied are those traditionally associated with small talk. They are
best characterised as reflecting the detail and minutiae of routine, domestic
family life – minor health concerns, what is flowering in the garden, meals
just eaten, and so on. Callers are in the position of needing to establish why
their calls are warranted, whether as part of a planned, routine series of
'keeping in touch' calls, or whether there is exceptional business to be attended
to in the call.

Coupland and Ylänne-McEwen draw from two different corpora of travel
agency talk, and their analysis reveals the different frames in which talk
about the weather is done. The weather is of course one of Malinowski's
examples of safe, ritualised topics available even to non-familiars. It is often
thought of as fodder for predictable commentary on a shared environment,
and it does indeed function this way at times in the data. Like Drew and
Chilton, the authors comment on how many instances of small talk are based
on local change, 'updating on recent happenings, movements and experiences'.

But the travel agency context involves other framings of the weather, allowing Coupland and Ylänne-McEwen to compare and contrast them and to examine linkages and shifts between them. The weather as a phatic resource mainly occupies liminal, timeout moments in the travel agency, when commercial business is suspended or carried on without speech. But we also see how weather as a topic can enable participants to go beyond polite and ritualised relations, at times into intimate exchanges about their lifestyles and preferences.

Coupland and Ylänne-McEwen also address the interplay between sociability and the promotion of positive, effective customer relations and the commercial goals of selling. (Both Cheepen and Kuiper and Flindall also take up this theme in their chapters.) Many and perhaps all commercial organisations will recognise the economic power of 'good service' and of their employees' 'social skills'. The travel industry perhaps has special reasons for prioritising 'the feelgood factor'. Small talk may mean big business. Of course, different types of service encounter will present different opportunities for small talk, and some are far more routinised than others. Kuiper and Flindall's data are supermarket checkout encounters and that talk generated during these limited moments of co-presence. Their argument is that the routine nature of the task in which the checkout assistants are engaged predicts the formulaic nature of the talk exchanged. Checkout operators have an 'inventory of formulae' which they enact to deal with the opening, payment and closing sequences. But overlaid on this inventory is a rather more 'free' form of talk, in which the operators, and their customers, display a limited form of creativity, at least within the confines of 'safe' and non-contentious topics.

The issue of cultural variation is again addressed in this chapter, with Kuiper and Flindall finding inter-cultural variation in the handling of such 'oral traditions', not least with regard to tolerating silence (cf. Jaworski's chapter). In the commercial context, this might suggest differences in the extent to which 'conversationalisation', in Fairclough's sense (see the general Introduction) is affecting public discourse globally. Fairclough's perspective worries over the social feigning that such talk represents. But Kuiper and Flindall interpret the frequency with which their dyads move out from formulaicity into more individually designed conversation as 'genuine' sociability, even in these fleeting encounters between strangers or distant acquaintances.

5

Calling just to keep in touch: regular and habitualised telephone calls as an environment for small talk
Paul Drew and Kathy Chilton

1   Introduction: telephone calls made just to 'keep in touch' as an environment for small talk

One widespread use which we make of the telephone is to keep in touch with one another. People may call each other up just to keep in touch with one another, and to maintain their relationship over distances of time and space. This is common among family members who live some distance apart, and are therefore unable to meet very frequently. Instead they may telephone one another, often on a regular basis, just to keep up with the week's doings and happenings, to find out how each is getting along, and to share and talk over the small events and concerns which make up their daily lives. In many families this is habitualised to the extent that there is an understanding or even an arrangement that one will telephone the other each week, perhaps on a certain day and at a certain time (or at least, during a certain period of the day). Such arrangements take account of what each knows about the other's routines: so, for example, a daughter might telephone her mother on Sunday evenings, at a time when she knows that her mother will have finished her evening meal, but before she settles down to watch some favourite television programme, and also before she (the daughter) has to bath her own daughter and put her to bed. These regular calls do not need to be made for any other more specific reason than to 'keep in touch'.

The existence of such habitualised and routinised telephone calls, and the part they play in maintaining contact between members of families who live some distance apart, was confirmed by our preliminary investigation of a corpus of telephone calls recorded by a family over an extended period (Frohlich, Chilton and Drew 1997). The corpus consists of over 300 calls made by a family during three sample 2-month periods spread over 3 years:

the family was professional class, and consisted of mother/wife, father/ husband, a daughter living away from home in another part of the country and a son living at home (until the final set of recordings, when he too left home). Approximately 10 per cent of calls in the corpus were between the middle-aged wife/mother of the household and her elderly mother living on the other side of the country. Although they would visit one another from time to time, these visits were not frequent: their principal means of staying in touch was to speak on the telephone at least once a week, usually on a Sunday evening. It appears that they took turns to call. For present purposes, our interest in these calls is that by virtue of this arrangement they needed to have no other reason to call than that this was when they usually spoke on the telephone, and that it was one's turn to call the other.

In such calls, the mother and daughter in our corpus – though this is supported by evidence from other corpora involving telephone calls between family members and close acquaintances – talk about what they have had or are going to have for lunch, each other's minor ailments, meeting or speaking to a mutual acquaintance during the week, suitable presents for upcoming birthdays, the weather, what is in flower in the garden, the week's or day's events (such as that they have been to church that evening) and what other members of the family have been doing. All this can be considered *small talk*, both in some vernacular sense, and also in so far as they are matters which would not ordinarily be newsworthy and hence constitute a reason for telephoning, at times other than the appointed regular weekly call. On this occasion, however, for the purposes of the weekly call, they may have no other or 'better' reason to call than to keep in touch; and they may expect their conversation to consist of nothing other than such matters of small talk.

So the habit of the mother and daughter in our corpus to speak on the telephone each week provides us with a collection of calls in which participants are not calling for any specific purpose; that is, they do not have a reason for calling, other than to *keep in touch*[1] – which is the phenomenon on which we focus in this study. Small talk of a certain kind, exchanging the news of daily life, seems to be particularly associated with such calls. In this respect, calling just to 'keep in touch' can be considered to be a *context* for talk – a context in which participants engage in small talk.

However, it is necessary to add a complicating factor to the picture: people who are close, and who talk regularly on the telephone just to stay in touch, may also occasionally call one another for some particular purpose, with some particular matter or business in hand. That is, the fact that two people have a relationship in which they stay in touch by calling each other regularly does not guarantee that every time one calls the other she will not have a particular reason for calling. She may do so: she may be calling to announce some especially urgent or momentous news, to request assistance, to arrange a forthcoming visit, or to find something out etc. Thus, if one is calling for a particular reason, then the context of their talk is different, reflected in the different character of the talk between them – for now, the conversation, for some part of the call at least, will be focused on the business which is the specific reason for calling, and will not consist simply of small talk.

In other words, the context of talk is not determined by people's exogenous, sociolinguistic identities (e.g. *mother* and *daughter*). It can, and does happen in our corpus that, when one calls the other at the time scheduled for their weekly call, she nevertheless happens to have some particular business to conduct. Thus the nature of the call, and hence the context of the conversation between them, is a contingent property. The matter of whether a call is going to be about some particular reason for calling, or just to chat, is negotiable in each call, no matter how close the relationship between the participants, or with whatever regularity they speak to one another over the telephone. This sense of the negotiability or contingent nature of context is captured in Heritage's proposal to:

> abandon our traditional concept of 'context' as something exogenous to interaction or as an external interpretative resource. Instead, we can begin to think of context as endogenously generated within the talk of the participants and, indeed, as something created in and through that talk.

> (Heritage 1983: 283)

Heritage is suggesting here an approach which has come to be adopted by a broad range of cognate perspectives which might be collected under the umbrella of 'interactional sociolinguistics' (as contrasted with variationist sociolinguistics). Instead of supposing that the ethnographic 'facts' of the relationship between participants (e.g. that they are members of a family) somehow 'explain' aspects of their conversation, we should aim rather to investigate how, in their talk, the participants orientate to their relevant identities. Schegloff (1992) has argued that it is not enough to show that participants possess certain (ethnographic) identities: our aim should be to demonstrate how certain of their identities come to be occasioned as 'procedurally relevant' for their talk, and what are the consequences of that for the kind of talk in which they engage.

Hence our analytical strategy in this chapter is to investigate how, when either mother or daughter telephones the other, they constitute the call as being one of their regular scheduled weekly 'keeping in touch' calls. We are focusing here on how the participants construct the context as being one in which the conversation will consist of that kind of small talk through which they stay in touch and keep up to date with each other's lives. Specifically, we show that the opening exchanges in these calls, together with the introduction of the first topic, is the primary environment for establishing that a given call is one of their regular weekly calls, and that there is no further special business or reason for calling. This is generally displayed through the small talk in which they engage immediately following the opening greetings.

2   Telephone call openings

There is ample documentation in the literature of the ways in which certain speaker identities, relationships, interpersonal relations, institutional identities and so forth are accomplished or made interactionally salient through the ways participants manage the openings of conversations (this literature, which includes research involving comparisons both within and across speech communities/cultures, is too large to cite exhaustively; but examples are Hopper 1992; Hopper and Drummond 1992; Hopper and Chen 1996; Coupland, Coupland and Robinson 1992; Schiffrin 1977; Schegloff 1986; and Scollon 1998). Specifically in the context of Anglo-American call openings, Schegloff (1986) has shown that the complex inter-relationships between 'call type' and 'relationship type' results in a range of organisational patterns which are all adaptations or modifications of a standard, canonical or 'unmarked' opening sequence. This canonical opening is characteristic of calls between people who have some 'unmarked' form of acquaintance; that is, they are neither particularly close or intimate (e.g. are not close family, nor intimate friends), nor are they strangers. They are known to one another, and have some acquaintance, but are not sufficiently close to be able, for instance, to recognise the other instantly just by hearing their voice. Similarly, the canonical pattern of call openings is associated with calls which are made neither purely for business, nor just to keep in touch: they occupy some middle position, in so far as callers have specific reasons for calling, but other things besides such reasons may be talked about (including topics of 'small talk').

Thus the canonical pattern of call openings which Schegloff has identified is not so much a template for all call openings. It is, rather, a neutral menu of possibilities, from which deviations – including omissions, attenuations and insertions – may be made to reflect the particular circumstances of the call, in terms of the relationship between callers, and the type or nature of the particular call. The canonical pattern of opening calls, as described by Schegloff, consists of a sequence of four paired actions, followed by what he terms the 'anchor position'; this is a slot in which the first topic, the 'reason for the call', is introduced. This sequence is summarised in Table 1 below, in which the schematic summary of the sequence (left-hand side) is illustrated by a call which begins canonically (right-hand side).

In the canonical opening the *caller* typically initiates the exchange of 'how are you?'s [iv], and also introduces the first topic, the 'reason for calling' in the anchor slot [v]. It is, of course, quite possible for the caller's initial 'how are you?' enquiry to occasion some 'first topic', introduced in their response by the one who has been called. Indeed the caller's enquiry 'how are you?' allows for this, by signalling that the caller has no business so pressing that he or she needs to move straight to the reason for calling.

Table 1

(source: Schegloff 1986: 115)

0 [i]	Summons	Phone rings
1	Answer	J: Hallo
2 [ii]	Identification/	B: Hallo Jim?
	Recognition	
3		J: Yeah
4		B: 's Bonnie
5 [iii]	Greetings exchange	J: Hi,
6		B: Hi,
7 [iv]	Exchange of 'how are	How are yuh
8	you?'s + responses	J: Fine, how're you,
9		B: Oh, okay I guess
10		J: Oh okay
11 [v]	First topic	B: Uhm (0.2) what are you doing New Year's Eve ...

If the caller wishes instead to indicate that the call is about some specific business, he or she may avoid introducing 'how are you?'s (and hence avoid the associated 'danger' that the topic he/she has called about may be delayed or sidelined by news which the called has), and move straight to introduce the reason for calling (in position [iv] in Table 1). Unless the called party has some particular urgent or important piece of news which should properly be announced at the earliest stage possible, he or she is likely to do an unelaborated response to 'how are you?', followed by a return 'how are you?', as J does in line 8 in Table 1. This enables the caller to respond briefly, and introduce his/her reason for calling (lines 9 and 11, Table 1).

This canonical pattern of telephone openings is based, then, on unmarked forms of relationships between caller and called, and of the kind of call it is. Calls between those who are either strangers, or very close friends or relatives, as well as calls made for a very specific purpose (business) or for no other reason than to keep in touch, appear to differ from this canonical pattern. For example, members of the public telephoning certain organisations, such as a bank, the police, an electricity board and so on, may choose not to self-identify, and are likely to omit greetings and 'how are you?' enquiries. As a result the opening sequence is greatly attenuated, and the business about which the call is being made is swiftly introduced (for examples and discussion, see Hopper and Drummond 1992).

At the other end of the continuum are the kinds of calls with which we are concerned in this chapter, namely the habitualised weekly calls between mother and daughter which are made for no particular purpose, or have no other business, than to keep in touch with one another. These kinds of calls appear to diverge from Schegloff's canonical pattern of openings in three principal ways.

- Certain sequences are attenuated and are therefore accomplished in a more compact form.
- Items are inserted into the openings before anchor or first topic position: these are normally accounts of one kind or another, often accounts for or remarks about departures from their normal routine (e.g. for calling out of turn, or on a different day, or time, than usual). These accounts may result in a return greeting or the 'how are you?' sequence being deleted altogether, or delayed.
- The party who initiates 'how are you?'s and who introduces the first topic is not restricted to the caller (as it is in the canonical openings). Indeed, in the regular weekly calls to keep in touch, the roles are reversed, and the one who has been *called* generally initiates these sequences; and either party may introduce the first topic.

3   Divergences from the canonical pattern of call openings

The openings of weekly calls to keep in touch are reduced, in comparison with the canonical form identified by Schegloff, principally through the ways in which identification and recognition are managed. As intimates who are in regular contact, Lesley and her mother typically use an unelaborated greetings exchange as a means of displaying recognition of one another. The tasks of identification and recognition are managed implicitly in the greetings exchanges, through intonational and prosodic properties of 'Hellos' displaying recognition: thus the sequence as a whole is reduced or attenuated through the omission of stage [ii] in the canonical pattern. This is illustrated in Example 1 below, in which Mum's prosodically characteristic *Hello:::* in line 2 serves not only as a greeting, but also as a claim to have recognised her daughter's voice, and as projecting that Lesley will recognise her without the necessity for her (Mum), as caller, to self-identify. Similarly Lesley's *Oh hello* in line 3 both returns Mum's greeting, and displays that she has indeed recognised the caller.

Example 1[2]

```
[Holt: 310]
0 Summons                    ((phone rings))
1 Answer                     Les:   Hello
2 Greeting                   Mum:   Hello:::
3 Greeting                   Les:   Oh hello
4                                   (.)
5 Remark about timing        Les:   I've been waiting for you:
```

Identification and recognition are accomplished, mutually, in an embedded fashion, in a quite minimal exchange of greetings tokens. This attenuated form of opening will be constant in all calls between them – even, as we shall see later, in calls when one calls the other, perhaps out of sequence or on a day other than that on which they usually talk on the phone, for some very specific reason or business. So this divergence from the canonical form, the attenuation of the sequence through omitting a separate slot for managing identifications and recognition, arises specifically from the type of relationship (intimates). Other divergences are associated with the particular circumstances of the call, including the type of call.

In line 5 of Example 1 it is evident from Lesley's remark that the call is one of their expected weekly calls, made by the one whose turn it is (Mum) at, or perhaps a little after, the appointed time. On occasions when the 'regular' weekly call is made in some way out of sequence (different time or day than usual, or not by the one whose turn it is) then, although the beginning of the opening is achieved in the same attenuated fashion, the 'irregularity' of the call is routinely addressed in the opening stages. That is, when calling just to keep in touch, but not at the usual time or in the usual sequence, the caller remarks on and accounts for the timing of the call, before the 'anchor' slot for introducing first topic occurs. Thus such accounts are done at an earliest opportunity: it seems that the point of doing so is to indicate that the call is 'just routine', in circumstances where the irregularity of the call's timing or sequence might initially render the nature of the call unclear to the recipient. In particular, the irregularity of the call might lead the one who is called to believe that there is some special reason (business) for this call: given the chance that the called party might detect from the unusual timing of the call that the caller has some particular purpose for calling, she (i.e. the caller) displays through an earliest possible account for calling at this time (or out of sequence) that the call is nevertheless one of their usual chats – and in this way, 'achieves' (in Schegloff's phrase) the routine nature of the call. So that the second divergence from the canonical opening pattern is that remarks accounting for the irregularity of the call's timing are inserted into the sequence, before first topic position, and usually immediately after the greetings sequence, as in Example 2.

Example 2

[Holt: S088:1:12:1]
```
1 Mum:        . . . eight.
2 Les:        Oh hello Mum
3 Mum:        Hello love
4 Les:        .hh I rang you today because we're off to Newcastle and
5             York tomorrow=
6 Mum:        =Are you ( . ) oh lovely mm hmm
7 Les:        How're you.
```

```
8 Mum:          Oh very well thank you mm hm
9 Les:          Is Auntie Laura still with you?
```

In lines 4–5 Lesley provides an account for calling 'today', in terms of circumstances which will prevent her calling on the usual day. In other turn/sequential environments, Lesley's account that *we're off to Newcastle and York tomorrow* might be interpreted as a news announcement. It occupies the slot where 'reason for a call' would normally be introduced and pursued if the call had been made for some specific, non-routine purpose or reason. However, Mum's response in line 6 is consistent with her analysis of Lesley's turn as a simple account for the irregularity of the call's timing, and as marking the call as being 'the routine call at an other-than routine time'. Similarly, in line 7, Lesley displays no sign that announcing the trip was intended to be a candidate first topic: she makes no attempt to topicalise this further, but simply resumes the archetypal opening sequence by initiating the 'how are you?' sequence.

Such accounts for calling at an unusual time or out-of-sequence are not always produced immediately after the initial greetings. They may be backed up into the 'how are you?' sequence, as in the following example: here Mum marks the call as routine by asking *How is things* in line 6, but then goes on in lines 9–10 to give an account for the abnormal timing of her call (i.e. morning, rather than evening).

Example 3

```
[Holt: S088:1:11:1]
 1 Les:          Hello:?
 2                        (.)
 3 Mum:          ↑Hello::
 4                            (.)
 5 Les:          hhOh ↑hello:, h
 6 Mum:          How is ↑things=
 7 ( ):          =hh
 8 Les:          hOh:: alright thank yo[u
 9 Mum:                               [Thought we'd have a change this
10               morning ring you this morni[ng
11 Les:                                     [Oh: I say Gordon's jus' come
12               home he's bin itta party all night.
```

It is significant that this account is nevertheless still marked as having some priority, to be done at an early opportunity and before the first topic: Mum achieves this by beginning it in overlap with the end of Lesley's response to her (Mum's) enquiry (see lines 8/9), thereby preempting a reciprocal 'how are you?' enquiry by Lesley. Once again, the recipient of the account, this time Lesley, makes no attempt to topicalise the account in any way, but instead offers her own candidate first topic (lines 11–12).

The third respect outlined above in which the openings of these routine calls to keep in touch diverge from the canonical form concerns which party initiates the sequence of reciprocal 'how are yous?' and the first topic. It will be recalled that, in the canonical form, the caller generally initiates both 'how are yous?' and the first topic (for an account of how 'how are yous?' play a phatic role in communication, specifically in a medical setting, see Coupland, Coupland and Robinson 1992). However, in the weekly calls to keep in touch, the attenuation of the openings through the omission of the identification/recognition sequence provides an opportunity, or a position, in which either party may initiate 'how are yous?' and subsequently open the first topic. Hence these roles are not restricted to caller. Indeed, an interesting pattern emerges in these data. Briefly, when the call is made at the appointed time and by the one whose turn it is, then it seems that it is almost invariably the *called* party who initiates the 'how are you?' sequence. But, if the call is made at an unscheduled time, and where there are possible grounds therefore for the recipient to believe that the other might be calling for some specific business, then the *caller* always initiates the 'how are you?' sequence.

Examples 4 and 5 show the openings of calls made at the scheduled time: in each case it is the called who asks how the caller is – the reverse of the canonical ordering of this role.

Example 4

[Holt: 99]

```
1 Les:          (     )
2 Mum:          Helloo:
3 Les: →        Oh hello how're you?
4 Mum:          Very well thank you love and you?
5 Les:          Yes tha:nk you
6 Mum:          That's good
7                        (0.5)
8 Mum:          We had torrential rain today
```

Example 5

[Holt: X(C):1:1:6:1]

```
 1 Les:          . . . ↑o
 2                        (0.3)
 3 Mum:          H' ↑llo::::[ (it's)
 4 Les:                    [Oh hello [Mum
 5 Mum:                              [ (me.)
 6                        (0.2)
 7 Mum:          ↑H[ello,
 8 Les: →          [How're you↑:
 9                        (0.5)
10 Mum:          ↑Oh: ↑thank goodn'ss the ↑li:ne's ↓clear toni:ght,
```

The same pattern, in which the recipient of the call is the one to initiate the 'how are you?' sequence, is evident also in those calls which have first been answered by someone other than the intended recipient. It frequently happens in households that the one who answers the telephone is not the person to whom the caller wishes to speak. Thus the answerer passes the call over to the intended recipient (this happened in 50 out of the 315 calls in our larger corpus). When this happens, the daughter (this only occurs in the daughter's household, since her mother lives alone) will come to the 'phone knowing that it is her mother who is calling; this is partly by virtue of the timing of the call (on the scheduled day, at about the usual time), and partly also because presumably whoever has answered will pass the call over saying something like 'it's your mother' (and she may even have overheard something of what the answerer has said on the 'phone to the caller). In these circumstances, there is generally a brief exchange of greetings, after which the called, i.e. the daughter, always initiates the 'how are you?' enquiries, as in the following example.

Example 6

[Holt: 2:9:1] (Mum is caller. The call was first answered by Lesley's husband)
```
1 Les:          Hello::,
2 Mum:          ↑Hello love,
3               (.)
4 Les: →        How're you ↑;
5 Mum:          ↑Alright thank you ↑love
6 Les:          Oh goo:d,
```

By contrast, when the caller telephones at a time other than at their usual weekly scheduled time, or 'out of sequence' (i.e. when it is the other's turn to call), it is the *caller* who initiates the 'how are you?' enquiries. This is illustrated in Example 3 above, where in line 6 Mum asks 'How is things' (see line 9–10 for her explicit orientation to her calling at a different time than usual). A further example is the following case, in which Lesley has called Mum on a Saturday evening, rather than the usual Sunday.

Example 7

[Holt: 2:2:4:1] (Lesley has called Mum on a Saturday evening)
```
1 Mum:          Hello::::?
2 Les:          Oh hello it's me:
3                   (.)
4 Mum:          Hello luv
5 Les: →        How are you::?.
6 Mum:          ↑Alright thank you: (.) 'n you?
7 Les:          Yes
8 Mum:          ↓Good
```

So the pattern which emerges is that when the call is made at the usual weekly day/time, by the one whose turn it is to call, the recipient (called) treats the call as just one of their regular calls to keep in touch, and as having no more specific purpose than that. This is displayed in her not leaving it to the caller to initiate the 'how are you?' enquiries: given that she understands that the caller has telephoned just to keep in touch, she can then invert the usual roles associated with enquiring after the other on the 'phone, and immediately ask after the caller. When, however, the caller has telephoned at an 'unscheduled' time, she orientates to the possibility that this may not be one of their routine weekly chats, and that instead the caller may have called for some specific reason. In which case, the recipient leaves it to the caller to determine the nature of the call; and she does so, initially, by *not* initiating the 'how are you?' sequence, but leaving that (and thereby the future trajectory of the call) to the caller.

Just as the attenuation of openings in regular weekly calls to keep in touch results in there being a position in which recipients of calls have the opportunity to initiate 'how are you?' enquiries (an opportunity which overwhelmingly they take), so also they may introduce the first topic. Recall that in the canonical openings, the *caller* initiates first topic (step [v] in Table 1). Recipients of 'unmarked' types of calls generally leave the first topic slot (the anchor position) to callers, as the position in which they can introduce the reason for their having called. However, the recipient of a regular weekly call to keep in touch may display her understanding that the caller has no such specific reason for calling, by being the one to introduce the first topic. Again, Example 3 illustrates this rather clearly; because, although Mum has telephoned earlier in the day than usual, it is evident from her remarking about that (lines 9–10) that she has no special reason for calling this early (she is calling at this time 'just for a change'). Thus it is evident to Lesley that this is nevertheless their routine weekly call: at which point she (Lesley) introduces the first topic, her son arriving home from an all-night party. And in the following example, in which Mum is calling at the usual time on a Sunday evening, Lesley introduces the first 'small talk' topic immediately after the greetings – thereby further attenuating the opening, by omitting the 'how are you?' sequence.

Example 8

[Holt: X(C):1:2:7:1]
```
 1  Les:         Oh hello[:,
 2  Mum:              [Me::,
 3                    (0.4)
 4  Les: →       .hhh ↑Oh: hello I've just ↑bin watching the ↑fi:lm on:
 5               Channel ↑Fou:r. Have ↑you- are ↑you see ↓ing i[t
 6  Mum:                                                    [What is it.
 7                    (0.4)
```

```
 8 Les:        .hhh Oh it's a ↑lovely film. i-It's -u it's about this
 9             ma:n who's got to get rid'v a turke:y (0.3).p.hhh an:d
10             eighty four pou:nds to a ↑poor family f'↑Christmas:.
11 Mum:        ↑Oh: hnh-[hn
12 Les:                  [An' he's having the most ↑awful difficulty: heh
13             heh
```

Conversely, if the caller is telephoning at the usual, scheduled time, but is calling for a specific reason, and not (just) for one of their regular weekly chats, then she will need to preempt any possibility that the recipient will introduce a first topic. This is illustrated in Example 9, in which Mum has called at their usual time on a Sunday evening: but this is the evening before she is travelling to visit Lesley and her family, and she has called specifically to alter the arrangements for collecting her.

Example 9

```
[Holt: X(C):2:2:5:1]
 1 Les:         . . . .↑'o?
 2              (1.8)
 3 Les:         hell ↑o:::,
 4              (2.2)
 5 Les:         HELLO:?
 6 Mum:         Hello:?
 7              (0.3)
 8 Les:         Oh hello Mu[m?
 9 Mum: →                  [↑Hello love .hh ↑Uh:m ( . ) Lesley:
10              (0.2)
11 Les:         Ye:s?
12 Mum: →       aa baat A↑bout tomorro:w
13 Les:         ih-Ye::s?
14 Mum:         I ↑think (.) probably it will be best if I can go on
15              (0.2) t'Yeovil.
```

Immediately after the greetings exchange (this is prolonged in lines 1–8 by some evident auditory difficulties), Mum signals that she has some specific reason for calling. She does this by marking the 'disjunction' from the opening sequence, with an inbreath, *Uh:m*, and then 'nominating' Lesley (this from the middle of line 9: this is a pre-sequence which engages Lesley's attention to some business at hand, through a summons, lines 9–11, alerting Lesley to the nature of the business, line 12). She has thereby secured the position to introduce her reason for calling (lines 12, and 14–15), by preempting any move by Lesley to initiate the 'how are you?' enquiries – for, if Lesley were to do so, the call would be developing the sequential trajectory of one of their usual weekly calls (on preemptions in this position, see Schegloff 1986: 133–44).

The attenuation of these habitualised calls to keep in touch, in comparison with the canonical form exhibited by 'unmarked' types of calls (between acquaintances but non-intimates), arises from the recognisability of the other's voice and hence the ease of identification between intimates. When this factor is combined with the timing of the calls – a call being made by whoever's turn it is to call, at the appointed time/day – the result is to lift the restrictions on which party initiates the 'how are you?' enquiries, and introduces the first topic of conversation. In the canonical form, the caller does both. However, in the weekly calls to keep in touch, the recipient of the call (the called party) is usually the one who is first to ask the caller how she is: and either of them may introduce the first topic. The fact that when one calls at an 'unscheduled' time, the called does not initiate the 'how are you?' enquiry, thus reverting to the pattern of canonical openings, is further evidence for participants' orientation to the difference between their habitualised weekly calls just to keep in touch, and calls made for a specific purpose. They construct the kind of call it is partly through the timing of the call: but only partly, because as we have seen, one may call the other at the usual time, but for a specific reason (Example 9); or one may call at a time other than the usual time/day, but only for the usual chat (e.g. because they cannot call on the usual day, as in Example 2). But a call is constructed as having no other purpose than to keep in touch in part also by the nature of the first topic. It is to that issue that we now turn.

4   First topics and 'small talk'

We saw in Example 9 that Mum moved quickly to introduce her reason for calling, immediately after the greetings exchange, thus preempting the exchange of 'how are yous?'. She did this as a means to display that, although she was calling at the usual weekly time, this was *not* the usual weekly chat. If she had waited until after the 'how are yous?', Lesley might have come to treat the call as one of their usual calls at the end of the week, and might even have introduced a first topic. So, however the opening of the call unfolds, it is the first item to be topicalised which works finally to confirm the call as either made for a specific reason, or the usual 'keeping in touch'. Which is to say that participants design and recognise the talk in first topic position as being either 'business' or 'small talk'. And that raises the question as to what is characteristic of 'small talk' topics, which enables them to be produced and recognised as such? What sort of things do people talk about when there is no natural candidate for the first topic, associated with the reason for calling (e.g. some news to be announced)?

Analysis of the first topics in these regular weekly calls between mother and daughter reveals that they fall into three broad categories.

- They report 'noticings' concerning the immediate, local environment.
- They report, or elicit a report from the other, about the 'day's happenings'.
- Or they involve requests for news updates about events or circumstances which were current when they last spoke.

These have in common a strong sense of being 'current' or proximate, either temporally (such as today's activities) or spatially (things observed in the immediate environment, such as a beetle crawling down the wall). So first topics designed to display the call as being one to keep in touch are recognisably 'small talk' in so far as they concern very proximate matters of the 'here and now' (even though subsequently the participants may go on to talk about more distal matters, or matters of a more enduring nature).

At a grammatical level, this sense of 'currency' is reflected in the prevalent use of the present tense in conjunction with the perfect and/or progressive aspect. This, particularly when used, as it often is, in combination with the intensifying temporal adverb 'just', has the effect of marking some event, activity, etc. as newsworthy precisely because of its immediacy or proximateness. So 'what has just been happening' or 'what I've just been doing' are frequently used as material for a first 'small talk' topic. Also, at a grammatical/lexical level, the use of a variety of deictic and elliptical references in first topics invokes a further sense of proximity – the closeness of the relationship between the interactants themselves. When one participant uses referential terms which rely for their interpretation on intersubjective understanding, and when her co-participant displays that she is able to make sense of such minimal and seemingly inexplicit references, then this reaffirms the proximate and closely aligned nature of the relationship.

4.1   Noticings concerning the immediate local environment

In our data, this first category of 'small talk' topics consist of two types: i) oh-prefaced environmental noticings, and ii) weather noticings.

'Oh-prefaced' environmental noticings take the form of inserted sequences, in which one reports something which has just occurred in her immediate local environment. These are produced as having been spontaneously noticed, either visually, as in Example 3, or aurally, as in Example 5. A little more of these fragments are shown here, to illustrate the ways in which these noticings are constructed as spontaneous and immediate.

Example 3a

```
[Holt: 1:11:1]
 1 Les:          hOh:: alright thank yo[u
 2 Mum:                                [Thought we'd have a change
 3               this morning ring you this morni[ng
```

```
 4 Les:                        [Oh: I I say
 5                       Gordon's jus'come home he's bin itta party all night.
 6 Mum:                  o[h: good gracious=Has he ↑gotta fat head
 7 Les:                     [.hhhhh
 8 Mum:                  °h[n°
 9 Les:                       [.hhhh W'l I don't ↑know'e looks ↑qui- I've only
10                       jus'seen im through the window'e looks fi:ne. ehh heh
11                       heh heh
```

Example 5a

[Holt: X(C):1:1:6:1]
```
 1 Les:                  How're you↑:
 2                             (0.5)
 3 Mum: →                ↑Oh: ↑thank goodn'ss the ↑li:ne's ↓clear toni:ght,
 4                             (0.5)
 5 Les:                  Oh:. wasn't it [°clear°
 6 Mum:                                 [↑It's been ↑aw↓ful this wee↑:k
 7                             (0.4)
 8 Les:                  Oh uh has ↑i:[t?
 9 Mum:                               [It seemed like a lot of pebbles in the wire all
10                       the time.
11 Les:                  .hhh ↑Oh: dea↓:r.
12 Mum:                  ↑Mm:.
13                             (0.3)
14 Les:                  .hhh Uh:m (0.2) .k Well ↑we got cut ↑off on Thursda:y,
```

In Extract 3a, Lesley reports seeing her son, Gordon, arriving home from a party; she uses this observation as a candidate first topic. Her report is constructed so as to display its being contemporaneous, through features such as being done in slight overlap with Mum's account for the timing of the call (lines 3/4), her reporting that he has *just* come home, and its being 'oh-prefaced' (on *oh* as indicating a change-of-state, see Heritage 1984). In Extract 5a Mum's noticing concerning the quality of the telephone line (line 3) again is constructed as spontaneous noticing, in that it is inserted into the slot where a response to the 'how are you?' enquiry (line 1) would otherwise be done. The positioning of this seemingly disjunctive 'small talk' topic then occasions Lesley's announcement about the problem with their telephone line (line 14). Aural noticings about items such as voice quality, background noise, etc. were commonly topicalised in our data, which points to the possibility that, if shared local resources are prime targets for the makings of small talk, then perhaps shared resources from the aural environment are more likely to trigger comment in telephone conversation in the absence of mutually accessible visible resources.

The second type in this category of noticings concerning the immediate local environment consists of remarks about the weather. These were frequent in our data, and generally occurred after 'how are yous?', and therefore in anchor position for first topic – where nothing else thus far (for instance, in responses to 'how are you?') had occasioned a particular first topic. Perhaps because of the availability of the weather as something to talk about, if something else has not emerged so far, and before they come up with a 'real' topic, Sacks (1992: 205) refers to weather talk as 'a kind of "false first topic" and specifically a "transitional first topic"'. It has the potential to move talk along from the paired opening sequences (greetings, 'how are yous?') into topical talk.[3] In the following example (which is the continuation from Example 4 above), nothing is topicalised in the exchange of 'how are yous?'; in the slot immediately after that sequence (though delayed by a half second) Mum reports the weather *today* (line 7). Lesley's subsequent reference to Cornwall (line 16) (where they had been on holiday the previous week) touches off a 'real' first topic by Mum, the beginning of which is shown in lines 20–1.

Example 10

```
[Holt: 99]
 1 Mum:        Helloo:
 2 Les:        Oh hello how're you?
 3 Mum:        Very well thank you love and you?
 4 Les:        Yes tha:nk you
 5 Mum:        That's good
 6                    (0.5)
 7 Mum: →      We had torrential rain today
 8                    (.)
 9 Les:        A::h now (.) I heard you had I told Mark you needed it
10 Mum:        For which we're very plea:sed yes
11 Les:        Yes w[::
12 Mum:             [(                    ) rain.
13 Les:        Yes but here we've had nothing but rain all the
14             week
15 Mum:        Oh dear.
16 Les:        And anybody out down in Cornwall would have been
17             very:: (.) e:r (0.6) wet I imagine
18 Mum:        huh huh ye:[:s
19 Les:                   [so [we're pleased]
20 Mum:                       [(           )] Oh our vicar's been
21             in Co:rnwall for a fortnight
```

In Example 11, despite the exchange of greetings, Lesley's account for the delay in coming to the phone (lines 3–8), the exchange of 'how are yous?' (lines 11–12: the exchange is incomplete, see line 14), and Lesley's remark about it being her turn to call her mother (line 13), to which Mum responds by giving an account for the unexpectedness of the call (lines 15–19), nothing has been topicalised out of any of this. Again it takes the introduction of 'weather talk', initiated by the call recipient in anchor position (line 20), to

generate the first 'real' topic, their gardens (the beginning of which is shown
in line 33).

Example 11

```
[Holt: 1:8]
 1 Les:     Hello:,=
 2 Mum:     =Hello,
 3 Les:     I'm sorry tuh keep you, I've just'been stickin:g .h
 4          something on the front a'the: uhm (0.3) cooker .h
 5          because:: uh: ( . ) the top a'the knob fell off.
 6 Mum:     Oh: I see[:,
 7 Les:              [A:nd uh I've got ( . ) UHU dripping down
 8          the cooker.
 9 Mum:     eu:kh hih-hih-hih
10              (1.0)
11 Les:     How are you:?
12 Mum:     Oh fine thanks love,
13 Les:     .hh [ I w'z go ]ing tuh ring you t'morrow ni:ght.=
14 Mum:         [And you?]
15 Mum:     =Oh:. Well I- I'm (.) go to church t'morrow evening,
16 Les:     Ye[s,
17 Mum:       [So I thought I ring you this evening. I haven'
18          been: going in the evening b't I'm going t'start
19          t'morrow
20 Les: →   Oh:- You know we had snow this evening,
21 Mum:     So did we::.
22              ( . )
23 Les:     Ye::[s.
24 Mum:         [We had th'most awful hai:l storm this afternoon:n
25 Les:     Oh:.
26 Mum:     Wz like u-half crow::ns c[oming dow]n.
27 Les:                             [ Ye::s.    ]
28 Les:     Ye:s.
29              (0.3)
30 Mum:     Terrible weather fer this time a'the ye[a:r,
31 Les:                                            [I kno:::w,
32              (0.3)
33 Les:     I mean flowers are not coming ou:t are the:y.
```

In summary, one type of 'small talk' associated with the openings of these
habitualised calls to keep in touch is the noticing of something in the immediate environment. These are made 'spontaneously' – displaying that what
is reported is current in the speaker's field of vision or hearing – by being
inserted into the opening sequence often before the 'how are you?' sequence
has been completed (i.e. after one has asked the other how she is, but before
the other has the opportunity to reciprocate). And their spontaneity is marked
through there being 'oh-prefaced'. Alternatively, in the event that nothing

has been topicalised before 'anchor position', participants may report on aspects of the local weather, which routinely invites reciprocal talk which may in turn 'touch off' further related topics.

4.2 Reports of the day's activities

The second category of 'small talk' topics involves one or other reporting something they have just done or been doing, or something they have done earlier that day: both are proximate activities, differing only in the degree of proximateness (the former being very proximate). One major difference between 'oh-prefaced' environmental noticings and other types of reportings is that it is only the 'oh-prefaced' type which can be inserted in a sequentially disjunctive position (e.g. in the midst of the exchange of 'how are yous?'). All other types of announcement must be made in an appropriate slot, which in the opening of telephone calls is generally the anchor position. It should be remembered, however, that this is also the slot where 'reason for a call' might otherwise be expected and sought: so it is important, if the call is to be one of their routine calls, that any item located here should not be interpretable as a 'reason for calling'. If the caller, or for that matter the called party, was to introduce some unexpected or particularly significant news in this position, it could be interpreted as a reason for calling – which would run the risk of transforming the nature of the call into one being made for a specific purpose. In other words, any item in anchor position is susceptible to being seen as having some kind of priority, unless the topical content is such that it is impossible to consider it as such. So, where interactants wish to ensure that candidate first topics are seen as 'routine', they can mark them as such by reporting incidents which, in the same way as 'weather talk', are immediately visible as 'small talk'. This means that activities reported are totally mundane, inconsequential and, to some extent, familiar in that they involve recurrent favoured themes and tales of entirely routine activities. These trivial topics seem to invoke the immutability and continuity of the relationship and, again like weather talk, they are potentially, at least, reciprocal and, at best, topicalisable.

Reports of immediately prior activities consist predominantly of remarks about *what I was doing when the 'phone rang*. As can be seen from the following examples, television programmes can be a useful 'first something to talk about'. This is partly because there is a mutuality associated with TV programmes – one mentions watching a programme which the other might have seen (Example 12, line 2), or one might display knowledge of the programme the other has mentioned (here, in Example 13, lines 12–13, by virtue of its being one in a series which the recipient has watched): in either case they have some mutual, shared focus of conversation. There is the potential to extend this 'small talk topic' of TV programmes (as happens after line 13 in Example 13[4]); but, like weather talk, it is equally possible to drop the topic fairly quickly if anything more interesting crops up.

Example 12

[Holt: X(C):1:2:7:1]

```
 1 Les:    .hhh ↑Oh: hello I've just ↑bin watching the ↑fi:lm on:
 2         Channel ↑Fou:r. Have ↑you- are ↑you see↓ing i[t
 3 Mum:                                                  [What is it.
 4                    (0.4)
 5 Les:    .hhh Oh it's a ↑lovely ↓film. i-It's -u it's about
 6         this ma:n who's got to get rid'v a turke:y
 7         (0.3).p.hhh an:d eighty four pou:nds to a ↑poor family
 8         f' ↑Christmas:.
 9 Mum:    ↑Oh: huh-[hn
10 Les:             [An' he's having the most ↑awful difficulty:
11         heh heh
```

Example 13

[Holt: 310]

```
 1 Les:    Hello
 2 Mum:    Hello::
 3 Les:    Oh hello (.) I've been waiting for you:
 4 Mum:    Have you?
 5 Les:    W[ell it's your turn
 6 Mum:     [how co-
 7 Mum:    Oh good mm hm (0.4) waiting to go to bed?
 8 Les:    No: ( . ) no:
 9 Mum:    O::h lovely
10                 (0.2)
11 Mum:    I've been watching First Born
12 Les:    ↑O:h now what happened because ( . ) uh we watched it
13         last week but we were watching something else this week
```

It is evident that, as intimates who are in regular contact with one another, mother and daughter are very familiar with each other's typical Sunday schedule. So it is possible as a matter of routine for either party to report, for instance, that they have been to church, or to enquire whether the other has been to church. This reporting of a quite predictable prior activity, or eliciting a report about the other's prior activity, works in much the same way as 'weather talk' or reports of immediate prior activities; like these, it may occasion subsequent talk on that topic, or it may be swiftly dropped. One example will have to suffice to illustrate such reports. Here in Example 14, Mum announces in 'anchor position' (line 1), immediately after the exchange of greetings and 'how are yous?' (not shown), that she has been to church. Lesley does not acknowledge Mum's announcement, but rather inserts an 'oh-prefaced noticing' (line 4) which is topicalised (lines 6–26) before Mum is finally able to resume her report (line 29). So, in this case Mum's visit to church and subsequent activities are topicalised at some length, Despite the disruption caused by the inserted sequence.

Example 14

```
[Holt: 16]
 1 Mum: →      We've been to church (.) we been to the c- (.) e:r
 2             er:m candlelight service tonight
 3             (.)
 4 Les:        Ooh I've got a la:rge black beetle looking at me
 5             he:re.
 6 Mum:        Oh have you=
 7 Les:        =I've got to shout to Mark excuse m[e.
 8 Mum:                                          [mm
 9 Les:        MA::RK
10                  (.)
11 Mum:        Huh huh huh
12                  (.)
13 Les:        MA:RK
14                  (0.5)
15 Mum:        He won't eat you
16 Les:        Aye?
17 Mum:        He won't eat you
18                  (0.2)
19 Les:        This beetle is eno:rmous
20 Mum:        Is it a big one?
21 Les:        Yea:h=
22 Mum:        A:h.
23                  (.)
24 Mum:        And e:r (.) I[:m
25 Les:                     [Bring the dustpan and brush quickly will
26             you (.) there's a huge black beetle down here
27 Mum:        Huh huh
28 Les:        You wha:t?
29 Mum:        And Donald and Joan and the children and Rose have all been
30             to tea:.
31             (0.4)
32 Les:        Oh that's ni:ce.
33 Mum:        So they've just gone.
34                  (0.4)
35 Les:        [(O ]h lov[ely
36 Mum: →      [i-  ]     [We went to the first (.) service you
37             see
38 Les:        ye:s=
39 Mum:        =At half past five and then they came back to tea
40                  (.)
41 Les:        ye:s.
```

42	Mum:	And now they've just all gone huhh.
43	Les:	Oh jolly good
44	Mum:	Mmm.

4.3   News updates

The final category of 'small talk' topics are those which arise in response to enquiries about news-updates. These have a sense of 'proximateness' in so far as they invite a co-participant to report on the current 'state of affairs' regarding something they talked about last time they spoke. As first topics, however, these requests for news-updates are triggered by 'other-attentive' enquiries: they are solicitous, and as such they do considerable relationship work. The enquiries are 'other-attentive' to two sorts of things – what is known about the other's schedule (people visiting, trips etc.); and problems (particularly concerning health) experienced by the co-participant or significant others. Sequentially, these news-update enquiries occur in two principal locations: they may replace the exchange of 'how are yous?', as in Example 15, or they may be made immediately after the 'how are yous?' sequence, and in a sense arising as a continuation of the 'how are you?' enquiry, as in Example 16.

Example 15

[Holt: 1:1:1] (Lesley's family have all departed on a skiing holiday)

1	Les:	Hello:,
2	Mum:	↑Hello:::::, It's me?
3		(.)
4	Les:	Sorry?
5		(0.2)
6	Mum:	It's me:?
7		(0.3)
8	Les:	Oh yeh. Sorry I couldn'hear you very[well Je]:m's m-
9	Mum:	. [O h :]
10	Les:	m-[Jem's
11	Mum: →	[Are the family o:ff?
12		(0.5)
13	Les:	SORRY?
14	Mum:	'Av your family gone o:ff?
15		(.)
16	Les:	Ye:s,
17	Mum:	Oh ↓goo:d,
18	Les:	<A:t um: half past three: this morning.
19		(0.3)
20	Mum:	↑Oh my wo:rd.
21	Les:	.hh Well it was gon'be half pas'o:ne but they realized
22		they'd of been: up at Gatwick fa:r too earl[y
23	Mum:	[Oh:: gosh
24		y'been up all ni:ght the;n

Example 16

[Holt: 2:9:1]
```
 1 Mum:          (    )
 2               (0.4)
 3 Les:          Hello::,
 4 Mum:          ↑Hello love,
 5               (.)
 6 Les:          How'r you ↑:
 7 Mum:          ↑Alright thank you ↑love
 8 Les:          Oh goo:d,
 9 Mum: →        (I hear) you're better no:w
10               (.)
11 Les:          Well yes but (.) it it takes a ↑long ti:me tih get rid'v
12               the uh:m (0.8) you KNOW you ↑do:n't seem t'get rid'v it
13               really,
14 Mum:          No:.
```

Because these requests for news-updates refer back to something talked about in a previous call, the majority of deictic and elliptical references are to be found in this type of initial topic. The shared knowledge lying behind the use and interpretation of such references, plus the closeness which is invoked by the use of other-attentive enquiries which are finely tuned to the detail of the other's life, help to foster a sense of relational proximity, hence intimacy. To summarise, then; news-update first topics are occasioned by other-attentive enquiries, rather than being instigated by the news-teller; as such the news cannot be interpreted as having the status of the reason for calling. In turn, the other-attentive enquiries themselves are not interpreted as being the reason for calling because the call will always have been marked as routine in some way, for example, by its timing or because the enquiries are instigated by the called party rather than the caller.

5   Conclusion

We have distinguished between two kinds of calls – those made for some specific purpose, to conduct some business, such as make an enquiry, to make an invitation or make an arrangement; and those regular and habitual calls which close friends or family make to one another, often at an (informally) scheduled day and even time each week, which do not need any specific purpose or business other than to make that weekly call. The purpose of the latter calls, which have been the focus here, is to 'keep in touch', to chat merely to keep up with the news of the daily events in each other's lives. We have seen that these 'keeping in touch' telephone conversations create an environment or context in which small talk is characteristic or typical. But, although 'keeping in touch' can be considered to be a context for talk, and for talk of a certain kind (i.e. small talk), it is only through the details of the organisation of the talk itself that a given call is constituted as being one or the other kind of call (that is, as about some particular business or matter, or just the regular chat). In particular, it is the opening sequences of a telephone call where participants display, recognise, negotiate and ultimately determine the type of call this is to be. In the openings of calls made to 'keep in touch' we can see various organisations and topics which participants employ in constituting the conversation as calling just to 'keep in touch', rather than that one is calling the other about some particular business.

The regularity of the informal schedule of these calls, reflecting the intimacy between the participants, is strongly orientated to, as for instance when, at an earliest opportunity in the call openings, accounts are offered or sought for any deviation from the usual day/time schedule. These accounts display that, despite the irregularity of the call's timing, the call is nevertheless their routine weekly call. One of our findings has been that the structure of openings in these regular and habitualised calls differs from the canonical sequential pattern observed by Schegloff for 'unmarked' telephone calls. The openings in these calls are typically attenuated, particularly in the identification and recognitional sequences. Moreover, whereas in the canonical openings it is the *caller* who initiates the 'how are you?' sequence, and initiates also the first topic, here the *called* generally initiates 'how are you?' enquiries, and possibly also the first topic. This reflects the recipient's understanding that the caller has not called for any specific 'reason'/purpose, as might be assumed in other kinds of telephone calls. Our data show that when a call is made at the weekly scheduled time, the called party routinely initiates enquiries about how the other is; but when the call is made at an unscheduled time or is made 'out of turn', then it is always the caller who initiates 'how are you?' enquiries.

The topics about which participants began speaking in these conversations, i.e. first topics, are all *proximate* in some sense, and built with a sense of 'currency', in so far as these topics concern and focus on the immediate local spatial and temporal environment of the speakers. These may involve either spontaneous visual or aural noticings, of happenings or events in their environment (including the current weather in their part of the country). They may report on current or immediately prior activities, such as watching a television programme; or they may report activities or events which occurred earlier in the day. They may also use other-attentive enquiries to elicit reports about some event or state of affairs in the other's life (e.g. their state of health) which was salient when they last spoke. In other words, one may request a news-update regarding what she knows, from their last conversation, was happening in the other's life, or was going to happen in the period between that last call and this.

These habitualised, regular telephone calls between people who know one another intimately, and call to keep in touch with each other, and to exchange news about their daily doings, are a context for small talk. We have seen here that participants display this kind of relationship, and this kind of call, through constituting their talk in the opening moments of a telephone call as 'small', as being about the this-and-that of their ordinary lives. We have shown that they do so not only through the content of what they say – the kind of things, or topics, they talk about; but particularly through the way in which the talk itself is structurally organised in the opening sequences.

Appendix: A glossary of the transcription symbols

Calls have been transcribed according to the conventions developed by Gail Jefferson, and widely used in conversation analysis. The transcription notation is set out in full in J. M. Atkinson and J. Heritage (eds), *Structures of Social Action: Studies in Conversation Analysis*. Cambridge: Cambridge University Press, ix–xvi. But for convenience they can be summarised as follows:

Aspects of the relative timing of utterances

Intervals either within or between turns, are shown as pauses in tenths of seconds, thus (0.7).

A discernible pause which is too short to be timed mechanically is shown as a micro-pause, thus, (.).

Overlaps between utterances are indicated by square brackets, the point of overlap onset being marked with a single left-hand bracket; and the completion of overlap with a right-facing bracket, thus:

```
Les:    Ye::[s.
Mum:       [We had th'most awful hai:l storm this afternoon:n
Les:    Oh:.
Mum: Wz like u-half crow::ns c[oming dow]n.
Les:                          [ Ye::s.   ]
```

Contiguous utterances, where there is no discernible interval between turns, are linked by an equals sign, thus:

```
Les:    .hh I rang you today because we're off to Newcastle and York tomorrow=
Mum: =Are you ( . ) oh lovely mm hum
```

Characteristics of speech delivery

Various aspects of speech delivery are captured in these transcripts by punctuation symbols (which, therefore, are not used to mark conventional grammatical units) and other forms of notation, as follows:

.	A period indicates a falling tone.
,	A comma indicates a continuing tone.
?	A question mark indicates a rising inflection (not necessarily a question).
:	The stretching of a sound is indicated by colons, the number of which correspond to the length of the stretching, thus, 'H' ↑l̲l̲o::::: (it's)'
.h	Inhalation is shown by a stop, followed by 'h', the length of the inhalation being indicated by the number of hs̲.
h.	Outbreath is shown by 'h' followed by a stop, the length being indicated by the number of h's̲.
(hh)	Audible aspirations are indicated in the speech in which they occur (including in laughter).
°°	Degree signs indicate word(s) spoken very softly or quietly, thus:

°Okay° where's the property:?

Sound stress is shown by underlining, those words or parts of a word which are emphasised being underlined thus: 'We had torre̲ntial ra̲in today'

Particularly emphatic speech, usually with raised pitch, is shown by capital letters (other than, as conventionally, at the beginning of turns), thus:

```
Les:  =I've got to shout to Mark excuse m[e.
Mum:                                     [mm
Les:  MA::RK
```

Marked rising and falling shifts in intonation (pitch) are indicated by upward and downward pointing arrows, immediately prior to the rise or fall.

```
Mum:  ↑O̲h: ↑tha̲nk goodn'ss the ↑l̲i:ne's ↓clear toni̲:ght,
```

If what is said is unclear or uncertain, that is placed in parentheses, thus:

```
Les:  (       )
Mum:  Helloo̲:
```

Notes

1. One might say, to fulfil the *obligation* to keep in touch. Sometimes the weekly call can be experienced as something like a chore, or a burden; but it is made because it is expected. And this expectation can be oriented to, as when, if one party has 'missed' making the regular call, the other calls and asks if everything is all right, or whether she has been ill – supposing that the reason for missing might have been trouble of some kind or an illness.

2. See Appendix.
3. Sacks goes on to note about weather talk that 'its placing after a how-are-you sequence is only after certain sorts of how-are-you sequences, and that its ends can be very similar to the ends of how-are-you sequences, and that with the weather we find something that we can really call a "transitional topic", a topic that is uninformative about what's on your mind and has "exchange" features in that even people in fairly local juxtaposition can exchange weather reports' (1992: 205).
4. Mum's mention of watching *First Born* in Extract 13 works as an account as to why she is making the Sunday evening call at a later than normal time, as well as a report of a prior activity. But by orienting to this as a candidate first topic rather than an account, Lesley manages to compensate for the rather reprimanding overtones of her earlier remarks in lines 3 and 5, i.e. 'I've been waiting for you:' and 'well it's your turn'.

References

Coupland, J., Coupland, N. and Robinson, J. D. (1992) 'How are you?': negotiating phatic communication. *Language in Society* 21: 207–30.

Frohlich, D., Chilton, C. and Drew, P. (1997) Remote homeplace communication: what is it like, and how can we support it? In H. Thimbleby, B. O'Conaill and P. J. Thomas (eds) *People and Computers XII* (Proceedings of HCI '97). London: Springer, 133–53.

Heritage, J. (1983) *Garfinkel and Ethnomethodology*. Cambridge: Polity Press.

Heritage, J. (1984) A change-of-state token and aspects of its sequential placement. In J. M. Atkinson and J. Heritage (eds) *Structures of Social Action: Studies in Conversation Analysis*. Cambridge: Cambridge University Press, 299–345.

Hopper, R. (1992) *Telephone Conversation*. Bloomington: Indiana University Press.

Hopper, R. and Drummond, K. (1992) Accomplishing interpersonal relationship: the telephone openings of strangers and intimates. *Western Journal of Communication* 56: 185–99.

Hopper, R. and Chen, C.-H. (1996) Languages, cultures, relationships: telephone openings in Taiwan. *Research on Language and Social Interaction* 29: 291–313.

Sacks, H. (1992) *Lectures on Conversation*, vol. 2. Oxford: Basil Blackwell.

Schegloff, E. A. (1986) The routine as achievement. *Human Studies* 9: 111–51.

Schegloff, E. A. (1992) On talk and its institutional occasions. In P. Drew and J. Heritage (eds) *Talk at Work: Interaction in Institutional Settings*. Cambridge: Cambridge University Press, 101–34.

Schiffrin, D. (1977) Opening encounters. *American Sociological Review* 42: 671–91.

6

Talk about the weather: small talk, leisure talk and the travel industry
Nikolas Coupland and
Virpi Ylänne-McEwen

Talk about the weather has, since Malinowski, been taken as a paradigmatic case of phatic communion. The weather appears to offer conversationalists a topic of talk, and a way of relating to each other, that falls within the usually accepted bounds of small talk. The weather, it might be argued, is a neutral topic, accessible to all participants, non-person-focused and uncontroversial. The weather seems well suited to filling out those moments in social inter-action when people are 'avoiding other problems' (Robinson 1972; 1985), merely maintaining a conversational flow, attending to non-transactional purposes and doing 'timeout talk' (J. Coupland, this volume; Guendouzi 1997). Malinowski is in fact quite specific about the weather as a phatic resource:

> Inquiries about health, comments on weather, affirmations of some supre-mely obvious state of things – all such are exchanged, not in order to inform, not in this case to connect people in action, certainly not in order to express any thought.
>
> (1972: 149; see also 1923)

> The breaking of silence, the communion of words is the first act to establish links of fellowship . . . the modern English expression *Nice day today* . . . [is] needed to get over the strange and unpleasant tension which men feel when facing each other in silence.
>
> (1972: 150)

Romaine (1994) also suggests that 'Talking about the weather is a stereo-type associated with speakers of British rather than American English . . . the weather is a safe impersonal topic that can be discussed between two strangers who want to be friendly but not too friendly' (23).

Our intention in this chapter is not to undermine these 'classical' readings of weather talk. Rather, we hope to elaborate on them and recontextualise them. We want, firstly, to ask what precisely is it about the weather that imbues it with the supposed attribute of 'neutrality', and to show how weather talk in fact functions in naturally occurring talk. We build an argument through examining selected extracts of audio-recorded interaction from two corpora of travel agency talk. We take these data to be, at one level, reasonably representative of the broader category of service encounters, where posted servers interact with clients who have, primarily, transactional goals (Tracy and Coupland 1990) for their talk. That is, analysis of timeout sequences in the data should give us a general perspective on the extent to which 'the weather' (if this proves to be a coherent topical category) does in fact feature in small talk, and especially on how it is deployed in specific instances.

But secondly, and because our data are specific to travel agencies, we have the opportunity to explore other, less obviously phatic, framings of 'weather' (including 'climate', 'environment', etc.), where people construct very different meanings and values around this theme in their talk. The data contain instances when speakers engage substantially with weather themes, in both personal and institutional capacities. Travel agencies and the tourist trade invest heavily in economic formulations of weather, and travel agency talk clearly shows how the weather can be very far from an incidental, neutral concern. We focus on the linguistic and pragmatic means by which particular frames are marked and achieved (cf. Goffman 1974; Tannen 1993). Observing how weather features in different discursive frames should help us to identify how the small talk frame for weather is constituted, and what its boundaries are. We hope at least to show that the 'phaticity' of the weather depends on accessing one set of cultural norms for work and leisure, and on norms for structuring social engagement, rather than on its inherent properties as a topic for talk.

The data

The two sets of audio-recorded data were originally gathered for very different purposes[1] and are separated by some nineteen years. Both, on the other hand, are uncontrolled samples of naturally occurring interaction in travel agencies in Cardiff, the capital city of Wales. The Coupland set of 51 complete interactions (date-marked '1977' in the extracts to follow) was recorded in one city centre travel agency and focuses on interactions involving one female assistant. The Ylänne-McEwen set (date-marked '1996') comprises 144 interactions, recorded in seven different agencies with ten different assistants (eight female and two male). Both corpora were gathered with the permission of travel agency staff and clients and transcribed orthographically (see the Appendix for transcription conventions). First names at the head of each extract are fictionalised names of the assistants principally involved in the particular encounters. Clients are identified by randomly allocated numbers preceded by 'C'; they are also given fictionalised names in the body of each extract. Contextual information is given at the head of each extract as an aid to interpretation. Our analyses of particular sequences are based on the transcripts in conjunction with the original audio-recordings, plus our own field notes (each of us was a present but non-participant observer of the original speech events).

Weather talk as small talk

In this first analytic section we focus on the 'classically phatic' frame for weather, weather talk as part of small talk. Extracts 1–4 illustrate how participants in travel agency talk occasionally talk about the weather as an element of their timeout talk. The occurrence of phatic weather talk is relatively rare in the two corpora, constituting a total of seven instances which make reference to local weather conditions on the day of the interaction or on previous days.

The weather in passing

One account for the weather's suitability as a topic for small talk is that the weather is 'merely' an environmental concern, a backdrop to situated and focused social action. It is a matter of passing concern, which we experience in states of transition between activities – such as eating breakfast and being at work. If small talk occurs on the street, speakers may be quite literally in passage, moving in different directions between homes and places of work or leisure. Speakers may comment 'in passing' about the weather, which is pertinent to their transitional states at the moment of their chance encounters. People on radically different trajectories will predictably comment on a briefly shared environment, the weather, as it is temporarily experienced by them together.

The weather is itself in transition. Its quality of unpredictability (especially in Britain) ensures that there will very often be a change-of-state to comment upon – cf. Malinowski's 'Nice day today', 'Warmer than yesterday', and so on. At the same time, it is a predictable unpredictability, since we have rather fixed normative expectations for the weather relative to the seasons – 'for the time of year'. The surface motivation for talking about the weather is likely to be that the weather has changed, or that it has broken our expectations. (It is in fact interesting to speculate that many forms of small talk will be based in commentaries on local change – updating on recent happenings, movements and experiences.) Weather talk can therefore play off the intersection of various dimensions of change and movement – people through space and between activities, temporarily interconnecting with shifting atmospheric conditions (cf. the perspective taken by Drew and Chilton, this volume, in their analyses of telephone data).

Extract 1

1996C136 From the closing sequence of a 10 minute encounter in which the client has come to confirm her holiday booking; recorded in mid January.

```
        Emma:       what'll happen now in about ten days to two weeks time (.) you'll get a
                    confirmation from (.) ourselves and Thomsons and on that it'll give you the
                    date that we have to receive the balance
                                                               [
        Mrs Davies:                                           yes that's
5                   right
     (22.0) (Mrs Davies puts documents in handbag and gets ready to go)
        Mrs Davies: looks lovely out there ((but)) it's not (slight giggle)
                                                          [
        Emma:                                            is it cold?
        Mrs Davies: ((2 sylls)) the wind is terrible I can't understand ((what's=
                                                         [ ]
10      Emma:                                            oh
        Mrs Davies: =happening))
        Emma:       mind you good day to have your washing out providing it'll=
                                                               [   ]
        Mrs Davies:                                            (slight laugh)
        Emma:       =stay on the line
15      Mrs Davies: well it wouldn't ( . ) pegs would fly away
                                      [   ]
        Emma:                         (slight laugh)
        Mrs Davies: oh! (sigh) that's it then (3.0) many thanks for all attentions=
        Emma:       =that's okay no problem at all ( . ) that's what I'm here for and if you've got
                    any queries or anything over the next couple of weeks
20                  just give me a ring
        Mrs Davies: ((4 sylls)) I'll probably be in again later I'm trying to book something for
                    my daughter
        Emma:       yeah! no problem at all
        Mrs Davies: ((right ho)) thank you!
25      Emma:       thanks Mrs Davies! bye bye!
```

Extract 1 captures something of this experience, as Mrs Davies prepares to leave the travel agency on a blustery day. After putting away the documents she has been referring to in the process of booking her holiday with Emma, the assistant, she comments that it *looks lovely out there*, referring and physically orientating to the external environment she is about to experience. Of course this is a rather literalist reading of how weather talk comes into play in this extract. A further quality of this moment is its highly marked transitional nature *within* the speech encounter. The utterance *looks lovely out there* breaks the 22-second silence following Emma's explanation of how the booking Mrs Davies has made will be confirmed, and the client's agreement marker. In terms of Schegloff and Sacks's classical analysis of conversational closings (1999/1974), the putting away of the papers is itself a possible pre-closing move, and weather talk begins the verbal closing and leaving sequence. The weather as topic occupies lines 7–15 of the extract, and is followed in line 17 by the client's sigh (*oh!*), retrospective appraisal (*that's it then*), and thanking (*many thanks for all attentions*), and other linked and patterned turns which achieve closing. At line 7, then, the transactional frame has been broken by non-verbal actions (putting papers away, postural orientation to the street) and by weather talk itself, but also by a key-shift to laughter (first audible in line 7; the weather sequence is also closed by slight laughter at line 16).

In Extract 1, weather talk is therefore done 'in passing' in the more general sense of occurring at a moment of discursive transition, and it is in fact a rhetorical device for marking and achieving transition – here, orientation to leave-taking. This general pattern is strongly represented in the data, as shown in Extracts 2, 3 and 4.

Extract 2

1996C025 Six minutes into the encounter; the assistant is giving information about holiday destinations. She is accessing the computerised booking system; recorded in mid May.

	Mrs Reed:	what about Halkidiki how much is that one please?
	Cathy:	there's nothing showing for Halkidiki at all
		[
	Mrs Reed:	no
	Cathy:	see if Thomsons have got anything for Halkidiki they normally do
5		quite a good programme this is just Aspro
	Mrs Reed:	yeah
(6.0)	(Cathy typing)	
	Mrs Reed:	((I would fancy the Thomsons)) they seem a bit better the Thomson than Aspro
		[
10	Cathy:	they
		do yeah they tend to be nice a bit better quality as well
		[
	Mrs Reed:	((they are)) yes yeah
(37.0)	(Cathy typing)	
	Mrs Reed:	it's quite close isn't it today?
		[
15	Cathy:	it is yeah don't know what to do really do
		you? (slight laugh)
		[
	Mrs Reed:	((it's too hot for trousers isn't it yeah))

(12.0) (Cathy typing)

       Cathy: Bristol to Corfu's a hundred and fifty five

                                                            [

20   Mrs Reed: ((4 syllables)) from Cardiff

Extract 3

1996C113 The client and the assistant are looking through various holiday options for a late deal holiday in July. The transcript begins near the beginning of the encounter, as the client sits down. The client has asked about late deals and Melanie is taking out brochures; recorded in early June.

       Mrs Hill: it's warm in this office isn't it? ooh!

                                       [

       Melanie: very warm yes ((it's extreme))(typing on computer terminal) X27 (1.0) I'll try and get my er little fan fixed soon

     .

     .

     . (Melanie confirms dates, departure airport and duration)

5   Mrs Hill: so I could afford to wait really erm

       Melanie: well I don't know if Airtours have gone down from the fee you had in mind it may not be worth you waiting

       Mrs Hill: mm

(12.0)

       Mrs Hill: I can't ((imagine)) how you can work in this (slight laugh) it's like a

10   sauna in here (.) it's really close

       Melanie: I don't suppose I notice it cos I've been here all day it was colder (.) earlier on

       Mrs Hill: I think what it is is cos it's erm (.) it's rained ((4 sylls)) it's got ((sort of like)) a really close atmosphere outside ((over there))

                                  [   ]

15   Melanie: mm

       Mrs Hill: ((that's why it's so much cooler))

       Melanie: second of July it'll search for me . . .

Extract 4

1996C086 The client is booking a day trip by coach. Three minutes into the encounter, Elizabeth, the assistant, is telephoning the coach company. It is a rainy and windy day in late May.

       Elizabeth: (on the phone) no could we have pick up point at Westgate Street on this one please?

(40.0) (Elizabeth on the phone waiting for a response)

       Mrs Hughes: we sat out the garden yesterday no tights and er just a blouse=

                                               [

5   Elizabeth: I know it's amazing isn't it!

       Mrs Hughes: look at today I was shocked when I got out of bed

       Elizabeth: that's right (.) no two days are alike are they?

       Mrs Hughes: no well hope it's better on this next week

10   Elizabeth: (on the phone) hello? (1.0) seats number (2.0) that's fine thank you Sally
                    bye (.) (to client) seats nineteen and twenty
      Mrs Hughes: oh right

In each of these sequences, talk about the weather features at moments
where the verbal enactment of travel agency business is temporarily suspended. These occur when non-verbal activity progresses the main transactional business, or where a pause in proceedings is enforced by the assistant
having to wait or search for information, or while she enters information
onto a computer. In Extract 2 weather talk is bounded by substantial pauses
at lines 13 and 18. In Extract 3 Mrs Hill's comment beginning *it's warm* (line
1) is made while the assistant looks for brochures. The client reformulates
her observation about temperature, beginning at line 9 after a 12-second
silence, and the sequence ends at line 17 when Melanie's computer accepts
her search request. In Extract 4 Mrs Hughes embarks on her comments
about warm weather at line 4 after a lengthy pause and the sequence ends at
line 10 when Elizabeth has to respond to a tour operator on the telephone.

As well as being moments of transition in terms of discourse structure,
these are liminal moments (cf. Goffman 1971; Urry 1990; Rampton 1997),
periods of relative indeterminacy when the normative constraints of travel
agency discourse are not fully operative. As Rampton argues, liminal moments are opportunities for social actors to re-evaluate and potentially reconstruct their participation in communicative events. For this reason they
tend to involve, in various ways, reflexivity. Weather talk is no exception,
and the comments offered about 'the weather' in each of Extracts 1–4 are
better described as comments about how environmental conditions impact
on speakers themselves and their activities. In Extract 1, Mrs Davies antici-
pates a degree of discomfort when she leaves and goes out into the wind; in
Extracts 2 and 3, participants comment how the heat is making the office
uncomfortable, and in Extract 4, that the weather is shockingly different
from the previous day. Weather talk introduces evaluative comments about
the circumstances of interaction and about participants' affective responses
to them. It breaks away from the achievement of transactional/instrumental
goals and focuses reflexively on details of how the transaction has been
contextualised and how it is being experienced.

The weather as shared experience

In transactional discourse speakers perform in their institutional roles – here
as client and assistant. In interstitial weather talk, they perform as individuals
and as 'co-experiencers of the weather' (cf. Ylänne-McEwen's [1996] analysis
of role-shifting as a pervasive characteristic of travel agency discourse). The
weather is, after all, likely to affect co-present talk participants simultaneously and more or less equally. To this extent it is an appropriate resource

for relational talk, talk which may achieve a degree of solidarity by emphasising shared feelings (positive politeness in Brown and Levinson's (1987) terms and psychological convergence in the terms of communication accommodation theory – Giles, Coupland and Coupland 1991). Even television weather forecasters have used this strategy, in Britain, to make comments of a 'purely interactional, social/entertaining nature', such as *combination of spring warmth and rain will send some of us scurrying into the garage to find our lawn mowers again* (Sifianou and Tzanne 1997: 364).

But, more specifically, speakers feel entitled to assume (at least within the UK context) that weather/environment conditions will draw similar, convergent responses from their listeners. Listeners will agree that a sunny day is 'nice', rain is 'horrid' or 'nasty', winter cold is 'bitter' and heat waves 'unbearable' (cf. Coupland and Coupland 1997). More dynamically and discursively, it is striking how speakers design their comments about the weather to elicit evaluative consensus. In each of Extracts 2, 3 and 4 the principal weather-evaluating utterance is structured as 'it's ADJECTIVE isn't it?' (Extract 2, line 14; Extract 3, line 1 [and probably line 10]; Extract 4, lines 5–6). The tag question with falling tone seeks confirmation of an uncontroversial claim, and each of the cited instances draws confirmation from the next speaker in the following turn. Mrs Davies in Extract 1 does not use the tagged format when she comments that *the wind is terrible* (line 9), and she does not get Emma's agreement in the next turn. But Emma, the assistant, does engage in similarly evaluative comments to Mrs Davies's. Her *mind you* (line 12) is not establishing a contrary claim about the wind, only posing a more positive formulation of its implications for Mrs Davies – 'looking on the bright side' of a minor trouble (see Coupland, Coupland and Giles 1991), but here in a formulaic and phatic manner. Matched laughter across speaker turns (lines 7 to 16) bolsters the degree of consensus achieved.

Sharing in weather talk, again as illustrated in the four extracts, can go well beyond consensual evaluation, towards intimacy. Through talking evaluatively about the weather, speakers can introduce details of their personal lives and feelings, and explore those of their addressees. The weather exchange in Extract 1 incorporates Mrs Davies's oblique self-presentation as being somehow disoriented (*I can't understand ((what's happening))*) and a brief portrayal of the drama of Mrs Davies's washing day. Extract 2 similarly touches on the theme of inability to cope (*don't know what to do really*). Extracts 2 and 4 involve mentioning of personal decisions about whether to wear *trousers* and wearing *no tights and just a blouse*.

This exchange is of course an exchange between females, and the intimacy being constructed here is based around rather stereotypically gendered themes. Many of the examples we will consider are open to similarly gendered readings. All of the assistants who appear in the data are female, as are all but two of the clients whose interactions we have extracted for this chapter, so gender-linked interpretations are possible at many points. But this characteristic of the data does not allow us to make any explicit comparisons along gender lines.

Weather mattering

Our interpretations so far have emphasised the social and relational utility of the weather as a topic of talk – its ubiquitous availability to speakers, and its ability to achieve consensus and sometimes intimacy. We have said that the weather is relevant to people transitionally. We have implied that, like all phatic talk in Malinowski's discussion of it, talk about the weather is ritualised and prefigured, and it may be that speakers actually have little investment in their comments about it, even when they voice strong affect. In the extracts we have considered so far, it is easy to believe that Mrs Davies may not actually find the wind as terrible as she claims, and that Mrs Hughes and Elizabeth may be overstating their 'shock' and 'amazement' at a cold day in late May. We might ask how relevant climatic conditions (heat, cold, rain, etc.) truly are to most people's daily experiences. Are people perhaps being rather systematically disingenuous in their weather evaluations, sacrificing veracity in the service of relational effect? (Brown and Levinson [1987] list exaggeration as one micro-strategy of positive politeness.) Perhaps weather states are generally of little consequence to us in our cocooned modern environments, despite our conventionally strongly valenced adjectives to describe it.

We could argue, along these same lines, that 'bad weather' is usually a relatively minor inconvenience, and 'good weather' a reason for only minor gratification. If we work in offices and live in houses, the weather is viewed from within relatively homogeneous and controlled environments. The weather is out there, relative to the spaces where 'things that matter' happen. Most modes of transport too, using glass, metal and heating/cooling devices, create controlled conditions very similar to home and office spaces. They create sealed 'environments' which insulate us from the broader 'environment'. That meteorological environment is made largely irrelevant by taken-for-granted technologies for indoor 'climate control'. This further suggests that we construe the weather as a rather distant and hardly significant dimension of randomness in our structured and managed lives. One hallmark of urban modernity is to have engineered spaces and devices for rendering the weather largely irrelevant to our routines – clothing, umbrellas, public transport, shopping malls, superstores, as well as some more extravagant instances, such as sports stadiums and pleasure domes with roofs. Isn't our exaggerated evaluation of weather states just 'hot air'?

Weather as a lifestyle constraint

The contrary case can be made, however, for weather mattering, and impacting on people's lifestyle choices and possibilities. Broadcast and print media are ardent propagators of the weather. This is probably because the weather is linked in many ways to our increasingly leisure-oriented lives, and to our bodily self-presentations in work and leisure.

In the travel agency encounter transcribed as Extract 5, the primary transactional function is for a client, Mrs Taylor, to collect her tickets. Much of the talk is filled out around issues of weather and clothing.

Extract 5

1996C091 The client is collecting tickets for her Scandinavian holiday. It is raining heavily outside. The client comes in and approaches the assistant's desk; recorded in late May.

```
     Mrs Taylor:  oh dear oh dear what a day!
     Bethan:      awful isn't it!
                        [
     Mrs Taylor:              that's right my name's Veronica Taylor and I've come to
                  collect tickets
                                [
 5   Bethan:                   all right (2.0) let's have a look
(Bethan goes to fetch tickets) (65.0)
     Bethan:      it's here in the ((3 sylls)) (slight laugh)
     Mrs Taylor: yes
     Bethan:      looking forward to it?
10   Mrs Taylor: oh gosh yes I'm trying to think what to pack ( . ) when you have this sort of
                  weather it puts you off (laughs)
     Bethan:      it's terrible isn't it I think you need one suitcase for the summer clothes and
                  then one suitcase for the winter clothes
     Mrs Taylor: (smiling) oh dear
15   Bethan:      (quietly) that's probably the best (louder) what you need to do is er to sign the
                  bottom of that . . .
(4.5 minutes later) (Bethan is writing the ticket)
     Mrs Taylor: it's very difficult to know what to take though because as I say er everywhere
                  seems to have had atypical weather ( . ) I've had friends
20                who've just come back from Turkey and they were cold and the Turkish people
                  there were saying we've never had this sort of=
                                     [              ]
     Bethan:                         ((it's funny though))
     Mrs Taylor: =cold in in you know May and em so I haven't ((dear oh dear))
                                [    ]
     Bethan:                    (slight laugh) oh yeah
25   Bethan:      don't really know what to do for the best
                                                          [
     Mrs Taylor:                                          yeah ( . ) take layers
     Bethan:       ˙ mm
     Mrs Taylor: two thin jumpers so that one jumper can go on top of the other one (laughs)
```

Bethan:	and the plastic mac and er (.) it'll probably be boiling when you=

```
                                    [ ]                              [
30 Mrs Taylor:                      oh yes                          that's=
   Bethan:      =get over there
   Mrs Taylor:  =right that's why I've got my plastic mac here
   Bethan:      right there we go
   Mrs Taylor:  good=
35 Bethan:      =all done
```

The first spoken exchange involves the client commenting on 'bad weather' and the assistant's endorsement of the evaluation. We can call *what a day!* (line 1) a *conventional weather focuser*. A speaker uses it to signal a strong affective evaluation of the weather (supported here by the *oh dear*s, encoding a negative appraisal) which is fleshed out semantically by the listener's appreciation of the respect in which the weather is extreme – hot, cold, foggy or, in this case, wet. The exchange establishes a degree of solidarity between participants – they orientate together to the weather and express a shared evaluation of it. The exchange obviously also opens the encounter (Laver's 'initiatory function' – see 1975; 1981), allows participants access to each other's identities and stances (Laver's 'exploratory function'), and forestalls the potential threat of non-talk (Laver's 'propitiatory function'). Speakers, even in this service encounter setting, are able to embark on talk by constructing a frame in which institutional roles are less salient than personal roles, as we noted above. This frame shifts in the following two turns (lines 3–5) where the institutional roles of client and assistant become operative. Specifically, Mrs Taylor announces her name and her goal for the encounter in institutionally relevant terms: she mentions collecting tickets, which is a familiar stage in the institutional procedure of booking a holiday. At this point, arguably, talk ceases to be 'small'.

As happens in many of the encounters in the two data sets, however, Bethan's question at line 9 reinstates the more personally orientated frame. It can be assumed by both participants that an assistant (in her institutional role) does not need to know whether a client (in her complementary institutional role) is looking forward to the holiday at the centre of their transaction. We can also assume that the assistant has no professional interest in this, because the transaction, in a legalistic sense, has already been completed. By implication, Bethan's line 9 question must be heard outside of the institutional frame. The personal details that Mrs Taylor offers in response, and her reinstating of the weather topic at line 10, are consistent with the frame-shift Bethan has triggered. Clothes, suitcases and packing preferences for variable weather seem to be themes more amenable to personal than professional judgement. Better evidence than our own judgement of thematic appropriateness is the sequential arrangement of talk at this point. The speakers produce multiple endorsements and elaborations of each other's comments in the interaction up to line 15 and again some minutes later, from line 18 up to the encounter's closing sequence (lines 33–6). The utterances *oh gosh yes* (line 10), *it's terrible isn't it* (line 12) and *that's probably the best* (line 16) all have retrospective reference and express agreement and mutual support. The smile (at line 14) and the repeated laughter (marked at lines 11, 24 and 28) again index support and shared experience, as forms of positive politeness. All of this talk clearly relates to travel, which is Bethan's professional domain, but Bethan's alignment to the topics in this sequence is a layperson's. Participants manufacture a social consensus in working out a shared response to a weather issue. They move towards intimacy in the detail of their accounts (e.g. in talk about how many jumpers to take, and about their inability to decide, and perhaps via an element of reflexive parody in mentioning the stereotypical tourist's *plastic mac*).

This weather talk, like the opening exchange of the encounter, deserves in one sense to be labelled small talk, at least in relation to the (few elements of) transactionally focused talk in this encounter. As we have suggested, the assistant has repositioned (de-professionalised) herself by constructing the personal frame. The weather and packing talk is almost infinitely extensible, unlike the bounded and structured non-verbal and verbal stages of the transaction itself (the institutional procedure of giving, receipting and collecting tickets).

Of course, the weather exchanges are not irrelevant to the transactional dimension of the encounter, because Bethan's 'personal' style may well help sell the next holiday. Business reputedly thrives on 'niceness' and it is ultimately impossible to separate 'customer relations' from the instrumental goals of selling. But our point about 'mattering' here is that, in the personal frame, the weather seems to be occasioning dilemmas and decisions which do genuinely engage these speakers. They claim, at least, that *when you have this sort of weather it puts you off* (lines 10–11, albeit mitigated by following laughter), *it's terrible* (line 12), *it's very difficult to know what to take* (line 18). As we mentioned earlier, we have no way of evaluating participants' actual commitment to these concerns, and the conversational key is certainly not fully serious (cf. our comment, above, about the *plastic mac*). But they sustain an interaction centred on these themes and represent them as recurrent concerns.

Certainly this is not desemanticised, phatic weather talk in the Malinowski sense. It is better described as 'relational travel talk' orienting to travellers' concerns about being 'suitably dressed' for the multiple climates that modern travel places around them. Knowing *what to do for the best* (line 25) here includes selecting clothes for climates, clothes from different usage categories (*the summer clothes* and *the winter clothes* – lines 12–13). This talk identifies what we might think of as a semi-technical competence associated with modern travel, proposing solutions to a recurrent difficulty of leisure travel. In line with Urry's, Featherstone's (e.g. 1991) and others' critique of how leisure is nowadays socially constituted, these exchanges represent leisure/travel as a 'challenge' and a 'task' – the lexicon of work more than of enjoyment.

Weather as a commodity

There is one pervasive manner in which weather talk in our data operates outside the domain of small talk. This is when the weather is represented as a saleable commodity, when clients and assistants attach commercial value to the weather as part of the holiday packages they are selling and buying. Extracts 6, 7 and 8 illustrate the marketised discourse of weather that abounds in travel agencies.

Extract 6

1996C044/C045 The clients have come to enquire about the price of a flydrive holiday to Florida; two minutes into the conversation; recorded in mid May.

	Cathy:	the cheapest one we've got was two forty nine today
.		
.		(Clients and Cathy talk about prices on Ceefax) (4.0)
.		
	Cathy:	any particular date in June?
	Mr Lane:	((no))
		(Cathy typing)
5	Cathy:	two weeks?
	Mr Lane:	er is it possible to extend it ((would it be)) possible to extend it to three?
	Cathy:	((I'll find out now for you))
(20.0)		(Cathy typing)
	Mr Lane:	is it so cheap at the moment because of the exchange rate?
10	Cathy:	er yeah because it's really out of season at the moment as well
	Mr Lane:	it's <u>out</u> of season
	Cathy:	well it's not peak season (.) so they tend to reduce their
	Mr Lane:	what's the weather like then?
	Cathy:	it's very warm it's actually er (.) May and June are probably the nicest time to
15		go because it doesn't get humid you know I mean July August is very very humid very humid out there
(5.0)		(Cathy typing)
	Mr Lane:	so ((winter is the best time do)) you reckon?
	Cathy:	er no I was out there in the summer I went out there August
(3.0)		
20	Mr Lane:	that's the trouble isn't it all the exotic locations for <u>us</u> are in the wrong time of year ((probably))
		[
	Cathy:	yeah (laughs)
	Mr Lane:	if you're ready to go on holiday everybody else is in the winter
		[ ]
	Cathy:	that's right yeah
(17.0)		
25	Cathy:	the cheapest one shown up on our screen is two hundred and seventy nine pound it's on the sixth of June (.) that's a flydrive but it's Orlando

Extract 7

1977C039 The client and the assistant have been discussing various holiday destinations. Sue is commenting on the merits of Majorca; recorded in September.

```
      Mrs Evans:  . . . the er beaches are very nice and it's not too commercialised
      Sue:        no not if you go up the north
      Mrs Evans:  yes
      Sue:        and they're much nicer beaches than Ibiza
                                    [
  5   Mrs Evans:                        and what kind of what kind of temperatures w
                  will we find in May?
                                    [
      Sue:                            be quite nice in May very nice it'll be about
                                              [ ]              [
      Mrs Evans:                              um             sunbathing?
      Sue:        oh gosh yes it'll be in the 70s in the in May be very nice
                                                            [
 10   Mrs Evans:                                                yes it's one reason
                  we don't want to leave it s too much later cos it'd be too hot for the=
                                              [
      Sue:                                    cos it'd be too hot then be nice in=
      Mrs Evans:  =children
 15   Sue:        =May though warm enough to you perhaps you need a cardigan at night but
                  it'd be warm enough during the day to sunbathe
      Mrs Evans:  and er what about the other Greek islands rather than you mentioned Corfu
```

Extract 8

1996C099 Opening of an encounter in which the client has come to enquire about late deals; recorded in late May.

```
      Bethan:    hi!
      Mr Banks:  hello! ( . ) I'm looking now don't know if there's any offers or anything for
                 one week for two people on either the eleventh twelfth or thirteen of June
      Bethan:    anywhere in particular?
  5   Mr Banks:  anywhere that's warm
      Bethan:    (laughs)
      Mr Banks:  better than here ( . ) erm no I've got a very open mind on it ( . ) I'd like to fly
                 from Bristol Birmingham or Cardiff that's the only thing
(5 minutes later in the interaction)
 10   Bethan:    what about Greece?
      Mr Banks:  yeah! don't mind is it very hot ((at the moment))?
      Bethan:    it's not going to be extremely hot
      Mr Banks:  no
      Bethan:    sort of the season is really sort of picking up (1.0) the end of May
 15              er is the start of their season really erm
                                              [   ]
      Mr Banks:                               mm
      Mr Banks:  so it's not going to be sort of a hundred and ten in the shade ((perhaps))?
                                                                            [
      Bethan:                                                               no
```

Mr Banks: ((I don't mind then))
(4.0)
20   Mr Banks: I'm surprised at how little there is
      Bethan: we've all been rushed off our feet here it's been crazy (.) sort of especially
                  when the weather sort of like started picking up over <u>here</u>
      Mr Banks: everybody thinks about going <u>abroad</u>=
      Bethan: =yeah and well it's been (.) crazy and (.) today and yesterday was s sort of
25   the quietest days you had in a long time
      Mr Banks: ((ghaw)) yesterday (laughs)
      Bethan: ((well)) everybody was too sort of frightened to come out (slight
                  laugh) weren't they the rain was just lashing down
      Mr Banks: I drove down to Birmingham yesterday morning (.) God I had to follow the
30   storm all the way up
      Bethan: incredible wasn't it
(10.0) (Bethan typing)
      Mr Banks: mm I just have to take those [computer printouts of holiday options] and
                  have a chat about it

There is systematic inter-linkage of the concepts of weather, time/season, value and demand in the speakers' evaluation of holiday destinations in these Extracts, with costs explicitly mentioned in Extract 6 (lines 1, 9 and 25). Low price and 'good weather' are the fundamental positives here, with convenience (of time and place) also referred to. The negotiations involve establishing the best available trade-offs between cost and weather. In these three extracts, 'good weather' in the resorts is represented, for example, by *very warm, in the 70s, warm enough* and *warm*, and 'bad weather' by *very humid, too hot for the children, extremely hot* and *sort of a hundred and ten in the shade.* Clients are buying weather they consider 'nice' (e.g. Extract 6, line 14; Extract 7, line 7) in relation to cost and convenience.

There are several distinctive lexico-grammatical patterns in the marketised representation of weather. The concept of *out of season* (Extract 6, lines 10 and 11) formalises the relationship of weather to money – the period when costs fall because of low convenience or less desirable weather. In fact, it is only in this marketised domain that 'the weather' is regularly lexicalised/nominalised as *the weather* (Extract 6, line 13; Extract 8, line 22), along with *temperatures* (Extract 7, line 5), as opposed to the conventional form with 'dummy "it"' – 'it's hot', etc. The frequent relativising of temperature assessments ('warm enough', 'too hot', etc.) indicates their commodification. The weather, and especially temperature, is being rather literally valued as a key attribute of the available product. There are common expressions such as those with *got* which express prospective purchasers' control and ownership of the weather. One example is when an assistant advises avoiding a particular time of year on the grounds that *you haven't got the weather then* (from the 1977 corpus, client 40 – not extracted here), meaning that the weather will not be warm. Clients sometimes say that they have open preferences for holiday destinations, except in respect of the weather. For example, again in the 1977 corpus (client 41 – not extracted here) when the client says *I don't mind where I go as long as it's sunny.*

With the guidance of travel agency assistants, clients are manipulating the variables of money, weather and convenience to construct and control the future experiences of their package holidays, much as they select a grade of hotel or a resort with specific facilities. In fact, weather is redefined as a tourist facility, indexed through bar-charts in travel brochures showing hours of sunshine per day by month in different resorts.[2]

Limits on space prevent us developing a more detailed account of different participants' contributions to the commodification of the weather. On the whole, as we have suggested, weather commodification is contained within transactional talk, where clients articulate their wants (e.g. in the 1977 corpus, client 40 says *that's what I need the sun*) and assistants offer expert advice on the characteristics of particular resorts and deals. On occasions, however, assistants are invited to give accounts from their personal experiences, rather than from their professional knowledge. Client 10 in the 1977 corpus elicits information about temperatures and asks *have you been there* [to Toronto] *in June?* In response, the assistant provides information relayed to her by a friend: *P went . . . it wasn't that hot* (and cf. Cathy's contributions from line 14 in Extract 6).

So again we see shading out of institutional and into personal talk, and even commodified discourses of weather take on the flavour of what we earlier called semi-technical laypersons' leisure and travel talk. The commercialisation of weather and of the natural environment has very clearly followed from the growth of the tourist institutions, as Urry (1990) has pointed out. But there are some indications in our data that commodified ways of talking about the weather and the environment are not strictly contained within the institutions themselves.

Overview: frames for weather talk

Weather talk in the travel agency data emerges as a functionally diverse and variably contextualised phenomenon, certainly not uniformly contained within the notion of phatic communion. Most obviously, on the basis of the data, we need to segregate Malinowski's phatic interpretation of weather talk from the commercially and transactionally relevant instances discussed in the previous section. In some modes of travel agency talk the weather is a fully commercialised theme. Clients buy and assistants sell weather as a core commodity of packaged holiday. Urry (1990) has documented the rise and fall of the British tourist resort in the twentieth century, and its fall owes much to the massive growth in the appeal of overseas package holidays in the post-war period, promoted and sold through travel agency businesses.

The discourses of commodified leisure audible in travel agency talk are part of a broad and powerful cultural value-set, probably represented across most of northern Europe. Climate, and particularly the sun, still define much of the appeal and marketability of the Mediterranean and other similar resorts. Ways of speaking evaluatively and comparatively about the weather (as we saw in Extracts 6 and 7) are central to this particular cultural ideology of leisure; the system of values for leisure which prioritises sun and heat (see Coupland and Coupland 1997; 2000) is expressed through these forms of talk. Weather in this frame is anything but 'small'; indeed it is big business.

Our comments on Extract 5 suggested that there is also an 'intermediate' frame for weather talk which, while linked to the tourist trade and commercialised travel, is focused more interpersonally than transactionally. In that extract we saw a client and an assistant engaging in sharing personal experiences about how to 'cope' with the weather in their decisions about clothes and packing. In this frame, weather achieves significance in relation to lifestyle choices. The Malinowskian account of small talk seems to be only partly relevant to instances like this one. Client and assistant certainly show no sense of commenting here on 'some supremely obvious state of things', as Malinowski suggested for phatic talk. On the contrary, they show high involvement and mutual support for each other's complaints and suggestions, even though there do appear to be conventional (and probably gender-linked) ways of speaking for achieving support. Just as leisure can itself no longer be thought of as the necessarily marked mode of social existence, relative to work as the unmarked category, we should be wary of assuming that talk involved in planning and responding to leisure travel is somehow insignificant. Malinowski's dictums have always carried the inappropriate implication that relational talk is peripheral and incidental, and of course the designation 'small talk' risks perpetuating this stance.

Extracts 1, 2, 3 and 4 come closest to illustrating Malinowski's phatic communion in the travel agency data, although we have emphasised the positive relational and procedural functions of weather talk here too. We argued that it is indeed appropriate to view many instances of weather talk in service encounters as being done 'in passing', outside the transactional movement of the speech events. But we would again resist equating 'non-transactional' with 'peripheral'. Weather talk has a clear structuring potential in these interactions. It provides a means for speakers to signal, for example, an orientation to concluding interaction, and partly through reinstating the relevance of the environment outside of the physical location where talk is currently set. To say that weather talk 'fills' spaces where transactional talk has been suspended is therefore to underestimate its role in the management of the encounter more generally.

Finally, we have made several comments about how weather talk can achieve relational intimacy, and of course this is central to Malinowski's sense of the term 'communion'. But the weather does not offer intimacy merely through the fact of talking together on a 'neutral' topic. We showed how, in the first four extracts, speakers make evaluations of the weather which they can expect to be consensually shared by addressees, because they are part of a conventional evaluative discourse in the speech community. We see this consensus being achieved, sequentially, in the data. More than this, comments about the weather seem, on the basis of the data, able to function as a bridge into intimate and self-disclosive talk, even in this relatively public and transactionally defined speaking situation. Through moving in and out of weather talk, speakers can reconstitute the normative expectations or frames on which their interactions are based. Weather talk, therefore, also has a metacommunicative potential.

In fact, many of these interpretations are presaged (as is often the case) in Goffman's theoretical commentaries on framing (1974) and public discourse (1971). He writes (1974: 573) that:

> The individual comes to doings as someone of particular biographical identity even while he appears in the trappings of a particular social role. The manner in which the role is performed will allow for some 'expression' of personal identity, of matters that can be attributed to something that is more embracing and enduring than the current role performance and even the role itself... There is a relation between person and role. But the relationship answers to the interactive system – to the frame – in which the role is performed and the self of the performer is glimpsed.

This is a perceptive claim, but it is also, relative to our data, empirically accurate regarding the management of weather talk. In travel agencies, where weather partly defines the commercial centrepiece of business transactions, weather talk is also a resource for speakers to move out of their institutional roles and to glimpse each other as individuals.

Appendix

( )	non-verbal, paralinguistic, prosodic and contextual information
(( ))	unintelligible or uncertain transcription
under<u>lined</u> syllables	unusually heavily stressed syllables
[	simultaneously starting talk
[ ]	overlapping talk
(.)	short pause (half a second or less)
(2.0)	longer pause, in seconds
=	contiguous utterances; also one speaker's turn as continuing across lines of transcript

...	words omitted from transcript
.	
.	
.	lines omitted from transcript
um, mm, er, erm, oh	filled pauses, hesitations or exclamations
?	speech act having the illocutionary force of eliciting information; also rising intonation
!	emphatic utterances

Notes

1. Coupland's recordings were made for the analysis of phonological variation in workplace settings; Ylänne-McEwen's data were analysed for politeness and relational processes. Full details of the recording techniques, demographic characteristics of assistants and clients, ethical considerations and so on are available in Coupland (1988) and Ylänne-McEwen (1996).
2. Dann (1996) identifies the heliocentrism of contemporary tourism, which is nevertheless a relatively recent phenomenon. Getting a sun tan, for example, was not considered desirable until the 1920s (see also Urry 1990). Coupland and Coupland (1997) comment on the hedonism implicit in the 'traditional' discourse of sun-use, and contrast this discourse with other, more ascetic forms of body culture.

References

Brown, Penelope and Levinson, Stephen C. (1987) *Politeness: Some Universals of Language Usage*. Cambridge: Cambridge University Press.

Coupland, Nikolas (1988) *Dialect in Use*. Cardiff: University of Wales Press.

Coupland, Nikolas and Coupland, Justine (1997) Bodies, Beaches and Burn-times: 'Environmentalism' and its Discursive Competitors. *Discourse and Society*, 8/1: 7–25.

Coupland, Nikolas and Coupland, Justine (2000) Selling control: Ideological dilemmas of sun, risk and the body. In Stuart Allan, Barbara Adam and Cynthia Carter (eds) *The Media Politics of Environmental Risks*. London: UCL Press.

Coupland, Nikolas, Coupland, Justine and Giles, Howard (1991) *Language, Society and the Elderly. Discourse, Identity and Ageing*. Oxford: Blackwell.

Dann, Graham M. S. (1996) *The Language of Tourism: A Sociolinguistic Perspective*. Wallingford, Oxon: CAB International.

Featherstone, Mike (1991) The Body in Consumer Culture. In Mike Featherstone, Mike Hepworth and Bryan S. Turner (eds) *The Body: Social Process and Cultural Theory*. London: Sage, 170–96.

Giles, Howard, Coupland, Justine and Coupland, Nikolas (eds) (1991) *Contexts of Accommodation: Developments in Applied Sociolinguistics*. Cambridge: Cambridge University Press.

Goffman, Erving (1971) *Relations in Public: Microstudies of the Public Order*. London: Allen Lane/Penguin.

Goffman, Erving (1974) *Frame Analysis*. Harmondsworth: Penguin.

Guendouzi, Jacqui (1997) *Negotiating Socialized Gender Identity in Women's Time-out Talk*. Unpublished PhD Thesis. University of Wales, Cardiff.

Laver, John (1975) Communicative Functions of Phatic Communion. In Adam Kendon, Richard M. Harris and Mary Ritchie Kay (eds) *Organization of Behavior in Face-to-Face Interaction*. The Hague: Mouton, 215–38.

Laver, John (1981) Linguistic Routines and Politeness in Greeting and Parting. In Florian Coulmas (ed.) *Conversational Routine: Explorations in Standardized Communication Situations and Prepatterned Speech*. The Hague: Mouton, 289–304.

Levinson, Stephen (1979/1992) Activity Types and Language. *Linguistics* 17, 356–99. Reprinted in Paul Drew and John Heritage (eds) (1992) *Talk at Work: Interaction in Institutional Settings*. Cambridge: Cambridge University Press, 66–100.

Malinowski, Bronislaw (1923) The Problem of Meaning in Primitive Languages. In C. K. Ogden and I. A. Richards (eds) *The Meaning of Meaning*. London: Routledge and Kegan Paul, 296–336.

Malinowski, Bronislaw (1923/1972) Phatic Communion. In John Laver and Sandy Hutcheson (eds) *Communication in Face-to-Face Interaction*. Harmondsworth: Penguin, 146–52.

Rampton, Ben (1997) Sociolinguistics and Cultural Studies: New Ethnicities, Liminality and Interaction. CALR Occasional Papers, no. 4. Centre for Applied Linguistic Research, Thames Valley University, London.

Robinson, W. Peter (1972) *Language and Social Behaviour*. Harmondsworth, Penguin Books.

Robinson, W. Peter (1985) Social Psychology and Discourse. In Teun A. van Dijk (ed.) *Handbook of Discourse Analysis*, vol. 1. London: Academic Press, 107–44.

Romaine, Suzanne (1994) *Language in Society*. Oxford: Oxford University Press.

Schegloff, Emanuel and Sacks, Harvey (1999) Opening up closings. In Adam Jaworski and Nikolas Coupland (eds) *The Discourse Reader*. London: Routledge, 263–74. (Originally published in *Semiotica*, 1974.)

Sifianou, Maria and Tzanne, Angeliki (1997) 'Lovely day, isn't it?': Weather Forecasts in Their Socio–Cultural Context. In Emilia Ribeiro Pedro (ed.) *Proceedings of the First International Conference on Discourse Analysis, University of Lisbon, 17–19 June 1996*. Lisbon: Colibri Editions and Portuguese Linguistics Association, 357–66.

Tannen, Deborah (1993) What's in a Frame? In Deborah Tannen (ed.) *Framing in Discourse*. New York: Oxford University Press, 14–56.

Tracy, Karen and Coupland, Nikolas (1990) *Multiple Goals in Discourse*. Clevedon: Multilingual Matters.

Urry, John (1990) *The Tourist Gaze: Leisure and Travel in Contemporary Societies*. London: Sage.

Ylänne-McEwen, Virpi (1996) *Relational Processes within a Transactional Setting: An Investigation of Travel Agency Discourse*. Unpublished PhD Thesis, University of Wales, Cardiff.

7

Social rituals, formulaic speech and small talk at the supermarket checkout
Koenraad Kuiper and Marie Flindall

Be not afeard; the isle is full of noises,
Sounds, and sweet airs, that give delight, and hurt not.

WILLIAM SHAKESPEARE, THE TEMPEST

1 Setting the theoretical scene[1]

It is sometimes assumed both by speakers and in the research literature that, once one has acquired a natural language, speaking it is essentially a way of implementing the knowledge of the language one has through a set of performance mechanisms which are essentially psycholinguistic (Chomsky 1986; Levelt 1989). However, it is clear from many studies that communicative competence involves more than the implementation of an internalised grammar in linguistic performance. A number of theorists have shown that linguistic performance must be contextually situated and have proposed generalised sets of parameters of situational constraint to permit contextual features to be described. These contextual features have the role of controlling or influencing aspects of linguistic performance (using that term in the Chomskian sense), e.g. Biber 1994; Crystal and Davy 1969; Hymes 1968.

However, such approaches do little to indicate the specific ways in which discourse is situated within a culture, and a culture within discourse. It is our belief that ethnographies of speaking become more valuable as they focus more closely on small-scale socio–cultural contexts and examine the language used there. Take, for example, newspaper discourse. One might write a generalised ethnography for newspapers looking at them within the domain of public writing. But within such an already constrained medium as a newspaper there are many genres each of which has its own rules and regularities. Classified advertisements, weather reports and forecasts, death notices, sports reports, cricket scoreboard summaries, stock market reports, obituaries, reports of house fires are all governed by quite restrictive conventions of what can be written and how it can be written. For instance, the phrase *damping down hotspots* can only be used near the end of a report on a fire. Each genre in turn is linked to its own cultural niche where it performs a socially sanctioned role. The newspaper turns out to be just an umbrella for such genres locating each discourse in its own socio–cultural niche. On this view, little of use can be said about newspapers in general as a way of showing how discourse is constrained and the way it is culturally located.

On the basis of such a view, it follows that to become a native speaker one must come to command, actively or passively, a very large number of such varieties of the language one has acquired. That command is a direct measure of one's enculturation (Herdt 1980: 57–69). It is easy to test this empirically by coming upon varieties of one's own language one does not know. To understand the personal advertisements in the *New York Times*, for instance, requires two things. One must know the linguistic code in which they are written, which includes a sizeable number of acronyms. One must also be aware of the cultural context within which these advertisements function as ways of commodifying the self (Thorne and Coupland 1998). How that is done and perceived differs from place to place. To advertise oneself in New York City is not the same activity as in Wales, or Christchurch, New Zealand. We, the authors of this chapter, are not native speakers of the New York personal advertisements variety of English. In the only sense that really counts, we do not understand this variety of our language.

If one thinks in this way about native speaker communicative competence, it becomes clear that there is little room for free and unconstrained linguistic performance in many situations. Perhaps conversations, which have taken a significant role in discourse analysis, are actually rather unusual forms of linguistic performance in being relatively unconstrained. In other words we do not concur with the view that 'conversation is the predominant medium of interaction in the social world' (Drew and Heritage 1992: 19). It may be one way to interact socially with others but there are other varieties of speech with are also typical of human performance. It may be that language use is often a 'formal procedure of a communicative but arbitrary kind, having the effect of regularising a social situation' (Firth 1972: 3). This is how Raymond Firth defines a ritual. Rituals can be seen as being essentially sequential acts which are socially significant (Kuiper 1996: 6). Some of these are claimed to be entirely without meaning, for example, the performance of Hindu religious ritual (Staal 1990). Some secular rituals such as auctions are clearly meaningful (Smith 1989). In attempting to understand each ritual in a culture one is not only 'doing linguistics' one is also 'doing anthropology'.

If social factors create powerful limitations on what can be said and how it can be said, it is likely that performing in a linguistically free and unconstrained way in many situations will result in social ostracism or worse – incarceration in a prison or psychiatric hospital. One has only to look at the results of directing obscenities at a police officer to realise that this is not just possible but highly likely. Saying, apparently genuinely, 'good-bye' when one meets people, one is likely to have one's state of sanity questioned.

The linguistic constraints on native speakers are often quite specific, taking the form of being required to know an actual form of words, an idiom or a formula or set of formulae which perform an essential cultural role, along with the norms for using such expressions. Apologies are a case in point. English has a set of formulae for apologising. To be a native apologiser in English, one must know at least some of these formulae and the situations in which one needs to use them. Not using them in such a situation or using a non-formulaic utterance can create long-term social problems (Ferguson 1976). For instance, if one is required to apologise having transgressed against someone and says to that person *Never mind* instead of *I'm sorry* then one may risk various consequences ranging from ostracism to physical violence.

If we think of the social purposes for which formulaic speech is required or desirable, they are quite extensive. They range from the very general to the highly specific, such as: greeting someone, e.g. 'How are you doing?'; astonishment, e.g. 'You don't say?'; sympathy, e.g. 'I really am terribly sorry'; or selling a lot at auction, e.g. 'Sold to number eighty-seven'.

Looking at language in this way is not new. It was the view of Malinowski (1922). To see ourselves in this way requires us to look at ourselves as an ethnographer from another speech community might. Then we would see how situated most of our speech is and how comparatively little room for linguistic manoeuvre there sometimes is.

In what follows we examine the situation of supermarket checkout operators who are a situation where they perform rituals of encounter (Firth 1972; Laver 1981; Salmond 1976) in the form of service encounters (Merritt 1976; Merritt 1977).

> By a service encounter I mean an instance of face-to-face interaction between a server who is 'officially posted' in some service area and a customer who is present in that service area, that interaction being oriented to the satisfaction of the customer's presumed desire for service and the server's obligation to provide that service.
>
> (Merritt 1976: 321)

The encounter ritual takes the linguistic form of a set of opening and closing moves, and the central section involves a set of moves for payment to be made by the customer. Since these service encounters are in the nature of 'ritual interchanges' (Goffman 1967), checkout operators utilise a formulaic speech genre for them.

We have shown previously (Kuiper 1996) that central to any formulaic tradition are discourse structure rules and an inventory of formulae. That being the case different performers in a tradition can utilise the tradition in their own ways to create a persona within the tradition which will manifest itself in the different ways that the discourse structure rules and formulaic inventory are used. It is our intention in what follows to document both the tradition and the individual linguistic personae of a group of supermarket checkout operators at two supermarkets in Christchurch, New Zealand.[2]

In New Zealand, checkout operators can and do build on the opening routine to begin a rather more free form of talk about matters which have nothing to do with the functions they are performing, namely checking out items through the barcode scanner, accepting payment for goods and so on. They can talk, for example, about the weather, their customers' pets or what they hope to do in the weekend. When this happens we have a form of institutional talk which is not relevant, at least directly, to the task at hand.

This kind of interchange might be seen as 'small talk', namely,

> discourse operating in a limited domain and dislocated from practical action and what Malinowski thought of as 'purposive activities' which include hunting, tilling the soil, and war in 'primitive' societies.
>
> (Coupland, Coupland, and Robinson 1992: 208)

At the supermarket checkout talk about the weather or one's weekend activities has no direct practical use other than as a form of social intercourse.

The encounter's openings and closings between operator and customer can also be viewed as a kind of small talk since only the exchange section dealing with payment for groceries is fully functional and there are other societies where verbal greetings and partings are much rarer at the supermarket. For example, in the Netherlands in one supermarket frequented for a period by the first author, the only thing normally said by the checkout operators was the formula *Spaart u airmiles?*, 'Are you saving airmiles?'. The rest of the transaction was accomplished in silence.

We will later have more to say on just what the purpose of these openings and closings are and how 'genuine' they are.

2   Setting the empirical scene

2.1   Macro socio–cultural aspects

In supermarkets the grocer has been replaced by a number of more specialised employees who perform the tasks which the grocer used to do by him- or herself or along with an assistant or two. The checkout operator is one of these more specialised staff. Checkout operators perform the following routine tasks. They tally the prices of the items selected by the customer and accept payment for the goods. They also in many cases pack the goods. This specialisation involves a transfer of labour costs from the retailer to the consumer. First the consumer selects the goods rather than asking the retailer to select them. The consumer places the goods on the 'counter'. This leaves much less time for speech than the protracted interaction between the old-time grocer and his or her customers who had time to talk over the merits of various products not to mention local news. The action at the checkout is reduced to a repetitive routine like that of an assembly line. However, in New Zealand, it is normally accompanied by a minimal amount of talk dealing with payment for the goods. Whenever one makes face-to-face payments, the ritual of exchange functions as the topic of such talk, the checkout operator being the agent for the retailer in accepting payment for goods and services purchased.[3]

Those who perform the tasks of checkout operator require training to handle the mechanics of the checkout such as the use of the cash register, the microphone used to call for assistance, the cashcard machine if there is one, and the barcode scanner which is now ubiquitous at (or, more correctly, in) checkouts. Such training is usually very brief, being of the order of an hour or two and a period of supervision thereafter. The interactions with customers are also brief, being of the order of a few minutes, with many customers being strangers.

In New Zealand the great majority of checkout operators are women, many of them young, many of them part-time. They are not infrequently either in secondary or tertiary education. Youth wage rates in New Zealand provide incentives for employers in retailing to employ young people where possible. If these young people are intelligent, so much the better.

2.2   Micro socio–cultural aspects

Let us look closely at what happens at the checkout. A small queue of shoppers is lined up at the checkout of a supermarket. As a customer enters the checkout lane, the customer comes potentially within view of the checkout operator behind the counter. Usually an earlier customer is being served at the time when the customer first begins to place his or her prospective purchases on a moving belt or counter. Normally the checkout operator does not acknowledge the presence of one customer until having farewelled the previous customer. Then he or she will make eye contact, however briefly, with the new customer and greet the customer: the opening linguistic move in the service encounter.

The actions which the checkout operators perform are almost entirely rule-governed. They begin by scanning each item on the checkout slide over the scanner. Occasionally items refuse to scan and are manually entered into the cash register using the barcode number wherever possible.[4] Items which are not barcoded have their price entered. Once all the items have been scanned the total is tallied by the cash register and the total is conveyed to the customer. The customer then pays in one of a number of ways; the goods are packed if they have not yet been packed and the customer leaves with his or her purchases.

A number of conditional steps have been left out of this description. For example, at most supermarkets in New Zealand cigarettes must be purchased at the checkout because of restrictions on their sale to minors. So, if the customer wants to purchase cigarettes, the checkout operator has a sub-routine to get them. Many supermarkets in NZ now sell alcoholic beverages. Again these cannot be sold to minors and so in some supermarkets the checkout operator must signal to the supervisor to gain approval to sell such products. Again this is a conditional sub-routine of the kind that says 'if reading a bottle or carton of alcoholic beverage into the barcode scanner, call for supervisor'. The various ways of exchanging money are also each governed by sub-routines. The checkout operator must find out if the customer wishes to pay by cash, cheque or plastic card. For each there is a specific routine to transact. At some supermarkets customers pack their own goods and they have two ways of doing so: they can use either boxes which are on a bench away from the checkout or they can use plastic bags which the checkout operator provides. Again there is a choicepoint here and a sub-routine to accompany it.

Besides this major routine and its many possible sub-routines, another routine is being transacted, a speech routine. The checkout operator and the customer meet each other at the checkout and after a short period of time take leave of each other. This routine has a beginning, middle and end like a conversation (Schegloff 1972; Schegloff and Sacks 1973). The beginning and end of conversations have a strong tendency to be formulaic because what needs to be done in them is a matter of social ritual.

We therefore have, at the checkout, people performing physical routines in the way they perform their checkout tasks and, potentially, linguistic rituals in conducting talk with the supermarket's customers (Coulmas 1981). This context for talk therefore provides a good testing ground for the prediction that routine actions which require routine speech tasks will have those routine speech tasks performed primarily using speech formulae. It also is an open question as to how those speech formulae, if they are used, come to be learned, given that there is little training of checkout operators for this aspect of their work.

3   Methodology

This study was undertaken in 1991 at two supermarkets from two different supermarket chains, in two different suburbs of Christchurch, New Zealand over a period of about a month. One was in a lower socio–economic suburb, the other in a higher socio–economic suburb. About two hundred interactions were collected as follows.[5] Nine checkout operators were recorded, two male and seven female. Not all are represented by the same number of interactions since our aim was to look mainly at the ritual elements of checkout speech.[6] Customers were informed of the project by a large notice at the beginning of the checkout aisle and informed that the other aisles were not fitted with recording equipment. After the recording sessions, the taped interactions were transcribed onto cards and thence onto computer. Given the aims of the study there was no attempt to control for social variables such as the age, socio–economic status or gender of the customers. Customers were recorded at random as they came through the checkout. We were interested in the formulaic inventory and discourse structure used by checkout operators, and recorded the customers to see how they contributed to the interaction, i.e. we were interested in the ritual aspects of the interactions rather than the sociolinguistic variables which accompanied them.

As usual in such circumstances the normal caveat about the effects of microphones on people who are being recorded may be entered. They are manifest on one or two interactions where the operator and customer discuss the business of being recorded and in one case how it is better to say as little as possible. Our intuitions (based on years of experience as a super-market shopper in the case of the first author and as checkout operator and supervisor in the case of the second author) tell us that much of the data is an accurate enough reflection of what goes on at the checkout when microphones are not present for the data to function as a starting point for the observations we shall be making about checkout speech.

4   What happens at the checkout: the tradition

As will be clear to all denizens of the supermarket the events at the checkout for any normal transaction constitute a finite system. In the normal course of events only certain things can happen and they happen in certain sequences and not others. That is not to say that unusual things cannot happen. It is just that they are not part of the routine. For example, an armed hold-up is not part of the routine but asking a checkout operator for a product one has not been able to find is a routine event, although not one that occurs with great frequency.

Talk at a Christchurch checkout normally begins with a greeting from the operator to the customer or, occasionally, with a greeting to the operator from the customer. The only times when greetings are omitted are when the customer pre-empts the greeting with a question. For example:

Extract 1[7]

1 Customer: Do you have today's paper?
2 Operator: No. We don't sell the paper. Sorry.

Not infrequently, even when the customer has pre-empted the greeting, the operator will return to it after the pre-emptive question has been dealt with.

Extract 2

1 Customer: Doing a swap?
2 Operator: Yes.
3 Operator: How are you?

In this latter extract the customer's first utterance is an enquiry about the obvious. One operator has just replaced another who has gone for a break. But the operator still greets the customer with 'How are you?' (line 3) after having answered the inquiry. Some customers, often older ones according to the observations of the second author, like to 'get in first' so as to indicate their preparedness to enter into a small talk phase as soon as possible.

Notwithstanding such pre-emptive moves by a customer the data suggests that the greeting by the operator is virtually obligatory.

More remarkable is the highly formulaic nature of these opening moves with 88 per cent (176/200) being generable by a single finite-state system.[8]

The greetings follow the rules for opening conversations of Schegloff (1972) and Smith (1991).[9] In many circumstances such as the telephone conversations used by Schegloff (1972), interlocutors must identify one another. At a checkout, participants omit identifying each other because their identities in so far as they have a bearing on the checkout conversation are

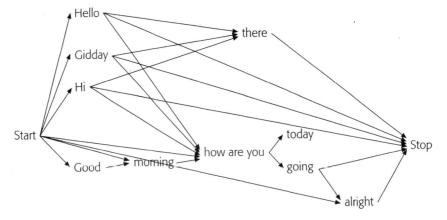

Figure 7.1   Greetings (starts plus information elicitation)

implicit. Operators wear name badges with their given names on them. Customers are seldom known to the operators and even when they are it is often not by name. Operators do not have to identify customers by name, as they would on the phone, since the person is standing in front of them. It also appears to be a convention of service encounters that one does not, as customer, identify oneself or get asked to do so by the person who is serving you. It is an interesting question why this should be the case.

'Once participants have identified each other, they must signal the start of the conversation' (Smith 1991: 50). This is often done by exchanging greetings. The typical opening words of supermarket greetings are words such as *Hi, Hello, Gidday, Good morning* and they are typical start formulae. Their function is to be the opening round in a verbal interaction and they are often one of an adjacency pair in symmetrical conversations. However, supermarket interchanges are not normally ones between equals and so in the majority of cases the start is uttered by the operator and in many cases the customer makes no reply to the start formula.

The start phase of a checkout interaction may be followed by a formula which is ambiguous. In some cases it is taken to be an information elicitation formula which aims 'to elicit information from the addressee' (Smith 1991: 64) and in other cases a formula elicitation formula in that it elicits not information but a formula in turn. In a majority of cases at the checkout there is one and only one such formula and it is *How are you (today)*? As Smith (1991: 64–5) indicates, following Firth (1972: 110) and Coupland *et al.* (1992), 'It is well-known to New Zealand speakers (and a source of confusion to non-native English speakers) that a response . . . may not be needed and, in fact, not even desired.' That certainly seems to be the case for some customers at the checkout since only some customers reply to the operator's information/formula elicitation formula (if there is one) at all. Of the 128 information/formula elicitation formulae, only 89 received replies. This is an unusual situation in that normally such formulae are part of an adjacency pair as Coupland *et al.* (1992) show.

There is a tendency in some cultures to feel that what is said by service staff during a 'start' phase of the kind of service encounter one has at the supermarket is insincere. At Disneyland, the smiling faces which constantly ask you how you are seem to be being friendly because Disneyland is a happy kingdom which trains all its staff (on pain of firing) to be ever cheerful. Certainly staff in many service situations are enjoined by the management to be friendly, cheerful and ever polite. It does not follow that all checkout operators are necessarily being insincere when they greet clients. In New Zealand we have the feeling (and that is all it can be) that most operators, given the transitory nature of their relationships with their customers, do want these to be genuine rather that superficial or artificial. In fact we feel that humans in general have this wish and that this desire will operate in tandem with the little training and exhortation there is for operators, in many cases, to create a genuine inquiry in the case of 'How are you today?'. It seems genuine in two ways, it is an opportunity for the operator to be positively polite and also creates an opportunity for the customer to begin a genuine conversation. If the formula 'how are you (today)?' was generally perceived as insincere, then it would be regarded as semantically empty having only pragmatic value as a move in a ritual. However, that it is not parsed as a semantically empty ritual move can be inferred from its capacity to function as the introductory move in a 'small talk' interaction where the customer responds to the inquiry as an information elicitation, i.e. by taking it literally.

At this point it is useful to distinguish between two kinds of talk that go on at the checkout: the matrix interchange which is obligatory, consisting of an opening, an exchange section and optionally a close, and the overlay 'small talk' which has the same opening but expands as the response to a perceived information elicitation. Many supermarket conversations have just a matrix interaction which is more or less functional and whose centre is transactional having to do with payment. However, if a reply to the information elicitation formula is forthcoming from the customer, it frequently signals that there will be overlay small talk as well. Of the 89 conversations in which the information elicitation received a reply, 70 lead to overlay talk. Thus only 19 elicited merely a formula by way of reply. There were only three overlay interchanges begun from a customer's initiative.

A reply by the customer to an information elicitation by the operator indicates that the customer is prepared for there to be more than a matrix interchange. It does not signal what the content of the overlay conversation will be as the following examples show:

Extract 3

1 O: Hi.
2 C: Morning.
3 O: How are you today?
4   You had a good week?
5 C: Yeh, very good, thank you.

Extract 4

1 O: And how are you today?
2 C: Good, thanks. It's nice and quiet this morning.
3 O: Yeah it is.
4 C: Well, I s'pose it might not be for you.

Extract 5

1 O: And how are you?
2 C: Good.

3 O: It's nice, that low salt margarine, isn't it? Have you
4   tried it?
5 C: ... low salt. I just picked it up ...
6 O: It's very – it's very nice.

There are a small number of checkout operators who go to more trouble to elicit an overlay conversation. One in particular has a series of formulae which she uses to break though to an unresponsive customer and she is frequently rewarded. She uses formulae such as *Have you had a good week?*, *How's your day been?* and *Glad for the change in the weather?* These information elicitations usually follow the more conventional *How are you (today)?* and by their greater specificity and lesser conventionality appear more genuine and spontaneous to the customer who is therefore under greater pressure to reply.

The topics for overlay talk, if there is any, tend to be selected from a small range, the weather being the most frequent. Other topics include: one of the customer's purchases which may be singled out for approbation, what the customer is going to do the rest of the day or weekend, what the operator is going to do the rest of the day. They are characteristically phatic (Malinowski 1922) and thus contrast with the matrix interchange which is functional in that its central content section deals with the exchange of money for goods purchased. Typical examples of overlay small talk are interchanges such as the following:

Extract 6

1 O: Hello. How are you?
2 C: Good, thanks. I've got all the goodies in there.
3 O: Oh, what've you got there? Fattening foods?
4 C: Yes, fattening foods.

Extract 7

1 O: Hi. How are you?
2   You had a good week?
3 C: S'pose so. Been alright. Glad the weather's come
4   right.
5 O: Yeah, 'bout time it did.
6 C: You're not wrong.

Extract 8

1 O: Hi, how are you today?
2 C: Good.
3 O: Have you had a good week?

4 C: Yep.
5 O: Survived the bad weather?
6 C: At least it's fine now, get the washing dry and the rest
7   of it.
8 O: Yeah.

Extract 9

1 O: Doing anything special for Easter?
2 C: No.
3 O: No.
4 O: You?
5 O: No – we've got friends coming from the North Island – so
6   – keep us pretty busy. Yes.

The overlay interchange, if there is one, normally occurs in the period between the time the operator starts checking the goods through the barcode reader until that is completed, at which point the exchange section of the matrix conversation must take place. In the absence of an overlay period of small talk everyone keeps silent until the exchange section of the interchange. On other occasions a short overlay conversation is followed by a period of silence until the barcode scanning is complete.

However, sometimes the overlay chat continues beyond the exchange section.

Extract 10

1 O: Hi, how are you?
2   Lovely day today.
3 C: Yes . . . you should be busy today.
4 O: Yes.
5 C: There's so many other shops open, though.
6 O: We were, um, very busy during the week.
7 C: Yes – oh, I think you'll always be busy . . . people still
8   eat, don't they?
9 O: Yes.
10 C: No matter what . . . what they still . . . taste food.
11 O: 's twenty-eight dollars eighty-five thanks
12   Doing anything special for Easter?
13 C: No, no . . .
14 O: No
15 C: . . . caravan. but . . . expensive . . .
16 O: Yeah, yeah. Twenty-eight, twenty-nine and one's thirty
17 C: . . . Doing up . . . house, fixing up the garden and things, you
18   know.

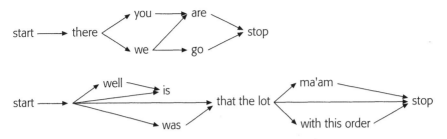

Figure 7.2   Introduction to exchange section formulae

19 O: Okay, well have a good weekend.
20   Thank you.

Not all the overlay small talk is on a single topic as Extract 10 shows with its four topics: a start on the weather (line 2), the business of the day for the checkout operator (lines 3–7), the fact that people have to eat (lines 7–8), and then what the customer is going to do for the Easter weekend (lines 12–18).

The start of the exchange section of the matrix interchange is sometimes signalled by a formula such as *Will that be all?* which indicates that the operator has tallied all the goods on the slide. Such formulae are also indirect requests for the customer to indicate whether they wish to purchase cigarettes. Occasionally the opening of this section may be signalled by a formula which merely indicates that the exchange section is about to start. For example, an operator might say *There we are* or *There we go*. One operator uses both.

The obligatory constituent of the exchange section is the operator's indication to the customer of the total value of the customer's purchases. This is always indicated by a formula.

The customer does not respond verbally to the cash call but provides payment in some form or other and the operator usually thanks the customer for it, again with a formula. If the customer uses a cashcard, the operator often asks whether the customer wishes to have any cash from the till along with paying for their purchases. Again this is done using a formula such as *Would you like any cash with that?*. The finite-state system which generates almost all the receipt of cash formulae is as follows:

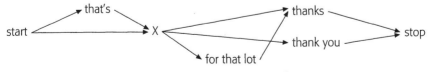

Figure 7.3   Cash-call formula

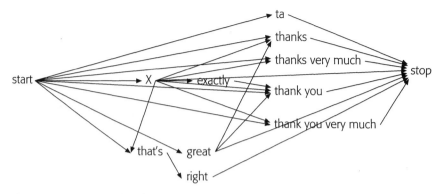

Figure 7.4 Receipt of cash formula

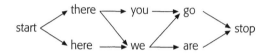

Figure 7.5 Introduction to change-counting formula

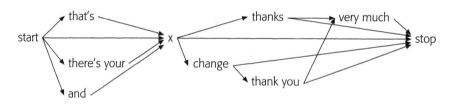

Figure 7.6 Change-counting formula

If there is change to be counted out, the operator then counts out the change and often again thanks the customer and again with a formula.

The exchange section is then complete and the customer leaves. But, following Schegloff and Sacks (1973), Smith (1991) suggests that departure also has a set of discourse constituents. Endings or leave-takings may start with back references to what has taken place earlier in the body of the interchange. Back references are normally 'thank you' formulae thanking the customer not for their money but for the whole transaction. They may also indicate that the transaction is complete by a formula such as *There you are*. This can mean that the operator thanks the customer four times; once when giving the total from the cash register, once when receiving the cash or card, once when counting out the change and a last *thank you* as a back reference to the whole transaction. There are times when the exchange section passes without a single reply from the customer as in the following interchange:

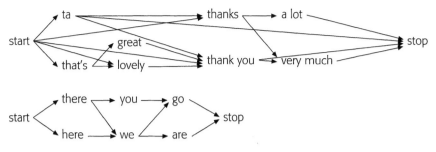

Figure 7.7   Back reference formulae

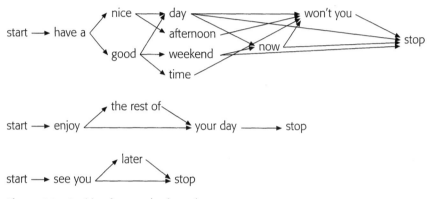

Figure 7.8   Positive face-stroke formulae

Extract 11

1 O: Is that the lot?
2   Twelve dollars fifteen, thank you.
3   Thank you very much.
4   There we are; seven dollars eighty-five change. Thank
5   you.
6   There we go, thank you.

This may again exemplify the strategy of not completing the adjacency pair which we remarked on earlier as a feature of some New Zealand English varieties, or it may reflect the service role of the operator and thus the customer's sense that speakers in such roles do not need always to be treated to bilateral courtesies.

A farewell may also contain positive face strokes (Brown and Levinson 1978) in which the operator wishes the customer well or, much less frequently, the customer wishes the operator well. *Have a nice day* is a typical version of such a formula.

Figure 7.9 Termination formula

Then, at the extreme end of the conversation, there may be a termination to parallel the introduction. *Bye*, or *bye*, *bye* are typical examples of such terminations.

It appears then that checkout operators avail themselves of a particular discourse structure for their matrix interchanges. This can be represented by a set of context-free rewrite rules (Scherzer 1974; Salmond 1976).[10]

Discourse structure of matrix conversation
Matrix interchange → Opening + Exchange + Close
Opening → (Start) + (Info./formula elicitation)
Exchange → Total + (Receipt) + (Change)
Close → (Back ref.) + (Positive face-stroke) + (Termination)

These rewrite rules generate, i.e. provide an explicit account of, how checkout speech formulae are used at each point in the discourse by indicating where the formulae may be used. Another way to see the rules is therefore as providing indices attached to each formula restricting where in a discourse sequence a formula may be used.

5   Checkout operator tradition and individual speech

The typical interchanges between customers and checkout operators look on the face of it as though they have little room for an individual operator to be different from others in that they are highly formulaic and the discourse structure of the matrix interchange is highly restrictive. In fact this is not the case. In checkout operator speech there is both a tradition and room for individual utilisation of that tradition. Let us begin by looking at the greeting. None of the operators uses every possible route through the greeting system. Each has his or her own preferred routes. It may be that these are a result of the relatively small sample but they are strongly suggestive of individuality. The finite-state diagrams in Figure 7.10 are the greeting routines of three different operators. To understand these diagrams one should compare the range of the possible formulae an operator might use and which are part of the checkout operator greeting tradition as given in Figure 7.1 with the range of formulae the particular operator uses as given in Figure 7.10.

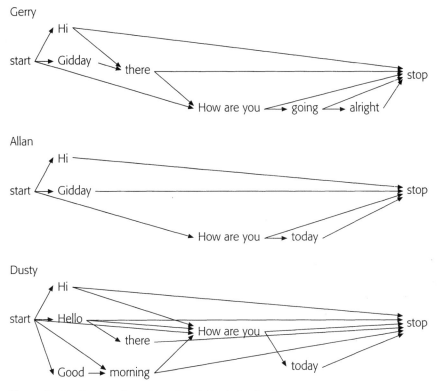

Figure 7.10 Greeting formulae of individual checkout operators

We could repeat this kind of filtering out of individual utilisation of the tradition for each phase of the matrix interchange but will take it that the above examples are indicative of how this can be done.

There are routes through the system in Figure 7.1 which do not appear in our data. For example, *Gidday, how are you today?* and *Good morning.* do not appear in the sample. However, we predict that operators can and will use such forms because that is the tradition on which they draw. It is likely that the only reason we have not recorded such greetings is that we have not collected enough data. In previous work on auctions Kuiper and Haggo (1984) found that subsequent recording 'safaris' usually found the 'missing' data and, normally, no formulae which were not generated by the finite-state diagrams. This is because formulaic speech is highly restricted, speakers utter the prescribed formulae, and little or nothing but the formulae in many contexts.

Not only that. Operators use particular tracks through their diagram with greater or lesser frequency and this pattern of preference creates an individual style. The frequency count for greetings generated by the finite state diagram in Figure 7.1 is given in Table 7.1.

Table 7.1 Greeting formulae used by each operator[11]

Greeting	Guy	Allan	Dusty	Leeanne	Gay	Elsie	Di	Shelly	Kris	Totals
How are you?	1:11%	5:31%	12:32%	5:38%	2:9%		1:5%	1:6%	2:9%	29
How are you today?		5:31%	5:13%		11:48%	4:24%	3:14%	1:6%	1:5%	30
How are you going?	1:11%									1
How are you going, alright?	1:11%									1
Alright?							1:5%			1
Hello.			2:5%	4:31%	6:26%	1:6%			3:14%	16
Hello there.			1:3%							1
Hello. How are you?			1:3%	1:8%					3	5
Hello. How are you today?							1:5%			1
Gidday		1:6%								1
Gidday. How are you?							1:5%			1
Gidday there. How are you going?	1:11%									1
Good morning. How are you?			4:11%							4
Hi	1:11%	5:31%	5:13%		2:9%		1:5%	1:6%		15
Hi there.	4:44%									4
Hi. How are you?			5:13%	3:23%	2:9%	11:65%	13:59%	8:50%	13:59%	55
Hi. How are you today?						1:6%	1:5%	4:25%		6
Morning.			3:8%							3
Morning. How are you today?								1:6%		1
Totals	9	16	38	13	23	17	22	16	22	176

Again similar tables can be constructed for each phase of the conversation. All operators are thus idiosyncratic in a limited kind of way. Many have formulae that they alone use. Some operators are clearly also much more flexible in their use of formulae than others. They use a greater range and they switch more frequently. The most creative in this regard is Dusty (D) who is an experienced operator and from North America. She goes to considerable lengths to farewell her customers sometimes using all three closing constituents such as *Thank you. Have a nice day. Bye bye* at the conclusion of a single interchange. She is also able to interpolate overlay small talk into a variety of niches. In one case, after a customer had found the supermarket to be out of her cat's favourite catfood, during and after the exchange section Dusty finishes with an enquiry about the cat (line 36), as a palliative to the customer's possible ill will at not having been able to purchase her cat's favourite catfood.

Extract 12

```
 1 O: Good morning.
 2 C: Morning.
 3 O: How are you?
 4 C: I'm fine, thanks.
 5 O: You look well. You look nice.¹²
 6 C: ... had – had ten days in hospital.
 7 O: Oh did you? You feeling better?
 8 C: I've had a new hip put in.
 9 O: Oh, well good for you. As – is – you going well
10     with it?
11 C: Yep.
12 O: Super.
13 C: Down to – ah – one crutch.
14 O: Good for you.
15 C: On my right side. Tell me, the Sheba pet food. You've
16     got beef cuts, beef and kidney, but no turkey in.
17     Turkey's the popular one.
18 O: Let me ask Murray for it – 'scuse me, Murray – in the
19     Sheba line of catfood will we be getting turkey?
20 M: We'd like to think so ... problems with the shipping ...
21     from America
22 C: I see you've got beef and kidney.
23     It's just come in – it was it's just come in ...
24 C: Well it must have, cos I didn't see it on Friday.
25 M: No ... only just arrived. In fact I didn't even realise
26     that myself.
27 C: Yeah well ...
28     So I wanted to buy turkey.
29 O: Yeah. Should be coming in very shortly. I'll know on
```

30   Tuesday
31 C: Okay, I'll go home and tell him.
32 O: Four dollars fifty, thanks.
33   Thanks.
34 C: Sorry.
35   . . . been out a lot . . .
36 O: That's your cat's favourite, is it?
37 C: Yes.
38 O: They all have their favourites.
39 C: . . . might be other cats also like it.
40 O: That's why – we're out.
41 C: Yeah. Thank you.
42   Okay.

The least flexible of the operators is Elsie (E) who had only been a checkout operator for a few days. Her small greeting range is matched by small ranges of formulae in every other part of the discourse structure of the checkout routine.

Most operators have strong modal preferences for a particular form and only use other tracks through their system occasionally. Allan and Guy occasionally use the stereotypically male greeting *Gidday* whereas only one of the women operators uses it and then only once.[13]

Each operator has the equivalent of a signature in the tracks through the general formulae of the tradition each chooses to use and the frequency with which he or she uses a given track. This signature is an index of their operator persona. This persona no doubt evolves differently over time so that some operators are more conservative maintaining their signature for long periods whereas other operators are more flexible.

The tradition which we have mapped as a set of discourse-indexed formulae and which operators draw on and utilise individually are not unique to supermarkets. The start formulae and information-elicitation formulae which form the opening are all used more widely than in supermarkets for the same purpose, namely meeting and parting. In the exchange section all the formulae are used in retailing in general and all operators at checkouts will have had ample opportunity to absorb them as passive recipients in their role as customers in retail transactions. The same is true for the close components of the matrix interchange which are used elsewhere for partings. They are in general use for the purpose for which they are employed in supermarket checkout interchanges or they are used in other retail settings. The formulae are therefore discourse function specific but not specific to a supermarket checkout tradition.

There is only one exception and this is the addition to the bag or box formula used chiefly by one checkout operator, *Do you want bags with that or are you going to box it?*. She appears to have constructed this addition herself since none of her colleagues uses it in quite this form.[14]

6 Conclusion

It is clear that supermarket checkout operators corroborate the hypothesis that where routine actions are accompanied by routine speech, such speech will be largely formulaic. We have also shown speakers will borrow appropriate formulae from elsewhere in their speech repertoire to perform the necessary functions in formulaic speech and that, even within such a tightly constrained environment as that which the routine actions and speech of checkout operators impose, there is room for individuality, idiosyncrasy and even for a small measure of creativity.

While these findings are of some interest in themselves, we wish to suggest that they may be generalised. There are many such oral traditions across the spectrum of a culture. The techniques we have used to map both the tradition itself in terms of its discourse structure rules and its formulae as discourse-indexed finite-state diagrams may allow a number of traditions to be modelled thus. It consequently allows the individual performers in the tradition to be modelled. This can be done by looking at which formulae they use, which tracks through the formulae diagrams they select and the frequency with which they select them. Our methodology can be used diachronically to see how an individual oral formulaic persona evolves. We hope that these techniques will provide useful tools, therefore, for the investigations of oral traditions in general.

What of the overlay conversations which constitute clear examples of small talk in the way it is defined by Coupland *et al.* (1992: 208)? Small talk at the checkout is framed by the rituals of greeting and leave-taking on the one hand (as it often is elsewhere) and the exchange section of the matrix interchange on the other. It fills the otherwise silent interstices with inconsequential talk; inconsequential in the sense that nothing practical generally follows from it. Socially, however, each instance finds common ground between speakers, server and served, on subjects which are as uncontentious as possible: the weather, catfood, generalisations about one's weekend activities. Occasionally a client will raise a matter of significance such as a recent hip replacement but the way this is discussed is always under the assumption that there will be no disagreement or nothing disagreeable said.

The fact that there are many interchanges at the supermarket which do not contain an overlay of small talk shows that the service encounter has primacy over small talk, as one would expect, but the fact that 70 (about 1/3) of the interchanges we recorded do have small talk overlays shows that, in New Zealand anyway, finding inconsequential common ground for a friendly chat between server and served is important. As we mentioned earlier, from casual observation it would appear that in identical physical circumstances at supermarkets in other societies, the norm is for there not only to be no small talk overlay but little or no talk at all.

We have also seen how small events such as the few minutes one spends at the checkout constitute a ritual event of considerable complexity. Such rituals are clearly learned and that learning is part of becoming an enculturated speaker. The small talk which can operate within this ritual is again, subject to convention as to its subject matter and the affability which governs its exercise. This illustrates our contention at the outset that these small scale socio–cultural events have much to tell us about what it means to be a native speaker of a language in a particular society.

Notes

1. The research reported in this paper was supported by research grants from the University of Canterbury. An earlier version of this paper was read at the 3rd NZ Language and Society seminar. Our thanks are due to the managers of the two supermarkets where we recorded and the operators and their customers who gave permission for their conversations to be recorded. We are also grateful to Justine Coupland for numerous helpful comments which have allowed us to refine our thinking and, we hope, make this study a better one to read.

2. This research was conducted some years ago. The intervening time has been allowed for so that, given the turnover of checkout operator staff at supermarkets in New Zealand, few of the operators if any would be identifiable from any transcripts we might use or be embarrassed by them.

3. This is not true in all countries. In the Netherlands the whole transaction may be accomplished without any talk.

4. Occasionally items lose their barcode labels.

5. The checkout operator was fitted with a lapel microphone and the customers were recorded using a semi-directional microphone, the two channels being fed into a Sony TCD 5M stereophonic cassette recorder. The hedge of *about* is necessary because some of the interactions were chats with supervisors and other operators which fell outside the normal transactional data we were using as the basis of this study. These interactions were not used for this study.

6. A number of operators were only 'on' for short periods filling in for others who were at a break.

7. We have given only an orthographic transcription of the speech we recorded since our interest was and is primarily in the formulae used by speakers.

8. Our use of a finite-state approach to the structural properties of formulae is explained in Kuiper 1996: 45–6. We take it that many formulae have variant forms and that a speaker who knows a set of structurally related formulae in fact knows the finite-state diagram which generates them and can thus select any of the available tracks through the diagram from left to right following the arrows. It may be that not all of the possibilities in

such a diagram will appear in a sample of speech recorded from a particular speaker. But the diagrams can be set up on the basis of a particular speaker's performance, as we will see later. Finite-state approaches to structural representation in syntax were first used by Chomsky (1957).

The eagle-eyed will notice that some of the finite-state diagrams below slightly overgenerate beyond the data actually collected and shown in the table. The diagrams are therefore to be read as claims about what the operators could say as well as what they do say from within their personal formulaic competence. Our claim is that the finite-state diagrams are a representation of the formulaic oral tradition which is available within the community of speakers. We will see later that different speakers have a preference for their own tracks through the diagram, each having a characteristic set of these.

9. We follow the rules of openings and closing devised by Smith (1991) because they are based in part on New Zealand conversational data and that seems the appropriate basis for seeing how conversations at New Zealand supermarkets are organised.

10. Context-free re-write rules generate, i.e. explicitly characterise, an allowable set of tree diagrams, e.g. in syntactic analysis. For our purposes we can regard these rules as those which the speakers have internalised and which they use to structure their discourse. We have shown the utility of such rules elsewhere (Kuiper and Haggo 1984; Kuiper 1996).

11. Each cell contains the raw number of these greetings used in the sample followed by its percentage of the total number of greetings used by this operator.

12. Justine Coupland (personal communication) suggests that these utterances 'seem to indicate prior acquaintance' otherwise they look 'unusually intrusive and beyond the bounds of "safe" talk . . . displayed here'. We feel a New Zealander can safely assume the the customer is older, having had a hip replacement operation. She would probably be a 'regular' at this supermarket. The acquaintanceship would only need to be of this order to make such utterances perfectly safe. The customer would be known from her previous visits to this supermarket. Beyond that no further acquaintanceship would be necessary. Again this may suggest a different metric for what constitutes verbal safety in New Zealand service encounters from that which prevails in the UK.

13. It would have been interesting to note at the time whether the interlocutor was male although this is not a concern of this study.

14. We have noted other examples of this kind of accretion to existing formulae in Kuiper (1992).

References

Biber, D. (1994) An analytic framework for register studies. In D. Biber and E. Finegan (eds) *Sociolinguistic Perspectives on Register*. New York: Oxford University Press.

Brown, P. and Levinson, S. (1978) Universals in language usage: politeness phenomena. In E. N. Goody (ed.) *Questions and Politeness: Strategies in Social Interaction*. Cambridge: Cambridge University Press.

Chomsky, A. (1986) *Knowledge of Language: Its Nature, Origin and Use*. New York: Praeger.

Chomsky, N. (1957) *Syntactic Structures*. The Hague: Mouton.

Coulmas, F. (ed.) (1981) *Conversational Routine: Explorations in Standardized Communication Situations and Prepatterned Speech*. The Hague: Mouton.

Coupland, J., Coupland, N. and Robinson, J. D. (1992) 'How are you?': Negotiating phatic communion. *Language in Society* 21: 207–30.

Crystal, D. and Davy, D. (1969) *Investigating English Style*. London: Longman.

Drew, P. and Heritage, J. (1992) Analysing talk at work: an introduction. In P. Drew and J. Heritage (eds) *Talk at Work: Interaction in Institutional Settings*. Cambridge: Cambridge University Press.

Ferguson, C. (1976) The structure and use of politeness formulas. *Language in Society* 5: 137–51.

Firth, R. (1972) Verbal and bodily rituals of greeting and parting. In J. S. La Fontaine (ed.) *The Interpretation of Ritual: Essays in honour of A.I. Richards*. London: Tavistock.

Goffman, E. (1967) *Interactional Ritual*. New York: Anchor Books.

Herdt, G. H. (1980) *The Guardians of the Flutes*. New York: Macmillan.

Hymes, D. (1968) The ethnography of speaking. In J. Fishman (ed.) *The Sociology of Language*. The Hague: Mouton.

Kuiper, K. (1992) The English oral tradition in auction speech. *American Speech* 67: 279–89.

Kuiper, K. (1996) *Smooth Talkers*. New York: Lawrence Erlbaum Associates.

Kuiper, K. and Haggo, D. C. (1984) Livestock auctions, oral poetry and ordinary language. *Language and Society* 13: 205–34.

Laver, J. D. M. H. (1981) Linguistic routines and politeness in greeting and parting. In F. Coulmas (ed.) *Conversational Routine: Explorations in Standardized Communication Situations and Prepatterned Speech*. The Hague: Mouton.

Levelt, W. J. M. (1989) *Speaking: From Intention to Articulation*. Cambridge, MA: MIT Press.

Malinowski, B. (1922) *Argonauts of the Western Pacific*. London: Routledge and Kegan Paul.

Merritt, M. (1976) On questions following questions in service encounters. *Language in Society* 5: 315–57.

Merritt, M. (1977) The playback: An instance of variation in discourse. In R. W. Fasold and R. W. Shuy (eds) *Studies in Language Variation: Semantics, Syntax, Phonology, Pragmatics, Social situations, Ethnographic approaches*. Washington, DC: Georgetown University Press.

Salmond, A. (1976) Rituals of encounter among the Maori: Sociolinguistic study of a scene. In B. Stolz and R. Shannon (eds) *Oral Literature and Formulae*. Ann Arbor, Michigan: Center for the Coordination of Ancient and Modern Studies, The University of Michigan.

Schegloff, E. A. (1972) Sequencing in conversational openings. In J. J. Gumperz and D. Hymes (eds) *Directions in Sociolinguistics: The Ethnography of Communication*. New York: Holt, Rinehart and Winston.

Schegloff, E. A. and Sacks, H. (1973) Opening up closings. *Semiotica* 7: 289–327.

Scherzer, J. (1974) Semantic systems, discourse structures, and the ecology of language. In R. W. Fasold and R. W. Shuy (eds) *Studies in Language Variation: semantics, syntax, phonology, pragmatics, social situations, ethnographic approaches*. Washington, DC: Georgetown University Press.

Smith, C. W. (1989) *Auctions: the Social Construction of Value*. London: Harvester Wheatsheaf.

Smith, J. (1991) *Salutations, Felicitations, and Terminations: a study in communicative performance*. MA thesis, University of Canterbury.

Staal, F. (1990) *Rules without Meaning: ritual, Mantras, and the Human Sciences*. New York: Peter Lang.

Thorne, A. and Coupland, J. (1998) Articulations of same-sex desire: Lesbian and gay male dating advertisements. *Journal of Sociolinguistics* 2: 233–57.

Small talk, sociability and social cohesion

Introduction to **Part III**

Justine Coupland

In the general Introduction, I was able to point to the origins of the argument that, functionally, small talk and its sub-genres attend to social and relational goals. In the third section of the book, we look much more closely at this issue, considering talk in two private contexts – families gossiping at dinner (Blum-Kulka), and groups of women exchanging stories about bad behaviour (Coates). The data allow the authors to provide much-needed detailing of what it means to work through 'social goals'. We see participants exploring and negotiating social mores, social stereotypes and social identities through small talk, and doing this as part of a wider process of debating and policing moral boundaries.

Blum-Kulka's chapter begins by exploring the 'human instinct for sociability', a very Malinowskian idea, in the context of the family dinner table. Her data give us insights into how children contribute to the small talk that is enjoyed in family communing. In the 'gossipy events' that she studies, adults lead children to accomplish both low-level and high-level socialisation processes. Blum-Kulka identifies different levels of domains of gossip, taking as her starting point those which exemplify Goffman's idealised 'happy conversations'. But she finds a tension between such sociability and socialisation goals, whereby children are taught a range of norms and skills, including table manners and indeed rules for conversational participation. The children's individual identities and their roles within family structures are moulded in these speech events. Socio–cultural values and ideals are also formulated and inculcated. When there are few personal or group-relevant implications at stake (when gossiping about celebrities, for example), 'pure sociability' can be entertained. But, when gossip focuses on relevant or even co-present others, there are multiple face-threats to all concerned. This more serious business uses gossip as a launch pad from which parents and other adults help children to make sense of their world. They have their stereotypes and preconceptions challenged and renegotiated through talk.

Coates takes up the gender politics of small talk, by looking at female small talk in private contexts of the sort that Goffman (1971) described as happening 'backstage'. This is talk that would be taboo in more public, frontstage contexts. Coates analyses women and girls talking, in particular exploring their use of narrative and reported speech. Her argument is that females use such talk to challenge frontstage norms of femininity (such as 'niceness' or 'loyalty') and to explore alternative selves. Small talk in these circumstances therefore offers the freedom of 'behaving badly'. Coates develops Bourdieu's (1991) notion of symbolic capital to make the claim that females and their discourse are assessed and constrained by powerful community norms. She points out that these norms dictate that frontstage norms of femininity need to be attended to, in some ways, even backstage. This is at least so in metapragmatic aspects of their talk, when women acknowledge that backstage talk constitutes 'bad behaviour'. That women recognise the 'badness' of their talk while relishing doing it recalls the familiar metaphor of forbidden fruit and, appropriately enough, Coates's analysis brings out the paradoxes and multiple layering of gendered power and powerlessness.

Coates does, however, see emotional catharsis and group-solidarity being achieved in backstage women's talk. The data show women and girls doing mutual support in *Schadenfreude* and in the celebration of bad female behaviour. The chapter ends on a challenging note, raising several conflicting possible readings. These backstage events may be a forum for non-ratified behaviour which, repressively, allows women to keep their frontstage performances normative and 'nice'. Alternatively, and more optimistically, women may be developing resources during backstage events. Talk on the backstage may act as a rehearsal for new sorts of frontstage behaviour and therefore for future social change. Girls and women may be preparing themselves to be, like boys and men, free to be bad in their frontstage performances. For the theme of this book as a whole, Coates's chapter intriguingly inverts the conventional delineation of small talk. Small talk has generally been associated with the 'niceness' and sociality that Coates refers to. But the backstage analysis allows us to see small talk used to challenge niceness and to celebrate anti-social norms.

References

Bourdieu, P. (1991) *Language and Symbolic Power*. Cambridge: Polity Press.
Goffman, E. (1971) *The Presentation of Self in Everyday Life*. Harmondsworth: Penguin.

8

Gossipy events at family dinners: negotiating sociability, presence and the moral order

Shoshana Blum-Kulka

If we believe Aristotle, the truly noble man does not speak much of himself nor of others, so as not to unduly engage in self-praise or condemnation of the other (cited in Statman 1994: 412). Other philosophers have a more sympathetic view of talk about others; for Hanna Arendt: 'We humanize what is going on in the world and in ourselves only by speaking of it, and in the course of speaking of it we learn to be human. Humanness . . . manifests itself in the readiness to share the world with other men' (Arendt 1968: 25, quoted in Spacks 1985: 257).

In its broadest sense, gossip is such sharing of the human world with other people. All its students agree that in some form it has to do with an exchange of information between at least two people about a non-present third party; yet they disagree as to its morality and social functions. Jewish tradition is especially critical of the type of gossip called 'bad tongue' (*leshon ha-ra*), where derogatory yet accurate information is passed about non-present others (Statman 1994). Current writing about gossip is more inclined to stress its humanizing functions. Many claim that there is no inherent meaning in the content of communications about others; whether or not a particular item of information will be evaluated as derogatory will depend on a host of factors, including the history of social relationships and the immediate social context within which the encounter takes place (Handelman 1973; Spacks 1985).

This ambivalence in attitudes to gossip is not only a theoretical matter; in studying forms of talk about others in the family what is striking is the degree of fluctuation in the nature of the talk: sometimes it is felt (to its distant observers listening to it later) to be the light, idle talk 'happy conversations' one associates with (Sacks 1992); at other instances one is struck with the gravity of the underlying moral issues at stake. Yet as in all narrative events in the family, it occasions the negotiation of personal, familial and cultural identities (Blum-Kulka 1997), the evaluation of specific events 'in terms of communal norms, expectations and potentialities; communal ideas of what is rational and moral, communal senses of the appropriate and the esthetic' (Ochs and Capps 1996: 30). Thus in interfacing self and society it has the power to serve as a medium of socialization *par excellence*.

This chapter explores gossip in the family through the prism of socialization; it asks what children might learn from participating in a multiplicity of forms of narration about others during dinner conversations. It is built around three theoretical issues: sociability, presence and morality. Our human instinct for sociability is presumably satisfied by relational focused, informal, egalitarian and non-goal orientated sociable talk. Examining co-narrations about non-present others in the family reveals the limits of sociability within this 'gossipy' frame. Sociability and gossip can go hand in hand, but might also be at odds with each other. The question is how participants in family meals interpret the notion of 'idle talk', how they engage in it and how they define its boundaries. Non-presence of story protagonist is considered a *sine qua non* of gossipy talk, and is often linked to the condition of all present being equally familiar with the person talked about. Both of these conditions are problematic in the intergenerational gathering of family meals; in the family 'presence' is negotiable, and levels of familiarity with gossipee varies between the participants and with subject matter. Furthermore, talk about non-present others can be light as well as serious, non-goal-orientated as well as topically focused. In the family truly idle talk seems to emerge only under conditions of low emotional involvement, as in the case of celebrity talk, while in all other gossipy narration it is underscored by issues of personal, familial and cultural identity. When such issues emerge at the discourse level co-narrations become overtly concerned with the negotiation of the moral order, interfacing self and society in the family arena.

In our quest[1] for gossip in the family we used the broadest definition of gossip possible, looking for exchanges in which information is passed about non-present others. We soon realized that even this definition is problematic; in multi-party talk 'non-presence' is a negotiable rather than absolute category, since participants may be transformed to symbolically non-present overhearers at any moment of the talk. Other aspects of gossip talk that would allow it to be defined as a 'local' representation of the gossip genre turned out to be just as problematic.

I propose to call the conversations examined here 'gossipy events' and to argue that such events constitute a sub-genre of family discourse. These events are 'gossipy' in the sense that they relate to (physically or symbolically framed as) non-present others, and may involve the social world outside the family. Yet, due to the variation in their topics and modalities, gossipy events are only loosely related to 'gossip' in sociological definitions of the term (Bergman 1993; Spacks 1985).

The dinner conversations examined come from two dinner conversations each of ten Israeli and ten Jewish-American middle-class, college-educated families with two to three school-age children, audio-taped (and, for the families who agreed, once also video-taped) in their homes in the United States and Israel. Each group included one single-parent family. A female (for the families included here) participant observer was present at all dinners. Sometimes other guests were present as well, including friends and family members. This is part of the data base that served for the analysis of cultural patterns of sociability and socialization in dinner talk (Blum-Kulka 1997). For the purposes of this study, we searched the transcripts of these meals for all talk about non-present others, including only talk extending over two turns. The search yielded a rich array of exchanges (83 in the Jewish American and 70 in the Israeli families) representing varied participation frameworks and subject matter, initiated and participated in by all present.

Protagonists and initiators

Who is being talked about? On a continuum of decreased intimacy from family, neighbours, friends, colleagues, teachers and to celebrities, the family is mostly concerned with a mid-point centred around friends and colleagues. In both Israeli and Jewish-American families, friends, acquaintances and colleagues are the protagonists of the majority of gossipy events (63 per cent for Jewish-Americans, n = 83, 66 per cent for Israelis, n = 70). Both adults and children initiate and participate in talk about teachers (in 16 per cent of the events for Jewish-Americans, 14 per cent for Israelis) and in talk about celebrities (Israelis 16 per cent, Jewish-Americans 7 per cent). As a rule neighbours get to be talked about very little in either group (in less than 4 per cent of events in each); non-present members of the family are more often the focus of gossip in the Jewish-American families (9.6 per cent) than in the Israelis (3 per cent).

Confirming previously established patterns in dinner talk (Blum-Kulka 1997), the choice of subject matter for gossipy talk shows little cultural variation. Just as in the choice of thematic frames and specific topics, the topical aspect of gossipy talk seems to derive mainly from the nature of the speech event and the shared socioeconomic background of the families involved. The social world evoked by adults and children in the family through gossipy talk is inhabited by relevant others; their relevance to the lives of different family members may vary at the onset of the exchange, but it is transformed to a family-shared relevance through talk. This process seems unique to the familial event; only at dinner can the friend of the 11 year old compete symbolically for gossipy space with the childhood friend of the mother of the family. Thus the nature of the speech event has a formative role on the choice of gossipy topics.

Cultural variation does emerge in considering patterns of initiation. The main initiators of gossipy talk in the Israeli families are the mothers (44.3 per cent) and the guests, who in this case are mainly the observers

(29 per cent). Children initiate 20 per cent of gossipy events, and fathers only 7 per cent. This is in line with overall paterns of participation in dinner talk (Blum-Kulka 1997: 59); we found that in the relatively informal and backstage ambiance of Israeli dinners, mothers talk more and initiate more topics than fathers (27 per cent of topic intiations vs. 9 per cent by men and twice the number of utterances), and observers take an active part in the conversation (initiate 28 per cent of topics and contribute 25 per cent of the talk). On the whole, the overall talking space taken up by the adults in Israeli families overrides the space allocated to children, yet children still play an important role in topic initiation (23.5 per cent) and overall participation (22 per cent).

On the other hand, at the relatively more formal Jewish-American dinner table, fathers are more prominent than the mothers (36 per cent topic initiations vs. 20 per cent by mothers), observers more reticent (contributing only 7 per cent of topics) and participating minimally in the talk, and children occupy a significant proportion of talking space (37 per cent of topic initiations, 38 per cent of utterances). Gossipy events deviate only little from these patterns; again, children play a major role in the talk (42 per cent), and observers a very minor role (4 per cent). At two of the Jewish-American meals examined, the guest included in two cases a grandmother and in another an uncle. From the 3 gossipy events initiated by 'guests' two were initiated by the uncle, one by the grandmother and none by an observer. The only general family discourse pattern *not repeated* is the division along gender lines: the contribution of women and men to gossipy events in this group is almost equal, with the men initiating 19 per cent and the women 22 per cent.

Children at all the meals are treated as ratified participants. Their rights of participation ensure the potential of dinner talk in general and gossipy events in particular as media of socialization, even if these rights may be modified or withdrawn in specific instances of the talk. Children get involved in the talk through initiating topics of their own, responding to adult elicitation (often about their day in school) and by contributing to adult-initiated topics.

In the Jewish-American families, the majority of the topics raised at dinner are child-focused, in the sense that they concern the children's lives both when initiated by or addressed to children. Children are allocated centre stage mainly when the topic concerns immediate family concerns from the recent past of their own or sometimes other members of the family. These patterns of participation are modified in gossipy events. Here age is of importance; preschoolers do not as a rule play a part in initiations, though sometimes may inadvertently supply the trigger for such an event. Thus in the course of an elicited dialogue with a 4 year old in an Israeli family about his friends in preschool, the child provides the information that one of the children has left the school. The information is new for some of the adults present, and it leads to a discussion of the recent events in the life of the family concerned ('Did they really move to Tel-Aviv?'). In the Jewish-American families, the 26 gossipy event initiations of the nine young school-age children (7 to 9) concern mostly stories about the misdemeanour or difficulties of other children or stories of what I call *'complainables'* with regard to teachers. Jewish-American teenagers (6 participants) talk more about peers than about teachers, and also participate more actively in adult-initiated gossipy events.

The cultural difference between the groups in the degree of child initiation of gossipy events seems to stem from cultural differences in overall participation structures. The Israeli group in general favoured the participation of the participant-observer; this trend is repeated in gossipy events, allowing less space for children's initiation and participation. The Jewish-American group shows a preference for child participation, and we see this trend reflected in gossipy events.

There is great individual variation between the families in both groups in number of gossipy events per meal: in the Jewish-American group, with a range of 4 to 19, (mean 10.5), in the Israeli families, a range of 1 to 20 (mean 8.9). Estimated proportions of gossipy talk from all dinner talk (based on a rough count of transcript lines) show a similar variation, ranging from 2 per cent to 33 per cent in the Jewish-American group, and from 4.5 per cent to 17 per cent in the Israeli group. Surprisingly, the age of the children in the family does not seem to affect the proportion of gossipy talk. Among the 'high-gossipers' with more than 10 events we find (in both groups) families with teenagers only as well as families with young school age children.

Negotiating felicity conditions for sociable talk: the dynamics of happy conversations

Sociability, as the essence of happy conversations, has no ulterior motive. It is fully orientated to the creation of an occasion where people derive pleasure from the company of others, one in which they are at perfect ease with each other. In sociable encounters, Simmel (1961) suggests, talking is an end in itself; talk is for talk's sake, lacking a purposive intention, an agenda of any kind. It is also talk which is fully democratic:

> This world of sociability, the only one in which a democracy of equals is possible without friction, is an artificial world, made of beings who have renounced both the objective and the purely personal features of the intensity and extensiveness of life in order to bring about among themselves a pure interaction, free of any disturbing material accent.
>
> (Simmel 1961: 159)

We enter into sociability as 'purely as "human beings", as that which we really are' (ibid.: 130) and thus it can become 'the most adequate fulfilment of a relation which is, so to speak, nothing but relationship, in which that which is otherwise pure form of interaction is its own self-sufficient content' (ibid.: 137). Goffman's (1981) idealized ordinary conversations are the enactment of such sociable events; they are non-goal-orientated, egalitarian and collaborative, according everyone the right to talk as well as to listen. Talk creates a unique focus of attention 'For talk creates for the participant a world and a reality that has other participants in it. Joint spontaneous involvement is *unio mystico*, a socialized trance' (Goffman 1967: 113).

This notion of happy conversations is echoed by the parents of the families studied in interview-talk about family meals: dinners are a 'social time' a time when 'we do talk uh about whatever happens to be on anybody's mind' (Blum-Kulka 1997: 36). Yet this idealized picture of sociable dinners is balanced by the understanding that dinners are also socializing events; parents are aware that they act as an opportunity space for teaching children table manners, forms of talk and cultural values. Dinner talk negotiates this tension between sociability and socialization goals through its variability of thematic frames and participation structures; thus the talk may move from the purely instrumental business of having dinner to highly non-immediate topics of culture and identity, and may allocate children the role of equal co-participants as well as that of momentary overhearers (Blum-Kulka 1997).

Subject matter, participation stucture and key

Are gossipy events in the family sociable? Can the thematic frame of 'gossipy talk' at dinner enact pure sociability? Arguably it can, but only under very specific felicity conditions of subject matter, participation structure and key. Conditions of subject matter have to do with the identity of the person talked about; the more he or she is socially and physically remote, the less the potential for personal involvement of the participants and hence the higher the chance for talk for the sake of talk. The second condition relates to the egalitarian principle: in sociable conversations, everyone's contribution needs to be treated with equal respect, and all can share in topics raised by each. Structural and negotiated asymmetries of power in the family, linked to social and discourse role and information states, present a problem to this requirement. Given the interdependent and asymmetrical relation between children and parents to start with, for children to participate in a conversation like equals they need to be accepted on an equal or near-equal footing with the adults either because of age (a teenager has advantage over a preschooler in this respect) or due to their equal or superior position in terms of knowledge. The third condition relates to the key of the interaction. Sociable encounters celebrate detached playfulness; talk about the private affairs of others may be sarcastic or critical in tone. The question is, does gossip talk in the family need to maintain an undertone of 'non-seriousness' to remain purely sociable?

Celebrity talk: a case of 'pure sociability'

These three conditions are fulfilled in 'celebrity talk', namely in gossip about the personal lives of public personae. As consumers of the media, children know as much, and often more than the adults in the family for example about the various bits of gossip surrounding a particular show and its makers. In the public sphere, as on talk-shows, the private lives of media celebrities are regularly topicalized. Well-known public personae, such as actors, singers and TV personalities, tell anecdotes from their life history in the course of their conversation with the host. In their thematic choice these stories satisfy the requirements of tellability in ordinary conversations in that in Sacks's terms it is the direct personal involvement of the teller in the story that grants him or her the right to tell it (Sacks 1978). Such stories are usually concerned with a presumably publicly unknown or at least not widely known aspect of the teller's life that contributes to building his or her image in her or his specific role as a public persona.

Family gossip along these lines is a prime example of interfacing of the public and the private. Thematically gossipy talk about celebrities shifts easily from evaluation of the virtual reality represented in the media, as when the children in one of the families discuss the last episode of a favourite soap ('*General Hospital* was so good' – 'What happened?') to gossipy talk concerning the personal lives and appearance of the actors and actresses. Celebrity talk has no age constraints: it surfaces in families with children of all ages. The subject matter of the talk may vary though with the age of the children. Thus in a family with a five year old the person discussed is the host on a program for children (Don Herbert, on *Mr Wizard*) who according to the father looks surprisingly young for his age ('. . . the guy gotta be seventy'). With older children celebrity talk may function as adult metacommentary to children's narratives. For example, in the course of a joint recounting of the story of a movie by two young teenagers the adults remark that the actress in the film, Jamie Lee Curtis, is the daughter of two well-known actors (Tony Curtis and Janet Leigh), noting that 'she looks like her mother, as a matter of fact'. Occasionally the interfacing of the public and private spheres is coloured by personal involvement, as when a discussion of Woody Allen films leads to a series of revelations by the mother ('His name is Allen Koninsberg'; '. . . he was married to Anita Glacer') known to her through her friendship with his sister some years back. On rare occasions (usually the TV was turned off during the dinners we taped), celebrity talk is directly anchored in the context of the show watched. In the following extract the family is discussing the pregnancy of an actress absent from the show broadcasted.

Example 1

Jewish-American family 6: Dina (17 f); Jack (12 m); Paula (observer); Uncle (mother's brother).[2] The family is watching television, the American drama, *Cagney and Lacey*, about two police women.

1 Mother:	Take the pot out of his hands.
%pau:	3:50
2 Uncle:	Okay [=! Laughs].
3 xxx:	This is Cagney.
4 Paula:	Too far out # no, no, no.
5 Uncle:	Uh, that's the [1:28] Cagney # and the other one is Lacey I like the other one.
6 Paula:	So Lacey's xxx
7 Uncle:	Yeah [2:84] xxx I guess she plays Lacey # her accent is [0:62] playing a Newyorker, she sounds really you know really does it good. She's pregnant that's why she's not really in this episode. She's on maternity leave.
8 Paula:	Oh, this must be an old one.
9 Uncle:	No, it's a new one. Is this a new one, Cortney? (com%: Cortney is his sister).
10 Mother:	Yeah xxx. xxx taking her place.
11 Uncle:	Then she's pregnant again? Didn't she already have a baby?
12 Paula:	Wasn't she pregnant during the Emmys last time?
13 Mother:	Yeah, and she was pregnant at the beginning of the season [0:90] this season. So now, she's taking her place 'cause she's on maternity leave.
14 Paula:	Oh.
15 Dina:	Who's taking her place?
16 Mother:	Michel Laurietti.

The exchange is initiated by one of the adults (the mother's brother), takes place mainly between the three adults present (mother, her brother and the observer) but the daughter's clarification query in turn 15 shows that she has been monitoring the talk all along. The 'on-line' nature of this exchange foregrounds its code-switching between the highly contextualized but disinterested meta-talk about the show ('this [episode] must be an old one'/ 'Is this a new one?') and the more involved language of gossip used to clarify the actress's number of pregnancies. All sociability criteria for family gossip are met: the gossipee is doubly removed from participation (being a media personality not even present on the show) and all participants, regardless of age, are treated as equals, with the contribution of each fully appreciated. The only criterion for gaining floor space is topically relevant knowledge; thus the mother has the longest turn because she can provide the crucial bit of the missing information. Furthermore, it is clear the issue is of no serious concern (note turn 11 'Didn't she already *have* a baby?'). As a result, celebrity talk in the family is a prime example of gossip as 'idle talk' (Gluckman 1963); it is chatty, light in tone and risk-free in terms of emotional involvement.

Risks of involvement

Less risk-free is gossip about familiar others. Detachment gets more difficult to maintain when the gossipee in question is a neighbour, a friend or a member of the family. The question is, can sociability prevail under conditions of emotional involvement? Examples from the family mealtime data show that personal involvement in the subject matter may well introduce a note of seriousness, endangering sociability. Gossip about relevant others carries the potential of threat not only to the face of the other, but also of threat to the speaker's own face. Liminal cases in our data come from talk about colleagues, family and friends. The next extract (from the same family at another meal) shows the 'soft shoulders' of happy conversations, the ease by which they can slide away from their main course of chatty, idle talk. The exchange is triggered by a phone call from a childhood friend of the mother (answered by the daughter, Dina) during which mother and friend are confirming prior arrangements for meeting in New York to attend the wedding of a mutual friend.

Example 2

Jewish-American family 6 (single-parent family): Dina (17 f); Jack (12 m); Paula (observer); Grandmother.

 1 Mother: She's gonna come back from New <u>York</u> with me.
 2 Dina: Oh, really?
 3 Mother: +^And she's gonna pick me up at the airport.
 4 Dina: That's <u>great</u>! What do you mean, she's gonna pick you up from # [//] when you get to JFK?
 5 Mother: No, we're gonna fly to Newark.
 6 Dina: Oh.
 7 Mother: And then >she's gonna come back with me on that Tuesday and that way Jack'll be back from Daddy's.
 8 Dina: Oooh <great> [>].
 9 Mother: <And um> [<] [1:22] and I'll be able [//] I think I'll just take the rest of the week off.
10 Dina: **I got the chills when I heard her voice+/.**
11 Mother: **I know isn't it ridiculous?**
12 Dina: **+^ Oh it's really bizarre, is her hair still long?**
13 Mother: **Someone said she looks like El Vira [1:15] you know El Vira the one that one that always wears [1:19] "the the the" [/] the witch [//] like a witch [//] she looks like a witch.**
14 Dina: **Sort of Dracula.**
15 Mother: **Yeah Dracula lady but she's [0:44] much prettier than El Vira. So that'll be better+/.**
16 Dina: **xxx?**
17 Mother: **She's already [//] she was 38 in May.**
18 Jack: **<u>Jasus</u> [2:15] She's older than you.**
19 Mother: **She's beautiful [0:40] and I mean we were friends she says <what's Jack like?> ['] so I said "remember Don when he was thirteen?"['] that's my**

ex-husband his dad 'cause we all were in [//'] we were in # public school together.

20 Paula: **Oh, yeah, wow.**
21 Mother: **Oh, Daddy would freak.**
22 Dina: **If he saw her?**
23 Mother: **If he saw her yeah he was[//] that was who he loved.**
            He said "I like Ellen, I only want you to be my friend" ['].
%act: general laughter.
24 Jack: **He said that to you? What a gap.**
25 Mother: **What a bargain.**
26 Dina: **Oh my God. She should have [//] she should have had him.**
27 Mother: **Really [2:38] she was smart.**
28 Dina: **God, that's so funny.**
29 Mother: **+^I'm really excited.**
30 Dina: **That's great.**
[Continued]

This example shows different levels of emotional involvement and information states among the participants with regard to the party talked about. It illustrates how involvement may introduce a serious undertone to the proceedings, endangering its sociability. We can see how talk about absent others serves not only to map for children the social world of the adults, but also to acquaint them with the emotional problems and attitudes of this world sometimes, as here, with direct relevance for their own lives. On one level, this is a happy conversation about an old friend both mother and daughter know well. Differing from Example 1, the tone of the conversation is of high emotional involvement shared by mother and daughter, expressed as 'shock' in hearing from an oldtime friend after presumably years of silence (see turns 10 and 11). On the onset this involvement does not endanger the light key of the conversation, nor does it reflect a critical stance towards Ellen, the woman talked about. In the intimate circle of mother and daughter seemingly derogatory statements about Ellen's looks (she 'looks like a witch', 'Dracula lady' are immediately qualified ('she's much prettier than . . .', 'she's beautiful') to express admiration. Jack's comment in turn 18 ('she's older than you') is a reminder that, despite appearances, this is not an intimate dyadic conversation. For the younger brother, the information about Ellen is new, and he is using it to delight in his mother's relatively young age ('she's older than you'). Paula's 'Oh, yeah, wow' reminds us that she too is new to the information about Ellen, and that the background information provided by the mother ('that's my ex-husband his dad 'cause we all were in public school together') is meant for her. As of turn 21, though the light tone is maintained (note the general laughter following the mother's disclosure in turn 23), the history of the past relations between the three protagonists evoked (mother, Jack's father and Ellen) touches potentially emotionally sensitive ground for all members of the family. For the younger child especially, talk about an absent friend of his mother evokes a web of complicated relationships and attitudes directly relevant to his life. Thus undertones of past and present emotional involvement with the protagonist of gossipy talk may introduce a note of seriousness, undermining the happy surfaces of sociable gossip.

More risks: shifts in participation frameworks and taboos on tellability

The second risk to pure sociability in gossipy events in the family stems from deliberate breaches of the presumably egalitarian principle by which all can share in the topics raised by each. When such breaches come from adults, we witness the parents going bald on record in exercising parental power to exclude children from a given exchange.

Example 3

Jewish-American family 4: Jordan (8 m); Sandra (4 f); Susan (observer).

  1 Father: Um [2:09] I had lunch at the [0:44] uh <u>Plárka</u> which is you know this "it's [/] it's called uh an upscale" [//] it's an upscale Greek restaurant. and uh +/.

  2 Mother: And you had # upscale Greek food?

  3 Father: Yeah! It was actually + . . . I had [0:82] an <u>octop</u>us salad. It was really good.

  4 Mother: 0 [=! laughs].

  5 Susan: 0 [=! laughs].

  6 Father: It was really good. Have you ever had octopus?

  7 Mother: <Yes!> [>]

  8 Father: <You've had squid> [<] but have you ever had octopus?

  9 Mother: I eat those things [1:81] &fr fried [//] deep fried so you don't know what it is <that you're eating> [=! laughs].

 10 Father: It's really good.

 11 Jordan: **Mommy <I have** xxx [0:88] oh> [>] [%com realizes he's speaking at the same time as father].

>12 Father: <Well anyway we had sit> [<] # sitting next to us at the other table was [1:00] Jim Baum acting Dean of L.A.S.

 13 Mother: Mmhm?

 14 Jordan: **Mommy?**

 15 Father: Plus [1:16] **<u>excuse</u> me** [%com to Jordan for interrupting]?

 16 Jordan: **Excuse <u>you</u>?**

 17 Father: +^ **I'm talking.**

 18 Jordan: **I know.**

 19 Father: **Yeah so you don't interrupt ok?**

 20 Jordan: **I don't have** xxx
    0 [=! giggles].
    <u>I</u> know.
    <<u>I</u> know.> [>] [=! giggles]

21 Father: <And ah> [<] + . . . anyway there's nothing to say except there was [0:47] Jim
              Baum [0:68] plotting [1:35] with two fellow co+conspirators.
              um+\.
22 Mother: Does he know your father?
23 Father: Well it [/] it turns out + . . . No I don't think he does.
              But um [0:75] one of the people he was talking to was [0:65] xxx man by the name
              of Ron Rozek who was the [0:97] Dean of the graduate college a few years ago
              who knows him and he stopped by to say hello.
              Ah [1:12] but # ah + . . . [04:84]
              I said Jim Baum [//] I my [0:53] [/] my back, I was sitting at the table and my
              back was to the table that Baum was sitting at and I told +/.
24 Mother: And you were worried.
25 Father: I said to them if xxx Baum were Dean I would not sit with my back to them.
26 Mother: 0 [=! laughs].
@End

This example illustrates a shift in participation framework *in the overall
macro context of the family meal*, excluding a child from a given gossipy event
despite his principled right as a ratified participant at mealtimes. We can see
from the overt sequence of the talk that 8 year old Jordan's attempts to
attract the attention of his mother (turn 11) are first ignored, and then
rejected by the father as an unwarranted interruption (turns 15, 17 and 19).
The question is, is the father's reprimand ('I'm talking' . . . 'Yeah so you
don't interrupt ok?') merely a reminder of turn-taking rules, as indicated by
Jordan's reaction ('I know', repeated twice and accompanied by giggles) or is
it also a move to exclude Jordan from the circle of ratified participants for
the topic at hand? There are several indicators in the discourse to suggest
the latter: as of the introduction of the topic, setting the scene ('I had lunch
at the Plarka today'), the father's utterances are designed for the adult audience of his wife and the observer. His choice of attribute for the restaurant ('upscale'), the banter involving the observer on the merits of sea food
(he turns to her in asking 'Have you ever had octopus?') and the way he
introduces the first character in the story ('acting Dean of . . .') are all
adult-orientated. The language and topic indeed seem beyond Jordan's
understanding, and he shows no signs of active listenership. Following the
side sequence with Jordan the father launches into his gossipy story ('there
was xxx plotting with two co-conspirators' turn 21) , restricting his audience
to his wife only, since not sharing all the needed background information
about the people mentioned, the observer (as the researcher listening to it
later) as well as the child could have difficulties understanding the point of
the story.

While Example 3 problematizes children's participation rights in a gossipy event, Example 4 problematizes the participation rights of all present in
such a specific event. It is not that some (the children) are not included in
the gossipy topic, but that an objection is raised to the topic being talked

about at all, children and adult alike. The 'breach' in this case is child-initiated. It is one of the children who by announcing 'it's her business' positions herself as the guardian of secrets, countering her sister's attempts to share with the family what must seem to her sensitive information concerning the life of somebody close.

Example 4

Jewish-American family 5: Dana (11 f); Ruth (9 f); Granny; Susan (observer).

1	Father:	Honey we can get you to gymnastics the problem is to get you <home from gymnastics.> [>]
2	Granny:	<Yeah right how> [<] are you gonna get home?
3	Father:	That's the biggest <u>prob</u>lem, if we had [0:57] a carpool.
4	Dana:	**Maybe <u>Shar</u>on.**
%com:		Sharon is the living-in au pair.
5	Granny:	**Oh, honey, Sharon would have been here [0:50] so she's doing something.**
6	Mother:	**I don't want to disturb Sharon, <she needed> [>] two days off.**
7	Dana:	**<Oh but she's+ . . . > [<]**
8	Father:	**Do you know what she's doing?**
9	Dana:	**I don't know.**
10	Ruth:	**She's going to the <u>doc</u>tor!**
11	Mother:	**I think she has a doctor's appointment.**
12	Ruth:	**And the psy<u>chi</u>atrist or [0:63] something.**
13	Mother:	**Is that right?**
14	Dana:	**I don't know [0:65] it's her business.**
15	Mother:	**Mm, mm it's her business.**
16	Ruth:	**She's going to the doctor I <u>know</u> she is. [=! raises her voice]**
17	Mother:	**That's right.**
18	Granny:	Well, you girls are [//] you better eat the stew because you're gonna have the stew tomorrow night for dinner.
19	Ruth:	Oh: no.
@End		

The hard core of the gossipy 'news' here concerns Sharon's appointment with the psychiatrist. This piece of information is arrived at very gradually, with both the grandmother and the mother providing first only the most general statements explaining Sharon's absence (turns 5 and 6). It is the younger sister, Ruth, who mentions a doctor's appointment, is supported by the mother, and then goes on to announce the news, namely that this appointment concerns a psychiatrist. The mother's confirmation check in turn 13 assures us of the novelty of this information. When next Dana positions herself as the guardian of Sharon's 'secrets', the mother clearly aligns with her daughter, echoing her words (turn 15). Ruth's insistence on raising the topic again (note the raise of voice in turn 16) is finally aborted by the grandmother's abrupt change of topic in turn 18.

Can sociability survive slander?

We have seen that the happiness of 'happy conversations' is vulnerable to high emotional involvement of some of the participants with the person talked about, to shifts in participation structure excluding parties from the circle of ratified participants and to taboos on the tellability of secrets. Yet, suprisingly, overtly derogatory subject matter does not necessarily endanger the sociability of the talk. Sociability may remain intact in cases of overtly derogatory talk about an absent other, provided it manifests a joint, collaborative spontaneous involvement of all family members in the topic at hand and preserves a playful key. The next extract illustrates a case of a family delighting in slandering a neighbour; making her relatively advanced age an issue, they call her names (*alte kuker*, e.g. 'old codger'), criticize her cooking and, as the conversation goes on (not quoted here), go on to criticize her appearance, her behaviour, her smell, her voice. Yet they do all this in the playful key of happy conversations. Sociability derives here from two sources: the nonseriousness of the talk and the way in which the participants align with each other and display their solidarity. As in the case of Jewish argument (Schiffrin 1984), overt form and/or content do not necessarily match underlying antagonistic attitudes.

Example 5

Jewish-American family 6: Dina (17 f); Jack (12 m); Uncle (mother's brother); Paula (observer).

 1 Dina: Aren't they good? [=! giggles]
 2 Paula: Mmm hmm.
 3 Uncle: I like these pickles They're better than Ruth's.
 4 Jack: Ooo [=! giggles]
 5 Dina: Oh <u>much</u> better than Ruth's.
 6 Jack: I never had one.
 7 Uncle: Ruth's a neighbour [1:50] she's a real {*alte kuker*} +/.
 8 Dina: {*alte kuker*} right [=! laughs].
          <she's such [/] she'a such a nose xx> [>].
 9 Uncle: <I called her an {*alte kuker*} to her face one day> [<] she got all insulted.
10 Paula: Oh, no [=! laughs]!
11 Uncle: I said 'Ruth you know you're such an {*alte kuker*}' [1:00] she got real insulted.
12 Paula: They are good. [=the pickles]
13 Jack: She's the <u>nosiest</u> person I know.
14 Mother: How could you say that? [%sarcastically]
15 Uncle: O [=! laughs].
16 Jack: Mom, do you want this? It's sour.
17 Uncle: 'Member when I called her an {*alte kuker*}[=! not laughing but very amused]?
18 Mother: She was <u>ve</u>:ry insulted, [=! laughs]
          <u>ve</u>:ry insulted.
19 Uncle: Yeah, well <the truth hurts> [>].
20 Jack: <What did she say> [<] to you?
21 Paula: Did she call you something back?

22 Uncle: A little {*pisher*} I don't know, something.
              She said "'<u>me</u>? Your calling me # an {*alte kuker*}" ['] [=! imitating].
23 Paula: Ooo [=! laughs]
24 Uncle: I kinda whispered it yknow # she wasn't supposed to hear it.
25 Paula: Oh, was anybody else around?
26 Jack: We xxx.
27 Uncle: Yeah, I guess there was a few people.
[continued]

This exchange cannot qualify as 'gossip' in the strict sociological definition of the term (e.g. Bergman 1993; Spacks 1985): it does concern a non-
present other, but it has little news and may be more importantly, is not
based on a shared degree of familiarity with the subject of the gossip. While
as a close neighbour she is apparently intimately connected to all members
of the family, she is a complete stranger to the observer. Yet there is a
connection – since all concerned are Jewish, they share an ethnic identity
manifestly of significance in licensing and mitigating the derogatory information passed.

Jewishness coupled with a relatively high degree of neighbourly intimacy
are both presupposed and evoked in this exchange. It is pickles ('Jewish'
food) that serves as the trigger for talk about Ruth. By noting that the ones
eaten 'are better than Ruth's' the uncle is admitting being highly familiar
with the taste of Ruth's pickles, and may be other food she prepares. In other
words, a background of close neighbourly relations is evoked and this relation is flavoured by shared ethnic identity. For example, mutual borrowing is
part of the relationship, as mentioned by Jordan later in the same conversation: '. . . and Ruth calls 'cause you know Ruth like wanna borrow something
[1:09] so she says send Jordan up' (in an extract not quoted here). The
language used in Example 5 is highly indexical for Jewish identity: the term
alte kuker ('old codger') is a borrowing from Yiddish and would not necessarily be familiar to non-Jews on the West coast, where this family lives. The
term is used several times, first as an all-encompassing membership categ-
orization device ('she's a real *alte kuker*' '*alte kuker* right', turns 7 and 8)
arrived at collaboratively by the uncle and Dina. Next, the term comes up
again in reported speech, as the uncle recounts the name-calling incident
with Ruth (turns 9, 11, 17 and 22). Significantly, she retorts by calling him a
'little *pisher*' (literally 'little pisser', also borrowed from Yiddish), drawing on
the exact same Yiddish vocabulary resource as the uncle. This way the reported incident becomes a brief reincarnation of ritual verbal duelling among
familiars, where, as in similar exchanges between Turkish boys (Dundes,
Leach and Ozkok 1986) the overt level of verbal aggression is playful rather
than serious.

Gossipy talk in the family sheds new light on two further issues related to
idle-talk in general: the presence/absence of the party talked about, and the
moral stance adopted by the family towards the new information passed.

Secrets, presence and alienation

According to Simmel (1950), keeping secrets is essential to social life; it is a constitutive element of social relationships not only that the participants know something about each other but also that they keep secrets too. Society rests on the teleological 'determined ignorance' of one person about another, an ignorance which is desirable even in intimate relationships. The secret offers a second, private world to the revealed, public one. Given these two worlds, in Bergman's formulation, gossip 'draws an essential part of its energy from the tension between what a person does publicly and what he or she seeks to keep secret as his or her private affair' (Bergman 1993: 53). This is, according to Bergman (1993), why it is impossible to gossip about young children. For young children the world has not yet split into a public and private one; it lacks the third structural condition (the two first being 'absence' and 'acquaintance') for a person to become the protagonist of gossip: *privacy.*

Family discourse indeed offers many instances of gossipy talk about children in their presence in a way that seems to indicate that the public/private distinction is not always respected when it comes to children. But there are two important qualifications that need to be added here; first, both 'absence' and 'privacy' are negotiable and shifting rather than absolute categories. Second, gossipy talk in the presence of the party talked about is not restricted to children; both in the family and elsewhere in multi-party talk the physical presence of anyone may be suspended, non-ratified symbolically through the telling of 'secrets' from the present/non-present party's life.

Children are particularly vulnerable in this respect. Children's 'secrets' may be made public when mothers tell stories to neighbours and family about and around their children, framing them as co-present others (Miller and Byhouwer Moore 1989) or when high-control mothers appropriate their children's speaking rights during pediatric consultations (Aronsson and Rundstrom 1988). Instances from the multi-party, intergenerational event of family dinners highlight the liminality of 'presence', the ease by which participation frames shift, changing the story protagonist's role from co-participant to overhearer in the course of a few turns of talk.

In the following example, extracted from dinner at the home of a bilingual American-Israeli family (Blum-Kulka 1997),[3] change in participation frames is further signalled through a language switch from Hebrew to English. As the family is sitting down to dinner, the mother and the observer are engaged in a conversation in Hebrew about pets. The observer tells about a cat that appeared on her doorstep one day and stayed in the house, when Nadav (6, m) remarks (in Hebrew) 'and we have a bird that died'. The comment needs to be repeated five times before an uptake comes forth ('yes' from the observer) and the child continues by stating 'and we buried her'.

The mother assumes the role of the author at this point, elaborating the history of the event ('Itai brought us a bird . . . and we fed her . . . and when they came back from school they found her dead . . .') evaluating it via the child's reaction ('it was a tragedy . . . *Nadav actually wept for a whole hour* . . . real tragedy'). The events are recounted with Nadav as a ratified co-participant; though he says little, the mother signals by her choice of pronouns ('brought *us . . . we* fed . . .') and language (Hebrew) that she is voicing a shared tale, one owned by mother and the two boys. But the evaluation offered introduces a note of distancing, a possible shift in participation frames – Nadav's 'secret', namely his crying, is framed as 'his' rather than 'our' event, thereby positioning him as the protagonist of gossipy talk.

But, where in the exchange I reported above the shift in participation frames is only hinted at, it goes through a full transformation ten minutes later when, following a stretch of instrumental dinner talk concerning food, the mother tells the story of the bird again, this time to the father, in English:

Example 6

American-Israeli family 3: Nadav (6 m); Itai (9 m); Marit (observer).

1	Mother:	Today we had a tragedy in the house, did you hear?
2	Father:	Yeh, I heard. How did she die?
3	Mother:	I would assume <that she dried up> [>].
4	Nadav:	<I xxxxxxxxxxxx>[<]
5	Mother:	The sun was awfully hot out there on the porch. She finally got up [0.6] <and walked around and couldn't find a place to take shelter> [>]/
6	Nadav:	<why there xxx why there xxx why there why there [%said in Hebrew]
7	Mother:	She didn't look that great this morning either. She might have been thirsty.
%com:		Nadav constantly chatters with Itai in the background
8	Father:	You came home + . .
9	Mother:	**The kids came home and found her + . .**
10	Father:	**Yeah.**
11	Mother:	**There was a whole scene here. Boy Nadav was hysterical.**
12	Father:	**Did he cry?**
13	Mother:	**He was hysterical for an hour Nadav.**
14	Father:	**Really?**
15	Mother:	**Itai had his friend at least [%'at least' said in Hebrew]** **I hate to think what would happen if he didn't have his friend here.**
16	Nadav:	**Oh [=! Laughs]**
17	Father:	**Sit straight and eat!**
18	Mother:	**Did it help you <Itai that Ze'ev was here> [>]?**
19	Nadav:	**<No no [/] no no no >[<]**
20	Itai:	**What?**
21	Nadav:	**Like the money.**
22	Father:	**I said to xx that I'd give you a pep talk yesterday. I explained to Taichy that [0.78] that birds die very easily that you'd be upset.**
23	Marit:	**What did you give her to eat? [% in Hebrew]**

[conversation continues in Hebrew among the adults only].

The shift in style, language, choice of pronouns and point of view from the earlier account clearly signals a change in participation framework. This is a story told by one adult to another, framing the protagonist child as at least an overhearer, if not an eavesdropper, to gossipy talk about his own 'hysterical' emotional reaction to the death of a bird. Note that Nadav's attempts to enter the conversation (turns 4 and 6) are completely ignored (though in turn 6 at least his comment is relevant to the topic), with the result that he embarks on a *byplay* (Goffman 1967) with his brother (turns 18 to 20), and is reprimanded for disruptive behaviour (turn 17). But the positioning of child-protagonists as overhearers is *highly transient*; thus the use of direct address can at any moment shift participation frames again, marking a transition to inclusion instead of exclusion. A first attempt is made here towards Itai, who is also included in the story (turn 18); the second, by the father in turn 22, this time explicitly to each of the children in turn.

One possible interpretation of such symbolic suspension of presence in gossipy events could be attributed to the structural asymmetry between adults and children. But this would be an oversimplification. It should be kept in mind that, despite the adult–child asymmetries in communicative competencies, most of the time at dinner adults engage in deliberate efforts to include children as ratified participants in the talk; furthermore, practices of symbolic exclusion are not limited to children as the protagonists of gossipy events. Standard categories of persons who are sometimes treated in their presence as *non-persons* – as if they were not there – include the very young, the very old and the sick (Goffman 1959: 152). The practice may also surface in close-knit groups of intimate or semi-intimate groups. For example, in the sheltered workshop for the elderly, described by Handelman (1973), members engage in gossipy encounters, during which information that can be perceived as derogatory is being passed about a physically present member who is made temporarily interactionally absent. But, as Handelman shows, such encounters may be oscillating or oppositional, rendering absence temporary through objections raised by the gossipee herself or himself who might than manage to re-enter the interaction and even gain ascendancy over the gossiper. In the following extract from a family dinner conversation, the family (including the father) is talking about movies, when the mother and children introduce a 'complainable' item concerning the father's behaviour in cinemas. The complaint carries the linguistic indicators of exclusion: third person reference to the father, choice of reference-term audience designing the message for the children ('Daddy'), and a slightly mocking tone of voice.

Example 7

American-Israeli family 8: Nira (13 f); Yael (13 f), a friend of Nira's); Aya (6 f); Nathan (5 m); Sarah (observer).

1 Father: Nira do you think I'll <like the movie. [>]?
2 Yael: <It's about a > [<] policeman whose wife and kids are murdered.
          [%said in Hebrew]
3 Mother: O [=! laughs]
4 Yael: They're murdered and he wants to find out who did it and some girl helps him
          +...
5 Mother: **Daddy would like it as long as it wasn't scary.**
6 Father: **It's not for me. I hate it, I hate things <like that> [>]. [%said in Hebrew].**
7 Nira: **<All right>[<] enough [%said in Hebrew]**
8 Nathan: **There was a movie +/.**
9 Mother: **Daddy likes it if it was scary then he could yell.**
10 Father: **No, I get scared of those things like the Goonies and <xxxxxx> [>]**
11 Aya: **<Daddy xxx> [>] Indiana Jones and [1.44] when Nira went to see it with him there was xx 'Ooohh' and everybody looks [0.93] and turns around and its a <u>grown</u>-up screaming.**
12 Nira: **xxxx**
13 Father: **But that's the end.**
14 Mother: **It's embarrassing to go to the movies with xxx. You'll never know when he'll <u>ye</u>:ll [=! laughs] from fright.**

The mother's choice of reference terms consistently excludes the father, specifically directing the talk to the children (turn 5) or to all present (turn 14). The father opposes the exclusion by contributing his viewpoint on the complainable item (turns 6 and 10) but fails to engage his wife in direct address (see 13 and 14). The older daughter's attempt to stop her mother (or change the topic) (turn 7) seems to indicate displeasure at having her father talked about this way, while the younger child (turn 11) takes pleasure from exactly the opposite direction, aligning with her mother in dramatically illustrating her father's fright in the movies. It is difficult to assess, lacking the history of the couple's relationship and their accumulated memory of previous conversations, how serious a face threat this exchange represents for the father. Judging by repeated listening to the tape, his tone is serious, lacking any sign of playfulness, while his wife's tone wavers between being just humorous to slightly mocking. Whatever its implications for the parties involved, the exchange shows that the suspension of presence can be maintained even in the face of opposition from the person talked about, and that the protagonists of such practices need not necessarily be children.

Goffman (1967) mentions four ways in which an individual can be alienated from a conversational encounter: *external preoccupation, self-consciousness, interaction consciousness* and *other consciousness* (1967: 117–25). These forms of alienation threaten the joint spontaneous involvement of successful interaction rituals, showing a failure on the part of an individual to fulfil his or her involvement obligations. Gossipy events concerning a physically present party can be added as another form of alienation, this time of the other rather than the self. In this sense alienation through exclusion is a further threat to sociability; 'idle talk' can lose its 'idleness' when involving potential face-threats to members present.

Moral dilemmas: teacher talk

A recurrent topic of talk about 'others' at dinner is talk about teachers. Predominantly (but not exclusively) initiated by children, such talk typically centres around complainable events from school-life. Such talk juxtaposes, in Habermas's (1987) terms a systemic 'institutional order' of the school on the public domain, with the private domain of the 'lifeworld' in the family. Children's critical talk about teachers poses a moral dilemma for the parents: do they object to such criticism, upholding the institutional order for their children and thereby positioning themselves as defenders of the system, or do they align with the children against the teachers, allowing teachers to be the protagonist of gossipy talk, thereby favouring solidarity formation in the lifeworld over the upholding of the institutional order of schools.

The solutions to this dilemma at the family dinner table range from weak upholding of the institutional order by avoiding affiliation with critical positions against teachers, to the other end of strong emotively coloured affiliation with children's critical positions. The process of negotiation over the meaning of recounted incidents leads on many occasions to a reframing of initial positions and to new understandings. Underlying these events are shared cultural background assumptions with regard to the necessity of schooling. There are indications in the discourse that children actually expect censorship from adults on complaints against teachers. Thus, in the following exchange, Shlomit (12) uses the recording of the dinner as a way to retract from her critical statement about a teacher:

Example 8

Israeli family 2: Shlomit (12 f); Ricky (10 f); Mira (5 f): Rachel (observer) Yoash (adult guest); Giora (9 m, child guest).
Shlomit and Yoash are discussing Shlomit's history teacher (a woman); Yoash has studied with this woman's husband, who is a professor of Judaic studies.
1 Shlomit: Does he talk a lot? She is a terrible talker.
2 Yoash: He is a very educated man.
3 Shlomit: **She is completely dumb.**
4 Yoash: **She is dumb?**
5 Shlomit: **Excuse me, it's being recorded.**
%com: **the children all laugh.**
[Translated from Hebrew]

Yoash's clarification query could be interpreted as a cue to elaborate as well as a hint of censorship. Shlomit treats it as a hint of censorship and apologizes for having used such a strong attribute by evoking the recording. In other words, she indicates an awareness of a public/private division; certain things are not said publicly about teachers, where 'public' might include the family dinner table.

The upholding of the of institutional order is expressed in the discourse through strategies of avoidance. Thus, when in a Jewish-American family Jordan (8 m) announces that his substitute teacher that day 'got mean', the father's first reaction is to half-jokingly prejudge the story by asking 'Why? What did you do to her today?' As Jordan goes on to complain that she didn't let the children out for recess, despite protest from all the kids that she is breaking the rule established by the regular teacher, the father reacts by changing the subject and asking when the regular teacher is coming back. In other words, in the controversy between the institutional version (the teacher having the authority to make decisions about recess) and the child's version (an injustice has occurred), the father chooses to withhold judgement, thereby rejecting the suggested challenge to institutional authority (Blum-Kulka 1997: 48).

Indications of an uncritical embracing of children's position against teachers come from unexpectedly harsh side remarks by parents at dinner, like 'she is awful' or 'he must be an alcoholic' (a mother's reaction to her son's mention of his teacher's constantly red nose). More typical is solidarity shown through a lack of protest, as in the following extract:

Example 9

Israeli family 1: Yoram (10 m); Nadav (11 m); Giora (9 m guest child); Rachel (observer).
The children are talking about their English teacher, using the English word 'teacher' as his nickname; the topic of teacher-talk is initiated by the guest child, Giora, who makes a comment about his hosts' home-class teacher, Rachel.

1	Giora:	Rachel the teacher must be very [/] very tough.
2	Nadav:	We terribly hate <'teacher'> [>] [% 'teacher' is said in English]
3	Mother:	<Teacher> that's what you call him {=! laughs].
4	Yoram:	Shnicer <visher> [>] [% rhyming nonsense words]
5	Giora:	<I actually> like him.
6	Nadav:	But we hate him. So we xxxx +/.
7	Yoram:	We sing # 'one two'
8	Nadav:	So we [0.72] nu what do you call it +...
9	Yoram:	Really he does not know how to teach xxx +/.
10	Nadav:	We fly airplanes [/] fly airplanes and when somebody is thrown out of class he gets back in and hides behind the desks.
11	Mother:	**Not very nice [=! quietly]**
12	Rachel:	The tea is excellent [//] yes, excellent.
13	Mother:	**Just a minute, why do you hate 'teacher'?**
14	Yoram:	'Teacher' does not know how to teach.
15	Nadav:	Last year he was a complete softy and this year he is tough.
16	Yoram:	But he does not know how to teach he says write it and that's it.

17	Giora:	There are two 'teacher'
18	Mother:	**Who is your 'teacher'?**
19	Giora:	It's Ya'acov actually I like Ya'acov.
20	Yoram:	No he is bad he doesn't know how to teach.
21	%com:	[the children recite together in English]
		'Teddy bear [bir] [//] teddy bear [bir] look around look around'
22	Yoram:	He has a new name 'mixer'.
21	Nadav:	You know where it comes # from this word from 'teacher'.
22	Mother:	**'shvicer'? [% 'a show off' in Hebrew, borrowed from Yiddish]**
		Say, does he teach you songs, this 'teacher'?
23	Children:	[% singing in English] 'Good morning to mother to father /oh xx absolutely
		good morning to brother to sister to flower.'
	%Par:	the children are making lot of noise
24	Giora:	Shsh don't yell.
@	End.	

The presence of the guest child, Giora, triggers the type of talk children presumably engage in among themselves when talking of teachers: calling the teacher names ('teacher', 'shnicer' 'mixer'), expressing negative attitudes ('we hate him'), complaining about his teaching ('he does not know how to teach'), showing off 'bad behaviour' ('we fly airplanes . .'.) and eventually getting caught up in a mocking performance of what they learnt at school from this very teacher. Giora's (the guest child) role as the nominated addressee of the talk can be seen by his protest in turn 5 ('I actually like him'), and his comments in turns 17 and 19. This framing presents the adults with the dilemma whether to interfere and sanction the children's talk, or hold back completely and act as silent overhearers. The mother's solution is a mid-way between this two options: she does interject with a mild protest, uttered very quietly ('not very nice', turn 11) but continues with a question (turn 13) that signals at least partial alignment with the children. She echoes the children's own words on 'hating' the teacher and uses their nickname for him, thereby orientating herself to their point of view and allowing for the possibility that they are right in their criticism. The line she takes is held up through a further repetitions of the nickname in turns 18 and 22 and her joining in the nicknaming game (turn 22). In asking about the songs he teaches (turn 22) she seems to distance herself from the children's point of view, perhaps suggesting in an indirect way that they do learn something from 'teacher'.

On the continuum from silence to solidarity in reaction to children's gossipy talk about teachers, Jewish-American families seem more inclined towards silence, and Israelis towards solidarity with the children. In interfacing the institutional, public world of schools with the lifeworld of the family, Israelis simultaneously engage in two opposing activities. On the one hand, they engage in boundary crossing through 'good gossip' about teachers. For example, on one occasion a mother tells her son about his teacher's physical problems, in the process praising her courage and stamina ('Do you know your teacher is something really special?'). On the other hand, they draw imaginary lines of solidarity between all pupils, past and present vs. all teachers, at school and at the University. Thus two adult guests at one dinner entertain the family with shared memories of their days at the University, making fun of their Latin teacher, who was particularly 'adept' at putting everybody to sleep from sheer boredom. In both groups teacher talk also occasions overtly socializing events, where children engage with adults in meaning making through negotiation in rich and formative ways.

Example 10

Israeli family 3: Dalit (9 f); Orna (8 f), Rachel (observer); Marcus (video-camera man).

1	Orna:	What a mean teacher we have for ballet, she is called Rosa and she yells at us all time and tells us we are *fuyot* [% 'awful', using a slang expression] [1:16] she is te:rrible.
		And Mom went to talk to the principal today.
2	Mother:	I have already told Rachel the whole story [=! laughs]
3	Orna:	Oh yes?
4	Rachel:	I think that mother was right but I understand that you actually felt very embarrassed because of this but you have # no reason.
5	Orna:	Why?
6	Mother:	You see you have no reason, Rachel says so too.
7	Rachel:	I think mother was right.
8	Orna:	Right, and she even came from Russia, the lady Rosa {% waves her hand in ballet movement]
	%com:	Orna's use of the logical connector 'even' (*afilu* in Hebrew) here is odd, as what she seems to mean (and is understood as saying) is 'because'.
9	Father:	So what if she came from Russia?
10	Orna:	And there they did not have even bread to eat, so mother told us.
11	Marcus:	They had only bread.
12	Mother:	They had bread and potatoes [=! laughs].
13	Father:	No they had potatoes as well.
14	Mother:	And here she needs to prepare a show at Beit Ha'am [% a show-hall in Jerusalem] with eh [1.72] white ballet dresses and +/.
15	Marcus:	But the best dancers in the world came from Russia, so that they do have + . . .
16	Orna:	Right.
17	Mother:	Right, she's a very good teacher only +/.
18	Orna:	But mean, all the time she xx +/.
19	Marcus	No may be she is mean.
20	Mother:	Her mentality.
21	Rachel:	She is very much a frustrated ballerina.
22	Orna:	She and da [//] she dances beautifully [0.66] but every second she yells at us, if we raise our feet # a bit if one finger is not straight, then she starts yelling at us that we are {*fuyot*} [% 'awful'] and we should straighten the finger.
23	Father:	xxxxxxx
24	Mother:	She'll send them to Siberia [=! laughs].
25	Rachel:	Oo [=! laughs]
26	Mother:	If she could she would do it.

27 Marcus:	The truth is that there are many very beautiful places in Siberia, but people certainly think +/.
28 Mother:	Listen, beautiful or not I have no desire to visit this place.
29 Dalit:	Why?
30 Mother:	Because of the connotations.
31 Orna:	What's 'connotations'?
32 Mother:	Associations when you think of Siberia.
33 Orna:	Yes?
34 Marcus:	Sure, because it's far away from all eh [/] from all the surroundings.
35 Orna:	Then surely Rosa would have sent us.
36 Mother:	To dance on the ice [2.34] with white frills.
37 Rachel:	I think its not connected so much to meanness but that it is a style.
38 Mother:	Mentality.
39 Rachel:	+, a style she was taught.
40 Mother:	Exactly.

There are several issues negotiated throughout this exchange: the child's embarrassment at her mother intervening in school, the ballet teacher's 'meanness', ethnic stereotypes with regard to Russian Jews as well as preconceptions about Siberia. It is an example of *theory-building* (Ochs, Taylor, Rudolph and Smith 1992) at its best; with the active participation of all present, guests and children included, a child's perspective on her teacher's behaviour is both supported and challenged in ways that lead to a re-appraisal and re-contextualization of the original complaint. One of the remarkable features of this co-construction of meaning is the full enactment of the sociability principle whereby everyone's 'overall evaluation of the subject matter at hand – whose editorial comments, as it were . . . is treated with respect' (Goffman 1981: 14, note 8). Another feature is related to its socializing functions; it demonstrates well how children may be assisted in their sense-making of the world by talking to adults, with people other than their parents making significant contributions to the process. As conversationalists argue and shift positions new perspectives emerge, until a consensual agreement is reached.

Affiliations shift with the talk, with the two guests (Rachel and Marcus) playing a central role in the meaning-making process and acting as challengers of stereotypes and preconceptions expressed by children and adults alike. The complainable item, as presented by Orna to the observer in turn 1, seems to centre on the teacher's unpleasant behaviour, but also mentions the mother's visit to the principal. Rachel's comment in turn 4 ('I think that mother was right') relates not to the overt complainable item but to an inferred one (presumably included in the 'whole story' told to her previously): namely the child's embarrassment at her mother's intervention. On the issue of the mother's visit Rachel emphatically aligns with the mother, with the two women presenting a closely synchronized team for the child. But on the issue of the teacher's behaviour, new alliances are formed. Orna's attempt to link the teacher's 'bad' behaviour to her Russian origins is at first fully backed by the mother, who seems to have been the originator of the idea that against the background of near-famine experienced back in Russia (as partly voiced by Orna, 'they did not have even <u>bread</u> to eat, so mother told us') she can't be expected to perform properly as a ballet teacher. In holding up this position the mother sidesteps her husband's opposition – 'So what if she came from Russia?' – and ignores Marcus's first attempt (turn 11) to change the direction of the talk.[4] Marcus's second attempt meets with much more success. When he mentions that the 'best dancers in the world came from Russia' (turn 15) both Orna and the mother concede his point and admit, as implied, that the generalization also holds for this specific teacher; as indicated by Orna's 'right' (turn 16) and the mother's admittance '. . . she's a very good teacher only. .' (turn 17). Following further protest (see turn 18) Orna even shifts to praise ('she dances beautifully', turn 22). But first disagreeing with her mother she insists on the teacher's 'meanness' (turn 18). Marcus, in accordance with the preference for agreement in conversation (Sacks 1987) aligns with Orna's position in turn 18, allowing for the possibility that this teacher might be an exception ('no may be she is mean', turn 19). The mother's adoption of Orna's perspective in blaming the teacher further emerges in her sarcastic comments about Siberia ('She'll send them to Siberia' . . . 'to dance on the ice with white frills', turns 24 and 36), but is eventually abandoned in favour of the more sympathetic explanation offered by Rachel ('I think its not connected so much to meanness but that it is a style', turn 37) she fully agrees with. Thus the ballet teacher's Russian origin, first used as grounds for blame, evoking negative stereotype of Russian Jews, is now transformed to a pardonable excuse for her seemingly harsh behaviour with the children. With several issues negotiated, this example shows that, when families engage in debate in the spirit of *communicative rationality* (Habermas 1971, cited in Layder 1994: 189), new understandings may be reached for all concerned, children and adults alike.

Conclusions

Gossipy talk in the family problematizes all three elements posited by Bergman (1993) as essential and constitutive for gossip: *acquaintance*, *absence* and *privacy*. Unequal distribution of knowledge between parents and children (or between family and guests) with regard to absent friends, relatives and acquaintances affects the genre in several ways. Beyond introducing a need to redress the balance in information states through the interjection of explanations (as in the case of the mother supplying information on a non-present 'Daddy' to the observer in Example 2), it also creates an imbalance in emotional attitudes towards absent others, affecting sociability. Thus the chatty, idle talk associated with sociable gossip among friends (regardless of whether its 'good' or 'bad' gossip) emerges in family discourse mainly when levels of emotional involvement are low, as when celebrities are concerned, and is less easily achievable when friends of the parents or children are concerned. A different set of issues arises when the 'acquaintance' in question happens to be a child's teacher: in addition to differences between participants in degrees of emotional involvement and knowledge, talk about teachers interfaces the public and private spheres in ways that might break up the family as a solidarity unit and position children and adults in opposition to each other.

The second condition, namely absence, poses a new set of problems. In the family as elsewhere, participants physically present may be symbolically made absent, turned into non-persons excluded from a given gossipy topic or even made the topic of such talk. The unique features of family discourse in this respect are the vulnerability of children as candidates for momentary exclusions, and the transient, fleeting nature of the acts of the symbolic suspension of presence.

In defining the type of knowledge transmitted through gossip (as related to privacy) Bergman insists that it is knowledge that '. . . actually makes a difference in the real and virtual social identity of the subject of gossip. Thus the gossip information must concern something that does not agree with the subject of gossip's self-presentation and whose "public disclosure" for the subject of gossip would probably evoke a feeling of embarrassment or shame' (Bergman 1993: 58). The spectrum of gossipy information discussed at the family dinners observed is much wider than this definition; though each event does intrude on the private sphere of another, probably due to the presence of children it is only rarely seriously indiscreet. Yet gossipy information can constitute in Brown and Levinson's (1987) terms, a face-threatening act in several ways: for the protagonist of gossip, the FTA touches on both negative face (infringing on the private sphere of another) and positive face (disclosing potentially morally contaminating information); such threats being especially poignant when the subject of gossip is someone physically present at dinner. For the deliverer of gossip, the face threat concerns positive face; disseminating indiscreet information about another reflects badly on its transmitter, as witnessed by the child who retracts because of the recording (Example 8).

Despite its problematic aspects, on the whole the genre of gossipy talk represents sociable talk, with important socializing gains for children. The presence and participation of children in this speech event is one of its most prominent features. We have seen that, by being treated as ratified participants for gossipy talk, children may gain access to adult perspectives on the tellability of gossipy news, offer their own perspectives on tellability and negotiate with adults the cultural and familial norms evoked in mapping the social world. Precisely because alliances and affiliations in gossipy talk in the family may cut across age lines, the genre offers children a rare opportunity for full participation in multi-party, intergenerational discourse forms.

Notes

1. I'm grateful to the two research assistants in the project, Anat Schelly and Ronen Avramson for compiling and transcribing the data.
2. Transcription follows the CHAT format (MacWhinney 1991) for the following conventions: < > = overlap; [>] = overlap follows; [<] = overlap precedes; # = noticeable pause shorter than 0.3 seconds; length of longer pauses is given in parenthesis in tens of seconds[/] = retracing without correction; [//] = retracing with correction; +/. = interrupted utterance; +... = trailing off, (incompletion); +^ = quick uptake (latching); +, = self completion; ++ = other completion; and = an incomplete word; [=! text] = paralinguistic material; [%com] = contextual information; xxx = inaudible utterance(s); number of xs stands for length of inaudible utterance in seconds. In addition, punctuation symbols indicate intonation contours, underline = emphatic stress; CAPS = very emphatic stress. Bold = is used to highlight segments of interest; @End+marks end of topical segment. {italics} = borrowed terms from another language. Data from Israeli families, originally in Hebrew, is presented in translation.
3. This and the next example come from the database of dinner conversations in American-Israeli families (Blum-Kulka 1997) and were not included originally in the analyses for this study. The frequencies quoted and all other examples in this study are based on the analyses of 'gossipy events' in the data from the mealtimes of twenty Israeli and Jewish-American families.
4. Note that by challenging the truth value of the previous propositon (Orna: '... they did not have even bread', Marcus: 'They had only bread'), Marcus is also conveying a metamessage on the importance of adhering to the maxim of quality (Grice 1975: 46 'Do not say that for which you lack adequate evidence'), introducing to the discussion the notion that validity claims of the objective, external world need to pass the test of factuality.

References

Arendt, H. (1968) *Men in Dark Times*. London: Jonathon Cape.

Aronsson, K. and Rundstrom, B. (1988) Child discourse and parental control in pediatric consultations. *Text*, 8, 159–89.

Bergman, J. (1993) *Discreet Indiscretions: The Social Organization of Gossip*. Hathorne, NY: Aldine de Gruyter.

Blum-Kulka, S. (1997) *Dinner Talk: Cultural Patterns of Sociability and Socialization in Family Discourse*. Mahwah, New Jersey London: Lawrence Erlbaum.

Brown, P. and Levinson, S. (1987) *Politeness: Some Universals in Language Usage*. Cambridge: Cambridge University Press.

Dundes, A., Leach, J. and Ozkok, B. (1972/1986) The strategies of Turkish boys' verbal dueling rhymes. In J. J. Gumperz and D. Hymes (eds) *The Ethnography of Communication*. New York: Basil Blackwell, 130–61.

Gluckman, M. (1963) Gossip and scandal. *Current Anthropology*, 4, 307–695.

Goffman, E. (1959) *The Presentation of Self in Everyday Life*. New York: Doubleday Anchor Books.

Goffman, E. (1967) *Interaction Ritual: Essays on Face to Face Behavior*. New York: Doubleday.

Goffman, E. (1981) *Forms of Talk*. Philadelphia: University of Pennsylvania Press.

Grice, H. P. (1975) Logic and conversation. In P. Cole and J. Morgan (eds) *Syntax and Semantics 3: Speech Acts*. New York: Academic Press, 43–59.

Habermas, J. (1971) *Towards a Rational Society*. London: Heinemann.

Habermas, J. (1987) *The Theory of Communicative Action Volume 2: Lifeworld and System: A Critique of Functionalist Reason*. Cambridge: Polity Press.

Handelman, D. (1973) Gossip in encounters: the transmission of information in a bounded social setting. *Man*, 8, 210–27.

Layder, D. (1994) *Understanding Social Theory*. London: Sage.

MacWhinney, B. (1991) *The CHILDES Project: Tools for Analyzing Talk*. Hillsdale, NJ: Lawrence Erlbaum.

Miller, P. J. and Byhouwer Moore, B. (1989) Narrative conjunctions of caregiver and child: A comparative perspective on socialization through stories. *Ethos*, 17, 428–49.

Ochs, E. and Capps, L. (1996) Narrating the self. *American Review of Anthropology*, 25, 19–43.

Ochs, E., Taylor, C., Rudolph, D. and Smith, R. (1992) Storytelling as a theory-building activity. *Discourse Processes*, 15, 37–72.

Sacks, H. (1978) Some technical considerations of a dirty joke. In J. Schenkein (ed.) *Studies in the Organization of Conversational Interaction* (ed. Gail Jefferson from unpublished lectures: fall 1971, 9–12). New York: Academic Press, 249–70.

Sacks, H. (1987) On the preference for agreement and contiguity in sequences of conversation. In G. Button and J. E. R. Lee (eds) *Talk and Social Organization*. Clevedon, UK: Multilingual Matters, 54–69.

Sacks, H. (1992) *Lectures on Conversation* Volumes 1 & 2, Oxford: Blackwell Publishers.

Schiffrin, D. (1984) Jewish argument as sociability. *Language in Society*, 13, 311–35.

Simmel, G. (1917/1950) *The sociology of George Simmel*. London: Collier-Macmillan.

Simmel, G. (1961) The sociology of sociability. In T. Parsons, E. Shils, K. D. Naegele and J. R. Pitts (eds) *Theories of Society: Foundations of Modern Sociological Theory* (reprinted from *American Journal of Sociology*, 55 (1911), 157–162). New York: The Free Press, 157–63.

Spacks, P. M. (1985) *Gossip*. New York: Knopf.

Statman, D. (1994) Gossip, 'bad tongue' and morality. *Iyunim Bexinux*, 43, 399–415 [in Hebrew].

9

Small talk and subversion: female speakers backstage[1]
Jennifer Coates

Introduction

In this chapter I want to examine the small talk – sometimes referred to as 'gossip' (see Jones 1980; Coates 1989) – of women and girls in spontaneous interaction with each other. In particular, I shall look at the use of narrative and of reported speech in small talk and at the way women friends play with different voices. I shall explore the role of this kind of informal talk in the self-presentation of women and girls, in the construction of alternative femininities. I shall draw on the work of Erving Goffman in this analysis, in particular on his notions of ritual and of frontstage and backstage (Goffman 1971). Like Goffman, I define myself as 'an anthropological fieldworker whose "tribe" [is] the unnoticed world of everyday interaction under our own noses' (Collins 1988: 44).

Conversation can be seen as a ritual, and the ritual of conversational small talk that occurs backstage plays a crucial role in the construction and maintenance of the self. This chapter will focus on those aspects of women's backstage performance of self which do not fit prevailing norms of femininity. I shall argue that the backstage talk possible only with close friends provides women with an arena where norms can be subverted and challenged and alternative selves explored.

Women and 'being nice'

In 1996, Jenny Joseph's poem 'Warning' was voted Britain's favourite post-war poem in a BBC poll. This is how it begins:

> When I am an old woman I shall wear purple
> With a red hat which doesn't go, and doesn't suit me.

And I shall spend my pension on brandy and summer gloves
And satin sandals, and say we've no money for butter.
I shall sit down on the pavement when I'm tired
And gobble up samples in shops and press alarm bells
And run my stick along the public railings
And make up for the sobriety of my youth.
I shall go out in my slippers in the rain
And pick flowers in other people's gardens
And learn to spit . . .

The poem's popularity suggests that its message – a woman threatening that in her old age she will overthrow the constraints of conventional femininity – has struck a chord with many women. The poem celebrates a woman who dares to challenge conventional norms, a women who declares that she will refuse to conform. Conformity here involves appearance, domestic duties and behaving 'nicely'; challenging these norms means behaving 'badly' and having fun.

I do not want to suggest that women never have fun and never behave 'badly', except backstage. In the 1990s there were many examples of young high-profile media women doing 'behaving badly' frontstage (examples are Denise van Outen, Ulrike Johnson, Zoe Ball).[2] The popularity of the television comedy series *Absolutely Fabulous*, where the two main characters behave outrageously, also suggests a growing fascination with, and tolerance of, women leading independent lives. But the reaction of the tabloid press to a recent incident, when Melanie Blatt of AllSaints exposed her abdomen on stage at a concert – she was 5 months pregnant at the time – indicates that, while women may now feel able to challenge the norms in public, such behaviour is still perceived as unladylike and shocking. In other words, the norms of conventional – hegemonic – femininity are still in place.

Doing femininity according to these norms crucially involves being 'nice'. The ideal of femininity, established in the nineteenth century, is the 'perfect wife and mother', the epitome of niceness (Purvis 1987: 255). Brown and Gilligan (1992) have explored in moving detail the struggles that girls have with the social pressure to be nice. Their study involved nearly one hundred girls between the ages of seven and eighteen, students at the Laurel School for Girls (a private day school in Cleveland, Ohio). They suggest that adolescence is, for girls, 'a time of disconnection' when they struggle 'over speaking and not speaking, knowing and not knowing, feeling and not feeling' (Brown and Gilligan 1992: 4). They show how a girl feels that 'people will not be nice to her if she is not nice to them' (op. cit: 60). But the girls interviewed by Brown and Gilligan are aware that being nice to others often involves them in hiding what they really feel, in not saying what they really feel. This dilemma continues into adulthood. Adult women feel under pressure to be nice, but also need to express the whole range of feelings, nice and less nice.

The same is not true for men. In the extract from the poem given above, for example, the woman's threat that she will learn to spit violates a norm about adult *female* behaviour in Britain today, not adult male behaviour: no one is shocked by the sight of a man spitting in the street or on the football pitch. Moreover, it seems that in the late twentieth century, while women feel obliged to try to behave nicely, male speakers will overtly deny niceness. A good example of this is Pilkington's (1992) study of the small talk of four groups of same-sex speakers. Her analysis of their talk revealed striking gender differences: 'The men ... frequently abuse one another ... [They] often made comments that indicated that they looked upon this abusive behaviour as a positive thing and polite behaviour as something negative. Jim says to Ray at one point, "Don't try to make out that I'm nice"; he then goes on to comment, "I like complete bastards" ' (Pilkington 1992: 57). The contrast between Jim's insistence that he is *not* nice and the struggles of the girls interviewed by Brown and Gilligan to conform to ideals of feminine 'niceness' is striking.[3]

It seems that, in the modern world, 'behaving badly' has positive connotations when associated with men, but negative connotations when associated with women. This means that certain kinds of behaviour are taboo for women. Yet the evidence of the poem I started with is that there is a strong desire in women to challenge these constraints.

Frontstage and backstage

So where is this challenge expressed? I shall draw on Goffman's (1971) dramaturgical metaphors of 'frontstage' and 'backstage' to explore the way women deal with aspects of the self which do not accord with conventional norms of femininity. For all of us, 'frontstage' performance is much more carefully controlled, and much more susceptible to prevailing norms of politeness and decorum. Informal personal conversations are widely acknowledged to be backstage activity. This does not mean that in interaction with friends we are not performing, but the distinction between performer and audience is blurred: there is a sense of 'all-in-together' and failures in performance cease to be a worry. 'There can be plenty of performance failures here [i.e. backstage]: in fact the sharing of such failures as they actually transpire is what makes up the "informality" of the talk, and the sense of ease and intimacy of selves that goes with it' (Collins 1988: 56). This means that burping or sneezing in the middle of an utterance to a friend will actually underline the friendliness of the encounter.

Given the constraints on appropriate behaviour for women in public spaces, even today, it is not surprising that women have always had a particular relish for the 'sense of ease and intimacy of selves' that goes with informal backstage talk. Goffman himself noticed that women interacting with other women provides a particularly good example of backstage. In *The Presentation of Self in Everyday Life* he quotes a long extract from Simone de Beauvoir's *The Second Sex*, which ends as follows:

> With other women, a woman is behind the scenes; she is polishing her equipment, but not in battle; she is getting her costume together, preparing her make-up, laying out her tactics; she is lingering in dressing gown and slippers in the wings before making her entrance on the stage; she likes this warm, easy, relaxed atmosphere . . . For some women this warm and frivolous intimacy is dearer than the serious pomp of relations with men.

> (De Beauvoir quoted in Goffman 1971: 115)

However, an important feature of all backstage talk is the tension which exists between front- and backstage norms. This is exacerbated in the case of women speakers by their position in society, in particular their relationship to symbolic capital (see Bourdieu 1977; Eckert 1993; 1998). According to this perspective, women need to gain symbolic capital on the basis of their character and their relationships with others. Women's symbolic capital is evaluated in relation to community norms, so it is very important that women attempt to control these norms. Penelope Eckert claims that all-female talk is 'the major means by which they do this' (Eckert 1993: 35). This means that women need to pay attention to frontstage norms of femininity even while letting their hair down backstage.

In this chapter I shall draw on a corpus[4] of both mixed and same-sex conversation gathered over the last fifteen years with the aim of exploring the speaking practices of (white, middle- and working-class) women and men with their friends, in pairs and in larger groups. Speakers ranged in age from twelve to fifty years old. The corpus consists of spontaneously occurring conversations, recorded with the agreement of participants in settings chosen by participants themselves: in the case of the women this was invariably the home, apart from one group of adolescent girls who recorded themselves in a room in their local youth club. (This contrasts with male participants who chose a wide range of settings: in their homes, in pubs, in a university office after hours, in a youth club, even in a garden shed in the case of one group of [dope-smoking] adolescent boys.)

Small talk – women backstage

Backstage talk can be described as 'performers' shop talk' (Collins 1988: 56). One of the things women friends do with each other is talk over their performance frontstage, describing the feelings that accompanied the performance. During such talk, women will often say things which contradict the polite front maintained during the performance. Such contradictions are an intrinsic part of backstage talk: 'A back region or backstage may be defined as a place, relative to a given performance, where the impression fostered by the performance is knowingly contradicted as a matter of course' (Goffman 1971: 114).

The following extract[5] from a conversation between two young women friends illustrates this nicely. One of the friends (Ann) has complained of having a bad day at work.

Example 1

```
1 Jude: why did you have a bad day?
  Ann:                          got into work this morning
```
```
2 Jude:                  oh dear/    ⌈how did you break them?
  Ann: and broke two mugs/    then ⌊er-
```
```
3 Jude:                      ⌈what did they say?
  Ann: dropped 'em/ <LAUGHS> ⌊then er I got all the bloody
```
```
4 Ann: snotty customers/ stupid people/ . had one lady who er
```
```
5 Ann: bought twelve glasses/ and I was wrapping them all up/
```
```
6 Ann: and she'd told me after I'd wrapped six of them up/
```
```
7 Ann: 'Can you take the price off the bottom of them'/
```
```
8 Ann: stupid cow/ 'Yes certainly Madam'/ so I unwrapped
```
```
9 Ann: them all and rewrapped them/
```

Ann's story of her 'bad day' makes very clear distinctions between frontstage and backstage. In her frontstage persona, she describes herself as answering the customer politely and doing what she is asked to do without question. The two speakers also implicitly acknowledge that breaking things at work is a failure of performance. At the same time, Ann intersperses her narrative with comments which tell Jude what she really felt at work. She refers to the customers she'd served as *bloody snotty customers* and *stupid people* (staves 3–4), and her comment *stupid cow* (stave 8) about one particular customer is juxtaposed with her acting out of her own super-polite persona saying to this customer *Yes certainly Madam*.

So in this example, Ann tells the story of her day to a friend and presents herself in a way which directly contradicts the impression she had carried off at work. At work, the exigencies of her role as a (female) shop worker require her to perform herself as 'nice'; at home, talking to a close friend, she performs a very different self, one who is not nice, who is rude about the customers and who resents doing what they ask. We have to infer that 'behaving badly' like this backstage – that is, owning our less nice, our more impolite and unsociable feelings – is accepted and even welcomed between friends, precisely because backstage is the appropriate arena for dropping your front, and because reciprocal admissions of 'not-niceness' reinforce solidarity.

I want to look now at the backstage talk of some very young speakers, three four-year-old girls. This example provides a very striking case of female speakers performing 'not-nice' selves, in the context of fantasy play. The three speakers here (G1, G2 and G3) are playing with dolls in the 'Wendy Corner' of their British nursery kindergarten class. The girls decide in their personae as Mothers that they need to bath the babies. They move through a sequence of utterances: 'G3 suggests the water is hot; G2 says "Let's boil the babies"; G1: "Yes let's boil them and boil them"; G2: "We'll boil them till their skins fall off"' (Cook-Gumperz in press).

This example comes from data collected by Jenny Cook-Gumperz in research exploring the role of play – specifically the role of talk in play – in the formation of gender identity. Girls' pretend play often involves games where girls enact domestic scenarios (see also Goodwin 1988; 1990). In modern western societies, learning to be a woman involves learning how to be a 'good mother', to the extent that 'An idealised figure of the Good Mother casts a long shadow' over the lives of girls and women (Ruddick 1989: 31; see also Weedon 1987: 33–4). Play has a key role in this learning. Cook-Gumperz argues that 'one important function of the game [of Mummies and Babies] is to allow the two girls, in their game talk, to explore their gender role as women' (Cook-Gumperz 1995: 416). But clearly, the game *is* a game and the girls are aware of this: they exploit the backstage nature of their play together away from adults (though in this case not away from the concealed tape-recorder) to explore the role of women as mother by pushing at the limits, and by acting out being *bad* mothers.

The expression of such violent and blatantly un-maternal feelings by four-year-old girls is simultaneously amusing and shocking. The expression of similar unmaternal feelings in relation to real children by adult women is much more shocking. The next example (Example 2) comes from a conversation between three women in their 30s who have been friends for many years.

Example 2

----

1 Anna: some people when they have children just think- just

----

2 Anna: assume that everybody loves kids/
  Sue: ⌈that everybody
  Liz: oh I know/ ⌊they do/

```
----------------------------------------------------------------------------
3 Anna:  they know ⎡all they have to ⎡do-
  Sue:             ⎢((xxx))          ⎢who wants to see them))
  Liz:             ⎣especially theirs/
----------------------------------------------------------------------------
4 Anna:  it's like Michael's sister was like that wasn't she?=
  Sue:                                                    =mhm/
  Liz:
----------------------------------------------------------------------------
5 Anna:  'you must love ⎡((2 sylls))/         they're so wonderful'/
  Sue:                  ⎣they were HORrible/
  Liz:
----------------------------------------------------------------------------
6 Anna:  and they were GHASTly children/
  Sue:
  Liz:                                   nobody ever says
----------------------------------------------------------------------------
7 Liz:   that do they/ <LAUGHING>
----------------------------------------------------------------------------
```

In this example, we see the three friends exploring the clash between the assumption that *everybody loves kids* (stave 2) and that all children are *wonderful* (stave 5) and the reality that some children are NOT wonderful – *they were horrible* (stave 5); *they were ghastly children* (stave 6). There is explicit acknowledgement that to call children 'horrible' or 'ghastly' is taboo – Liz says *nobody ever says that do they* (staves 6–7). This is an interesting comment, since the three women are in fact saying precisely that. Liz's remark can be understood to mean 'nobody ever says that when they are frontstage'. The frontstage performance of Woman/Mother entails certain sorts of behaviour and precludes others. Saying 'children are wonderful' is expected, but saying 'children are horrible' is taboo. The fact that these women feel able to express subversive views with each other demonstrates the backstage nature of women's friendly talk. These women exemplify very clearly Goffman's (1971: 115) description of backstage as a place where '. . . the performer can relax; he [*sic*] can drop his front, forgo speaking his lines, and step out of character'. These women are relaxed: they have dropped their front, and stepped out of character.

Having agreed that they have negative feelings about some children, the three friends go on to consider their attitude to children in general. This next extract from their conversation is initiated by Anna, the only one of the three who does not have children.

Example 3

```
----------------------------------------------------------------------------
1 Anna:  can I just ask you two as mothers/ did you used
----------------------------------------------------------------------------
2 Anna:  to feel particularly fond of children before you
----------------------------------------------------------------------------
```

```
 3  Anna:  had them?=
    Sue:              =no/=    how can I say that? I used to
    Liz:              =no/                    .
```

```
 4  Anna:                          ⎡you did didn't you/
    Sue:   work with them/<LAUGHS> ⎣but no/
    Liz:
```

```
 5  Anna:
    Sue:                                        no/
    Liz:   I didn't/ I wasn't very maternal at all/ –    no/
```

```
 6  Anna:  cos Janet and I without ⎡children   .
    Sue:
    Liz:                           ⎣you just get used to them/
```

```
 7  Anna:  you know you feel- you DO feel a bit mean sometimes/
```

```
 8  Anna:  but I just can't understand that assumption that people
```

```
 9  Anna:  have that everybody loves-
    Sue:                         .          you can't go round-
    Liz:
```

```
10  Anna:                        ⎡((xx)) certain children    .    I
    Sue:   I wouldn't expect     ⎢anybody to ( (xxx)) my child/
    Liz:                         ⎣no I wouldn't/
```

```
11  Anna:  really like/ but parents ⎡like that ((just))-
    Sue:
    Liz:                            ⎣I think it's-    I think
```

```
12  Anna:
    Sue:
    Liz:   it's a-  .  a fallacy as well that you like every
```

```
13  Anna:                         no/  .  that's right/
    Sue:         ⎡mhm/                          I still
    Liz:   child/⎣cos you don't/
```

```
14  Anna:                          <LAUGHS>
    Sue:   quite often don't like children/ <LAUGHS>
    Liz:                                        actually
```

```
15  Liz:   I think you particularly dislike your own/
```

Here we see a subtle shift from the proposition 'some children are horrible'
to the proposition 'I don't like every child' (*I think it's a fallacy as well that you
like every child*, Liz, staves 11–13), and from here to the even more taboo
proposition 'I don't like children' (Sue and Liz both say *no* in stave 3 in
response to Anna's question *did you used to feel particularly fond of children*

before you had them?, and Sue says *I still quite often don't like children* in staves 13–14). This shift is marked syntactically by a change in grammatical subject. The earlier propositions involved sentences where the subject of the sentence is children, for example, *they were horrible* or *they were ghastly children* (note that the women's involvement is not marked syntactically in these sentences). By contrast, the later propositions position the women as the (pronominal) subjects, through the use of 'I' or the impersonal pronoun 'you'. Liz's final utterance (*actually I think you particularly dislike your own*, staves 14–15) marks a further step in bringing the propositions close to home: here Liz not only has women as the pronominal subject (*you*) but transforms the children from some generalised group to specific children – 'your own' – in other words, precisely that sub-set of children who, in your frontstage performance, you are not allowed to be un-maternal towards.

The backstage talk we see here is highly subversive. Dominant discourses of femininity (and of motherhood) do not allow for the expression of negative feelings about children. Anna, Sue and Liz support each other in sustaining a radically different discourse, one which challenges the idea of women as loving, caring, nurturing beings for whom having children is the ultimate experience of their lives.

The next two examples come from conversation between a different group of women friends, women who are about 10 years older than Anna, Sue and Liz, and who live in the north of England rather than the south. One of the women – Meg – tells a story about meeting an old friend, Jean, who she has felt estranged from since her divorce. She then goes on to tell a story about the rivalry between her son and Jean's son, where she openly expresses her negative feelings towards Jean's husband, Stan, and her unconcealed pleasure at their son's failure to get a brilliant degree, despite his early promise.[6]

Example 4

[Stan's] one of those few- one of the few people in the world that I feel deeply spiteful
    towards,
and it's all to do with his son and my son.
3 My son's a little bit older than his son,
    but when they were both young lads about fourteen or something,
    he said to me, 'Well you know Jacob isn't of the same calibre as Max,
6 and <u>Max is a genius</u> <SLOW AND PRECISE>
    and er you know thi- not many people are blessed with having a genius as a child.'
    [Sally: *oh god.*]
9 [Bea: *was he still wetting the bed at this stage?*]
    but it was true that Max's incredibly creative child,
    he could do absolutely everything,
12 he w- he made fantastic meccano models,
    and he was the brightest boy they'd ever had in his- in the previous school,
    and he went to Birkenhead School ((on a)) scholarship.
    [. . .]

15 Well he became a religious maniac
   which I thought was a lovely come-uppance because they're socialists and Marxists
   and it was very difficult for them to cope with.
18 Anyway Max got a 2.2!
   [Jen: *oh fantastic! I always thought he was dull as ditchwater.*]

The talk that follows this story shows Meg working hard to contextualise it; in other words, she feels the need to make clear that she would only behave in the way the story portrays in particular circumstances.

Example 5

----
 1 Meg: you know how er to some people you kind of e- exaggerate
----
 2 Meg: about your children/ most people you play them down
----
 3 Meg: and say what absolute rogues and rotters they are/
----
 4 Meg: but one- one- the the the she- they represent the few
----
 5 Meg: people that I f- feel I have to boast about my ⌈children/
   Bea: ⌊mhm/
----
 6 Meg: so I gave this .hh SPLENdid account of my kids you see/
----
 7 Meg: and I er I went on about this ex- extraordinary job that
----
 8 Meg: Jacob's got or GOing to have/ and of course he's
----
 9 Meg: nowhere near this job working ⌈in a Trade Union/
   Bea: ⌊this Trade Union/
----
10 Meg: <u>cos I just think it sounds nice you see</u>/ <LAUGHING>
   Bea: yes/
----
11 Meg: and I could see that Jean also thought it sounded nice/
----
12 Meg: because they are very political people/ ⌈((xxxx))
   Bea: ⌊mhm/
   Jen: yes it would
----
13 Meg: yes/   ⌈absolutely/
   Jen: absolutely fit their idea of what their ⌊son should-
----
14 Meg: and then I said 'oh what did you say Max was doing?'/
----
15 Meg: and she said 'oh he's working at Harwell'/
----
16 Meg: I thought 'oooh god' you know/ ((it's something with
   Bea: ((2 sylls))
----
17 Meg: ⌈nuclear-)) yes/ a ⌈tomic/   .   I mean he may be
   Sally: ⌊oh yes/ nuclear/ ⌊gosh/

```
18 Meg:  on the side of n- antinuc ⌈but-
   Bea:                                            ((doesn't sound
   Jen:                               ⌊oh I doubt it/ I very much
   Sally:                                          ((xxxxxxxxxxxxx
```
```
19 Meg:
   Bea:   like it))
   Jen:   doubt it/ it's part of the Establishment=
   Sally: xxxxxx))                              =yes it is/
```
```
20 Meg:  mhm/
   Bea:          ⌈i- isn't it awful the way
   Sally:     oh ⌊gosh/
```
```
21 Bea:  you DO get set up with some people though/
```
```
22 Bea:  where you- you- you'd actually take pleasure-
```
```
23 Bea:  instead of taking pleasure in the triumphs
```
```
24 Bea:  of their children=      and thinking oh isn't it-
   Meg:                  =yeah/
```
```
25 Bea:  it- . you know isn't it wonderful that's Emma's got
```
```
26 Bea:  distinction in her . violin exam or something/ [ . . . ]
```
```
27 Bea:  you think 'yeah – she fails! innit great!' <GROWLY VOICE>
   Meg:                  yeah/
```
```
28 Bea:  you know/i- i- i- ⌈it's horrid/ but I've got people
   Sally: yeah/            ⌊it's horrid/ yes/
```
```
29 Bea:  that I feel like that/
```

This discussion is followed by a story from Bea, which continues the theme of delighting in the failure of a friend's – or ex-friend's – child. Serial story-telling, where speakers in turn tell anecdotes on a common theme, is a common feature of friendly talk (see Galloway Young 1987; Shepherd 1997). In women's talk, serial story-telling often takes the form of reciprocal self-disclosure (Coates 1996a; 1996b).

Example 6

```
  I feel like that about a friend of mine who lives in New York
  who's- well she refers to her son as her little star,
3 and that doesn't help.
  and when I arrived at the- at the – at her apartment to stay,
  and she and her husband were both out at their exciting jobs in publishing,
6 and this lad of s- of seven or eight let me in,
  and asked if he could make me some coffee.
```

(Sally: *oh he _is_ a little star then*)
You know he IS a little star,
9 and he's so perfect that you just want to jump up and down 'im
and see if he'd squish you know,
[. . .]
and I'm so hoping that something marvellous will happen
12 and he'll run away from home
and – or you know something will squelch this . . .

These two stories and the discussion which accompanies them are again classic backstage talk: the women friends feel able to let down their fronts, to drop their normal 'nice' scripts. Both stories tell of ex-friends who offended or irritated the narrators in one way or another, and both stories declare the narrator's pleasure in the failure (real or imagined) of the ex-friend's offspring. Meg's presentation of Stan through reported speech portrays him negatively – as a parent who is insensitive to others (through his comparison of his son and Meg's) and who has ridiculously inflated ideas about his son (the reality being that he only got a lower second class degree). Speakers exploit reported speech to adopt a variety of voices, and to animate characters in their stories in ways which fit the bias of their story. Reported speech has an important evaluative function in story-telling (Maybin 1996) and women talking backstage explore alternative femininities through playing with different voices.

One thing that stands out about these two stories is that both Meg and Bea describe their feelings with relish: they make no attempt to hedge what they are saying. Meg says *[Stan's] one of the few people in the world that I feel deeply spiteful towards.* Admitting to feeling 'deeply spiteful' about someone is not part of women's normal frontstage performance. Bea's story reveals her irritation with (and possibly envy of) her New York friend, in particular her exciting job in publishing and her son who she calls a 'little star'. (This phrase irritates her since it contravenes the norm that mothers should be modest about their children's talents and should refrain from eulogising them in public.) Bea's remark *and he's so perfect that you just want to jump up and down 'im and see if he'd squish you know* (lines 9–10) is not only not-maternal and not-nice, it also betrays feelings of violence which are outside the range of 'normal' femininity. But Bea's words express a fantasy, and so are more comparable to the little girls' *let's boil the babies* than to Meg's gloating over Stan's son's mediocre degree.

Celebrating deviant women

The evidence I've looked at so far involves women exposing their not-nice selves to each other either through discussion of not-nice, un-feminine feelings, or through recounting past actions which show them behaving 'badly', or through sharing fantasies about behaving 'badly'. I now want to look at another strategy common in women's talk which has an important role to play in the expression of 'not-niceness'. It has been widely observed that women monitor and attempt to control community norms through discussing *other* women's behaviour (Goodwin 1990; Eckert 1993; 1998; Coates 1996a). These observations have often focused on the way groups position themselves in opposition to the values or attitudes betrayed by third parties, that is, by querying or criticising or even condemning the behaviour of others. But this same strategy – the discussion of others' actions – can be used as an opportunity to celebrate 'bad' behaviour, and has the great advantage of simultaneously keeping the speakers at one remove from such overtly 'bad' behaviour. The next example (Example 7) is an extract from a conversation about Anna's mother who, Anna claims, is 'such a character' (stave 6).

Example 7

```
--------------------------------------------------------------------------
 1 Sue:   it's not kind of your normal family when you go up to
--------------------------------------------------------------------------
 2 Anna:                            ⌈.hh she used to be-
   Sue:   Anna's Mum's/ she's- she's ⌊quite an exciting lady/
--------------------------------------------------------------------------
 3 Anna: she used to be ⌈so-        she used to be so
   Liz:                 ⌊are they Liverpool born and bred?
--------------------------------------------------------------------------
 4 Anna: beautiful when she was ⌈young my mother/
   Sue:                         ⌊yes/
--------------------------------------------------------------------------
 5 Anna: so beautiful/   %no    ⌈no%/
   Sue:                         ⌊but she I mean she's a great laugh/
--------------------------------------------------------------------------
 6 Anna:                 oh she's such a character/
   Sue:   she's great fun/
--------------------------------------------------------------------------
 7 Anna:                        mhm/  -
   Sue:   yeah/ she really is/  .          she was the one
--------------------------------------------------------------------------
 8 Sue:   who went out and said to those people
--------------------------------------------------------------------------
 9 Anna:
   Sue:   'Did you know Susan's a vegetarian?' <WHISPERS>
   Liz:                                        <SHRIEK OF LAUGHTER>
--------------------------------------------------------------------------
10 Anna: she's a ⌈really-
   Sue:          ⌊      (xxxxxxxxxxxxxxxxxx laughing)
   Liz:          ⌊as if this was a crime/
--------------------------------------------------------------------------
11 Anna: she's a major embarrassment/
   Sue:                         yeah/ <LAUGHING>
--------------------------------------------------------------------------
12 Anna: do you know what she did recently?
--------------------------------------------------------------------------
```

This question leads into a series of stories, all told by Anna, which demonstrate Anna's mother's eccentricity: in the first, the mother pulls a jogger's tracksuit bottoms down after he claims that her dog has bitten him;[7] in the second she puts up tents in the garden with electricity and TV because a visitor is allergic to her cats; in the third Anna herself meets a boy on the beach who announces that Anna's mother is adopting him. At this point Liz comments: 'It must really be fun to have a mother like that' and Anna tells the fourth story, which recounts how her mother arrived at her ex-husband's funeral:

Example 8

```
    when my father died last year
    she came down to the funeral
 3  and she got a train <LAUGHING> . she got a train that got into Euston at about-
    she got the sleeper
    and it got into Euston about six thirty in the morning,
 6  and she said to Henry and I 'I'll get the train to Esher,
    just make sure that the answering machine's not on and that you're up,
    so that somebody can come and get me from Esher station',
 9  and I was staying with my stepmother to keep her company,
    so it was all in Henry's hands,
    and of course he forgot,
12  he was fast asleep in bed,
    so my mother gets to Esher station at seven thirty in the morning.
    and there's no Henry
15  and its pouring with rain
    so.what does she do?
    she walks round the corner,
18  sees that there's a milk depot, a Unigate milk depot,
    and she walked in,
    and she asked one of the milkmen to give her a lift to the house, <LAUGHING>
21  and she arrived on a milk float <LAUGHING> for my dad's funeral. <CHUCKLING>
```

As the fuller transcript below shows, Anna's friends respond to this story with a great deal of laughter, some of it almost uncontrollable:

Example 9

```
-------------------------------------------------------------------------
1 Anna: so what does she do? she walks round the corner/
-------------------------------------------------------------------------
2 Anna: sees that there's a milk depot-  a Unigate Milk depot/
  Sue:                        <LAUGHS>
-------------------------------------------------------------------------
3 Anna:
  Sue:  <LAUGHS> oh yeah/ <LAUGHS>
  Liz:  <SHRIEKS WITH LAUGHTER> 'I've been on a milk fl-
-------------------------------------------------------------------------
```

---

4 Anna: <u>and she walked in and she asked one of the</u>
  Liz: milk lorry'/

---

5 Anna: <u>milkmen to give her a lift to the house</u>/ <LAUGHING>

---

6 Anna: <u>and she arrived on a milk float</u>
  Sue: <u>I bet she did</u>/ <LAUGHING>   <LAUGHS>
  Liz: <LAUGHS>

---

7 Anna: <u>for my dad's funeral</u>/ <LAUGHING> <u>oh my god</u> <LAUGHING>
  Sue: <LAUGHS>
  Liz: <LAUGHS>

---

8 Anna:
  Sue: .   <u>oh I love it/it's so funny</u>/ <LAUGHING>
  Liz: <LAUGHS>

Sue's comment: *oh I love it/ it's so funny/* (in stave 8) is an explicit recognition of the positive pleasure such a story provides. Anna's mother, who features in many stories told by Anna to her friends, is an unconventional character who allows for the discussion of unusual, un-feminine behaviour – and for the celebration of such behaviour. Note that the three friends position Anna's mother as out of the ordinary (*it's not kind of your normal family when you go up to Anna's Mum's* – Example 7, staves 1 and 2), yet speak of her in positive terms (*she's quite an exciting lady* – Example 7, stave 2; *she's a great laugh/ she's great fun/* – Example 7 staves 5–6; *oh she's such a character* – Example 7, stave 6).

The story concerns an everyday event – a family funeral – but the ingredients are unconventional from the start, since the dead man will be mourned by both his ex-wife (Anna's mother) and his second wife (Anna's step-mother). What makes the story so funny is the incongruity of an older woman dressed for a funeral travelling in a milk-float. The fact that this is a third-person narrative, not a personal account, is potentially liberating, as the friends themselves are not implicated in the behaviour described.

Backstage constraints

Although backstage behaviour is much more relaxed than frontstage, there are still constraints. Being backstage 'does not mean that friendly talkers are exempt from problems of framing and staging' (Collins 1988: 56). Moreover, even as the blurring of performer and audience typical of backstage talk produces solidarity among talkers, so it is still important that speakers present themselves as 'good persons', both to protect their own face and that of fellow speakers. In any context, whether formal or informal, a speaker will select the 'least self-threatening position in the circumstances' (Goffman 1981: 326).

This means that, even in talk between close women friends, where self-disclosure is reciprocal and taboo feelings can be acknowledged, speakers have to pay attention to their performance, to the extent that speakers confirm in themselves and each other a sense of being a 'good person'. This is obviously a tricky task where the topic under discussion involves speakers presenting themselves as 'not nice'.

It is noticeable that in many conversations where we find women performing selves that could be seen as un-feminine and not-nice, the participants themselves comment critically on the behaviour they have revealed. In Example 5 Bea describes as *awful* the feeling which she and her friends are all admitting to: *isn't it awful [author's emphasis] the way you DO get set up with some people though where you- you- you'd actually take pleasure- instead of taking pleasure in the triumphs of their children [. . .] you think 'yeah – she fails! innit great!' <GROWLY VOICE>*. This is followed by a discussion where Mary (who arrived after Meg's and Bea's stories (Examples 5 and 6) were told) also expresses unhappiness with the idea that we take pleasure from other people's failure, even though she agrees she has done this.

Example 10

```
----------------------------------------------------------------------------
1 Mary:   but I don't like feeling like that=
  Meg:                                    =no I don't like
  Jen:                                    =oh it's horrid/
----------------------------------------------------------------------------
2 Mary:              you know/
  Meg:   feeling like that/        but um ⎡((I think it's
  Bea:                                    ⎣well it seems
----------------------------------------------------------------------------
3 Mary:  ⎡but I DO do  it/  ⎡a lot/
  Meg:   ⎮xx))              ⎮yeah/ =yeah/ oh I feel it
  Bea:   ⎣like we all do feel like ⎣that=
  Sally:                           =yes/
----------------------------------------------------------------------------
4 Mary:              yeah/
  Meg:   a lot/ I feel it most- more than I don't feel/
  Others:                    <LAUGHTER>
----------------------------------------------------------------------------
5 Mary:  the older I get the more of a horrible bitch I get/
----------------------------------------------------------------------------
6 Mary:  <LAUGHS>
----------------------------------------------------------------------------
```

This discussion is a clear demonstration of the tension between the need to express not-nice feelings and the need to keep a foothold in the conventional frontstage world where women are always nice and mothers are always loving. On the not-nice side, Bea (staves 2–3) asserts that they all feel these not-nice feelings about other people's children, and simultaneously Mary admits *I do do it a lot* (stave 3). Meg (staves 3–4) pushes this further by claiming that she is more likely to feel 'bad' rather than 'good' feelings about other people's children, an admission which is received with supportive laughter by the others. On the other hand, Mary's claim that she doesn't like feeling *like that* (stave 1) is supported emphatically by Meg and Jen, and Mary later labels herself as a *horrible bitch* (stave 5). In other words, rather than celebrating the fact that as she gets older she feels freer to behave badly, Mary frames her behaviour as a negative, un-feminine development.

This tension between front- and backstage norms is a feature of all backstage talk. As I've argued already, it is exacerbated in the case of women speakers by their position in society, in particular their relationship to symbolic capital (Bourdieu 1977; Eckert 1993; 1998). Because women's symbolic capital is evaluated in relation to community norms, women need to pay attention to frontstage norms of femininity even while indulging in small talk backstage. As a result, in women's backstage talk we find women relaxing and letting down the conventional, 'nice' front they normally maintain frontstage. But we also find women expressing ambivalence about these alternative, subversive aspects of their identities. This may be done by explicit self-labelling, as we saw with Mary's remark in Example 10 *the older I get the more of a horrible bitch I get*. Alternatively, it may be expressed in the uneasy response of fellow-speakers. The next example comes from a conversation involving four fourteen year old girls. Clare's explanation of what a jockstrap is leads into her disclosing her fantasies about a boy in their class:

Example 11

```
-------------------------------------------------------------------------------
1 Hannah: Clare/ what's a jock strap?
-------------------------------------------------------------------------------
2 Hannah:
  Clare:    it's a jo-  .  it's what men use/ it's their
-------------------------------------------------------------------------------
3 Hannah:
  Clare:    like their equivalent to a bra/ and they hold
-------------------------------------------------------------------------------
4 Hannah:
  Clare:    their dick up with it ⌈((and their balls))/
  Jess:                            ⌊cos like when they do tie
-------------------------------------------------------------------------------
5 Hannah:
  Clare:
  Jess:     it round and they walk round/ you know/ <LAUGHS>
-------------------------------------------------------------------------------
6 Hannah: especially when people do things like ice hockey
-------------------------------------------------------------------------------
```

---

7 Hannah: ⌈and stuff like that/ where it could get harmed
  Becky: ⌊oh/

---

8 Hannah: easily/ or like- <LAUGHS> or it could get put
  Clare: like DEAN! ((xxx))

---

9 Hannah: under a lot of –   ⌈strain-
  Clare: I can imagine ⌊Jason like

---

10 Hannah:
   Clare: putting gel on his hair/   you know/ and he's
   Jess: <SHRIEK>

---

11 Hannah:
   Clare: sort of trimming it . and- and combing it
   Jess: ugh/

---

12 Hannah: ⌈Clare!
   Clare: every day/ . so disgusting/
   Becky: <LAUGHS> ((it's ⌊you who's

---

13 Clare: I can imagine him doing
   Becky: being)) disgusting Clare/

---

14 Clare: that though/ he's so s- vain/ he's such a bastard/

As this extract reveals, Clare's self-disclosure is met with negative reactions by her friends. Jess responds by shrieking in horror (stave 10) and making disgusted noises (*ugh* – stave 11); Hannah exclaims *Clare!* in a disapproving tone (stave 12); Becky says *it's you who's being disgusting Clare* (staves 12–13), though she laughs with amusement rather than disgust. We should also note that, while Clare discloses these fantasies about Jason grooming his pubic hair, fantasies which position her as daring and unconventional, she simultaneously presents herself as finding this vision of Jason *disgusting* (stave 12). Moreover, after her friends react disapprovingly, she defends her position with the claims that Jason is both *vain* and *such a bastard*, claims which justify her fantasy.

The girls' small talk here is clearly playful: the talk following the extract above continues to focus on Jason and boys and there is no sense that Clare has really shocked her friends. It is more that in this group of friends she is often the one who voices the more daring position. The four friends play with ideas of good- and bad-girl behaviour; because they are backstage they can explore bad-girl behaviour but, as here, they balance such talk with comments and stories which anchor them in a more conventional femininity.

Even when the talk is of third parties behaving 'badly', as in Anna's story of her mother (Example 8 above), there is some ambivalence expressed. While Sue and Liz are openly celebratory about Anna's mother (cf. Liz's comment *it must be really fun to have a mum like that*), Anna herself tempers her stories with remarks such as *she's lunatic* and *she's absolutely nutty*. While these comments are said affectionately, in a context where Anna overall expresses amused admiration of her mother, the choice of the words 'lunatic' and 'nutty' position the mother at the abnormal end of some imaginary spectrum, and distance her from Anna and her friends (who therefore are positioned as more 'normal').

Our need to position ourselves as relatively 'normal' as well as nice is a constant restraining factor. Women continually monitor both their own and other women's performances in a variety of ways. None of us is ever free of the need to keep up some sort of front; as Goffman puts it, 'by and large, it seems [the speaker] selects that footing which provides him [*sic*] the least self-threatening position in the circumstances, or, differently phrased, the most defensive alignment he can muster' (Goffman 1981: 325–6).

Backstage: safety-net or revolutionary cell?

In this chapter I have explored the ways in which women express not-nice aspects of themselves, despite frontstage pressures to conform to prevailing norms of femininity. I have argued, following Goffman, that backstage is a region which allows the performer to drop her front and talk openly with fellow-performers about aspects of herself which don't fit her frontstage role. Backstage interaction fulfils a vital need in women's lives to talk about behaving badly, whether this means recounting incidents where we ourselves behaved badly, or whether it means fantasising about such behaviour, or whether it means discussing and celebrating the unconventional behaviour of other women. In other words, backstage talk allows women to support each other in challenging or subverting frontstage norms, and in exploring alternative selves.

However, the data I have collected suggest that women feel obliged to balance such subversion by adopting, often simultaneously, more conventional discourses where they express ambivalence about, or label negatively, these less conventionally feminine aspects of themselves. Different discourses give us access to different femininities and we are all unwittingly involved in the ceaseless struggle to define gender. As Weedon puts it: 'The nature of femininity and masculinity is one of the key sites of discursive struggle for the individual' (Weedon 1987: 98).

The evidence of the conversations I have recorded is that women take great pleasure in exploring aspects of themselves which cannot normally be expressed frontstage. The 'warm, easy, relaxed atmosphere' (De Beauvoir quoted in Goffman 1971: 115) of backstage provides women with a relatively safe space to express less conventionally feminine, less 'nice' aspects of themselves. Women, like men, need to assert their right to wholeness, to having not-nice as well as nice feelings. Jenny Joseph's poem 'Warning' is a rare frontstage assertion of such feelings. It is testimony to women's desire to have the right to be not-nice that the poem is such a favourite.

It remains to be seen whether the overt expression of alternative and subversive femininities backstage only serves to perpetuate the hetero-patriarchal order, by providing women with an outlet for the frustrations of frontstage performance. Or is it possible that such backstage rehearsals may eventually lead to new frontstage performances?

Notes

1. This chapter is a revised and expanded version of a paper published in the *Journal of Sociolinguistics* (volume 3, number 1), which was itself based on a paper presented at Sociolinguistics Symposium 12, University of London, March 1998. I'd like to thank all those who have given me feedback about the paper, particularly Jenny Cheshire and Justine Coupland.
2. I am grateful to Justine Coupland who suggested this line of argument.
3. Further glimpses into contemporary laddishness are afforded by Cameron 1997; Gough and Edwards 1998; Kaminer and Dixon 1995.
4. The following table gives details of the corpus (further details and an account of the methodology employed can be found in Coates 1996a, chapter 1). I am grateful to all those who allowed themselves to be recorded or allowing me to use their talk as research material. I am also grateful to colleagues and students who have made data available to me, and to those who have helped me with transcribing the data. The names of all particip-ants have been changed.

Number of	All-female	All-male	Mixed	Total
Conversations	20	20	10	50
Speakers	26	33	29	88
Hours of talk	19 h 45 m	11 h 40 m	6 hours	37 h 25m

5. For transcription conventions see below.
6. Narratives are presented in the format devised by Wallace Chafe (1980), where each line represents an 'idea-unit'.
7. This story – *My mother and the jogger* – can be found in Coates 1996a: 100–1.

Transcription conventions

The transcription conventions used for the conversational data are as follows:

A slash (/) indicates the end of a tone group or chunk of talk, e.g.:

got into work this morning and broke two mugs/

A question mark indicates the end of a chunk of talk which I am analysing as a question, e.g.:

how did you break them?

A hyphen indicates an incomplete word or utterance, e.g.:

he's got this twi- he's got this nervous twitch/

you feel- you DO feel a bit mean sometimes/

Pauses are indicated by a full stop (short pause – less than 0.5 seconds) or by figures in round brackets (longer than 0.5 seconds), e.g.:

certain children   .   I really like/

[he] left a video (2.0) in a video recorder/

A broken line marks the beginning of a stave and indicates that the lines enclosed by the lines are to be read simultaneously (like a musical score), e.g.:

```
----------------------------------------------------------
A:   the squidgy stuff that they put on pizzas/
B:                                           Mozzarell ⌈ a/
C:                                                     ⌊ Mozzarella/
----------------------------------------------------------
```

An extended square bracket indicates the start of overlap between utterances, e.g.:

```
----------------------------------------------------------
A:   and they have newspapers and ⌈ stuff/
B:                                ⌊ yes very good/
----------------------------------------------------------
```

An equals sign at the end of one speaker's utterance and at the start of the next utterance indicates the absence of a discernible gap, e.g.:

```
----------------------------------------------------------
A:   because they're supposed to be=
B:                                =adults/
----------------------------------------------------------
```

Double round parentheses indicate that there is doubt about the accuracy of the transcription:

and he went to Birkenhead School ((on a)) scholarship

Where material is impossible to make out, it is represented as follows, ((xx)), e.g.:

you're ((xx))- you're prejudiced/

Angled brackets give clarificatory information about underlined material, e.g.:

nobody ever says that do they <LAUGHING>

you think 'yeah – she fails! innit great!' <GROWLY VOICE>.

Capital letters are used for words/syllables uttered with emphasis:

you DO feel a bit mean sometimes/

The symbol [. . .] indicates that material has been omitted, e.g.:

no/ [. . .] don't think I've done anything really that bad lately/

% indicates quietly (%% very quietly)

References

Bourdieu, Pierre (1977) *Outline of a Theory of Practice*. Cambridge: Cambridge University Press.

Brown, Lyn Mikel and Gilligan, Carol (1992) *Meeting at the Crossroads: Women's Psychology and Girls' Development*. Cambridge, MA: Harvard University Press.

Cameron, Deborah (1997) Performing gender identity: young men's talk and the construction of heterosexual masculinity. In Sally Johnson and Ulrike Meinhoff (eds) *Language and Masculinity*. Oxford: Blackwell, 47–64.

Chafe, Wallace (1980) The deployment of consciousness in the production of narrative. In Wallace Chafe (ed.) *The Pear Stories: Cognitive, Cultural and Linguistic Aspects of Narrative Production*. Norwood, NJ: Ablex, 9–50 .

Coates, Jennifer (1989) Gossip revisited: an analysis of all-female discourse. In Jennifer Coates and Deborah Cameron (eds) *Women in their Speech Communities*. London: Longman, 94–122.

Coates, Jennifer (1996a) *Women Talk. Conversation Between Women Friends*. Oxford: Blackwell.

Coates, Jennifer (1996b) Women's stories: the role of narrative in friendly talk, Inaugural Lecture, Roehampton Institute London.

Collins, Randall (1988) Theoretical continuities in Goffman's work. In Paul Drew and Anthony Wootton (eds) *Erving Goffman. Exploring the Interaction Order*. Cambridge: Polity Press, 41–63.

Cook-Gumperz, Jenny (1995) Reproducing the discourse of mothering: how gendered talk makes gendered lives. In Kira Hall and Mary Bucholtz (eds) *Gender Articulated: Language and the socially constructed self*. London: Routledge, 401–19.

Cook-Gumperz, Jenny (in press) The interactional accomplishment of gender and girls' oppositional stances: young children between nursery life and school life. In Bettina Baron and Helga Kotthoff (eds) *Gender in Interaction*.

Eckert, Penelope (1993) Cooperative competition in adolescent 'girl talk'. In Deborah Tannen (ed.) *Gender and Conversational Interaction*. Oxford: Oxford University Press, 32–61.

Eckert, Penelope (1998) Gender and sociolinguistic variation. In Jennifer Coates (ed.) *Language and Gender: A Reader*. Oxford: Blackwell, 64–75.

Galloway Young, K. (1987) *Taleworlds and Storyrealms*. Lancaster: Kluwer Academic Publishers.

Goffman, Erving (1971) *The Presentation of Self in Everyday Life*. Harmondsworth: Penguin Books.

Goffman, Erving (1981) *Forms of Talk*. Oxford: Blackwell.

Goodwin Marjorie (1988) Cooperation and competition across girls' play activities. In Alexandra Dundas Todd and Sue Fisher (eds) *Gender and Discourse: The Power of Talk*. Norwood, NJ: Ablex, 55–9.

Goodwin, Marjorie Harness (1990) *He-Said-She-Said: Talk as Social Organisation among Black Children*. Bloomington IN: Indiana University Press.

Gough, Brendan and Edwards, Gareth (1998) 'The beer talking': four lads, a carry out and the reproduction of masculinities. *The Sociological Review*: 409–35.

Jones, Deborah (1980) Gossip: Notes on women's oral culture. In Cheris Kramarae (ed.) *The Words and Voices of Women and Men*. Oxford: Pergamon Press, 193–8.

Kaminer, Debra and Dixon, John (1995) The reproduction of masculinity: a discourse analysis of men's drinking talk. *South African Journal of Psychology*, 25 (3): 168–74.

Maybin, Janet (1996) Story voices: the use of reported speech in 10–12 years olds' spontaneous narratives, *Current Issues in Language and Society* 3 (1): 36–48.

Pilkington, Jane (1992) 'Don't try and make out that I'm nice'. The different strategies women and men use when gossiping, *Wellington Working Papers in Linguistics* 5, 37–60; reprinted in Jennifer Coates (ed.) (1998) *Language and Gender: A Reader.* Oxford: Blackwell, 254–69.

Purvis, June (1987) Social class, education and ideals of femininity in the nineteenth century. In Madeleine Arnot and Gaby Weiner (eds) *Gender and the Politics of Schooling.* London: Hutchinson, 253–75.

Ruddick, Sara (1989) *Maternal Thinking: Towards a politics of peace.* London: The Women's Press.

Shepherd, Jenny (1997) *Storytelling in Conversational Discourse: A Collaborative Model.* Unpublished PhD thesis, University of Birmingham.

Weedon, Chris (1987) *Feminist Practice and Poststructuralist Theory.* Oxford: Blackwell.

Professional and commercial applications

Introduction to **Part IV**

Justine Coupland

We have already seen small talk 'at work' in previous chapters – in Holmes's business settings and in the service encounters analyses by Coupland and Ylänne-McEwen and by Kuiper and Flindall. But the two final chapters, in this fourth section of the book, engage more with the professional viewpoint on the value of small talk. Cheepen's chapter focuses on the promotion of good customer relations, to commercial ends; Ragan's chapter focuses on the promotion of positive health outcomes, through the promotion of solidarity.

Ragan argues that small talk is pivotal to the achievement of instrumental goals, specifically health care delivery during practitioner–patient consultations. As many other authors have done, she questions the notion that any talk is, ultimately, 'smaller' than any other. In her data analysis she shows that talk which communication theory has traditionally assigned to the category 'relational' (and side-lined in comparison with 'instrumental' talk) services no lesser needs. She is following a strong recent theme in health communication in the USA, which emphasises the importance of medical practitioners attending to patients' social, emotional and psychological concerns in addition to their biomedical ones. This is the agenda of holistic medicine. Ragan puts the case that, through small talk, the profound asymmetry of the provider–patient encounter can be attenuated.

Her focus is on two specific modes of small talk: humour achieved in verbal play, and reciprocal self-disclosure. The co-patient role adopted by the doctors in some of these data examples is reminiscent of the 'shifts of alignment' illustrated earlier by Coupland and Ylänne-McEwen, where travel agents temporarily suspend their professional stances to talk as 'co-consumers'. Ragan concludes that the mutuality and affinity achieved via small talk in her data bear directly on medical outcomes. She refers, for example, to reduced anxiety during medical procedures, and patient satisfaction and compliance in the longer term. She ends, in common with many of the other contributors, with an insistence that we need a complex, multi-dimensional approach to communicative functioning in professional settings, where 'task' and 'relationship' concerns are co-relevant and inter-related.

Cheepen similarly begins her chapter by reflecting on the inter-related dimensions of 'task-directed' and 'person-directed' dialogue. The clearest instance of person-directed dialogue is 'full-blown conversation', which Cheepen conceptualises as an activity people engage in 'purely because they want to'. Cheepen's earlier work with Monaghan (1990) on informal conversation provides detailed analysis of its formal characteristics (see Chapter 11, References). The data used in this chapter show speakers in task-directed dialogue (telephone service transactions) engaging in transitory, ritualised social bonding during 'side sequences' or 'small islands' in talk. It is these islands, Cheepen comments, that 'underline the human nature of the dialogue' and give it the flavour of friendliness.

Many companies, however, have replaced human telephone operators with automated voice systems, and these also come under scrutiny in Cheepen's research. She observes that such companies are anxious to preserve client loyalty by providing 'friendly' and 'natural' interaction. The tenor of automated talk is, then, a sensitive, economically salient issue. Cheepen's chapter therefore goes on to compare human/human with human/machine dialogue, in respect of small talk. The differences in realisations of ritualised aspects of telephone service encounters, such as openings, confirmation/checking sequences and closings, across human/human and human/machine systems is examined. In general, the design of automated system utterances limits customer's own use of relational talk, such as scripted politeness moves. In addition, they are not well suited to dealing with problem scenarios, where politeness and facework are, for human interactants, high-priority aspects of dialogue. Comments about incidental details of the call, or verbal play, are aspects of human telephone exchanges that promote the attributions of friendliness and approachability that companies want to promote.

Finally in the chapter, Cheepen reports a small-scale study where users evaluate two automated answering systems. She finds that telephone service users prefer to use automated systems which do *not* have the supposedly 'human' and 'friendly' discourse features (such as politeness tokens and personal pronouns) which automated dialogue designers have been concerned to incorporate into them. Cheepen concludes that there remains a considerable gap between human and surrogate small talk. For the moment, at least, it seems that computer-based initiatives have not yet threatened the immutably human and humanising nature of small talk.

10

Sociable talk in women's health care contexts: two forms of non-medical talk
Sandra L. Ragan

Introduction

Whereas 'small talk' traditionally has been relegated to a peripheral, conventional, and more or less purposeless form of discourse (Malinowski 1923; Robinson 1972), enacted by speakers in ritualistic fashion and marginalized as insignificant relative to talk that serves instrumental purposes, I suggest in this chapter that so-called 'small talk' in the context of several women's health care situations is pivotal to the achievement of instrumental, i.e. medical goals. In fact, the following analysis of conversation in three types of women's health-care encounters questions the very notion that discourse in the institutional context of female health care provider–female patient can be neatly segmented into task (instrumental) talk and relational (small) talk. Rather, I argue that interpersonal and organizational communication scholars (and traditionally sociolinguists) have perpetuated a false dichotomy (see also Tracy and Naughton, this volume) by categorizing the discourse goals of interactants in institutional contexts as task OR relationship. In the following analyses of medical discourse between female providers and female patients, sociable talk, i.e. relational communication between provider and patient, is tantamount to task, in that the 'task' of these health-care interactions is not merely to interview, examine, diagnose and treat/prescribe; it is also to co-create a relational climate that facilitates these critical medical achievements as well as promoting patient cooperation/compliance after the encounter. Instead of being separate discourse goals whose achievement is accomplished independently of the other, so-called task and relational goals in these contexts are inextricably enmeshed and interdependently achieved.

For the purposes of demonstrating this argument, utterances and sequences of talk that would *appear* to be serving extra-medical (non-task) goals will be extracted from the discourse for analysis. Yet my contention throughout the chapter is that sociable or relational talk between provider and patient does not constitute 'small talk' in its traditionally denigrated connotation. In fact, I question the very notion that any talk is 'smaller' than any other; the 'task' in medical encounters necessarily entails the co-enactment by participants of what many have labeled 'small talk' or 'phatic communion' (Malinowski 1923). Regardless of the labeling of so-called extra-task talk as 'sociable', 'relational,' 'small,' or 'phatic' (labels that would appear almost synonymous), such talk serves no 'small' function, as the following analyses will detail.

The conversational data for this piece include discourse extracts from three different health-care contexts for women in the southwestern region of the US: (1) 41 audio-taped interactions between a female nurse practitioner and her female patients at a university health clinic; (2) 53 audio-taped interactions between a female medical doctor and her female patients in a general practitioner private practice setting; and (3) 24 audio-taped inter-actions between three female radiology technicians and their female patients in a breast care clinic. All women in these studies are Euro-Caucasian and predominantly middle-class.[1]

A patient-centered model of medicine

The biomedical model of medicine, in which power resides solely in the medical provider who attends only to the patient's presenting medical (or biological) symptoms, has long been the established model in Western medical practices (see, for example, Brody 1992; Sharf and Street 1997). Analyses of discourse in medical settings in which practitioners have focused on bio-logical and biotechnical approaches to disease have demonstrated that the social and psychological concerns of patients related to their health care have been repeatedly marginalized and ignored (Waitzkin 1991). As early as 1977, psychiatrist George Engel called for a more comprehensive and integ-rated approach to medical practice that he termed the biopsychosocial model. Yet only recently has this reconceptualization of medical care, which pro-motes a more active and co-equal role for patients in clinical encounters, gained much attention in actual health care practices (see Sharf 1988; Deber 1994; Stewart *et al.* 1995).

In 1997, the leading journal in the communication discipline dealing with health care, *Health Communication*, published a special issue on 'The Patient as a Central Construct in Health Communication Research'. Articles in this issue pointed up the need for the medical community to acknowledge patients' health-related social and psychological concerns, to admit of the patient's need to co-determine treatment options, and to empower the patient to co-participate in the management of his/her health care. These authors (Sharf and Street; Vanderford, Jenks and Sharf; Lambert, Street, Cegala,

Smith, Kurtz and Schofield; Lammers and Geist; and Rimal, Ratzan, Arnstron and Freimuth) as well as other researchers in health care communication (Beck, Ragan and DuPré 1997; Morris and Chenail 1995; Street, Gold and McDowell 1995; Frankel 1995) do not advocate the replacement of the biomedical model with a more patient-centered approach to medicine merely to redress the power imbalance between provider and patient. Their recommendation for a more comprehensive, co-equal or partnership model of health care interaction stems from a strongly held belief that a patient-centered approach to health care interactions will promote improved health outcomes, particularly if 'health' is conceptualized as multi-faceted and comprised of social and emotional as well as physiological components.

Patient-centered medicine and the creation of a provider–patient relationship

Much recent research in health care communication has focused on aspects of the interpersonal communication between provider and patient as Thompson (1994) recently reviews. Dissatisfaction with providers' lack of interpersonal skills and a perceived lack of provider concern for the patient overwhelmingly result in patients' dissatisfaction with their medical encounters; but, more importantly, patients' *satisfaction* with their health-care interactions is positively linked to compliance, to improved psychological and medical outcomes, and to avoidance of malpractice litigation (for a review of this literature, see Thompson 1994). Although research findings that correlate satisfaction with the provider–patient encounter with these critical health outcomes are sketchy at this point, extant research evidence does suggest that the lack of emphasis on relational factors in health-care encounters is both a common and undesirable feature of medical interaction. Numerous studies point out that interpersonal competence on the part of the health-care provider leads to improvements in patients' health outcomes (e.g. Doyle and Ware 1977; Heszen-Klemens and Lapkinska 1984; Kaplan, Greenfield and Ware 1989; King 1991). Further, some research suggests that patients may not be able to discriminate between their overall satisfaction with provider care and their satisfaction with provider communication (Thompson 1994). It would appear that technical and interpersonal proficiencies of health care providers are interwoven inextricably into patient perceptions of and satisfaction with their health care encounters.

A patient-centered approach arguably necessitates interpersonal, relational talk in medical encounters, for it advocates that the patient's 'lifeworld' must be taken into account by the provider, and that interactants must wrestle with the dialectical tension of talk that is 'social' and talk that is 'medical' (Mishler 1984; Clark and Mishler 1992). It is that 'social' talk, co-created by both interactants, and the resolution of the tension between so-called social or relational goals and medical goals, that this chapter addresses.

The difficulties of creating relationship in a non-egalitarian encounter

In addition to the perplexities of creating relationship in an encounter whose goals traditionally have been viewed as purely instrumental (i.e. biomedical) by many health-care providers and patients alike, additional complications are foregrounded in the context of women's health care. First, however, one must note the inherent paradox of relational talk in a non-egalitarian, institutional interaction. All patients, male and female, confront health-care providers who have been trained to be expert in their fields, who conduct the interview, examination, diagnostic and treatment procedures of medical care in their own environment, and who are constrained by numerous and frequently contradictory institutional and extra-institutional mandates (e.g. in the USA, at least, those imposed by health insurance groups). Health-care providers decidedly assume charge of health-care interactions, with many patients collaborating in this control by subscribing themselves to a model of medicine that deifies its practitioners and renders patients powerless and passive.

Pomerantz, Ende and Erickson (1995) in their analysis of conversations in a medical clinic aptly discuss the dilemma of being an expert in a society that exalts the democratic ideology of egalitarianism. Whereas experts should be granted more authority and respect than non-experts, all persons should be respected for their opinions as well as permitted to voice these. In a teacher–student interaction, for example, the teacher finds ways to maintain authority in a non-authoritarian manner – Wetherell, Stiven and Potter (1987) term this 'unequal egalitarianism'. Similarly, Goffman (1961) refers to 'role distancing' as an attempt to mitigate the force of authority by 'making nice'; e.g. to disguise the boldness of a request by framing it as suggestion rather than as order. Not only does such a conversational move redress power imbalances, but it may also achieve the needed cooperation of the non-expert (or subordinate) – Goffman's example is one of a surgeon who politely requests rather than demands a scalpel from his surgical nurse, thus facilitating her necessary cooperation for a successful surgery. As Pomerantz *et al.* note, such a strategy as 'making nice' does not change power relations, but 'it does lubricate the interaction, easing the face-threatening force of unmitigated commands' (p. 164).

Whereas there is no a priori superior–subordinate role assignment in a provider–patient encounter, western culture and the biomedical model of health care have imbued the health-care provider with the status of expert and authority. A more patient-centered, consumer-orientated model of health care entails patients interacting in health-care encounters in a more egalitarian manner; i.e. asking questions, being forthcoming about symptoms, questioning diagnoses and prescriptions, etc. Yet, particularly for women patients, such assertive behaviors are often at odds with women's socialization as nurturers, supporters and confrontation-avoiders. Research findings in women's health care further point up that when women *do* engage in question-asking, for example, caregivers frequently ignore their questions or cut them off – maneuvers which communicate that such assertiveness is dispreferred and which function to augment women's passivity and silence in their health-care interactions (e.g. Corea 1977; Fisher 1986, 1991, 1993, 1995; Todd 1993; Todd and Fisher 1993; West 1984). In addition to studies that show that a consumerist stance is devalued by many health-care providers of female patients, other research findings suggest that patients' pursuit of emotional and psychological concerns in their health-care interactions is cut short by providers who interrupt, quickly reinstate a medical topic or fail to respond altogether to the patients' seemingly extra-medical issues.

Thus, a quandary exists: given that the patient-centered health-care model appears to ensure better health outcomes than the traditional biomedical model; given that such a model inherently encompasses the patient's social and psychological lifeworld as well as his/her presenting medical symptoms; given that relational communication serves to illuminate this lifeworld and that relationships are co-constructed by interactants through their verbal and nonverbal behaviors, yet also given that health-care interactants (both providers and patients) generally approach health care from a perspective that reifies power imbalance and that denigrates relationship, how can pro-viders and patients negotiate their interactions effectively? We suggest that as health-care interactions are socially constructed and emergent rather than static and role-dependent, both providers and patients can engage in talk that facilitates the accomplishment of the multiple medical *and* social goals of the health-care encounter. Through discourse that otherwise might be labeled insignificant or at best peripheral to the alleged, superordinate medical goals of interview, diagnosis, examination, and treatment – that is, the dis-course of relational communication or 'small talk' – the profound asymmetry of the provider–patient encounter can be mediated. The following analysis details how two features of 'small talk' in female provider–female patient interactions – the use of humor and verbal play and the employment of extra-medical self-disclosure that promotes identification – function to pro-duce positive facework, affinity and perceptions of relationship in contexts that are intrinsically face-threatening and potentially devoid of relational pleasantries.[2]

The management of face threat in relational communication in women's health-care contexts

The corpus of data collected from the health-care interactions of three women's health contexts – a university health clinic, a breast care center and an MD's private practice office – demonstrate that, contrary to expectations for a dearth of social or relational talk in such interactions, discourse is replete with so-called 'small talk'. Such sociable talk upon initial inspection might appear to be superfluous, completely peripheral to the medical aims of the provider–patient encounters. Yet I argue that the 'small talk' of women's health-care interactions, at least for the conversations analyzed, serves to ease the face-threatening feature of gynaecological and prenatal care and also to facilitate the attainment of supposedly more serious and purposive medical goals. Smith-DuPré and Beck (1996), Goldsmith (1992) and others have noted how achievement of some interaction goals facilitates the accomplishment of other goals. For example, Goldsmith (1992) reports that the neglect of facework in comforting behavior undermines the attainment of other goals: 'threats to face are not merely unwanted side effects in the support process; they threaten the very outcomes that are believed to link supportive interactions to physical and psychological well-being' (p. 277).

The following analyses display how women health-care providers and women patients utilize the conversational devices of verbal play and non-medical self-disclosure to promote rapport and to facilitate the achievement of relational and medical goals.

Humor and verbal play

As DuPré (1998) notes, the role of humor in establishing relationship in medical encounters has been investigated by numerous studies (Robinson 1975; Coser 1959, 1960; Ragan 1990; Beck and Ragan 1992; Smith-DuPré 1992). Humor not only produces affinity between provider and patient: it performs a face-saving function; it mitigates physiological stress; it promotes the feeling that one may 'relax with safety' (Hayworth 1928: 370), and it even works to ensure better patient treatment, in that patients who can laugh have been found to receive better medical care (e.g. Coombs and Goldman 1973).

In the context of a breast care center, for example, DuPré (1998) explains how humor is used by both radiology technicians and female patients to mitigate the anxiety and fearfulness of a procedure that might reveal devastating results, that is perceived as uncomfortable and even painful by many patients, and that can be face-threatening due to the necessity to disrobe and to display one's breasts in a series of awkward positionings. Patients undergoing mammography, for example, frequently comment on breast size and on the discomfort of the exam, as in these extracts:

Extract 1[3]

1 Patient: There's not very much to put on there
            ((compression begins))
2   You're going to squash what I have left! (laughter)

Extract 2

1 Patient: I'm flat-chested. They aren't very big so:: ((laughter))

Extract 3

1 Patient: ((commenting on presence of researcher)) Won't bother me if she
2 can stand to look at these big boobs. ((smile))

Extract 4

1 Patient: I started [with breast implants] in '67. The first ones
2 were pretty but not as pretty as the ones in '72.
3 Provider: You wanted the new model, huh? ((both laugh))

DuPré (1998: 93)

In other instances from DuPré's (1998) data, technicians and patients jokingly commented on the patient's breasts or on the X-ray procedure itself, as in these extracts:

Extract 5

1 Provider: Need your arm outta your right sleeve.
2 Patient: Sorry. I'm just standin' here waitin' for mother ta tell me what to
3 do! ((both laugh))

Extract 6

1 Provider: This machine has automatic compression it=
2 Patient: =does itself and doesn't stop 'til it gets there, huh?!
3 I don't know that that's such a good idea! ((both laugh))

In collaborating to joke about the patient's concerns with her breasts and the awkwardness of the X-ray procedure itself, technician and patient construct interaction that may function to ameliorate anxiety and that promotes the notion that 'we're in this together and it's really not so fearful'. As DuPré (1998: 96) notes, such humorous incidents convey from the patient's perspective, 'I won't take the fact of my nudity very seriously and you needn't either. Let's laugh and lighten up a bit.' In addition to cueing possible discomfort about her nudity, such laughter more plausibly is the result of what Jefferson (1984) terms 'troubles resistivity' – telling one's troubles, yet laughing in order to display that one is coping. On the part of the radiology technician, DuPré comments that humorous statements function to acknowledge the patients' feelings while at the same time keying or rekeying (Goffman 1974) the experience as 'not so bad'. Frequently, technicians offered advance humorous cues to the patient, apparently to ward off any negative affect, as in these extracts:

Extract 7

1 Provider: We told you to wipe your deodorant off and we got
2   goop all over you. Don't you feel lovely now? ((both laugh))

Extract 8

1 Provider: See how easy it is for me to tell you to relax? ((patient laughs))

Extract 9

1 Provider: Are ya havin' fun yet?
2 Patient: ((sudden grin)) well ((pause)) no.

DuPré (1998: 97–8)

Nurse practitioners in the university clinic setting similarly utilized humorous small talk to help relax patients during pelvic examinations and to frame the exam as non-face-threatening (Ragan and Pagano 1987; Ragan 1990; Ragan and Glenn 1990; Beck and Ragan 1992; Beck and Ragan 1995). In many instances, practitioner and patient collaborated to redress the potential face threat of the exam, as in the following extract from a gynaecological examination:

Extract 10

1 Provider: Are you doin' okay?
2 Patient: he heh heh alright yeah::: (2.7)
3 Provider: NOT always the best thing to do is it
4 Patient: he he [heh (a little)
5 Provider: [NEVER (just the) thing to spend your after[noon]
6 Patient: [heh heh heh]   heh [he heh]
7   I can think of a lot of other things heh heh heh
8 Provider: heh heh heh oh Yes:
9 Patient: definitely=
10 Provider: =heh heh heh heh

In gynaecologic exam interactions, we argue, the rapport engendered through the joint construction of such playful small talk facilitates the performance of the exam in that it eases the patient's possible embarrassment and discomfort and encourages her to relax. Further, the sense of relationship and the perception of the health-care provider's concern for the patient that develops through such verbal playfulness may create a climate of trust that promotes patient cooperation with the exam procedure as well as compliance with the practitioner's health-care directives (Ragan and Pagano 1987; Ragan 1990; Beck, Ragan and DuPré 1997).

These playful keyings of health-care interactions in both the breast care center and the university health clinic acknowledge patients' possible anxieties about mammographies and pelvic examinations in ways that suggest that their situation is at most uncomfortable but certainly not unbearable. As DuPré (1998) remarks in her analyses, humor in the breast care center context appears a particularly functional means of managing 'the delicate balance between hurting and helping' (p. 98). Further, from ethnographic observations of the interactions between radiology technicians and their patients, DuPré notes that the use of humor changed the tone of an interaction to a more relaxed, less formal, more playful and more conversational one. The rapport built between technician and patient through humorous banter in these interactions likely enhances the patient's cooperation with the exam process, thus facilitating the technician's acquisition of accurate X-ray images and the ensuing diagnostic reading that may prove critical to the patient's well-being and even to her ultimate survival.

Beck, Ragan and DuPré (1997) discuss the co-accomplishment of relationship by women patients and their female health-care providers via such conversational activities as humor and verbal play and personal disclosures, these features of interaction being prominently displayed in the facework and social affinity reflexively enacted by provider and patient. In the following excerpt, for example, nurse practitioner and patient collaborate in a playful exchange that signals to each that they share a common conceptualization of the nature of a pelvic examination:

Extract 11

1 Provider: All done (2.4) that's it (3.5)
2 Patient: hhh gee that wuz fun [(.1) heh heh heh heh] heh heh (1.2)
3 Provider: [heh heh heh heh heh]
4   oh you wanna do it again? Heh heh heh heh=
5 Patient: =heh heh heh (.)
6 Provider: okay so I'll run all this stuff to the lab.

That the nurse practitioner recognizes the patient's sarcastic use of 'fun' in line 2 by extending the joke in line 4, displays and reflexively enacts what Burke (1950) terms identification – a rhetorical strategy marking mutuality and promoting connectedness and a sense of partnership between interactants. Humor in this context creates social solidarity not only by producing shared laughter at the jointly acknowledged absurdity of wishing to repeat a 'fun' pelvic examination; it also enacts the role-distancing, 'making nice' behavior (Goffman 1961) that reduces face threat and enhances the performance of medical tasks with patient cooperation.

Extra-medical self-disclosure in women provider–women patient interactions

In similar manner, extra-medical self-disclosure by female providers in the three women's health-care contexts investigated appears to result both in positive relational and medical outcomes. Whereas the biomedical model of medicine assumes a standard format in health-care encounters of 'provider asks questions, patient discloses information', the female practitioners in our corpus of data frequently violated the medical norm of non-reciprocal self-disclosure by revealing personal information. Such disclosures, as with other features of so-called 'small talk' in health-care interactions, at first glance appear superfluous chitchat, perhaps even counter to the medical goals of the situation and inappropriate for health-care professionals socialized to maintain distance from their patients. (I am reminded of a revered and popular female general practitioner in my early adult years who, when I complained of a lump at the base of my neck, took my hand, placed it on her own neck, and exclaimed, 'That's nothing. Feel *this* one!' Instead of thinking that my medical concern was being summarily dismissed, I immediately grinned, relaxed and knew that, in her own inimitable fashion, my doctor was assuring me that my lump was not of medical concern.)

In the medical encounters analyzed, provider self-disclosure is not treated as inappropriate or 'unprofessional' by women patients, in that it elicits reciprocal patient disclosure which promotes both relational and medical goals. The following extended excerpt from an interaction between a female MD and her female, college student patient, presenting with fever blisters, is an exemplar of the positive use of provider self-disclosure:

Extract 12

```
 1 Provider: Um, the typical dosage that they suggest for it is 200 milligrams
 2           five times a day. Now that's kind of a pain.
 3           You can also get it in 800 milligrams that's really used
 4           more for genital herpes=
 5 Patient:  =mm hmm
 6 Provider: We just happened to have some of the 800 milligrams at home
 7           from the drug rep sent us, so I took that for this, and I,
 8           I don't know if I should even be telling you this
 9           because a typical dose is 200 five times a day, but I
10           took that, I took one of those, and it just knocked it
11           out=
12 Patient:  =really?
13 Provider: Yeah, and I just know for a busy college student it might
14           be hard to take [something five times a day]
15 Patient:                 [five times a day]
16 Provider: So, if you want, we can try the 800=
17 Patient:  =that would be great because=
```

18 Provider: =that might be easier, lemme because then you would take it
19   less often=
20 Patient: =mm hmm=
21 Provider: =you know, maybe=
22 Patient: =well=
23 Provider: =once to twice a day=
24 Patient: =my sleeping schedule's so strange it's hard for me to take
25   it something three times a day [unintelligible]
26 Provider: [right] right=
27 Patient: =right=
28 Provider: =yeah=
29 Patient: =yeah=
30 Provider: =Okay, well, let me getcha a prescription for that. It
31   helps. Um, at least it sure cuts down on, you know, the
32   root of it and everything, so yeah. If you know that
33   something's coming up that you just can't have a fever
34   blister for=
35 Patient: =yeah=
36 Provider: =you can always take a few, you know, you can take one for
37   a couple of days to make sure, if you're getting your
38   pictures done [or something like that]
39 Patient: [well, it's real] um I get em I know from
40   stress, but if I'm out in the sun, they're all on my
41   face. So it's kinda nice if I get sunburned=
42 Provider: =right=
43 Patient: =then I know I I it's just=
44 Provider: =you're gonna uh=
45 Patient: =I know if I get sunburned I'm gonna get one=
46 Provider: =you're gonna get one. Right yeah yeah=
47 Patient: =so=
48 Provider: =yeah, yeah, you can take those, and in that instance, they
49   should prevent it, and I can't promise a hundred per cent=
50 Patient: =oh I know=
51 Provider: =but it will [[tape cuts off]]

(Beck et al., pp. 89–90)

The doctor in the above instance appears to shift from the conventional MD role to a 'co-patient' role by confessing in line 8 that 'I don't know if I should even be telling you this' and then by sharing her own history of taking a mega-dose variety of the medication under discussion (lines 6–11). The doctor's subsequent acknowledgment of the patient's lifestyle as a 'busy college student' (line 13) connects her self-disclosure about her own experience with the drug and its availability in 800 milligram form by making it relevant to the patient's life circumstances. The provider then offers a negotiative move in line 16 – 'So, if you want, we can try the 800' – thus amplifying her role as co-participant. At that point, the patient in line 17 declares her preference for the 800 milligram dose and discloses (lines 24–5) that her sleeping schedule would prohibit her compliance with a five times daily drug regimen. At line 30, the doctor announces the achievement of a collaborat-ively produced treatment decision – 'let me getcha a prescription for that'.

The above interaction is an excellent example of how a discourse-created partnership can be collaboratively enacted by caregiver and patient through reciprocal self-disclosure. Not only does such disclosure foster identification and mutuality; it literally initiates a sequence of conversational events that culminate in a patient's participation in her health-care treatment decisions, with the ensuing possibility that she will cooperate with the treatment plan and get well.

The doctor in the above interaction provides an excellent example of what Branch and Malik (1993), Street *et al.* (1995), and Frankel (1995) discuss as a health-care provider's taking advantage of 'windows of opportunity'. Astute listening skills, an open-ended interviewing style and attention to the patient's psychosocial concerns, coupled with nonverbal attentiveness, provide these 'windows' for patients to discuss quality of life issues that impact on medical decision-making (Street *et al.* 1995). Similarly, Markakis, Suchman, Beckman and Frankel (1993) discuss 'empathic opportunities' – an MD's response to any patient expression of moderate to strong negative affect. For example, in the following extract, a patient has complained of dizziness, and the MD has just asked what he was doing at the time he first felt dizzy:

Extract 13

1 Provider: What were you doing at the time?
2 Patient: I (don't know) I just went to getting dizzy and I started crying, I
3   told Bobby I wanted to go to the hospital or somewhere so – I
4   finally felt a little better and just got into bed and went to sleep.
5 Provider: Okay. Tell me a little more about the itching.

(Frankel 1995: 244)

Whereas the 'cost' of pursuing such empathic opportunities is negligible (Stewart, Brown and Weston 1989; Beckman and Frankel 1984), the 'reward' may be great for providers and patients alike. As Frankel (1995) notes in his work on clinical interviews, the traditional focus on the structure of clinical discourse may have made us overly scientific in developing a theory of such discourse, such that we may have excluded 'what may be the most funda-mental dynamic feature of interviews, the act of caring and the feeling of being cared for' (p. 255).

Smith-DuPré and Beck (1996) explore in depth how the female MD in Extract 12 fosters patients' involvement and empowerment in their health-care interactions through self-disclosures that facilitate 'a less threatening, more symmetrical exchange of intimate information' (p. 79). For example, in the excerpt below in which a female patient is tearfully apologizing to her doctor for going off her antidepressant medication, Smith-DuPre and Beck claim that the doctor's disclosures facilitate face-preservation of her patient, encourage the patient to take an active role in her own health care and establish relational affinity and mutuality:

Extract 14

```
 1 Patient:   ((crying)) I should never have stopped the medicine
 2 Provider:  That's okay. That was a reasonable thing to do.
 3 Patient:   I know you told me to do that and I did just the opposite.
 4            Gonna kick me out? ((tearful but laughing))
 5 Provider:  (smiling)) Oh no! You're kicking yourself enough.
 6            It's just so common I mean I'm the same way I mean I can
 7            just see a lot of you in me and I've had to lea:rn stuff.
 8            But you just you take it all in you in yourself and take
 9            responsibility for stuff that you don't need to and
10 Patient:   I do
11 Provider:  and try to make everybody happy and please everybody and
12            and uh ( . ) that's not healthy
13            ((both laugh))
14 Provider:  I mean honestly. That's just that's the way our
15            personalities are and that that stems from childhood
16            stuff. Everything does. A lot of people don't believe
17            it but it does.
```

Smith-Dupre and Beck's (1996) analysis notes that the patient places herself in a risky, potentially face-threatening stance by admitting that she did not comply with her physician's instructions to continue taking the antidepressant medication. While the doctor responds reassuringly in line 2, the patient in lines 3–4 jokingly invokes a conventional notion of MDs as authority figures – 'I know you told me to do that and I did just the opposite. Gonna kick me out'? The MD responds in line 5 as if this were an invitation to deny such an authoritarian role and to do forgiveness, which she enacts by noting that the patient is already punishing herself enough (line 5). Then, beginning with line 6, the doctor self-discloses about how she identifies with the patient in that she has tended in the past to behave in an unhealthy way herself (line 12). This act treats the patient's initial confession as inoffensive, thus preventing a possible loss of face and contributing to 'an interactional climate that is safe for patient participation and expression of patient goals and concerns' (Smith-DuPré and Beck: 84). In fact, later in this same doctor–patient encounter, the doctor recommends to her patient both psychological counselling and a self-help book that she herself has started reading; yet she offers these suggestions in ways that make it acceptable for the patient to decline them, as she has also 'declined' the Prozac medication for her depression. Again, through her own self-disclosures, the doctor acknowledges that emotional issues (both the patient's and her own) are components of one's overall health and appropriate topics for health care interactions.

Conclusion: toward a theory of small talk

Smith-Dupré and Beck (1996) conclude from their analyses of female doctor–female patient interaction that the multiple medical and relational goals of health-care communication should be viewed 'reflexively rather than hierarchically. Relational goals (such as face preservation, identification, role attainment and politeness) do not constitute extraneous enterprises for the physician and his or her patients. Instead, the very display and treatment of relational goals can work to suggest preferences for how the encounter should ensue, how the participants should view one another, and how medical goals may be expressed and accomplished' (p. 87).

This commentary and the preceding analyses of verbal play and extra-medical self-disclosure in female provider–female patient interactions point to a problematic for researchers (and for practitioners) who attempt to discretely delineate categories of 'small talk', or, for that matter, who believe that they can distinguish between 'task (or instrumental or medical) talk' and 'relational (or non-instrumental or social) talk'. In the health-care interactions between female providers and female patients discussed in this chapter, so-called 'small talk' arguably facilitates so-called 'task' (i.e. medical) goals of the encounters, in that the co-achieved facework, mutuality and affinity that are the relational byproducts of verbal play and non-medical self-disclosure, bear directly on medical outcomes – e.g. ease of medical procedures, disclosure of pertinent medical information, accuracy of diagnosis and increased likelihood of patient compliance. The enmeshment of 'small talk' and 'non-small talk' in these health-care interactions displays the concurrent, interdependent and reflexive achievement of so-called medical *and* relational goals.

An apparent conundrum rests in our conventional definition of *task* and our insistence on believing that the 'work' of interaction is not as inherently relational as it is instrumental. No talk in any context can be considered 'small' if, in fact, we subscribe to a belief that task and relationship co-exist as inextricable features of every encounter. As Bateson (1972), Goffman (1974) and numerous other scholars have described in their theories of metacommunication, all messages communicate both information and relationship. The absence of what is perceived to be relational or 'small talk' in both social and work interactions does not mean that relationship is not being communicated to interactants. All social and institutional discourse reflexively define relationship for the interactants, whether 'small talk' is present or not. In health-care interactions, the absence of 'small talk' does not signify necessarily that partnership between provider and patient is lacking, yet such implicit relational messages as provider control, professional distance and devaluation of the patient's social-psychological world *can* be assumed in its absence, to the detriment of the patient's (and, perhaps, the provider's) well-being. Thus, rather than perpetuating the false dichotomy that purports to separate out 'task' and 'relationship' talk, it would appear wiser to see discourse as dialectic, as serving 'both-and', not 'either-or' purposes (see Baxter and Montgomery 1996 for further discussion of dialectical theory in interpersonal communication).

Coda

Feminist sociolinguistic theorists, who suggest that 'phatic communion' is to be valued rather than devalued, might also point out the futility, if not the fatuousness, of trying to discover the 'either-or-ness' of discourse rather than acknowledging its 'both-and-ness'. If all communication has task and relationship dimensions, what is 'small talk' if not a component of the relationship dimension that psychologically characterizes the entirety of the discourse (and which, therefore, could be argued as being the more important, more serious, more believable and more authentic part of the message?) Yet, aside from the impossibility of discriminating between 'small talk' and 'large talk', there is little to gain theoretically or practically from the ideological warfare that value-grades talk that is allegedly instrumental, business, powerful, serious (i.e. so-called 'men's talk') as superior to talk that is relational, social, powerless, frivolous (i.e. so-called 'women's talk'). I contend that women *and* men use discourse to enact the professional and personal lifeworlds and goals highly valued by both genders: women *and* men construct life choices through conversational interaction; women *and* men: make purchases from; negotiate deals with; solicit professional services of; become friends with; and make love to people who promote credibility, trust and liking through 'small talk'.

Notes

1. These data were collected by the author and/or by three of her former PhD students, Dr Michael Pagano, Dr Christina Beck and Dr Athena DuPré. The author gratefully acknowledges the prior analytic work of Pagano, Beck and DuPré and its contribution to the perspectives and analyses herein.
2. These conversational features were chosen for analysis not necessarily because they occurred more frequently than other forms of sociable or relational talk in women's medical discourse, but because they appeared to be relationally and medically significant. We do not make the claim, however, that additional kinds of relational talk are not also important in facilitating medical and relational goals in women's health-care contexts.
3. The following symbols are used in the transcriptions in this chapter:
   [ ]   Brackets are used to indicate overlapping utterances. Left brackets note the beginning of an overlap, and right brackets close or end the overlap.

=	This sign denotes a 'latching' of two contiguous utterances that do not overlap.
___	Underlining represents stress/emphasis.
:	A colon stands for the extension or stretching of the sound that it follows.
-	A hyphen following a sound marks a cut-off, a definite stopping of sound
?	A question mark indicates rising pitch at the end of a word or phrase ending, not necessarily a grammatical question
^	An arrow pointing upward shows a marked rise in pitch.
.	A period indicates a sliding or falling pitch at the end of a word or phrase, not necessarily a grammatical sentence.
,	A comma denotes a continuing intonation, a subtle or slight stretching of sound with a small upward or downward pitch that shows possible completion.
^ ^	A carat sign or degree sign preceding and following a word or phrase indicates that it was said more quietly than the surrounding talk.
>>	The sideways chevrons bracket talk that is spoken faster than the surrounding talk.
<<	The sideways chevrons bracket talk that is spoken slower than the surrounding talk.
(0.4)	Single parentheses enclosing numbers represent pauses in a conversation. The numbers express seconds and tenths of seconds. Brief pauses are expressed as (.).
( )	Single parentheses enclosing words or blank space surround doubtful hearings.
hhh	Hs indicate audible outbreaths, sighing or nonverbal laughter.
.hh	A superscripted period followed by hs denotes audible inbreaths.
(( ))	Double parentheses are used for descriptions of nonverbal behavior or nonspeech sounds.

These transcription symbols are adapted from the notation system developed by Jefferson (Sacks, Schegloff and Jefferson 1974).

References

Bateson, G. (1972) *Steps to an ecology of mind*. New York: Ballantine.

Baxter, L. and Montgomery, B. (1996) *Relating: Dialogues and dialectics*. New York: Guilford.

Beck, C. S. and Ragan, S. L. (1992) Negotiating relational and medical talk: Frame shifts in the gynecologic exam. *Journal of Language and Social Psychology*, 11, 47–61.

Beck, C. S. and Ragan, S. L. (1995) The impact of relational activities on the accomplishment of practitioner and patient goals in the gynecologic exam. In G. Kreps and D. O'Hair (eds) *Communication and health outcomes*. Cresskill, NJ: Hampton Press, 73–86.

Beck, C. S., Ragan, S. L. and DuPré, A. (1997) *Partnership for health: Building relationships between women and health caregivers*. Mahwah, NJ: Erlbaum.

Beckman, H. B. and Frankel, R. M. (1984) The effect of physician behavior on the collection of data. *Annals of Internal Medicine*, 101, 692–6.

Branch, W. T. and Malik, T. K. (1993) Using 'windows of opportunity' in brief interviews to understand patients' concerns. *Journal of the American Medical Association*, 269, 1667–8.

Brody, H. (1992) *The healer's power*. New Haven, CT: Yale University Press.

Burke, K. (1950) *A rhetoric of motives*. Los Angeles, CA: University of California Press.

Clark, J. A. and Mishler, E. G. (1992) Attending to patients' stories: Reframing the clinical task. *Sociology of Health and Illness*, 14, 344–72.

Coombs, R. H. and Goldman, L. J. (1973) Maintenance and discontinuity of coping mechanisms in an intensive care unit. *Societal Problems*, 20, 342–55.

Corea, G. (1977) *The hidden malpractice: How American medicine treats women as patients and professionals*. New York: William Morrow.

Coser, R. L. (1959) Some social functions of laughter: A study of humor in a hospital setting. *Human Relations*, 12, 171–82.

Coser, R. L. (1960) Laughter among colleagues: A study of the social functions of humor among the staff of a mental hospital. *Psychiatry*, 23, 81–95.

Deber, R. B. (1994) The patient–physician partnership: Decision-making, problem solving and the desire to participate. *Canadian Medical Association Journal*, 151, 423–7.

Doyle, B. J. and Ware, J. E. (1977) Physician conduct and other factors that affect consumer satisfaction with medical care. *Journal of Medical Education*, 52, 793–801.

DuPré, A. (1998) *Humor and the healing arts: A multimethod analysis of humor use in health care*. Mahwah, NJ: Erlbaum.

Fisher, S. (1986) *In the patients' best interests: Women and the politics of medical dicisions*. New Brunswick, NJ: Rutgers University Press.

Fisher, S. (1991) A discourse of the social: Medical talk/power talk/oppositional talk. *Discourse and Society*, 2, 157–82.

Fisher, S. (1993) Doctor talk/patient talk: How treatment decisions are negotiated in doctor–patient communication. In A. Todd and S. Fisher (eds) *The social organization of doctor–patient communication*. Norwood, NJ: Ablex, 161–82.

Fisher, S. (1995) *Nursing wounds: Nurse practitioners/doctors/women patients and the negotiation of meaning*. New Brunswick, NJ: Rutgers University Press.

Frankel, R. M. (1995) Some answers about questions in clinical interviews. In G. H. Morris and R. N. Chenail (eds) *The talk of the clinic: Explorations in the analysis of medical and therapeutic discourse*. Hillsdale, NJ: Erlbaum, 233–58.

Goffman, E. (1961) *Encounters: Two studies on the sociology of interaction*. Indianapolis, IN: Bobbs-Merrill.

Goffman, E. (1974) *Frame analysis: An essay on the organization of experience*. New York: Harper and Row.

Goldsmith, D. (1992) Managing conflicting goals in supportive interaction. An integrative theoretical framework. *Communication Research*, 19, 264–86.

Hayworth, D. (1928) The social origin and function of laughter. *Psychological Review*, 35, 367–84.

Heszen-Klemens, I. and Lapkinska, E. (1984) Doctor–patient interaction, patients' health behavior and effects of treatment. *Social Science and Medicine*, 19, 9–18.

Jefferson, G. (1984) On the organization of laughter in talk about troubles. In J. Atkins and J. Heritage (eds) *Structures of social action: Studies in conversation analysis*. Cambridge: Cambridge University Press, 346–69.

Kaplan, S. H., Greenfield, S. and Ware, J. E. (1989) Impact of the doctor–patient relationship on the outcomes of chronic disease. In M. Stewart and D. Roter (eds) *Communicating with medical patients*. Newbury Park, CA: Sage, 228–45.

King, P. E. (1991) Communication, anxiety, and the management of postoperative pain. *Health Communication*, 3, 127–38.

Malinowski, B. (1923) The problem of meaning in primitive languages. In C. K. Ogden and I. A. Richards (eds) *The meaning of meaning*. London: Routledge and Kegan Paul.

Markakis, K., Suchman, A. L., Beckman, H. B. and Frankel, R. M. (1993) Coming to terms with empathy: Raters of the lost art. Paper presented at the annual meeting of the Society of General Internal Medicine, Washington, DC.

Mishler, E. G. (1984) *The discourse of medicine*. Norwood, NJ: Ablex.

Morris, G. H. and Chenail, R. J. (eds) (1995) *The talk of the clinic: Explorations in the analysis of medical and therapeutic discourse*. Hillsdale, NJ: Erlbaum.

Pomerantz, A. H., Ende, J. and Erickson, F. (1995) Precepting conversations in a general medicine clinic. In G. H. Morris and R. J. Chenail (eds) *The talk of the clinic: Explorations in the analysis of medical and therapeutic discourse*. Hillsdale, NJ: Erlbaum, 151–69.

Ragan, S. L. (1990) Verbal play and multiple goals in the gynaecological exam interaction. *Journal of Language and Social Psychology*, 9, 67–84.

Ragan, S. L. and Glenn, L. D. (1990) Communication and gynecologic health care. In D. O'Hair and G. Kreps (eds) *Applied communication theory and research*. Hillsdale, NJ: Erlbaum, 313–30.

Ragan, S. L. and Pagano, M. (1987) Communicating with female patients: Affective interaction during contraceptive counseling and gynecologic exams. *Women's Studies in Communication*, 10, 45–57.

Robinson, V. M. (1975) Humor and the health professions: Cultivating humor as a tool in teaching, communication and intervention in the helping process by health professionals. Unpublished doctoral dissertation, University of Northern Colorado, Greeley.

Robinson, W. P. (1972). *Language and social behaviour*. Harmondsworth, UK: Penguin.

Sacks, H., Schegloff, E. A. and Jefferson, G. (1978) A simplest systematics for the organization of turn taking in conversation. In J. Schenkein (ed.) *Studies in the Organisation of Conversational Interaction*. New York: Academic Press, 7–55.

Sharf, B. F. (1988) Teaching patients to speak up: Past and future trends. *Patient Education and Counseling*, 11, 95–108.

Sharf, B. F. and Street, R. L. (1997) The patient as a central construct: Shifting the emphasis. *Health Communication*, 9, 1–11.

Smith-DuPré, A. A. (1992) Humor in the hospital: An ethnographic study of the communicational aspects of humor shared by patients and caregivers. Unpublished master's thesis, University of Southwestern Louisiana, Lafayette.

Smith-DuPré, A. A. and Beck, C. S. (1996) Enabling patients and physicians to pursue multiple goals in health care encounters: A case study. *Health Communication*, 8, 73–90.

Stewart, M., Brown, J. B. and Weston, W. W. (1989) Patient-centered interviewing, part III: Five provocative questions. *Canadian Family Physician*, 35, 159–61.

Stewart, M., Brown, J. B., Weston, W. W., McWhinney, I. R., McWilliam, C. L. and Freeman, T. R. (1995) *Patient-centered medicine: Transforming the clinical method.* Thousand Oaks, CA: Sage.

Street, R., Gold, W. R. and McDowell, T. (1995) Discussing health-related quality of life in prenatal consultations. In G. H. Morris and R. J. Chenail (eds) *The talk of the clinic: Explorations in the analysis of medical and therapeutic discourse.* Hillsdale, NJ: Erlbaum, 209–31.

Thompson, T. L. (1994) Interpersonal communication and health care. In M. L. Knapp and G. R. Miller (eds) *Handbook of interpersonal communication.* Thousand Oaks, CA: Sage, 696–725.

Todd, A. D. (1993) Exploring women's experiences: Power and resistance in medical discourse. In A. D. Todd and S. Fisher (eds) *The social organization of doctor–patient communication.* Norwood, NJ: Ablex, 267–85.

Todd, A. D. and Fisher, S. (eds) (1993) *The social organization of doctor–patient communication.* Norwood, NJ: Ablex.

Waitzkin, H. (1991) *The politics of medical encounters: How patients and doctors deal with social problems.* New Haven, CT: Yale University Press.

West, C. (1984) 'Ask me no questions . . .': An analysis of queries and replies in physician–patient dialogues. In S. Fisher and A. D. Todd (eds) *The social organization of doctor–patient communication.* Norwood, NJ: Ablex, 127–60.

Wetherell, M., Stiven, M. and Potter, J. (1987) Unequal egalitarianism: A preliminary study of discourses concerning gender and employment opportunities. *British Journal of Social Psychology*, 26, 59–71.

11

Small talk in service dialogues: the conversational aspects of transactional telephone talk[1]
Christine Cheepen

1 Transactional and interactional dialogue

All dialogue, whether spoken or written, can be viewed in terms of its overall communicative goal. That is, we can categorise dialogues according to what the dialogue participants are trying to achieve. At the most general level, this means that dialogue can be seen primarily as either task-directed – i.e. concerned with achieving some change or development 'in the world', otherwise known as 'transactional dialogue', or person-directed – i.e. concerned with achieving some change or development in the relationship between the dialogue participants – otherwise known as 'interactional dialogue' (Brown and Yule 1983; Cheepen 1988; Cheepen and Monaghan 1990).

Analysts (and, indeed, dialogue participants) are, in general, able to categorise without too much difficulty the *primary* goal of a dialogue as either transactional or interactional. It is rare, however, in the case of human–human discourse, to find a dialogue which is *purely* one or the other. From the point of view of the dialogue analyst, a close inspection of the transcribed text of an overwhelmingly transactional dialogue, for example, will often reveal the presence of material which, although subsidiary to the main thrust of the talk, is unambiguously interactional. Dialogue participants are, in many cases, unlikely to reflect in any great detail on the overall nature of the dialogue in which they have taken part but, even so, it is not uncommon to hear comments such as 'It wasn't so much an interview – more of a chat really', or 'I thought it was just a chat, but he obviously had a hidden agenda'.

It is, of course, possible to think of dialogues which are apparently *either* transactional *or* interactional. Consider, for example, the dialogue associated with buying a train ticket, which clearly has as its primary purpose the goal of buying/selling the ticket or, on the other hand, the dialogue which constitutes 'sweet nothings' (though this may fall into a category which puts it outside what we would normally regard as 'a dialogue' – and may be more properly categorised as 'a state of talk' (Goffman 1967)). In practice, however, if we consider how such dialogues actually progress, we find that even in these rather extreme examples there are likely to be cross-over features between task-direction and person-direction. In the case of buying a train ticket, the core transactional content which functions solely to achieve the buying and selling activity will almost inevitably be accompanied by other talk, more characteristic of person-directed talk, such as 'good morning, please can I . . .' 'thanks', 'bye' and the like. And even the sweet nothings are likely to contain (or perhaps shade into) transactional elements of talk.[2]

Conversation is the most overwhelmingly interactional kind of dialogue, because its purpose is the creation and maintenance of social relationships between the participants, and 'informal conversation between equals is the archetypal speech event involving two or more speakers' (Coates 1996). It will be useful, at this point, to explain in a little more detail how I use the term 'conversation', as this will throw some light on how I view the relationship between conversation and small talk.

First, conversation is essentially unscripted talk. This is a non-controversial point; theatrical performances which rely on a script would never be described – by a discourse analyst, an actor or a theatre-goer – as conversations of any kind. Certainly, while describing a theatrical performance it would be reasonable to refer to 'a conversation' *between the characters*, but this is not the same thing at all; a conversation may take place within a play, but a play cannot be a conversation.

The unscripted nature of talk, however, is not sufficient to identify the talk as conversation. Another essential feature of conversation is the overall aim of the talk. On the one hand it is possible to take the view that conversation has *no* overall aim, in that it is not conducted to achieve anything which can be described in terms of 'getting things done' in the ordinary sense. The other side of this coin is to view conversation as something people do, not to earn money, not to put groceries in the cupboard, not to get the car fixed, but *purely because they want to*. This helps to distinguish conversation from other types of dialogue, as it highlights the social bonding aspect of the talk. In fact, social bonding *is* the overall aim of conversation – a situation which is clearly not the case with other kinds of dialogue. It is important to bear in mind, of course, that social bonding through talk can take many forms. Sometimes it will occur as friendly, loving, verbal strokes, but it can also take the form of arguing, teasing or other more aggressive kinds of communication – what Malinowski, in his discussion of phatic communion, describes as 'the bonds of antipathy' (1923: 316).

Finally, and most importantly, the defining feature of conversation – which is intimately connected with the social bonding aspect – is what I would call the *discoursal equality* of the participants. Within any 'conversation' (in the sense I am using this term here), the participants operate as equals. This means that they have equal rights to talk and listen, to choose (and change) topics, to tell and evaluate stories (Cheepen 1988). In practice, this equality is put into operation by the participants *taking turns* at doing all these things, so that control is handed from one to the other throughout the talk, and the participants regularly exchange roles during the encounter.

This clearly distinguishes conversation from other kinds of unscripted dialogue where, although there will inevitably be different turns at talk, and a sequence of different topics (or subtopics) for discussion, the allocation of turns at talk and the selection of topics will be overwhelmingly the responsibility of one participant only. In an interview, for example, the interviewee will certainly have plenty of opportunity to talk, but this will be at the explicit invitation of the interviewer, and the range of topics will undoubtedly be planned by the interviewer in advance of the encounter. Even in a business meeting, where the participants may recognise one another as equals, there will still be one who controls the agenda (usually the one who is on 'home ground').

Conversation, then, is overwhelmingly social, interactional talk, which differentiates it from those other genres of dialogue where transactional goals predominate, and where the participants collaborate through talk to carry out a task or a set of tasks. Within transactional talk, however, speakers typically do linguistic work which often resembles conversation. Sometimes this will arise after the transactional goals have been accomplished, when the participants will collaborate to move smoothly on into a full-blown conversation. This situation can arise at the end of a business meeting, a tutorial, or some similar encounter where the participants may already know one another socially. It is extremely unlikely, however, to occur in something like a job interview, where the task agenda, the timing of the encounter, and the discoursal roles and responsibilities are very clearly delineated. The participants here are tightly constrained to the preset agenda, and do not have the option to move on into conversation.

The possibility of participants moving into full-blown conversation is, however, not the only way in which the discoursal characteristics of conversation are manifested in transactional talk. Typically, transactional encounters (except perhaps the most minimal, such as buying a train ticket during rush hour) include small sections of the dialogue where the participants appear to be exchanging talk which is focused not on the transactional task but on the interactional bonding of the speakers. This may surface as brief, friendly, semi-ritualised phatic tokens – informal greetings such as 'hi there', or more extended sequences, which occur as 'interactional islands' in the predominantly transactional flow of the talk. This kind of talk is usually initiated by the 'superior' participant (e.g. the interviewer, the doctor, the teacher) but can then also be used by the 'inferior' participant. As this kind of talk is, in a sense, 'outside' the transactional agenda, and because it tends to occur in comparatively *small* 'islands' within the larger sections of directly transactional dialogue, it can be seen as 'small talk'.

Previous research work on the various functions of spoken language in the office context. Monaghan (1992) has indicated how overwhelmingly transactional dialogue is peppered with small talk which is reminiscent of conversation (Holmes, this volume). In an efficient office, business tasks are not accomplished by simply 'getting down to business' – and this is even true of relatively low-level tasks like dictation. It is usual, for instance, to find discoursal items such as greetings included in a dictation tape. At first glance it may appear that an opening utterance on a dictation tape such as 'hi Susan' is simply a 'small talk extra', but in practice this serves as a clear signal of 'beginning of dictation session', and is therefore functioning to promote the transactional goal of successful dictation/transcription.

Small talk does not occur only in the opening phases of transactional dialogues – it tends to permeate the whole dialogue. Elsewhere in this volume it has been pointed out that public discourses are becoming increasingly 'conversationalised', so that dialogue participants tend to expect that what are essentially transactional dialogues will contain substantial linguistic material which is primarily interactional (Fairclough 1995; Habermas 1984). This means that transactional talk is increasingly characterised by a level of informality and 'pseudo-intimacy' which is derived directly from the discoursal patternings found in unscripted, casual conversation. The result is what we have come to consider as a flavour of friendliness about our transactional dialogues - even when those dialogues are focused on the most mundane of transactions, such as telephone banking, bill paying and the like.

Transactions can, of course, take place in a wide variety of social contexts – the participants may be well known to one another or be strangers, the setting may be formal or informal (depending on the overall goal of the encounter), the situation may be more or less power-laden in favour of one participant over the other.

Telephone-mediated, service dialogues are among the most overtly transactional dialogue types – their overall goal is clearly transactional, the relationship between the caller and the agent is highly 'business-orientated' and focused on achieving the transactional goal, and the participants are strangers with no shared social background other than knowledge of their generalised social roles. Even these dialogues, however, contain numerous small talk tokens which display a strong dependence on the discoursal patterns which characterise informal, friendly conversation. As we will see in succeeding sections, the small talk aspect of service dialogues with human agents occurs as a liberal sprinkling of lexico-grammatical signals of informality which underline the human–human nature of the dialogue. Examples from telephone calls to an electricity call centre will illustrate how these signals cluster at important structural points in the dialogue – particularly openings, closings and confirmation sequences. Examples will also be given where participants indulge in lengthier sections of small talk which occur as 'side sequences' (Jefferson 1972) in the dialogue.

2   Service dialogues and the growth of call centres

Over recent years there has been an increasing tendency for many transactional dialogues to be conducted by telephone, and there is now a proliferation of call centres dealing with service dialogues in domains such as telephone banking, insurance services, bill payment for utilities and a range of other commercial services.

The relationship between conversation and service dialogues of this kind is a complex one, primarily because of considerations of equality – and more importantly inequality – between the participants in a service dialogue. Callers accessing a service are, in one sense, superior to the agent who is answering the call (following the principle of 'the customer is always right' or at least of trying to give the customer what they want). The agent is, however, the participant who has the specialist information, and can therefore be seen as superior in that sense. In terms of controlling the discourse, however, it is always the agent who carries the responsibility and the caller who relies on the agent to do just that. In service dialogues, although the caller may be notionally the superior, discoursal superiority is firmly with the call centre agent.

It is important, of course, for callers not to feel that they are being patronised, and to feel that they have some status in terms of the encounter. Agents in service dialogues must therefore ensure that the caller is made to feel comfortable during the encounter. This is done by the use of small talk which echoes the linguistic friendliness and bonding talk of conversation, and serves to maintain the 'face' of the caller (Goffman 1955). The 'house style' may impact on the way friendliness is signalled – some organisations, for example, operate on a first-name basis, and the agents will address the callers by their first names, while other organisations prefer their agents to address callers by title plus last name.[3]

Recent technological developments in automatic speech recognition have led to an increasing number of organisations that provide telephone access to transactional dialogues where the human staff who normally act as agents within call centres are replaced with automated systems. This means that callers now frequently participate in transactional dialogues where their interlocutor is a machine. Where this is done, the service provider is anxious to retain their existing clients (and, of course, to attract new ones). To do this, they must overcome the dislike the majority of callers have for human–machine dialogues,[4] and ensure that callers continue to receive an acceptable level of service.

To make the changeover to an automated dialogue service as smooth as possible from the point of view of the callers, the service provider is generally anxious to carry as much 'human-ness' as possible through to the automated dialogue. British Telecom, promoting their automated voice services, refer to providing the system with a 'friendly... dialogue style' (*BT Voice Services – Now You're Talking*). The recent European EAGLES initiative, in its handbook on Spoken Dialogue Systems, recommends that automated dialogue systems should have a 'warm and friendly personality' (Gibbon *et al*. 1997). Designers of automated dialogue systems (who are, in the main, software engineers who are currently specialising in dialogue systems) are, generally speaking, under considerable pressure from their commissioning clients to develop automated systems which will mimic the linguistic behaviour of human agents, and within the research and development community there is a general consensus that automated systems should be as 'natural' as possible. Aust (1996) takes an extreme position here, stating 'ideally the caller should not realise he is talking to a machine'.

As later examples will show, this has resulted in an ever-increasing number of automated dialogue systems which are liberally peppered with linguistic signals of informality and friendliness – or what I am referring to here as small talk – which attempt to emulate the natural give and take of the interactional islands within human–human transactional talk. Section 8 below will take up this issue and challenge the wisdom of attempting to make machines sound like human agents.

In the following sections of this chapter we will look at some examples of how small talk arises in human–human and in human–machine service dialogues, paying particular attention to three areas of the dialogue – openings, closings and confirmation sequences, and also consider cases where side sequences of small talk occur. The human–human examples will be drawn from a corpus of call centre dialogues with a utilities provider. The information in the corpus is confidential and, in order to ensure anonymity, we have therefore amended all names to their syllabic equivalents. We will look at how different kinds of small talk are incorporated into automated systems in different topical domains. Finally, we will describe the results of some recent experiments on how human callers react to the inclusion of 'natural' small talk in automated dialogues, and consider the implications for dialogue design.

3 Openings

3.1 Openings in human agent service dialogues

An example from a call to an electricity call centre staffed by human agents will illustrate how a human agent typically opens a service dialogue:

Example 1

Blankshire Electricity, Mary Smith speaking – how may I help you?

This opening formula is typical of transactional telephone dialogues where members of the public ring in for a particular service or set of services. It is worth remembering that staff in call centres are trained to answer a call in a particular way. This opener functions primarily in a transactional way, but interactional signals are present, which give a *flavour* of small talk to the opening.

The first section 'Blankshire Electricity' is purely transactional. It functions to tell the caller which service they are connected to. The second section 'Mary Smith speaking' (which is not used by all call centres) is both transactional and interactional. It signals to the caller that the agent is, in a sense, the 'right' person to talk to – i.e. someone who can probably answer questions and deal with problems on their own authority and initiative, as opposed to, say, a switchboard operator, who can only forward the call to some more senior figure. An additional transactional function here is to give the caller sufficiently detailed information to be able to call again and ask for the same person if a problem should arise. There is also, however, an interactional function in the announcement of the agent's name – which is the underlining of the human-ness of that agent.

In addition to this there is also an aspect of this section which communicates to the caller what we can think of as a kind of textual meaning related to the expected pattern of the dialogue which will ensue. It indicates, in fact, that the dialogue may be fairly lengthy and complex. If the expectation by the service provider was that the dialogue would be brief and simple then there would be little advantage in the agent giving her name. When the agent does give her name she is signalling that she is trained for and prepared to participate in a dialogue of some complexity.

The third section of the opening – 'how may I help you?' is a formulaic structure which signals the transactional function 'you may ask me questions', and also 'and I am in a position to be able to answer them'. It also functions textually, by using an interrogative form, which both requires an answer and simultaneously hands the next turn at talk to the caller (Schegloff 1968). Ritualised politeness is clearly communicated by this formula, and some directly interpersonal material is also included in the form of the personal pronouns 'I' and 'you' so, as with the announcement of the agent's name, we can see the flavour of small talk in this formulaic catering for the human-ness of the dialogue participants.

3.2   Openings in automated service dialogues

In the automated systems currently in commercial use in Britain there is great consistency in the way the dialogue opens. A telephone banking system illustrates a typical opening:

Example 2

Welcome to the XXX Telephone Banking Service . . .

The inclusion of 'welcome' (an item found at the beginning of almost all commercially available automated dialogues) functions transactionally as the first signal that the caller is connected to the system. It is also clearly intended as some kind of interactional signal – a marker of politeness. Although highly formulaic – unlike the informal friendliness of much small talk – politeness must be considered essentially interactional, rather than transactional, because it is not directly focused on the transactional goal of the talk, and also because politeness is an attitude which expresses human respect and consideration for another human; it does not characterise our dealings with machines.[5]

If we consider the way a non-automated service dialogue opens, we can see that this is not, strictly speaking, an attempt to emulate human dialogic talk – the item 'welcome' in initial position is not normally found in human utterances except, perhaps, in a formal, monologic speech. Even then it will, in the majority of cases, be prefaced by other introductory material such as 'I'd like to welcome you all . . .'. In automated dialogues, however, this is the normal opening item in the system's first utterance, and this has great significance for the caller.

When dialling a telephone service, a caller often does not know in advance whether the call will be answered by a human agent or an automated system. Indeed, in many cases the caller may well be expecting to talk to another human being and be unaware that the service has been automated. If that is the case, then s/he will expect to hear the pattern illustrated in Example 1 above – an announcement of the name of the service followed by some kind of invitation to ask a question.

For current automated systems, particularly those of any complexity, this is not a practical design, because the range of possible responses the caller might make is too large (and too uncertain) for the underlying speech-recognition technology to cope with. Designers cannot, then, simply allow callers to ask questions in 'free format', but must guide the callers to respond with items which the system can recognise and deal with. In our telephone banking example, this is done immediately after the 'welcome' section, by giving the caller a restricted set of choices of what to say next:

Example 3

. . .
For an account balance, say 'one'.
To order a statement, say 'two'. (etc.)

Clearly, for a caller who is expecting to deal with a human agent, this does not match with the expectations s/he has about how the dialogue is likely to proceed. On the contrary, such a caller will expect, after an agent's offer of 'how may I help you?', to take over the control of the dialogue by introducing the next topic of conversation, whether that is getting an account balance, ordering a statement, or some other business s/he wishes to conduct. The caller must, then, revise those expectations considerably on encountering an automated system.

The use of 'welcome' in initial position is extremely useful here, because it signals to the caller from the very outset of the dialogue that the system is an automated one – it is an opening which only a machine would deliver, so all expectations about how the dialogue can proceed must be revised to accommodate this. It appears, then, that designing dialogues to open in this way is an unambiguous signal of automation, which, appearing first in the talk, allows the caller the maximum possible time to adjust to this provision, and to adopt expectations about the future structure of the dialogue which are appropriate for talking with a machine. When the caller hears the list of menu options, s/he has already been prepared (by the preceding 'welcome' signal) to take part in a strictly controlled dialogue. In most cases, callers respond to such cues 'successfully' – i.e. in such a way that the dialogue does not break down, and the overwhelming majority are successful in completing their transaction. This indicates that the system's opening prompt is sufficiently robust to allow transactional success. All automated systems are provided with repair and correction mechanisms, so that when problems do arise for the caller at this point – e.g. the caller says nothing – these mechanisms are initiated by the system (e.g. 'I didn't hear you say anything. Here are the options again'), the caller understands what is required, and the dialogue is usually then rescued.

4   Closings

4.1   Closings in human agent service dialogues

Example 4

[A=Agent, C=Caller]
 [1]A right right that's fine then
 [2]C is that alright (inaud)
 [3]A OK
 [4]C tomorrow then
 [5]A tomorrow yeh I'll ring the showroom anyway today to let
 [6]   them know and then there won't be any problem when you go in
 [7]C OK then thanks a lot
 [8]A OK can you just take some ID with you and everything
 [9]C OK then (inaud)
 [10]A alright

[11]C bye
[12]A bye

(Call Centre Corpus)

Note here the high incidence of repetition of closing signals – 'OK', 'bye', 'then' (which functions as a closing signal when used in conjunction with other similar tokens as in this example) – coupled with the explicit references back to (and reinforcement of) topics which have clearly already been dealt with earlier in the dialogue (the sequence beginning 'tomorrow . . .' [line 4]).

Clearly, this highly repetitive kind of closing sequence (which is very typical of human telephone transactions) owes much to the patternings which characterise conversation – the kind of speech event in which the speakers are concerned primarily with interaction rather than transaction.[6] It illustrates the tendency of human beings to express solidarity with one another through the exchange of language more or less regardless of the overall purpose of the talk.

The linguistic expression of personal solidarity may well be (and certainly appears to be) appropriate for inclusion in what is a highly transactional dialogue when the dialogue participants are both human beings. Undoubtedly it makes carrying out the transactional business which is the goal of the encounter more pleasant for both speakers – it is, in fact, a clear example of speakers *indulging in* small talk.

4.2   Closings in automated service dialogues

Closings in automated systems differ substantially from closings in human–human dialogues. As Example 4 above illustrates, human interactants adopt a very small talk-orientated approach, underlining the interactional, friendly aspects of the dialogue by numerous repetitions of closing signals. This lengthy procedure also, however, functions transactionally as a 'preclosing' (Schegloff and Sacks 1973), so that, during the repetitive exchanges, both parties have the opportunity to open a new, previously unmentioned topic of talk if required. When the closing finally occurs, it is clear to both parties that all appropriate topics have been covered and the dialogue is complete.

This transactional functionality provided in human agent service dialogues is not possible in automated systems. Instead, they typically allow the human caller only one opportunity to raise a new topic, and then close without further delay. Consider the following example from a commercial telephone bill payment service:

Example 5

[1] If you require further assistance please say 'yes', otherwise remain
[2] silent.

[3] <pause>
[4] Thank you for calling XXX. Goodbye.

Unlike the closing (potentially preclosing) sequence between a caller and a human agent, the caller here has only one opportunity to treat this sequence as a preclosing, and to reopen the dialogue by raising a new topic. Once the final section (beginning 'Thank you' [line 4]) begins, then the opportunity to reopen the dialogue is lost. If the caller then remembers that s/he does want to access another part of the service there is no option to do this in the current encounter – the only possibility is to let the system disconnect and to ring again.

Note that the final part of the system utterance here contains interactional material in the form of politeness markers 'Thank you' and 'Goodbye'. Clearly this provides some transactional functionality, because it indicates that the pause during which the caller has their one opportunity to raise a new topic has now elapsed and the call will now terminate, but the selection of conventional politeness tokens to signal this (rather than, for example, a direct instruction such as 'replace the receiver') illustrates the reliance of the dialogue designer on the human–human model of conversation.

5 Confirmation

Confirmation occurs frequently in telephone-mediated service dialogues of any complexity. It serves three major functions

- channel checking
  i.e. are you still there?
- discourse monitoring
  i.e. have we reached a boundary in the talk?
- information verification
  i.e. have I got this number right?

The most cursory observation of conversational data reveals, however, that confirmation is a very strong feature of this kind of purely interactional dialogue (Cheepen 1988, Cheepen and Monaghan 1990). It appears that human beings, in their bonding dialogues with other human beings, are accustomed to exchanging confirmation sequences with great frequency.

Example 6

[1]K: ... painting the skirting board white and when I opened the tin
[2]   it weren't white was it was yellow says brilliant white on the pro
[3]C: you're kidding what the wrong colour

(Cheepen and Monaghan 1990, Tape – Dresses)

Example 7

[1]G: I was having a drink with him in the pub you know like one
[2]   does and (inaud)
        . . . .
[3]T: was it in a pub he bought you a drink (inaud) I thought it was
[4]   (inaud)
[5]G: our beloved leader has bought me a drink this evening. I think
[6]   that means I'm gonna be sacked

(Cheepen and Monaghan 1990, Tape – Dawsons)

Example 8

[1]D: . . . . . . with food I mean they will actually. help themselves to
[2]   salad – and have – almost everything
[3]C: whatever's in the salad servers I can't believe it
[4]D: virtually yes I mean they w . they will avoid . chunks of onion
[5]C: yeh
[6]D: but erm – more or less anything else

(Cheepen and Monaghan 1990, Tape – Celia)

The familiarity – one might say omnipresence – of confirmation in conversational talk is such that the linguistic constructs which humans use to signal it are very deeply ingrained in their dialogic behaviour, so it is not surprising that confirmation also features so frequently in transactional talk. Over the telephone, of course, where participants have no visual clues that what they are saying is correctly understood, there is also a strong transactional need for confirmation sequences.

As the following examples will illustrate, the confirmation structures which are built into many current commercial automated systems bear very little resemblance to those which speakers naturally produce (and appear to expect) when engaged in dialogue with other human beings. In the following sections, I will present some examples of confirmation in transactional telephone dialogues between human speakers, outline some of the problems these indicate for the design of automated dialogues, and compare them with some confirmation sequences currently being used in automated systems.

5.1   Confirmation functioning as channel checking

Telephone dialogue participants typically check (and confirm) that the communication channel is open at the beginning of the discourse, with the matched openers hello/hello. They also carry out the same procedure when there has been some break in the talk, as in the following extract:

Example 9

[1]A just bear with me a moment please
[2]C yes

AGENT CONSULTS RECORDS
[3]A hello
[4]C hello

(Call Centre Corpus)

Automated dialogues do not provide for this. Instead, when the system is retrieving information from elsewhere, it is usual for music to be played and, when the dialogue resumes, there is no opportunity for the caller to contribute a confirmation to the talk.

5.2 Confirmation functioning as discourse monitoring

There are clearly observable areas of human–human dialogue where participants are involved in agreeing 'where they've got to' in the discourse, and where they both give clear signals that a particular section (i.e. a particular topic or subtopic) has come to an end. Consider the following example, which occurs towards the end of a problem/solution structure.

Example 10

(simultaneous speech is indicated by underlining)
[1]A it's your bill then isn't it Mr Brown
[2]C right
[3]A yeh you've got a reminder – yes a actually
[4]C so (inaud)
[5]A that was issued . you see before – we fitted the token meter
[6]C but
[7]A so just ignore it
[8]C it said contact you immediately . right it said to contact you
[9]   immediately
[10]A yeh well that's thank you very much for ringing
[11]C yeh
[12]A and the wires have got crossed they've sent the reminder out . but
[13]   that's why we've fitted the token meter anyway isn't it
[14]C yes that's (inaud)
[15]A well
[16]C (inaud)
[17]A yeh . so thank you Mr Brown for ringing up
[18]C right (inaud)
[19]A now in future (continues with new topic)

(Call Centre Corpus)

Note here how the participants' turns at talk begin to 'die away' (indicated by 'inaud' [line 14]) as they reach a consensus that the problem/solution sequence is concluding, and the repetition of the typical tokens of confirmation – echoic, often overlapping responses of 'well' (line 15), 'yeh' (line 17). Note also that, in this particular example, although she goes on to introduce a new topic of talk (or, more precisely, a new subtopic, related to the previous one) after the problem has been solved – i.e. what will happen 'in the future' (line 19), the agent includes what might be considered a 'pre-preclosing' twice in her turns – 'thank you very much for ringing' (line 10) and 'thank you Mr Brown for ringing up' (line 17), presaging the closing which occurs later in the dialogue – 'thanks for ringing then . bye bye'.

This patterning is never found in automated dialogue systems. Typically, confirmation of 'where we are in the dialogue' is done by a variety of formulaic system prompts, which tells the user which menu is currently available and how to move to other menus.

Example 11

here are the film times for the week beginning Thursday the twentieth of March

Example 12

to hear the film times again, say THREE after the tone,
to book seats for any of the films currently showing, say FOUR after the tone

With this mechanism, the system simply signals to the caller what the options are, and no negotiation is possible. A caller talking to a human agent will always have the option to interrupt the agent and to introduce their own topical agenda. This sometimes occurs when callers have serious complaints, and will say, for instance, 'I'm not satisfied with this, let me speak to your manager'. In an automated system this facility is not generally available, unless one of the menu options is to speak to an operator. Very often, however, systems are not designed in this way.

5.3   Confirmation functioning as information verification

Example 13

[1]A what's the address then please you're moving out of
[2]C I'm moving out of six Bullerforte Road
[3]A Bullerforte
[4]C yeh
[5]A how do you
[6]C B
[7]A spell that
[8]C B-U-double L
[9]A yes
[10]C E-R
[11]A yes

[12]C F-O-R-T-E – Bullerforte Road
[13]A Road where's that please
[14]C Cole Green Hatfield
[15]A Hatfield just bear with me a moment please

(Call Centre Corpus)

Confirmation in this fragment is carried out over a lengthy section of the dialogue, and participants collaborate closely to construct the sequence as a joint production. Note the characteristic overlapping of turns at talk, which is so pronounced that the sequence resembles, in many respects, a round song. Close matching is evident even in the talk which is not directly focused on the detail being confirmed – note the opening two utterances of the fragment, where 'moving out of' (line 1), first uttered by the agent, is echoed by the caller in response.

The way confirmation is stretched out over a quite lengthy chunk of the discourse and across many turns at talk in this example, along with the characteristic echoing of turns or partial turns at talk, clearly illustrates what normally happens when the dialogue is between a human caller and a human agent – this is the 'natural' way human speakers do confirmation. This complex and elegant patterning is not, at present (nor in the foreseeable future) a possibility in an automated system. As the following example, from an experimental, in-house directory enquiries system at BT Research Laboratories will show, a much stricter format is used in automated dialogues.

Example 14

[S=System, C=Caller]
[1]S And now say the surname
[2]C Foster
[3]S And now spell the surname
[4]C F-O-S-T-E-R
[5]S Is the surname Foster?
[6]C Yes

(Attwater *et al.* 1996)

This practice of asking for a spelling to confirm recognition of the name before problems arise is clearly designed to ensure that the caller is made aware of the system's procedures to achieve accurate recognition. It is not, however, how humans naturally do confirmation. This system has been designed to expect a yes/no response to the confirmation question 'Is the surname Foster?' (line 5) with a yes/no response. Other dialogue systems in use in the public sector make this an explicit requirement. Consider the following fragment from a telephone banking system.

Example 15

Was that banking account number XXXX? Please answer yes or no.

The usefulness of getting a yes/no answer in these situations is clear. It is essential that important details such as account numbers, names, addresses and the like are correctly understood by the system. Given the problems which can (and do) arise in any speech recognition system, where a caller's input may be misrecognised, it is very helpful indeed if, at this point in the dialogue, the only recognition vocabulary which is operational is the yes/no vocabulary. However poor the quality of the input signal, it is unlikely that the system will be unable to distinguish between the only two items it is 'listening for'. From the point of view of the caller, however, this may be far from ideal. A number of researchers have noted the difficulties which arise when callers are requested to respond with *only* a yes or no (Cheepen 1994; Foster *et al.* 1992), and this resistance to giving such a terse answer can often lead to further problems with the underlying speech-recognition technology. A response of 'umm, well no' or similar will, for example, cause severe disruption to a system which is set up to recognise *only* a yes/no response at this point, and the communication may break down completely.

6   Side sequences of small talk

The previous sections have illustrated how transactional dialogue is punctuated throughout with interactional lexicogrammatical fragments which give the overall dialogue a flavour of interpersonal friendliness. As well as this, however, it is not uncommon to find that participants in service dialogues will indulge in lengthier sections of small talk which occur as 'side sequences' (Jefferson 1972), where topics are discussed which fall outside the transactional topical agenda of the discourse, and which do not contribute directly to the overall transactional goal (though friendliness and approachability in the human agent may well contribute to encouraging the caller's good opinion of the organisation, and may further the long-term transactional goal of retaining the caller as a customer). Consider the following examples.

Example 16

[1]A but you said something about you wanted to change the change the
[2]   name Miss Ward
[3]C yeh the name should now be it's Mrs M Franton . now
[4]A Mrs
[5]C M Franton

[6]A Franton
[7]C F . R A N T O N
[8]A T O N
[9]C yes – you sound full of cold
[10]A do I
[11]C yes
[12]A yes yes I've started with a bit of one yeh
[13]C (laugh)
[14]A keep smiling for me and I might not get one
[15]C (laugh)
[16]A (laugh) I'll do that for you then Mrs M Franton and I'll send you a
[17]   direct debit mandate out for twenty-one pounds

(Call Centre Corpus)

The underlined section of this extract is a side sequence of small talk. It arises 'out of the blue', and has no obvious connection with the preceding topic (which the agent, in fact, returns to after the matched laugh tokens at the end of the side sequence [lines 15, 16]). This is a clear example of the conversationalisation of public discourse. The side sequence plays no part in furthering the overall goal of the discourse – in fact it appears to interrupt what is a legitimate, local transactional goal (changing the name of the account holder). The only function of this side sequence, is apparently an interactional one – it signals an atmosphere of human friendliness between the participants.

A similar situation occurs in the next example, which is taken from an advertisement currently being run on a national radio station for a telephone banking company. The advertisement consists largely of extracts from calls taken by human agents at the bank call centre. The callers are all actors who are primed to ask questions which give the agents appropriate opportunities to describe the advantages of banking with a company where all transactions are carried out by telephone. The agents in the extracts are actually employed in the call centre, and are unaware that the calls they are dealing with are specially set up to be used in an advertisement – from their point of view they are simply dealing with incoming enquiries from members of the general public.

Example 17

. . . . .
[1] Male Caller   and you can pay all my bills and sort out all my
[2]   business
[3] Female Agent   yes that's right
[4] Male Caller   so basically you can organise my whole life
[5] Female Agent   (laugh) yeh . not sure about your love life
[6]   though (laugh)

Again, this is clearly a side sequence – its topic does not contribute to the overall transactional goal of the talk, and it appears to function purely inter-actionally, signalling informality and 'a bit of fun' between the agent and the caller.

The interesting point about this example is that the extract (as well as others) has been chosen by the company to feature in a radio advertisement which attempts to persuade potential new clients of the advantages of chang-ing to the telephone banking company. Certainly, the transactional advant-ages of using telephone banking are illustrated by the other extracts used in the advertisement (staff on call 24 hours a day, lower bank charges, etc.), but this particular extract, with its small talk side sequence (lines 5,6), has also been selected as a selling point which will appeal to new customers. This illustrates the importance service providers attach to the signalling of friend-liness in service dialogues and, perhaps, throws some light on why service providers who move onto automated dialogue systems are so anxious to retain that quality in the dialogue, even when the agent is not a human being but a machine.

7   The 'naturalisation' of automated dialogues

As we have seen in the preceding examples, dialogue in automated systems is managed very differently from the way talk is organised in service dialogues where there is a human agent. Interactional signalling – what in human–human dialogue occurs as highly characteristic small talk – is still present, but it is considerably reduced. Signals of politeness, friendliness and a degree of informality, such as 'goodbye', 'please' and 'I'm sorry' are used, but the long sections of discourse which provide their immediate context in human–human dialogue cannot be catered for in automated systems, due to the constraints of the underlying speech recognition technology. The overriding concern in automated dialogues is (and must be) to ensure that transactional information is correctly exchanged, and this can only be guaranteed if callers are restricted in the range of input tokens they can use.

Service providers are nevertheless anxious to give their automated sys-tems a friendly flavour, so, along with the rather minimalist tokens of friend-liness, etc. which are sprinkled through the system prompts, they also, in some domains, use other, more general signals of the system 'personality' (Gibbon et al. 1997). This is particularly evident in automated dialogues which are operating in leisure domains, where it is common to encounter signals such as a distinctive, 'up-beat' tone of voice (similar to that often used in TV advertising). Such systems frequently use special, 'leisure-orientated' vocabul-ary items, as in the following two fragments taken from an automated sys-tem used at Jarman Park Leisure Centre, Hemel Hempstead, Hertfordshire:

Example 18

hot shot . it's a new sports concept . with something for everyone – twenty . ten pin bowling lanes – interactive golf ranges – American pool tables – satellite tv . and much more – it's a world of sport . game on

Example 19

for the young . who don't want to miss out on all the fun . there's a great new kids' activity centre and crèche for two to twelve year olds – fully trained nursery nurses will take care of your little ones . leaving you free to have your own kind of fun

Building automated dialogues which include such signals of supposed human-ness is, of course, a complicated and difficult task, which involves the service provider in considerable cost, both at the initial design stage, and during any subsequent alterations to the system. It is evident, however, even from a cursory sampling of the automated systems which are currently in operation, that such signalling in automated dialogues is, for designers and for service providers, an important priority, which warrants such financial outlay.

The implication here must be that designers and service providers assume that providing dialogues of this style is an important factor in *usability* – i.e. that 'naturalness' in the dialogues will make them more accessible, attractive and easy to use for the human callers who interact with them. In the following section I will question the validity of this viewpoint, and consider a set of recent experiments which investigated to what extent this kind of 'naturalness' really does promote usability.

8   Experiments with 'naturalness' in automated dialogues

In the course of an ESRC-funded project at the University of Surrey, the research team carried out a set of experiments to investigate how the inclusion of 'naturalness' tokens function in automated dialogues, *from the point of view of the users* (Williams and Cheepen 1998). The results were unexpected and give rise to serious questions about the validity of the current approach to dialogue design.

8.1   Design of experiment

The experiment focused on how callers reacted to two automated dialogue systems – one with an interactional strand built into the system prompts – we called this the 'original' version, and one where the interactional strand had been removed – we called this the 'denatured' version. Both versions were interfaced with an underlying dummy database of bank account information.

The experiment was carried out in two phases – the first using 12 subjects and the second using an additional 22 subjects. The subjects were all members of the general public and had no particular expertise with automated dialogue systems other than occasionally using answer phones or perhaps booking cinema seats through an automated system. All subjects were required to use both versions of the system, and were given a set of banking tasks to carry out via the automated dialogues. The subjects were not informed of the difference between the two versions.

To find out what callers' perceptions about the dialogues were we were careful not to lead our informants in any way. We therefore kept our questions as general as possible, in order to allow the subjects the greatest possible leeway to express their own evaluations without guidance from us. After using each version of the dialogue, the subjects were asked

How did you get on?
What did you think of it?
Why?
Would you use a similar system if your own bank introduced one?

After using both versions of the dialogue, the subjects were asked

Which did you prefer?
Why?

8.2   System utterances

The original version was the set of system utterances – or *prompts* – which were recorded for a telephone banking system which is currently in use in a commercial situation.

The interactional material in the original version (which was similar to that found in many current commercial systems, including operational telephone banking services) fell into three major categories:

- politeness tokens
  e.g. please, thank you
- personal pronouns
  e.g. I, you, your
- conversational constructions
  e.g. in a moment I will ask you to tell me the account number

To produce the denatured version, all this interactional material was removed from the prompts. In some cases this was simply a matter of removing an explicit politeness token, for example *After the tone please select the account* became *After the tone select the account*, and some personal pronouns were simply replaced by the, for example *speak your Telephone Banking number* became *speak the Telephone Banking number*. In other cases, however, in order to avoid using personal pronouns, the grammatical structures were also changed, for instance *I'm sorry I didn't understand that* became *Not understood*.

Throughout the 'translation' process the team kept the denatured version as close to the original as possible, and no substantive additions were made to the original prompts. Where more than minimal changes were required in order to denature the prompt, the alteration was always in the direction of reducing the prompt, rather than augmenting it, while retaining all the transactional content necessary for the caller's task to be achieved. From a purely transactional (i.e. directly goal-driven) point of view, then, the denatured version of the system provided the same functionality as the original.

8.3   Results of the experiment

In terms of overall transactional success, there was no apparent difference between the versions. That is, there was no difference in the number of caller errors, the number of abandoned calls, misrecognitions or other undesirable occurrences. There was a slight difference in the time taken to complete the calls using the different systems – the denatured was quicker – but the difference was not statistically significant because, although some system prompts became shorter because words were removed, the business of translating from original to denatured sometimes involved adding extra words, for instance when using a passive construction instead of an active one, in order to remove items like personal pronouns.

There was, however, a noticeable difference in callers' perceptions of usability when comparing the two systems. Although the subjects did not notice what the difference was between the systems (i.e. presence or absence of naturalness tokens) 8 of the 12 subjects in the pilot phase and 8 of the 18 in the main phase preferred the denatured version. Only one subject in the main phase preferred the original version. Overwhelmingly, the subjects gave as their reason for preferring the denatured version their impression that it was quicker. They expressed this by commenting negatively on the original version, which they described as 'long-winded', and found irritating. Some even commented that the denatured version was 'more user-friendly'.

9   Conclusions and recommendations for dialogue design

The experiments showed that, in spite of the good intentions of designers and service providers, the end users of automated systems simply do not like taking part in dialogues where machines simulate the behaviour of human agents. Certainly, the general public use the systems which are currently in operation (very often they have no choice) but, when asked to choose between a machine which is 'conversational' and one which is not, their clear preference is for the 'machine-like' version.

The conclusions of the research team here were that the experiment represented a situation where there was a failure of *appropriate* naturalness. In other words, the experiment showed that the inclusion of small talk (of even the most minimal kind) is not 'natural' in dialogue *when one of the participants is a machine*. The human-like tokens which are at present incorporated into automated dialogue systems – certainly in the domain of telephone banking, where we conducted our experiments – are inappropriate for such a context.

Naturalness is not an absolute, it is, rather, an emergent property of a dialogic context. Although human beings may enjoy the natural, small talk-orientated give-and-take of dialogue with another human being, they do not appreciate this in the human–machine context, where relationship building between participants is at best an irrelevance and at worst an impediment to full usability.

Further experiments should be carried out, in a variety of different topical domains, in order to establish to what extent our finding that 'less is more' should be the guiding principle for designing automated dialogues which are appropriately natural. At present, our findings clearly indicate that the human–human model of transactional dialogue is not suitable for the human–machine discourse context. The message to dialogue designers must be, therefore that, while automated systems need to incorporate the full range of transactional functionality appropriate for their particular domains, the inclusion of small talk is counterproductive. Callers in dialogue with human agents are happy to include in their talk sections which cater for the humanness of the agent; callers in dialogue with a machine prefer to treat the system as a tool – not as a simulation of a human interactant.

Notes

1. This paper has arisen partly out of ongoing research on an ESRC-funded project, Guidelines for the Design of Advanced Voice Dialogues, under the Cognitive Engineering Programme, project number L127251012. Partners in the project are the University of Surrey, UK and Vocalis Ltd, Cambridge, UK.

    Thanks to Lucy Cheepen for advice on how human agents in Call Centres are trained to respond to incoming calls.

2. Although we are reluctant, in a scholarly paper of this kind, to suggest what they might be.

3. The decision about how to address callers is also closely tied to the particular service being provided. Agents in banking call centres are likely to use title plus last name, while more leisure-oriented services may address callers by first name only.
4. There are still many people who are reluctant even to leave messages on answering machines.
5. It is possible to hear people who are having trouble with starting the car (or the computer) saying 'please, please', but I would argue that this is more properly categorised as a plea to the Almighty.
6. Remember the transcript of the telephone call between Prince Charles and his mistress, Camilla Parker-Bowles, in which their closing sequence lasts longer than two minutes.

References

Attwater, D. J. et al. (1996) Dialogue design in advanced speech applications. BTRL Research publications.

Aust, H. (1996) Dialogue Modelling. In *Communication*, Proceedings of The Fourth European Summer School on Language and Speech: Budapest.

Brown, G. and Yule, G. (1983) *Teaching the Spoken Language*. Cambridge: Cambridge University Press.

Cheepen, C. (1988) *The Predictability of Informal Conversation*. London: Pinter Publishers.

Cheepen, C. (1994) Friendliness and user friendliness in speech-driven interface design. IPrA, *Pragmatics* 4: 1.

Cheepen, C. and Monaghan, J. (1990) *Spoken English: a practical guide*. London: Pinter Publishers.

Chervell, J. (1997) 'I just called to say I love you'; Love and desire on the telephone. In K. Harvey and C. Shalom, *Language and Desire: encoding sex, romance and intimacy*. London: Routledge.

Coates, J. (1996) *Women Talk*. Oxford: Blackwell.

Fairclough, N. (1995) *Critical Discourse Analysis*. London: Longman.

Foster, J. C., Dutton, R., Jack, M. A., Love, S., Nairn, I. A., Vergeynest, N. and Stentiford, F. (1992) Design and evaluation of dialogues for automated telephone services. *Speech and Hearing*, Proceedings of the Institute of Acoustics Autumn Conference. Windermere, UK.

Gibbon, D., Moore, R. and Winski, R. (eds) (1997) *EAGLES Handbook on Spoken Dialogue Systems*. Berlin: Walter de Gruyter.

Goffman, E. (1955) On face work: an analysis of ritual elements in social interaction. In J. Laver and S. Hutcheson (eds) (1972), *Communication in Face-to-Face Interaction*. Harmondworth: Penguin Books.

Goffman, E. (1967) *Interaction Ritual*. New York: Anchor Books.

Habermas, J. (1984) *Theory of Communicative Action*; Vol. I: *Reason and the Rationalisation of Society* (trans. T. Mcceetry). London: Aeinernann.

Jefferson, G. (1972) Side sequences. In D. Sudnow (ed.) (1972) *Studies Insocial Interaction*. New York: The Free Press.

Malinowski, B. (1923) The problem of meaning in primitive languages. In C. le Ogden and I. A. Richards (eds) *The Meaning of Meaning*. London: Routledge and Kogan Paul, pp. 146–52.

Monaghan, J. (1992) Fundamental research underlying the design of an automated dictation system. *Speech and Hearing*, Proceedings of Institute of Acoustics Autumn Conference. Windermere, UK.

Schegloff, E. A. (1968) Sequencing in conversational openings. In J. Laver and S. Hutcheson (eds) (1972) *Communication in Face-to-Face Interaction: selected readings*. Harmondworth: Penguin.

Schegloff, E. A. and Sacks, H. (1973) Opening up closings. In R. Turner (ed.) (1974) *Ethnomethodology*. Harmondworth: Penguin.

Williams, D. and Cheepen, C. (1998) 'Just speak naturally': designing for naturalness in automated spoken dialogues. *Proceedings of CHI*. (OK relay) Los Angeles.

Index